JAMES EDWARD
OGLETHORPE

OXFORD
UNIVERSITY PRESS
AMEN HOUSE, E.C. 4
London Edinburgh Glasgow
New York Toronto Melbourne
Capetown Bombay Calcutta
Madras Shanghai
HUMPHREY MILFORD
PUBLISHER TO THE
UNIVERSITY

JAMES EDWARD OGLETHORPE
from the painting by an unknown artist, now in the
Library of Oglethorpe University, Atlanta, Georgia

James Edward
OGLETHORPE
IMPERIAL IDEALIST

BY

AMOS ASCHBACH ETTINGER

OXFORD
AT THE CLARENDON PRESS
1936

PRINTED IN GREAT BRITAIN

AMICO MEO
DEI MINISTRO
GULIELMO CAROLO SCHAEFFER
GEORGIAE OGLETHORPEIANAE
INDIGENAE

PREFACE

ONE hundred and fifty years ago there died in the manor house of Cranham Hall, Essex, an Englishman whose career spanned wellnigh a century, who had touched life at many points, and whose interests had not been confined to the Mother Country but had led him to America, an English gentleman who was not unhonoured in the company of his peers: James Edward Oglethorpe.

Despite his fame there have been no more than a bare half-dozen biographies of him in the succeeding century and a half, while the best sources for his life have come to light only in the last two decades.

If, despite Austin Dobson's dictum that Pope's famous couplet has 'done more to preserve the memory of the founder of Georgia than all the records of the Office at Westminster', we accept the postulate that history—and biography—should be rewritten, these musty archives, together with the Boswell papers and countless other documents but recently unearthed, can be read afresh to present a clearer picture than has yet appeared of one who, to-day more than ever before, deserves his Boswell.

This study has gradually evolved from an essay which was awarded the Beit Prize in Colonial History for 1929 in the University of Oxford; and its origins have led me to strive the more for accuracy and wide reference. Like Boswell, 'I have sometimes been obliged to run half over London in order to fix a date correctly; which, when I had accomplished, I well knew would obtain me no praise, though a failure would have been to my discredit'. For, as Sir John Fortescue so well expressed it, 'the chief pleasure of an historical student is to discover things for himself'.

Yet although the responsibility for these pages is mine, I can well repeat Pope's phrase: 'Whatever the success may prove, I shall never repent of an undertaking in which I have experienced the candour and friendship of so many persons of merit'; and I owe a debt of gratitude to those who have led me into the many and varied pleasant fields whence I was able to gather so rich a harvest.

In the United States of America, where this work originated, I am particularly indebted to five great sources: for many years my friend, Mr. Howard Seavoy Leach, Librarian of Lehigh University, Bethlehem, Pennsylvania, has given me *carte blanche* among his collections of printed historical and literary materials.

Because their kindness has enabled me to complete an entirely new chapter in the life of Oglethorpe, I am under special obligation to Colonel Ralph Isham of Princeton, New Jersey, the generous owner of the Papers of James Boswell, and to Dr. Frederick A. Pottle of Yale University, their learned editor.

Of equal importance for new light from the enemy's point of view on Oglethorpe's Georgian career was the aid given me by Dr. James A. Robertson, Executive Secretary of the Florida Historical Society, to whom I am grateful for the Society's transcripts of Spanish archival records.

For first-hand knowledge of the archives of South Carolina I am indebted to the State Archivist, A. S. Salley, junior, of Columbia, South Carolina.

My fifth group of benefactors were Georgians. Oldest of my friends in Oglethorpe's colony, Mayor Thomas Gamble of Savannah introduced me to the custodians of Georgia's historical treasures. To Mr. and Mrs. Wymberley Jones DeRenne and Dr. and Mrs. Craig Barrow I owe thanks for *entrée* to the DeRenne Library at Wormsloe, Isle of Hope; to Mr. William Harden and Mrs. Marmaduke Floyd I am obliged for aid at the Georgia Historical Society; while the Rev. C. A. Linn, Ph.D., allowed me to use his unpublished study on the Salzburgers, and Mr. Edmund H. Abrahams guided me to the sources for the early history of the Jewry in Savannah. To these and to many other friends in Savannah I owe sincere thanks not only for academic assistance, but also for the finest flavour of Southern hospitality. And I have happy memories of an instructive inspection of Fort Frederica and Saint

Simon's Island under the guidance of Mrs. Margaret Davis Cate of Brunswick. In Atlanta my debt is equally great. To President Thornwell Jacobs of Oglethorpe University I owe not only certain portraits and much discussion on various points, but a sustaining interest and zeal; and my labours in the Georgia period of Oglethorpe's career were considerably lightened by the aid of the State Historian, Miss Ruth Blair, and her assistant, Miss Iverson Dewes.

Considerations of space forbid my naming all the individuals throughout the United States who aided me, but I must here make bare acknowledgement to Mr. R. B. Adam of Buffalo, New York, for access to his Johnsonian library; Dr. John C. Fitzpatrick, Washington, D.C.; Dr. W. N. Schwarze, custodian of archives and President of Moravian College for Men, Bethlehem, Pennsylvania; Dr. H. E. Bolton of the University of California; Mr. W. S. Lewis of Farmington, Connecticut; Dr. S. M. Pargellis and Dr. F. W. Hilles of Yale University; Dr. D. M. Little of Harvard University; Dr. K. C. Balderston of Wellesley College; Dr. L. F. Stock of the Carnegie Institution, Washington, D.C.; Dr. R. S. Crane of the University of Chicago; Dr. Verner Crane of the University of Michigan; and the staffs of the American Antiquarian Society; the American Philosophical Society; the New York Public Library; the Library of the Mount Airy Lutheran Theological Seminary, Philadelphia; the Virginia State Library, Richmond; the Library of Congress, Washington; the Sterling Library, Yale University; the Widener Memorial Library, Harvard University; the Massachusetts Historical Society; the Historical Society of Pennsylvania; the Library of the University of Pennsylvania; and the Charleston, South Carolina, Free Library.

In England my obligations are equally heavy. To His Majesty, King George V, I beg to express my appreciation for his gracious permission to use the Stuart Papers and those of the Duke of Cumberland at Windsor Castle, where for personal courtesies I would thank His Majesty's

PREFACE

Librarian, Mr. O. W. Morshead, Miss M. Mackenzie, and the members of the staff.

In London I am under permanent obligation to the officials and staff of the literary search room at the Public Record Office and to the staffs of the Manuscript Room, Newspaper Room, and Main Reading Room of the British Museum. For generous assistance I must thank His Majesty's Secretary of Works and Public Buildings; Mr. W. E. Ottewill of the India Office; Professor P. Geyl of the University of London; Mr. Anthony R. Wagner, Portcullis, of the College of Arms; Mr. J. A. R. Pimlott; Sir Charles Petrie, Baronet; Dr. J. Johnston Abraham; Mr. C. W. Stewart of the publishing house of Faber and Faber; Mr. W. C. B. Tunstall; Mr. and Mrs. Richard Holworthy; Mr. E. Redman; Dr. Hubert Hall and Miss M. B. Curran of the Royal Historical Society; and the staffs of Lambeth Palace Library; Fulham Palace; Sion College; the Royal Academy of Arts; the Royal Society; the Victoria and Albert Museum; and the Society for the Propagation of the Gospel.

Beyond London I would express my thanks to the Earl of Home; Baron Ponsonby of Shulbrede Priory; Lord Tweedsmuir, still better known as Colonel John Buchan; Mr. Aleyn Lyell Reade; Miss Olive Lloyd-Baker, custodian of the papers of Granville Sharp; Mr. Arthur Bryant; Dr. Henry Guppy and Dr. Moses Tyson of the John Rylands Library, Manchester; Mr. and Mrs. George Hughes of Oglethorpe Manor, Tadcaster, Yorkshire; Mr. E. V. Swanton of Haslemere; and the officials of the Scottish National Library, Edinburgh, and the Yorkshire Archaeological Society, Leeds.

Great as is my debt to these, I owe most to a group of scholars at Oxford. For his sustaining interest in this study of a son of Corpus Christi College, I would pay tribute to the memory of Dr. Percy S. Allen. To his successor, Sir Richard Livingstone, and to Lady Livingstone and Mr. J. G. Milne, the Librarian of the College, I owe much, while to the officials and staffs of the Bodleian Library,

PREFACE

the Camera, and Rhodes House Library I am indebted for unhampered access to all pertinent matter in university records, manuscript collections, and printed books. I would also acknowledge the generosity and encouragement of Professor R. Coupland, Beit Professor of Colonial History, and Dr. R. M. McElroy, Harmsworth Professor of American History. And not the least of my gratitude is due Mr. L. F. Powell, who, while engaged on his own labours in the revision of Birkbeck Hill's edition of Boswell's *Life*, found time to aid me with friendly interest. Finally I would express my thanks to the officers and staff of the Clarendon Press.

Although my chief obligations lay in Great Britain and America, I must not forget the debt I owe to Dr. Ludwig Bittner, the very capable and courteous Director of the Haus-, Hof-, und Staats-Archiv, Vienna, Austria, for important references to the reports of the Imperial Minister to England.

To many others who gave thought and time to my inquiries I can but make this general acknowledgement of sincere appreciation.

Owing to circumstances beyond my control I was unable to gain access to the archives of the Society for Promoting Christian Knowledge, and to the manuscripts of the Associates of the late Rev. Dr. Bray, documents dealing with Oglethorpe's philanthropic projects and connexions. I was likewise unable to view the manuscripts in the Phillipps Collection at Cheltenham, but a thorough survey of the catalogue of the Library leads me to believe that the loss has not been great.

One debt remains to be acknowledged. It would have been impossible for me to complete this study had not my Father and Mother, not without sacrifice, supported and upheld me on every hand. Without their interest and continued aid this volume could not appear.

A. A. E.

ALLENTOWN, PENNSYLVANIA
1 September, 1935

CONTENTS

I. A YORKSHIRE HERITAGE . . . 1
II. A JACOBITE YOUTH 47
III. THE MEMBER FOR HASLEMERE TO 1743 . 81
IV. THE ORIGINS OF THE GEORGIA MOVEMENT 110
V. GEORGIA: THE FIRST PHASE: ADMINISTRATION 129
VI. GEORGIA: THE SECOND PHASE: RELIGION . 153
VII. GEORGIA: THE THIRD PHASE: IMPERIAL DEFENCE 207
VIII. THE 'FORTY-FIVE AND OBLIVION . . 255
IX. *OTIUM CUM DIGNITATE* IN JOHNSON'S LONDON 291
INDEX 331

LIST OF ILLUSTRATIONS

JAMES EDWARD OGLETHORPE, from the painting by an unknown artist, now in the Library of Oglethorpe University, Atlanta, Georgia . *Frontispiece*

THE FLEET PRISON COMMITTEE, from the painting by WILLIAM HOGARTH, 1729, in the National Portrait Gallery . . . . . *Facing page* 90

THE GEORGIA COUNCIL, from the copy by A. E. DYER of W. VERELST'S painting, now hanging in Rhodes Memorial Hall, Atlanta, Georgia . . ,, 146

MAP OF THE DEBATABLE LAND, 1670–1763, taken by permission from H. E. Bolton and M. Ross, *The Debatable Land* (University of California Press, 1925) . . . . . . ,, 172

GENERAL OGLETHORPE, from the mezzotint by T. BURFORD, *circa* 1743 . . . . ,, 224

SAMUEL JOHNSON, from the painting by SIR JOSHUA REYNOLDS, 1778, in the Tate Gallery . . ,, 292

JAMES BOSWELL, from the portrait by SIR JOSHUA REYNOLDS, 1786, in the National Portrait Gallery ,, 312

JAMES EDWARD OGLETHORPE, aged 88, at the sale of the Library of Dr. Johnson, from the pen-and-ink sketch by S. IRELAND, 1785 . . . ,, 324

CHAPTER I
A YORKSHIRE HERITAGE

IN his brilliant survey of English History, George Macaulay Trevelyan has interpreted the eighteenth century as the age of the individual. Acknowledging that its corporate institutions were 'half asleep', he asserts that 'the glory of the Eighteenth Century in Britain lay in the genius and energy of individuals acting freely in a free community'.[1]

That being true, not the least among the stars of Britain's firmament was one whom Austin Dobson has so happily dubbed 'a paladin of philanthropy': James Edward Oglethorpe.[2]

Unlike Athena, who sprang full-armed from the brain of Zeus, the future founder of Georgia was blessed with an heritage of which he was justly proud. Never were the psychological canons of heredity more sustained than in his case, for James Oglethorpe came of a family the history of which for over six centuries accorded strictly with the primary postulates of heredity and environment. From his ancestors he derived three cardinal attributes: an abiding loyalty to the Crown; his military profession; and the parliamentary tradition.

The studies in family origins by the late Dr. John Horace Round and his caustic criticisms of spurious genealogies have established the fact that the available records of the eleventh to the fifteenth centuries are by no means unassailable,[3] but from them we can gather at least a marked indication of the character and position of the family of Oglethorpe in the West Riding of Yorkshire.

Tracing a lineal descent from Ligulfe, Theane of Oglethorpe in the reign of Edward the Confessor, an Oglethorpe maintained, at the cost of his life, the forlorn

[1] Trevelyan, G. M., *History of England* (London, 1926), p. 506.
[2] Dobson, Austin, *A Paladin of Philanthropy* (London, 1899).
[3] Round, J. H., *Peerage and Pedigree* (2 vols., London, 1910), i. preface; ii. 307–84; *Family Origins* (edited by W. Page, London, 1930), *passim*.

hope of the Anglo-Saxons against the Norman invaders under William the Conqueror.[1] Twenty years later the manor of Oglethorpe in Bramham, West Riding of Yorkshire, is found recorded in the *Domesday Book* as Ocelestorp or Oglestorp, the thorp or village of one whose personal name in various dialects was, alternatively, Acwulf, Aculf, Acolf, Ocele, Ogle, or Ugelbert;[2] and towards the end of the twelfth century a William de Hocclestorp and Hugh, his son, were witnesses of a charter grant in Yorkshire.[3] With the passing of years the family gained in wealth and repute, so that the thirteenth century found a Petrus de Ockelesthorp a tenant on the Yorkshire estates of the Earls Percy of Northumberland, and Elyas Oclestorp, Hugh de Occlesthorp, Nicholas de Oclestorpe, and Nicholaa, his wife, prominent in their county.[4] The

[1] Theophilus Oglethorpe, junior, to Ralph Thoresby, Westbrook Place, Godalming, Surrey, June 27, 1707, Lancaster, W. T., editor, *Letters addressed to Ralph Thoresby* (Thoresby Society Publications, xxi, Leeds, 1912), pp. 150–1; Fanny Oglethorpe to the Duke of Mar, Paris, Dec. 23, 1717, the King's Collection of Stuart Manuscripts in Windsor Castle. The Rev. Mark Noble, in his nineteenth-century notes on 'Knights created by the Sovereigns of England from Henry VIII to George III', affirms, however, that the Oglethorpe family came into England with the Conqueror, MSS. English History (Bodleian Library, Oxford), e. 39, p. 31. See also Thoresby, Ralph, *Ducatus Leodiensis; or, the Topography of the Ancient and Populous Town and Parish of Leedes* (1st ed., London, 1715), pp. 254–5; (2nd ed., edited by Whitaker, T. D., London, 1816), pp. 252–3.

[2] *The Domesday Book* (4 vols., London, 1783–1816), i. 329 *b*, 373 *b*; Jaynes, H., editor, *Facsimile of Domesday Book relating to Yorkshire* (London, 1867), pp. lxiv and lxxviii; Moorman, F. W., *Place Names of the West Riding of Yorkshire* (Thoresby Society Publications, xviii, Leeds, 1910), p. 141; Morris, John, 'The Name of Oglethorpe', *Georgia Historical Quarterly*, xi. 216–49, 291–320, which attacks Moorman's assumption that Oglethorpe is Old English, and makes it Scandinavian; Johnston, J. B., *The Place Names of England and Wales* (London, 1914), p. 386; Searle, W. G., *Onomasticon Anglo-Saxonicum* (London, 1897), *passim*; Turner, J. H., *Yorkshire Place Names as recorded in the Yorkshire Domesday Book, 1086* (Bingley, no date), pp. 51, 92, 107, 113–14, 280; *Yorkshire Archaeological and Topographical Association Journal*, iv. 244. For the variations of the name of Oglethorpe, see *Register* 4 D 14 at the College of Arms, London, p. 76.

[3] *Coucher Book of the Cistercian Abbey of Kirkstall, West Riding of Yorkshire* (Thoresby Society Publications, viii, Leeds, 1904), p. 86 note.

[4] *The Percy Chartulary* (Surtees Society Publications, cxvii, Durham, 1911), pp. 86, 91; Cannon, H. L., editor, *The Great Roll of the Pipe, 26 Henry III*,

increasing prosperity of the family is evident in the career of John de Okelesthorp of Bramham who in 1308 and again in 1316 was ordered as a landed proprietor to furnish fourteen feudal soldiers to King Edward II for his campaign against the Scots,[1] and who in 1328 was a plaintiff in two cases dealing with estates in Bramham.[2] By 1376 a Willelmo de Ogilsthorp was rated as one of the landed gentry in the city of York,[3] and in 1492, while Christopher Columbus was making possible the transatlantic career of one of his scions, John Oglesthorp, Esq., was serving as a member of the jury at an inquest held at York Castle by Henry VII.[4] The records of the four-

1241–1242 (New Haven, Connecticut, 1918), p. 26; *Coucher Book of the Cistercian Abbey of Kirkstall*, p. 137 and note; Brown, William, editor, *Yorkshire Inquisitions* (Yorkshire Archaeological and Topographical Association Record Series, lxii), p. 62; Parker, J., editor, *Yorkshire Fines, 1232–1246* (Yorkshire Archaeological and Topographical Association Record Series, lxvii), p. 76; Baildon, W. P., editor, *Notes on the Religious and Secular Houses of Yorkshire* (2 vols., Yorkshire Archaeological and Topographical Association Record Series, xvii, Leeds, 1895; lxxxi, Leeds, 1931), i. 154; ii. 32–3; Page, W., editor, *Victoria County History of the North Riding of Yorkshire* (2 vols. and index, London, 1914–25), iii. 204. For a marriage contract of Adam Thwaites and his father-in-law, Hugh Okelesthorpe, April 18, 1260—whereby Thwaites agreed not to sell any of his land without his father-in-law's permission under penalty of going naked through the market-place of Harewood, *quando plenius fuorit*, on seven Saturdays—see Harleian MSS. (British Museum), 4630, p. 427; and MSS. Gough Nichols (Bodleian Library, Oxford), Top. York, f. 1, 'Notes relating to Yorkshire, collected by me, John Watson, M.A., F.S.A., 1762', p. 13.

[1] For the commission of array, June 13, 1308, see Harleian MSS. (British Museum), 4630, pp. 427–8; and MSS. Gough Nichols (Bodleian Library, Oxford), Top. York, f. 1, 'Notes relating to Yorkshire', p. 13. See also *Kirby's Inquest, or the Survey of the County of York* (Surtees Society Publications, xlix, Durham, 1867), pp. 50, 214, 285, 345; and *Inquisitions and Assessments relating to Feudal Aids: 1284–1431* (6 vols., London, 1899–1920), vi. 190.

[2] *Index of Placita de Banco, 1327–1328* (Public Record Office Lists, xxxii, part ii), p. 787.

[3] *York Memorandum Book. Part I (1376–1419)* (Surtees Society Publications, cxx, Durham, 1912), pp. 4, 9. For his will see Add. MSS. (British Museum), 29677, 'Paver's Extracts of Wills', f. 11. See also f. 60 and Add. MSS., 29683, f. 105; and Add. MSS., 29684, f. 35.

[4] Bilson, John, 'Gilling Castle', *Yorkshire Archaeological and Topographical Association Journal*, xix. 184. In addition to previous citations see also the Dodsworth MSS. (Bodleian Library, Oxford), ii, ff. 7 *b*, 34; vi, f. 55 *b*; viii, ff. 50 and 50 *b*; xxvii, ff. 57 *b*, 110 *b*, 171 *b*; cxvii, ff. 67 *b*, 86; cxl, ff. 5–15;

teenth and fifteenth centuries, in short, yield abundant evidences of the substantial and expanding influence of the family in countless legal documents, contracts, deeds and estate papers, wills and charters, each of which would make dull reading, but all of which put together manifest the high social, financial, and political station of James Oglethorpe's Yorkshire ancestors.

If in the eleventh to the fifteenth centuries the Oglethorpes consolidated their position in their native haunts, often by judicious matrimonial alliances with wealthy or influential neighbours, the sixteenth century witnessed not only further and greater family unions and the creation of new groups, but also the expansion of the Oglethorpe influence into the Church, Parliament, and the University of Oxford. John Oglethorpe of Oglethorpe, Yorkshire, known to be living in 1464, had four sons, the first, William, destined to be the ancestor, nine generations removed, of James Oglethorpe; the third, Robert, who founded the Oglethorpes of Rawdon; the fourth, Andrew; and the second son, George, whose line was of greater importance during the sixteenth century.[1] George

clii, ff. 125, 154, 155 *b*; Manning, O., and Bray, W., editors, *The History and Antiquities of the County of Surrey* (3 vols., London, 1804–14), i. 637; Page, W., editor, *Victoria County History of Yorkshire* (3 vols. and index, London, 1907–25), i. 478; ii. 228, 282, 293, 297–8.

[1] For the Oglethorpe genealogy see the *Register* of the College of Arms, London, 4 D 14, pp. 75–87; MS. 526 (Yorkshire Archaeological Society, Leeds), Paver's 'Black Book of Yorkshire Families', ff. 80 *b*–85; Harleian MSS. (British Museum), 1110, 'Miscellaneous Pedigrees by William Penson, Lancaster Herald', ff. 9 *b*, 10; 1420, f. 177 *b*; 1571, ff. 131, 131 *b*, 229 *b*; 4630, pp. 427–32; 6070, ff. 136–7; Add. MSS. (British Museum), 18011, 'Visitation of Yorkshire, 1584, by Robert Glover, Somerset Herald', ff. 157, 184 and verso; 26739, 'Pedigrees of the West Riding of Yorkshire', ff. 271–2; and 'Paver's Genealogical Records of Yorkshire'; Add. MSS., 29644, f. 132; 29646, ff. 51–6; 29648, ff. 184 verso–187 verso; 29651, f. 179. See also MSS. Rylands (Bodleian Library, Oxford), e. 13, f. 28 verso; and the following printed records: Foster, J., editor, *Glover's Visitation of Yorkshire, 1584/5, and St. George's Visitation, 1612* (London, 1875), pp. 52, 175, 237, 260, 275, 277, 281, 303, 313–15, 559, 590–1, 633; Norcliffe, C. B., editor, *Visitation of Yorkshire in the Years 1563 and 1564* (Harleian Society Publications, xvi, London, 1881), pp. 4, 46, 321, 330; *Dugdale's Visitation of Yorkshire, 1665* (Surtees Society Publications, lii, London, 1859), p. 262; Bannerman,

Oglethorpe in early manhood moved to Newton Kyme near Tadcaster where, it seems, some time before his formal marriage, there was born a son, Owen Oglethorpe, who was destined to high endeavours in the realm of learning and in the Church.[1] Because he was thus deemed to be illegitimate, Owen Oglethorpe was never recognized by the seventeenth- and eighteenth-century relatives of James Oglethorpe. As James's brother, Theophilus, wrote in 1707, Owen 'was an Oglethorpe but of a spurious race', and so his coat of arms 'must certainly be distinguished from the rest of the family by some mark of bastardy'.[2] But in the sixteenth century no such attitude prevented Owen Oglethorpe from making his impress upon Oxford. Successively an undergraduate and Fellow of Magdalen, Reader in Logic and Moral Philosophy in the University, Doctor of Divinity, and holder of innumerable minor church offices, Owen Oglethorpe in February 1536 was elected President of his college by the Fellows, in accordance with the manipulations of Thomas Cromwell and the royal wishes of Henry VIII. For seventeen years he held sway over this band of scholars, during which time he became a member of the select committee of Oxford and Cambridge divines who held the memorable reformation disputation with Cranmer, Latimer, and Ridley; and in 1551 he not only survived charges brought against him by ten of the Fellows, but was elevated to the Vice-

---

W. B., editor, 'The Oglethorpes of Oglethorpe. From the Visitation of Yorkshire, 1584–1585', *Miscellanea Genealogica et Heraldica*, 4th series, v (London, 1914), 224–5; Harwood, H. W. F., editor, 'The Oglethorpes of Oglethorpe. From Dugdale's Visitation of Yorkshire, September 12, 1665', *The Genealogist*, New Series, xx (London, 1904), 172–5; Harwood, *The Genealogist*, New Series, xxxii (London, 1916), 189.

[1] The only supporter of Owen Oglethorpe's claim to legitimacy is Foster, *Glover's Visitation of Yorkshire, 1584/5*, p. 314. For the solution of the problem of his birth and legitimacy see Harleian MSS. (British Museum), 1110, 'Miscellaneous Pedigrees by William Penson, Lancaster Herald', f. 9 b.

[2] Theophilus Oglethorpe, junior, to Ralph Thoresby, Westbrook Place, Godalming, Surrey, June 27, 1707, Lancaster, *Letters addressed to Ralph Thoresby*, pp. 150–1.

Chancellorship of the University.[1] Having ingratiated himself with his royal master, Owen Oglethorpe likewise had received a succession of ecclesiastical preferments, including the post of Canon at Windsor, but the death of his Protestant patron and the advent of Queen Mary in 1553 brought in its train the tragic and sanguinary Counter-Reformation. As a clerical politician, Owen Oglethorpe, however, saw to it that the change did not retard his own career for, by assiduous attention to the new Queen, he now became Bishop, first of Carlisle, and then of Lincoln, Dean of Windsor, and, by commission of 'Philipp and Mary', Scribe or Register of the Order of the Garter.[2] Pliable as he undoubtedly was, Oglethorpe, as Bishop of Carlisle, repressed the north from indulging in the Marian persecutions which so shook the south of England.[3] As one contemporary phrased it, he was a

[1] For Owen Oglethorpe's Oxford career see Gutch, John, editor, *Anthony à Wood's History and Antiquities of the Colleges of Oxford* (2 vols., Oxford, 1786–90), i. 316–17, 324, 429; appendix, pp. 83, 91, 268; Gutch, John, editor, *Anthony à Wood's History and Antiquities of the University of Oxford* (2 vols. in 3, Oxford, 1792–6), ii. 124–5; Boase, C. W., editor, *Register of the University of Oxford* (2 vols. in 5, Oxford Historical Society Publications, Oxford, 1884–9), i. 137; Foster, J., editor, *Alumni Oxonienses. Early Series, 1500–1714* (4 vols., Oxford, 1891–2), iii. 1087; Macray, W. D., editor, *A Register of the Members of St. Mary Magdalen College, Oxford* (New Series, 8 vols., London, 1894–1915), i. 133, 169; ii. 16, 18, 55–62; Mallet, Sir Charles E., *A History of the University of Oxford* (3 vols., London, 1924–7), i. 393; ii. 39, 89, 96–7, 104.

[2] Rymer, Thomas, *Foedera* (20 vols., London, 1704–35), xv. 420–1, 577; Hardy, Sir T. D., editor, *Syllabus to Rymer's Foedera* (3 vols., London, 1869–85), ii. 795–6, 798, 802.

[3] For Owen Oglethorpe's clerical career see the Lansdowne MSS. (British Museum), 980, 'Bishop Kennett's Collections', xlvi, ff. 312, 322; *Yorkshire Archaeological and Topographical Association Journal*, xiv. 402–4; Hill, A. du B., 'The Rectors of East Bridgford', *Thoroton Society Transactions*, xxvii (Nottingham, 1924), 87–8; Nichols, J. G., *The Topographer and Genealogist*, i (London, 1846), 505; Markham, Sir C. R., *King Edward VI; An Appreciation* (New York, 1908), p. 217; Lee, F. G., *King Edward the Sixth, Supreme Head* (London, 1889), p. 209; Smith, W., *Old Yorkshire* (4 vols., London, 1881–3), i. 95; Foster, C. W., editor, *Lincoln Episcopal Records, 1571–1584*, Lincoln Record Society Publications, ii (Saltergate, 1912), 243; Cole, R. E. G., *Chapter Acts of the Cathedral Church of St. Mary of Lincoln, 1520–1536*, Lincoln Record Society Publications, xii (Horncastle, 1915), 197; *Lincolnshire Notes and Queries*, v (Horncastle, 1898), 205, 235; vi (Horncastle,

bishop 'qualified with a moderate temper',[1] and it was this moderation, or vacillation, if you will, which explains his part in the coronation, in January 1559, of Queen Elizabeth who, five years before, had been lodged at Oglethorpe's house by her regnant rival, Mary. The Virgin Queen, having decided to be a Protestant, failed to gain the consent of Nicholas Heath, Archbishop of York, who, with all of the other bishops, save one, stubbornly refused to crown her. The dignity of the great Queen was saved by the defection of Bishop Oglethorpe who, on condition that she conform to Catholic ritual during the ceremony, to which she agreed, performed the coronation. Once crowned, however, Elizabeth, objecting to the elevation of the Host, brusquely deprived him of his office and cast him into prison where, in 1560, he died.[2]

1899), 144; *Letters and Papers, Foreign and Domestic: Henry VIII*, viii. 295; x. 38; xv. 9; xvi. 97, 603; xviii. 492; xix (part i), 491; xxi (part i), 778; Campbell, Lord, *Lives of the Lord Chancellors and the Keepers of the Great Seal of England* (4th ed., 10 vols., London, 1856–7), ii. 208–9; Froude, J. A., *History of England* (12 vols., New York, 1870), vii. 40; Dixon, W. H., *Royal Windsor* (4 vols., London, 1878–80), iii. 208–9; *Calendar of State Papers, Rome*, i. 61; *Calendar of State Papers, Spanish*, i. 17; Salter, H. E., editor, *A Cartulary of the Hospital of St. John the Baptist* (3 vols., Oxford Historical Society Publications, Oxford, 1914–17), i. 142; Tighe, R. R., and Davis, J. E., *Annals of Windsor* (2 vols., London, 1858), i. 590–3; *North Country Wills*, ii (Surtees Society Publications, cxxi, Durham, 1912), 18; MSS. Ashmolean (Bodleian Library, Oxford), 1123, f. 176 *b*; 1131, f. 52 *a*; Catholic Record Society Publications, i. *Miscellanea*, pp. 7, 10, 31, 34; ii. 59.

[1] *Memoirs of the Life of Mr. Ambrose Barnes* (Surtees Society Publications, l, Durham, 1867), p. 280.

[2] On the coronation of Queen Elizabeth see especially the following articles in the *English Historical Review*: Bayne, C. G., xxii. 650–73; xxiv. 322–3; xxv. 550–3; Wilson, H. A., xxiii. 87–91; Pollard, Prof. A. F., xxv. 125–6; and Ross, G. Lockhart, xxiii. 533–4. Also Bruce, John, editor, *Annals of the First Four Years of the Reign of Queen Elizabeth. By Sir John Hayward Kent, D.C.L.* (Camden Society Publications, Old Series, vii, London, 1840), p. 27; Nichols, John Gough, editor, *The Diary of Henry Machyn, Citizen and Merchant-Taylor of London, From A.D. 1550 to A.D. 1563* (Camden Society Publications, Old Series, xlii, London, 1848), pp. 103, 221, 378; Ditchfield, P. H., and Page, W., editors, *Victoria County History of Berkshire* (4 vols. and index, London, 1906–27), ii. 111; Pocock, Nicholas, editor, *Troubles Connected with the Prayer Book of 1549* (Camden Society Publications, New Series, xxxvii, London, 1884), pp. 131–2; Pocock, Nicholas, editor, *A Treatise on the Pretended Divorce between Henry VIII and*

A century and a half later Theophilus Oglethorpe, junior, complained that, because Owen Oglethorpe had crowned Queen Elizabeth,

the ignorant have it an honour to descend us from a Bishop when realy wee are not. I do not find our family mentioned in any history except Owen Ogle., nor do I expect it, for to be chronicled in our British annals they must be monsters, great favorites, or great rebells, etc., none of which, God be thanked, our family has been.[1]

While Bishop Oglethorpe's career overshadowed those of his Yorkshire cousins, Theophilus was not quite correct in assigning all others of that period to the realms of oblivion. Another Owen Oglethorpe, of Newington, Oxfordshire, corresponded with the great Lord Burghley; served in two Elizabethan Parliaments, for Wycombe, Bucks., in 1588, and for Wallingford, in Berkshire, in 1597; regularly furnished troops; and was knighted at Whitehall on the coronation of James I in 1603.[2] In Yorkshire Andrew Oglethorpe in 1567 had taken part in the 'Rising of the North' as a Marian Catholic, only to be killed three years later, and in 1572 Henry Oglethorpe of Bishopsfield, near York, was noted as one of the 'Princepall gentlemen in Yorkshyre', worth one hundred marks per annum in lands. Unfortunately for Henry his staunch faith led to his arrest as a recusant and he was held a prisoner at Hull. Ten years later it was recorded that 'he do remayne

Catharine of Aragon, by Nicholas Harpsfield, LL.D., Archdeacon of Canterbury (Camden Society Publications, New Series, xxi, London, 1878), p. 9; *Acts of the Privy Council of England*, New Series, iv. 106; v. 378; vii. 42, 79–81, 91, 96, 100–2; Strickland, Agnes, *Lives of the Queens of England* (8 vols., London, 1866), ii. 81, 123; iv. 144, 150–1.

[1] Theophilus Oglethorpe, junior, to Ralph Thoresby, Westbrook Place, Godalming, Surrey, June 27, 1707, Lancaster, *Letters addressed to Ralph Thoresby*, p. 151.

[2] Lipscomb, G., *History and Antiquities of the County of Buckingham* (4 vols., London, 1847), iii. 643; Willis, B., *Notitia Parliamentaria* (London, 1750), pp. 118, 137; Nichols, J., *The Progresses, Processions, and Magnificent Festivities of King James the First* (4 vols., London, 1829), i. 215; Birch, Thomas, *The Court and Times of James the First* (2 vols., London, 1848), i. 83, 410; Shaw, W. A., editor, *The Knights of England* (2 vols., London, 1906), ii. 119, 147.

obstinate', but by 1585 he had fled to Oxfordshire, where he kept the faith as late as 1592, while Catholic records show that other members of the Oglethorpe clan remained true to their religion until the end of the seventeenth century.[1] Even as Bishop Owen Oglethorpe and the Newton Kyme branch of the house had wandered afield in England, other, hardier sons of Oglethorpe of Oglethorpe had migrated to Ireland where, early in the seventeenth century, we read of Sir Robert Oglethorpe, Baron of the Exchequer, a member of historic Gray's Inn, London, and plain Martin Oglethorpe, adventurer.[2]

The wanderings of various scions of the old Yorkshire family had not, however, decimated their ranks at home: through a greatgrandson of old John Oglethorpe, Richard, who died in 1546, and thence through William, his son,[3] the line descended to a second William Oglethorpe who became a leader in the community, being listed among the Gentry of Yorkshire in 1584 as William Oglethorpe, Esquire, of Oglethorpe Grange, Barkeston Ashe, and who in 1588 contributed fifty pounds towards the defence of

---

[1] For other Yorkshire Oglethorpes see the *Index of Inquisitions*. I. *Henry VIII to Philip and Mary* (Public Record Office List, xxiii), p. 170: Richard Oglethorpe, 38 Henry VIII, York; p. 324: Thomas Oglethorpe, 5 Edward VI, York; II. *Elizabeth* (Public Record Office List, xxvi), p. 260: Andrew Oglethorpe, 12 Elizabeth and 20 Elizabeth, York, John Oglethorpe, 21 Elizabeth, Oxford, and William Oglethorpe, 22 Elizabeth, York. For Catholic Oglethorpes see Cartwright, J. J., *Chapters in the History of Yorkshire* (Wakefield, 1872), pp. 72, 150, 157, 160; Smith, *Old Yorkshire*, iv. 84; *MSS. of the Marquis of Salisbury* (Historical Manuscripts Commission Reports [hereinafter cited as H.M.C. Reports]), i. 468; iii. 106; iv. 273; *MSS. of the Right Honourable F. J. Savile Foljambe of Osberton* (H.M.C. Reports, xv, Appendix, part v), pp. 37, 81; *MSS. of the Earl of Egmont* (H.M.C. Reports), i. 50–5; Catholic Record Society Publications, i. 130–2; vi. 258, 282–3; xi. 265; xiv. 94; xviii. 58, 86, 94, 108; xxii. 17 and note 2, 25 note, 111–14; xxiv. 23.

[2] *Calendar of State Papers, Ireland*, 1606–8, pp. 116, 123, 161, 618; 1647–60, *passim*; *Calendar of State Papers, Carew*, vi. 31, 179, 384; Fletcher, R. J., editor, *The Pension Book of Gray's Inn, 1569–1669* (London, 1901), pp. 129, 131, 133, 153, 162.

[3] William Oglethorpe, senior, died in 1594. Crossley, E. W., editor, *Index to the Original Documents of the Consistory Court of York, 1427–1658* (Yorkshire Archaeological and Topographical Association Record Series, lxxiii, Leeds, 1928), p. 19.

England against the Spanish Armada.[1] This William Oglethorpe, junior, in 1580 had married Anne Sotheby of Pocklington, Yorkshire, who on January 5, 1588, bore him a namesake, William Oglethorpe the third. By 1605 this youth was at Sidney Sussex College, Cambridge,[2] and by 1610 a member of Lincoln's Inn,[3] while in 1608 he contracted a brilliant alliance with Susan, daughter of Sir William Sutton, Baronet, of Averham, Nottinghamshire; and the first of their nine children, Sutton Oglethorpe, born in 1612 at the old homestead in Bramham, Yorkshire, was destined to be the grandfather of James Edward Oglethorpe.[4]

Although loyalty to the Crown had been an abiding attribute through five generations of Oglethorpes, it fell to the lot of Sutton Oglethorpe to permit loyalty and

---

[1] Robert Oglethorpe contributed £25. Add. MSS. (British Museum), 29694, 'Paver's Genealogical Records', ff. 32 verso, 43; Stowe MSS. (British Museum), 165, 'Loans to Queen Elizabeth by Gentlemen in the Various Counties of England, 1588', ff. 30–1; Colman, F. S., *History of the Parish of Barwick-in-Elmet in the County of York* (Thoresby Society Publications, xvii, Leeds, 1908), p. 145 note.

[2] Venn, J., and Venn, J. A., editors, *Alumni Cantabrigienses, Part I (to 1751)* (4 vols., Cambridge, 1922–7), iii. 277; Venn, J., and Venn, J. A., editors, *The Book of Matriculations and Degrees . . . in the University of Cambridge, 1544–1659* (Cambridge, 1913), p. 498. A John Oglethorpe also entered Sidney Sussex College in 1656, taking his B.A. degree in 1569 and M.A. in 1663.

[3] William Oglethorpe the third died in 1668 after a lengthy career as attorney in the King's Bench Court. *The Records of the Honourable Society of Lincoln's Inn* (2 vols., London, 1896), i. 153; Ellis, Sir Henry, editor, *The Obituary of Richard Smith, Secondary of the Poultry Compter, London; Being a Catalogue of all such Persons as he knew in their life; Extending from A.D. 1627 to A.D. 1674* (Camden Society Publications, Old Series, xliv, London, 1849), p. 77.

[4] Harwood, 'The Oglethorpes of Oglethorpe', *The Genealogist*, New Series, xx. 172–5; Foster, *Glover's Visitation of Yorkshire*, pp. 170, 275; *Dugdale's Visitation of the County of York, 1665*, p. 151; Norcliffe, C. B., editor, 'Paver's Marriage Licences', *Yorkshire Archaeological and Topographical Association Journal*, xi. 242; Brigg, William, editor, *Yorkshire Fines for the Stuart Period: I. 1603–1614* (Yorkshire Archaeological and Topographical Association Record Series, liii, Leeds, 1915), pp. 29, 35, 44, 53, 86, 103, 120, 147, 207, 210, 222; Lister, J., editor, *West Riding Sessions Rolls, 1597–1602* (Yorkshire Archaeological and Topographical Association Record Series, iii, Worksop, 1888; liv, Leeds, 1915), i. 146 note, 215; ii. 17, 297–8, 369; Speight, H., *Lower Wharfedale* (London, 1902), pp. 376–83.

valour to supplant discretion and to justify, by his material martyrdom in the hey-day of Cromwell and the Commonwealth, the royal grant of arms to the Oglethorpes of Oglethorpe in 1596.[1] The rise of Oliver Cromwell as leader of the Puritan insurgents, together with the executive excesses of Charles I, could have but one result and, in the ensuing conflict, Sutton Oglethorpe became an important royalist figure in Yorkshire, performing valiantly for his King. Not only did he serve himself, but he saw to it that his cousins and other relatives by marriage supported the royalist cause. As commander of Beverston Castle, near Bristol, in 1644, he held out against the parliamentary forces until, as some would have it, he was captured one day off guard while calling on a young lady at a neighbouring farm-house. Although a contemporary damned him as 'a man rendred odious to the countrey by strange oppressions and tyranny, and who has lost himself basely',[2] Colonel Sutton Oglethorpe at some later date gained his release, for in 1648 he aided Sir Philip Musgrave to raise troops in the Five Northern Counties for the seizure and subsequent defence of Carlisle.[3]

[1] *Register* of the College of Arms, 4 D 14, p. 75; Rylands, W. H., editor, *Grantees of Arms, named in Docquets and Patents to the end of the Seventeenth Century* (Harleian Society Publications, lxvi, London, 1915), p. 185.

[2] Scott, Sir Walter, editor, *Somers's Tracts* (2nd ed., 13 vols., London, 1809–15), v. 347.

[3] Harwood, H. W. F., editor, *The Genealogist*, New Series, xxiii (London, 1907), 68; MSS. *of Sir Reginald Graham, Bart.* (H.M.C. Reports, vi), p. 329; *Yorkshire Diaries and Autobiographies in the Seventeenth and Eighteenth Centuries* (Surtees Society Publications, lxv, Durham, 1877), p. 13 note: *Dyurnall* of Captain Adam Eyre, 1646–1647; Duckett, Sir George, Bart., 'Letters of the Yorkshire Commissioners of Sequestrations, etc., to Cromwell, 1655–1666', *Yorkshire Archaeological and Topographical Association Journal*, vi. 93; Clay, J. W., 'The Gentry of Yorkshire at the Time of the Civil War', *Yorkshire Archaeological and Topographical Association Journal*, xxiii. 376; Burton, Rev. Gilbert, *Life of Sir Philip Musgrave, Bart.* (Carlisle, 1840), p. 12; Beach, Mrs. W. H., *A Cotswold Family: Hicks and Hicks Beach* (London, 1909), pp. 211–13; *Transactions of the Bristol and Gloucestershire Archaeological Society*, xxii (Bristol, 1899), 9; xxxvii (Bristol, 1914), 11; Curwen, J. F., *The Castles and Fortified Towers of Cumberland, Westmorland, and Lancashire North-of-the-Sands* (Cumberland and Westmorland Antiquarian and Archaeological Society Publications, Extra Series, xii, Kendal, 1913), p. 472.

But fortune now turned against the Oglethorpes. Several of that name fell in battle near Oxford and in 1651 Sutton Oglethorpe himself was arrested, tried, and imprisoned as a recalcitrant royalist, and fined £20,000 by Parliament. For some years before the conflict the Oglethorpes had been accustomed to ease their financial burdens by quietly selling various small parcels of land to their neighbours, the Fairfaxes; and now the Manor of Oglethorpe was to cancel the fine. On September 15, 1653, Sutton Oglethorpe conveyed the entire property to Henry Fairfax of Bolton Priory, whose brother, Ferdinando, second Lord Fairfax, had commanded the Northern Forces for Parliament from 1640 to his death in 1647; whose nephew, Thomas, Third Lord Fairfax, was Commander-in-Chief of the Roundheads; and whose great-great-granddaughter, Anne, a century later in Virginia, married George Washington's brother, Lawrence, and subsequently Colonel George Lee.[1] Thus, after a tenure of six centuries, full of honour and dignity, the Oglethorpes had lost their heritage and patrimony. What more could befall them?

Yet even the loss of his estate and his own temporary

[1] By George Lee Anne Fairfax became the grand-aunt of General Robert E. Lee, Commander-in-Chief of the Confederate Army in the War between the States, 1861–5. One of Sutton Oglethorpe's fellow royalists was Colonel Henry Washington, a member of an avowedly royalist family whence sprang, nigh a century later, Lawrence Washington and his brother, George. Day, W. A., editor, *The Pythouse Papers* (London, 1879), p. 7 note. For the business relations of the Oglethorpes with the Fairfax family see MSS. Fairfax (Bodleian Library, Oxford), 32, f. 181; MS. 41 (Yorkshire Archaeological Society, Leeds): Fairfax MSS. c; g, pp. 13–15; m, pp. 33, 37–9; MS. 529 (Yorkshire Archaeological Society, Leeds): Collection of Yorkshire material made by George Sherwood, Bundle 3. For the Fairfax pedigree see Stowe MSS. (British Museum), 640; *Dugdale's Visitation of Yorkshire*, p. 151; Harwood, H. W. F., editor, 'The Family of Fairfax of Oglethorpe', *The Genealogist*, New Series, xviii (London, 1902), 174–9; Johnson, G. W., editor, *The Fairfax Correspondence: Memoirs of the Reign of Charles the First* (2 vols., London, 1848), i. cxxv note; Markham, Sir C. R., *Life of Robert Fairfax of Steeton* (London, 1885), p. 135; Speight, *Lower Wharfedale*, pedigree insert facing p. 169; Farrer, W., and Brownbill, E., editors, *Victoria County History of Lancashire* (8 vols., London, 1906–14), iv. 349 note.

imprisonment did not fill Sutton Oglethorpe's cup of woe. In the peaceful days of 1635 he had married a young widow, Frances Mathew Pickering, daughter of John Mathew and granddaughter of the late Archbishop Mathew of York. In 1637 she had borne him a son, Sutton Oglethorpe, junior,[1] who at sixteen was to sadden his parents by engaging in the royalist plot of Lord Howard of Escrick, so that he was seized, imprisoned, tried, convicted, and banished from Britain. Only after a humble petition by his distracted parents to the Protector himself, in 1657, was the hot-headed youth permitted to return under bond.[2] Although impoverished by Cromwell's zeal, Sutton Oglethorpe managed to send his namesake to Oxford and, in due course, to Gray's Inn, London. In 1663, after the Restoration of Charles II had brightened the prospects of the family, the young lawyer took his Oxford M.A., and on April 11, 1664, at twenty-six, rashly married Elizabeth Robinson, an orphan of twenty-one, in London.[3] Sutton Oglethorpe, junior, was now compelled to seek a livelihood and, falling back on the debt

---

[1] Clay, J. W., editor, *Paver's Marriage Licences* (Yorkshire Archaeological and Topographical Association Record Series, xl), p. 73; Cook, R. B., editor, *The Parish Registers of St. Martin, Coney Street, York* (Yorkshire Parish Register Society, Leeds, 1909), p. 62.

[2] *Calendar of State Papers, Domestic*, The Commonwealth, 1657, p. 49; 1659–60, p. 35; Birch, Thomas, editor, *Collection of the State Papers of John Thurloe, Esq., Secretary, First, to the Council of State, and afterwards to the Two Protectors, Oliver and Richard Cromwell* (7 vols., London, 1742), iv. 614; *Depositions from the Castle of York, relating to Offences committed in the Northern Counties in the Seventeenth Century* (Surtees Society Publication, xl, Durham, 1861), p. 46 note.

[3] *A Catalogue of All Graduates in Divinity, Law, and Physick; and of all Masters of Arts and Doctors of Musick, who have regularly proceeded or been created in the University of Oxford, Between October 10, 1659, and October 10, 1770* (Oxford, 1772), p. 258; Harwood, 'The Oglethorpes of Oglethorpe', *The Genealogist*, New Series, xx. 172–5; Armytage, G. J., editor, *Allegations for Marriage Licences issued from the Faculty Office of the Archbishop of Canterbury at London, 1543–1869* (Harleian Society Publications, xxiv, London, 1886), p. 78; Cokayne, G. E., and Fry, E. A., editors, *Calendar of Marriage Licences issued by the Faculty Office, 1632–1714* (Index Library, xxxii, London, 1905), p. 31; Chester, J. L., editor, *The Parish Registers of St. Mary Aldermary, 1558–1754* (Harleian Society Publications, *Registers*, v, London, 1880), p. 30.

that Charles II owed his family, was eventually made Master of the Stud and, in 1684, Collector of the King's Customs at Carlisle. He in turn had two sons, Sutton the third, who became page of honour to Charles II, and on the King's death was commissioned a Cornet in the Cavalry; and John, who was appointed an Ensign in the Army. Sutton Oglethorpe, junior, lived to the ripe old age of ninety and, as the family had finally left Yorkshire by 1680, died in London in 1727 and was buried in Wandsworth Parish Cemetery in Surrey.[1]

Although he played a prominent part in the Commonwealth period for so young a man, Sutton Oglethorpe, junior, was not to prove the most important offspring of his father. In addition to two daughters, Elizabeth and Ursula, old Sutton Oglethorpe, the first, had another son, Theophilus. It was Theophilus Oglethorpe, born at Oglethorpe Hall in Bramham, Yorkshire, and baptized on

---

[1] *Calendar of State Papers, Domestic*, Charles II, 1663–1664, p. 260; 1667, p. 149; 1673–1675, p. 311; 1676–1677, p. 447; 1682, p. 625; MSS. English History (Bodleian Library, Oxford), Payments for Services to Charles II and James II from the Accounts of the Office of the Treasurer of the Exchequer, b. 4, f. 125; b. 6, f. 124; b. 7, f. 129; b. 8, ff. 127, 129; b. 10, ff. 99, 107; b. 11, f. 96; b. 12, f. 97; b. 14, f. 81; b. 15, ff. 33, 41; b. 18, f. 77; b. 19, f. 87; b. 20, ff. 59, 65; b. 21, ff. 12, 61 verso; b. 99, ff. 8 verso, 14 verso; b. 100, ff. 5, 14: Payments to Sutton Oglethorpe, Master of the Stud, 1679–1687, and Collector of Customs at Carlisle, 1688; and to Sutton Oglethorpe, his son, as page, 1682–1685; Akerman, J. Y., editor, *Moneys Received and Paid for Secret Services of Charles II and James II, from 30th March, 1679, to 25th December, 1688* (Camden Society Publications, lii, London, 1851), pp. 60, 64, 70, 125; *Calendar of Treasury Books*, iv, 1672–1675, pp. 338, 556, 564, 651, 669, 825; v, 1676–1679, pp. 35, 202, 361, 552, 718, 800, 978; vii, 1681–1685, pp. 197, 222, 470, 473, 735, 897, 1118, 1128, 1376, 1449, 1503; viii, 1685–1689, pp. 76, 484, 573, 587, 623, 625, 711, 780, 817, 2012; S.P. 44 (State Papers, Domestic, Entry Books, P.R.O.): 164, Military Commissions, 1679–1687, p. 216; Dalton, Charles, *English Army Lists and Commission Registers, 1661–1714* (6 vols., London, 1892–1904), ii. 15, 106, 165; Squire, J. T., *The Registers of the Parish of Wandsworth, Surrey* (Lymington, 1889), p. 335; *Yorkshire Wills* (Yorkshire Archaeological and Topographical Association Record Series, lx), *passim*. In 1662 Sutton Oglethorpe was recorded as 'late of Oglethorpe in the Countie of York'. Platt, G. M., and Morkill, J. W., *Records of the Parish of Whitkirk* (Leeds, 1892), p. 44. See also pp. 34, 88, 128. A Sutton Oglethorpe, Esq., is listed among the Gentry of Yorkshire as living at Firby, North Riding, about 1673, Add. MSS. (British Museum), 29694, 'Paver's Records', f. 61 verso.

September 14, 1650,[1] who was the first of his line to embody within himself all three attributes of his family: loyalty to the Crown; the profession of arms; and the parliamentary tradition. At the Restoration Sutton Oglethorpe, the patriarch, had wisely determined to rely on royal favour for his sons, and Charles II did not fail his old supporter. Despite the pleadings of the Treasury, Charles, in the words of a recent biographer, 'was not of the stuff of which economists are made',[2] and so could never bear to reduce or abolish the numerous pensions, debts, or outright gifts which he had lavished on the survivors or heirs of his father's loyal aides. The royal favours to Sutton Oglethorpe, junior, and his two sons have been described. Thirteen years younger than his brother, Theophilus was to gain even more. Having secured his first training as 'a Captain at the Age of Eighteen under the Famous Marshal Turenne in France',[3] he was given a Captain's commission in England in 1675 and assigned to command a company in the Horse Guards. This was no time for a weakling in the army, for Charles was confronted with both continental campaigns and a recurrent rising of Scottish Covenanters and the imminence of civil war. Theophilus Oglethorpe was in his element, and late in 1675 was sent, on full pay from both England and France, to aid Louis XIV for two years. His reward in 1678 was a promotion from 'Lieutenant to the First Troop of Granadeers' in the Guards under the Earl of Feversham to the rank of Major of the King's Own Regiment of Dragoons, and Brigadier of the Duke of York's Troop of Horse Guards. As such Oglethorpe commanded the Dragoons at Morpeth in Northumberland and saw action on September 14 of that year at Crookham, near Flodden Field, where began the struggle between the Cavaliers of

[1] Harwood, 'The Oglethorpes of Oglethorpe', *The Genealogist*, New Series, xx. 172–5.
[2] Bryant, Arthur, *King Charles II* (London, 1931), p. 169.
[3] *Register* of the College of Arms, 4 D 14, p. 68, Statement by Lady Eleanor Oglethorpe, April 21, 1716.

Charles II and the rugged Scottish Covenanters which was not ended until the Duke of Monmouth and the Earl of Feversham, with Oglethorpe commanding his own troop of dragoons as the advance guard, suppressed the rising at Bothwell Brigg on June 22, 1679. Victory brought further recognition, for Theophilus now sought and obtained not a few escheated estates forfeited by unfortunate Scots, grants which amply compensated him for his father's misfortunes under the Commonwealth. Early in 1680 he was expected to proceed in June to Tangier in command of England's North African outpost of three Guards regiments,[1] but fate, in the guise of a young lady, intervened and the warrior became the courtier.[2]

When in 1670 Charles II of England and Louis XIV of France met at Dover to conclude the treaty of alliance which the former's sister, Henrietta, Duchess of Orléans, had fostered, there appeared among the latter's maids of honour a twenty-year-old daughter of a noble but impoverished family in Brittany, named Louise Renée

---

[1] In June, 1682, £250 were paid out to 'Coll. Oglethorp' for 'Tangier, two years'. MSS. English History (Bodleian Library, Oxford), b. 10, f. 65.

[2] *Calendar of State Papers, Domestic*, Charles II, 1673–1675, pp. 567, 575; 1676–1677, pp. 206–7, 209; 1677–1678, pp. 251, 260; 1678, p. 270; 1679–1680, pp. 53–4, 56, 172, 228, 232, 410, 457, 470, 584; S.P. 44 (State Papers, Domestic, Entry Books, Public Record Office, hereinafter cited as P.R.O.): 164. Military Commissions, 1679–1687, pp. 48, 57; Add. MSS. (British Museum), 28082, Army Lists, f. 108; Dalton, *English Army Lists*, i. 204, 240, 254–5, 263, 273; Arthur, Sir George C. A., *Story of the Household Cavalry* (3 vols., London, 1909–26), i. 149 note, 157 and note, 161; Scott, Sir S. B., *The British Army* (3 vols., London, 1880), iii. 306; Barrington, Michael, *Grahame of Claverhouse, Viscount Dundee* (London, 1911), pp. 62–3; Akerman, *Moneys Received and Paid for Secret Services*, p. 1; Ralph, J., *History of England during the Reigns of King William, Queen Anne, and King George the First* (2 vols., London, 1744–6), i. 464; *Register of the Privy Council of Scotland*, 3rd series, vi. 118. For the following references I am indebted to R. C. Bosanquet, Esq., of Rock Moor, Alnwick, and his lucid letter of Aug. 20, 1932: Bosanquet, R. C., *Cavaliers and Covenanters: The Crookham Affray of 1678* (Newcastle-upon-Tyne, 1932), p. 41; McCrie, Thomas, editor, *Memoirs of William Veitch* (Edinburgh, 1825), pp. 69–72, 215 f.; Dalton, Charles, *The Scots Army* (2 vols., London, 1909), ii. 119 and note 2.

de Penencovet de Quéroualle.[1] Charles paid her so much attention that when the tragic death of Henrietta soon after deprived Louis of his chief support in maintaining the pact, Louise was made a pawn in the diplomatic manœuvres of the French King, who, to please Charles and keep him faithful to the alliance, sent her to London where she was soon dubbed 'Madam Carwell'. In the pungent phrase of Charles's biographer, 'virtue, duly tempered to meet the needs of a great occasion, had proved the handmaid of diplomacy',[2] and an infatuated monarch promptly created his favourite Duchess of Portsmouth. As such, Louise acquired a retinue worthy of her rank, wherein there served as her maid a winsome Irish colleen from Tipperary named Eleanor Wall. Born in 1662, Eleanor was the daughter of Richard Wall, or Du-Vall, of Rathkenny, who had lost his all in service for his King, having been 'transplanted' to the wilds of Connaught by the Commonwealth in 1656. Her mother was Catharine, daughter of Maurice Roche of Killcoman, Tipperary. Despite this ancestry, whence she claimed descent from Richard Seigneur de Val Dery, a colleague of William the Conqueror, and kinship through the de la Roche family with the house of Argyll,[3] Ellen, as she soon was called, accepted this post of necessity, but used her adversities to carve out for herself an amazing career. By 1679 the power of 'Madam Carwell' was at its zenith[4]

[1] *MSS. of the Marquis of Ormonde* (H.M.C. Reports, ii), p. 176; Forneron, H., *Louise de Kéroualle* (translated by Mrs. G. M. Crawford, London, 1887), p. 229; Lemoine, J., and Lichtenberger, A., 'Louise de Kéroualle, Duchesse de Portsmouth', *Revue des Deux Mondes*, xiv (Paris, 1903), 114–46, 358–96; Cartwright, Julia (Mrs. Henry Ady), *Sacharissa: Some Account of Dorothy, Countess of Sunderland* (2nd ed., London, 1893), p. 221; Hartmann, C. H., *Charles II and Madame* (London, 1934), chaps. xiv–xviii, particularly p. 315.

[2] Bryant, *Charles II*, p. 221.

[3] For Eleanor Wall's ancestry see her own statement of April 21, 1716, in the *Register* of the College of Arms, 4 D 14, p. 68; and her obituary notices in the London *Daily Journal*, June 26, 1732, p. 1; *Daily Post*, June 26, 1732, p. 1; *Grub-Street Journal*, June 29, 1732, p. 3; *London Journal*, July 1, 1732, p. 3. See also Thoresby, *Ducatus Leodiensis*, pp. 254–5.

[4] Much light is shed on the importance of the Duchess of Portsmouth during these years in Barillon's reports to Louis XIV from London. See

and, as was natural at the court of Charles II, her seventeen-year-old maid, by holding the key of admittance to her favour, had become a personage of vital importance to Louise's ardent admirers, most of whom, like the Duke of Monmouth and Henry Sidney, soon found that access to their idol often depended on courtesies to Ellen Wall.[1] In April 1680 on the death of Mistress Dorothy Chiffinch who with her husband, William, had controlled Charles II's domestic arrangements at Whitehall since the Restoration,[2] Eleanor Wall was promoted to the post of Head Laundress and 'sempstriss' to the King at a stipend of two thousand pounds a year, and given lodgings in the rear of the palace, near the stairs leading to the barges on the Thames and directly opposite the quarters of the dashing young Major of Dragoons, Theophilus Oglethorpe.[3]

The courtship was ardent and successful. The young

Baschet's Transcripts, in the Public Record Office, London, from the Archives des Affaires Étrangères, Paris.

[1] James, Duke of York, later James II, to Colonel George Legge, later First Baron Dartmouth. Edinburgh, Nov. 22, 1680: 'I see you have had some conversations with Mrs. Walle, you would do well to continue it, for I do realy beleve hir to be my friend', *MSS. of the Earl of Dartmouth* (H.M.C. Reports, xi, Appendix, part v), i. 53; Blencowe, R. W., editor, *Diary of the Times of Charles the Second, by Henry Sidney, afterward Earl of Romney* (2 vols., London, 1843), i. 170, 190–1; ii. 22–3; Cartwright, *Sacharissa*, p. 221.

[2] On the Chiffinch family see Fea, Allan, editor, *Memoirs of Gramont* (London, 1906), pp. 335 note, 336 note; Quennell, Peter, editor, *Memoirs of the Count de Gramont* (London, 1930), p. 337; *MSS. of the Late Allan George Finch* (H.M.C. Reports), ii. 81–4.

[3] The warrant of her appointment as Laundress, signed by Charles II, is dated Nov. 10, 1680, Add. MSS. (British Museum), 5750, f. 35. Her salary began in April, L.S. 1 (Lord Steward's Department, Controller of the Household, P.R.O.): 22, Accounts for 1680. See also E. 351 (Declared Accounts from the Pipe Office): 3111. Pipe Roll for the Wardrobe, Sept. 1679–Sept. 1680; and A.O. 1 (Audit Office), Bundle 2361, Roll 111. Accounts of the Great Wardrobe for 1680. For further contemporary light on her position and promotion see Francesco Terriesi to the Secretary of State, Florence, London, June 23, 1681, Add. MSS. (British Museum), 25362, Despatches of the Florentine Minister to England, v, ff. 144–5; *Calendar of State Papers, Domestic*, Charles II, 1679–1680, p. 40; 1680–1681, pp. 84, 229; Carte MSS. (Bodleian Library, Oxford), cclxvi, f. 39 a, Memorandum by Thomas Carte of conversation with Anne Oglethorpe, September 10, 1750, concerning her mother's associations with Louise Quéroualle, Duchess of Portsmouth, at the Court of Charles II.

couple had no economic embarrassments: Eleanor retained her advantageous posts with both King and Duchess; Theophilus, secure in the royal favour, had such diverse interests as a coal-mine and further forfeited estates in Scotland.[1] They were young and in love, and life was good; and one could always look forward to another promotion! Observing the example of John Churchill and Sarah Jennings, on whose marriage in 1678 the former continued to address his wife as Miss Jennings, Ellen Wall decided to retain her maiden name for a time, and married her Theophilus some time in 1680;[2] and happiness came in a prompt succession of sturdy sons and daughters: Lewis, born in February 1681; Theophilus, junior, 1682; Anne Henrietta, 1683; and Eleanor, in 1684.[3] It is a singular fact that, at a court notorious through the ages for its blatant immorality, the worst that could be said of Ellen had been that, prior to her marriage, she had ardently admired the Duke of Monmouth;[4] and no taint of suspicion or mention by that scandal-monger, Gramont, ever attached itself to either Theophilus or Eleanor Wall Oglethorpe. And yet an issue now arose which threatened to close the former's

[1] For reference to coal-mine see William Daggett to John Wentworth, London, Dec. 22, 1679, *MSS. in Various Collections* (H.M.C. Reports), ii. *MSS. of Mrs. Wentworth*, p. 395. For forfeited estates see *MSS. of the Duke of Buccleuch and Queensberry* (H.M.C. Reports, xv, Appendix, part viii), i. 139.

[2] In the accounts of the Controller of the Household she is listed as Elinor Wall until Oct. 1681 (L.S. 1:23–24); in the Declared Accounts of the Audit Office, she is 'Elianor Wall, nunc Elianor Oglethorpe' in March 1681 (A.O. 1, Bundle 2361, Roll 112); while in the Declared Accounts from the Pipe Office, the name changes after Sept. 1681 (E. 351:3112–3113). See also *MSS. of Sir H. Verney, Bart.* (H.M.C. Reports, vii), p. 479; *MSS. of the Marquis of Ormonde* (H.M.C. Reports, vii), p. 744.

[3] For the sequence and dates of birth see Shield, Alice, 'The Loyal Oglethorpes', *The Royalist*, ix (London, 1898), 41. For confirmation of Lewis Oglethorpe's birth in Feb. 1681 see *Journals of the House of Commons* (hereinafter cited as *Commons Journals*) (in progress, London, 1742—), xiv. 26. Thoresby affirms that the first five Oglethorpe children were born 'in St. James's House', Thoresby, *Ducatus Leodiensis*, pp. 254–5.

[4] For Ellen Wall's attitude towards Monmouth see Lemoine and Lichtenberger, 'Louise de Kéroualle, Duchesse de Portsmouth', *Revue des Deux Mondes*, xiv. 372.

career, an issue based, of all conceivable causes, on religion!

For reasons of state, Charles II had deemed it wise to conceal his own Catholic predilections, but not so his brother and heir apparent, James, Duke of York, whose honest convictions were often made the justification for many a surreptitious movement of revolt. The surcharged atmosphere of 1678 and her association with the Dukes of York and Monmouth had completely won the ardent lass from Tipperary, now heart and soul in the Catholic cause. It therefore was not strange that Theophilus Oglethorpe, who had valiantly aided Monmouth to rout Scottish Covenanters for Charles, should be drawn into the Duke of York's circle. Theophilus had been a messenger for the 'Papists' of 1674 and his name was associated with the Popish Plot revealed by Titus Oates in 1678, while Ellen's was linked with the Fitz-Harris case arising out of the attempts to bar James from the succession to Charles, and the Duchess of Portsmouth's intrigues for Monmouth against the Duke of York. But the services of Major Oglethorpe at Bothwell Brigg so impressed his sovereign that all was forgiven. In 1681 one of the court ladies wrote to her cousin that 'the King is taking away two dishes from his table, but yet I hear of a new game of cards at Court that he usually ventures two or three hundred guineas a night at'.[1] With such a king timidity was a sin and the Yorkshire warrior entered the lists for royal favour—and won. It was Theophilus Oglethorpe who brought the news that Parliament would recognize James the Catholic as heir apparent; it was he who was promoted to Lieutenant-Colonel in the Horse Guards and Master of the Horse to the King; and it was he who received further intestate or escheated estates. In 1681, for at least the third time in his brief career, he engaged in a brawl at St. Martin-in-the-Fields, wherein, according to the Court record, he 'slew and murdered the said

[1] *Portland MSS.* (H.M.C. Reports, xiv, Appendix, part ii), iii, *Harley MSS.* i. 368.

John Richardson by then and there giving him with a rapier a mortal wound near the navell, of which he died on the following day at St. Paul's, Covent Garden'; but the consequences were light: Acquitted of murder but 'Found Guilty' of manslaughter, Theophilus Oglethorpe 'asked for the Book, read it, and was branded', and no further punishment ensued.[1] The Colonel's position was unassailable, and to importunate courtiers he became as necessary as his wife had been while maid to the Duchess of Portsmouth.[2]

[1] Jeaffreson, J. C., editor, *Middlesex County Records*, iv (London, 1892), 150. Theophilus Oglethorpe had been in a quarrel in 1669 and had fought a duel in Picardy, France, in 1678. Dr. William Denton to Sir R. Verney, no place, Oct. 27, 1669, *MSS. of Sir H. Verney, Bart.* (H.M.C. Reports), p. 488; Lord Preston, British Ambassador to France, to Colonel Oglethorpe, Paris, December 23, 1682, *MSS. of Sir F. Graham, Bart.* (H.M.C. Reports, vii, part i), p. 276; *MSS. of the Marquis of Bath: Coventry Papers* (H.M.C. Reports, iii), p. 229; Duke of Ormonde to the Earl of Arran, London, Jan. 9, 1683, Carte MSS. (Bodleian Library, Oxford), l, f. 307.

[2] For new light on the Popish Plot see Hay, M. V., *The Jesuits and the Popish Plot* (London, 1934), chaps. v–vii. For the most authoritative survey of Jacobitism see Petrie, Sir Charles, Bart., *The Jacobite Movement* (London, 1932). For this portion see pp. 47–56. A strong German survey is found in Michael, Wolfgang, *Englische Geschichte im achtzehnten Jahrhundert* (3 vols., Berlin and Leipzig, 1920–35), ii. 283–409. The above paragraph is compiled from the following sources: Baschet's Paris Transcripts. P.R.O. Bundle 149, f. 156 (Archives, vol. 142, f. 484): Barillon to the King, London, June 16, 1681; Add. MSS. (British Museum), 27402, The Confession of Edward Fitz-Harris, f. 167; Add. MSS. 27277, f. 148; London *Current Intelligence*, June 11, 1681, p. 2; *MSS. of Sir William Fitzherbert, Bart.* (H.M.C. Reports, xiii, Appendix, part vi), pp. 58, 60; *MSS. of the Marquis of Ormonde* (H.M.C. Reports, vii, Appendix, part i), p. 744; *Calendar of State Papers, Domestic*, Charles II, 1680–1681, pp. 74, 96, 131, 154, 306, 309, 337, 512, 610, 615, 619; 1682, p. 430; *Calendar of Treasury Books*, vii, 1681–1685, pp. 352, 361, 488–9, 510, 551, 634–5, 674; viii, 1685–1689, pp. 101, 162–3; *MSS. of Sir H. Verney, Bart.* (H.M.C. Reports), p. 479; *MSS. of the Marquis of Ormonde at Kilkenny Castle*, New Series (H.M.C. Reports), iv. 586–91; v. 551; vi. 54, 75, 249, 263, 399, 509; *MSS. of Mrs. Frankland-Russell-Astley* (H.M.C. Reports), p. 48; *MSS. of Sir N. W. Throckmorton* (H.M.C. Reports, x, Appendix, part iv), p. 172; Feiling, Keith, and Needham, F. R. D., editors, 'The Journals of Edmund Warcup, 1676–1684', *English Historical Review*, xl. 252; Chamberlayne, Edward, *Angliae Notitiae; or, the Present State of England* (20 vols., London, 1669–1704), xii (1682), 205, 228; xiv (1684), 203; Kennett, White, *Complete History of England* (2nd ed., 3 vols., London, 1719), iii. 386; Oldmixon, J., *History of England during the Reigns*

Once involved, however, the Oglethorpes could not repudiate the cause. Theophilus found himself enmeshed in the activities of the notorious Count Königsmark during 1681 and 1682,[1] and both he and his wife were implicated with Monmouth, Robert Ferguson, and Lord Howard of Escrick in the Rye House Plot of 1683 to assassinate Charles; although one contemporary, the Earl of Ailesbury, counted him a supporter of the King.[2] Charles's only reaction to all such rumours of disloyalty was to bestow still more honours on the Oglethorpes. When in the summer of 1684 the Founders and Coppersmiths Company, one of the great Livery Companies of London, received its new charter, Colonel Theophilus Oglethorpe was appointed Master by the King.[3] Retaining thus in divers ways a close affiliation with the court, it happened that, as Charles lay dying early in February 1685, Eleanor Wall Oglethorpe, who with her husband now had quarters in St. James's Palace, was in the room next to that of the

of the Royal House of Stuart (London, 1730), p. 658; Ralph, *History of England*, i. 564, 598–601; Grey, Hon. Anchitel, editor, *Debates of the House of Commons, 1667 to 1694* (10 vols., London, 1769), ix. 181; Dalton, *English Army Lists*, i. 277, 313; Luttrell, Narcissus, *A Brief Historical Relation of State Affairs, from September, 1678, to April, 1714* (6 vols., Oxford, 1857), i. 149, 170; Toynbee, Paget, editor, *Reminiscences written by Mr. Horace Walpole in 1788* (Oxford, 1924), p. 125 note; Kitchin, G., *Sir Roger L'Estrange* (London, 1913), pp. 340–1; Ailesbury, Thomas, Earl of, *Memoirs* (2 vols., Roxburghe Club, London, 1890), i. 62, 74; Cartwright, J. J., editor, *Memoirs of Sir John Reresby* (London, 1875), p. 278; Thompson, E. M., editor, *Correspondence of the Family of Hatton* (2 vols., Camden Society Publications, New Series, xxii–xxiii, London, 1878), ii. 11.

[1] Oglethorpe even saw Count Königsmark off to the Continent in 1682 but, despite this, was released in May from his obligations as a bondsman for the Count, *Calendar of State Papers, Domestic*, Charles II, 1682, pp. 79, 86–7, 101, 103, 113–14, 116, 118, 127, 129–30, 136–7, 142, 170, and especially 212; *Calendar of Treasury Books*, vii, 1681–1685, p. 577; *MSS. of the Marquis of Ormonde*, New Series (H.M.C. Reports), vi. 338.

[2] Ailesbury, *Memoirs*, i. 74. See also a letter of 1683 by Colonel Oglethorpe on government efforts to preserve the *de facto* administration, *Calendar of State Papers, Domestic*, Charles II, July–December, 1683, p. 209 (State Papers, Domestic, P.R.O., Charles II, vol. 429, no. 162).

[3] Hazlitt, W. C., *The Livery Companies of the City of London* (London, 1892), p. 494. Hazlitt errs in identifying Colonel Oglethorpe as James Edward Oglethorpe.

King. While Theophilus Oglethorpe and Henry Sidney stood guard at one door of the royal bedroom, Eleanor herself watched the other as a priest came to administer Extreme Unction to the prodigal son of the Church.[1] And on that same day, February 6, 1685, while Charles II by his death was placing the destinies of England and the Oglethorpes in the hands of James, Duke of York, the Borough of Morpeth in Northumberland chose Theophilus Oglethorpe as its Member of Parliament.[2] His candidacy, in the district where he had gained a name for himself in the campaigns of 1678 and 1679 against the Scottish Covenanters, had been urged upon him by James himself, in whose favour he was now secure. Little wonder then that, when in the late spring of 1685 the turbulent Duke of Monmouth, capitalizing on his personal popularity and success against the Covenanters, emerged from his exile in Holland and raised the standard of rebellion

[1] It should be noted that the presence of the Oglethorpes at the death of Charles II is not recorded by any historian of the period, nor in Barillon's reports to Louis XIV (Baschet's Paris Transcripts, P.R.O. Bundle 160, ff. 36–42: French Archives, vol. 154, ff. 107 ff., 119 ff.); but Dr. Crawfurd refers to the fact that there were others in the room besides Father Huddleston. Crawfurd, Raymond, *Last Days of Charles II* (Oxford, 1909), p. 43. The version in the text is based on 'A Memorandum of Thomas Carte's Conversation with General Oglethorpe, February 3, 1749', Carte MSS. (Bodleian Library, Oxford), ccxxxvii, f. 35. Carte had heard this story 'several times before from him, his sister Anne, and mother, Lady Oglethorpe'. According to this narrative, Eleanor Wall Oglethorpe asserted that Charles II, due to his inability to swallow and his general physical condition, was unable to complete the ceremonies of the Church and so 'died in the Church of England'; whereupon King James, deeming it to his own political advantage to have his brother remembered as a Catholic, betrayed deep anger at her, and his minister suspended for a time her pension of nine hundred pounds. On the other hand, John Wesley in 1772 recorded in his *Journal* that Lady Oglethorpe had told his elder brother, Samuel, that 'I never left the room from the moment the King was taken ill till the breath went out of his body, and I aver that neither Father Huddleston nor any priest came into the room till his death'. Curnock, N., editor, *The Journal of the Rev. John Wesley, A.M.* (8 vols., London, 1909–16), v. 491.

[2] London *Gazette*, April 13, 1685, p. 2; *A Complete List of the Lords Spiritual, ... etc., in the Parliament of 1685* (London, 1685); *A True List of Members of Parliament, which met, May 19, 1685* (London, 1685); Gray, *Debates of the House of Commons*, viii. 367, 373–9; Bean, W. W., *The Parliamentary Representation of the Six Northern Counties of England* (Hull, 1890), pp. 543, 561.

against Catholic James II, Colonel Theophilus Oglethorpe forsook the halls of Westminster and promptly took the field for his King!

With the death of Charles II and the coronation as James II of his patron, the Duke of York, Theophilus Oglethorpe passed the next three years in a state of glorious ecstasy, replete with honours and royal recognition for himself and his Ellen, who were to attain their greatest distinctions and emoluments as a result of Monmouth's Rebellion of June 1685. Having been permitted by his forbearing father to escape after the Rye House Plot to Holland, where he found a haven with William of Orange, James Scott, Duke of Monmouth, son of Charles II by Lucy Walters, noted the death of his father and landed in Dorsetshire on June 11. Gathering a force of six thousand men, he proclaimed himself king as James II, but within a month the royal troops had pursued the invader and, routing his forces at Sedgemoor on July 6, had captured Monmouth himself, who, unable to pierce the stern soul of the regnant James II, was executed nine days later. Theophilus Oglethorpe's activities in this campaign have drawn high praise[1] and severe censure.[2] For his rout of

[1] Atkinson, C. T., *Marlborough and the Rise of the British Army* (New York, 1921), p. 79: Oglethorpe's attack 'dispirited and alarmed' Monmouth; Arthur, *Story of the Household Cavalry*, i. 180–2, 185–94: Oglethorpe was 'indefatigable' in his watching which helped to create Sedgemoor, but by the time Monmouth was in retreat, was 'perhaps a little stale'. See also MSS. Clarendon (Bodleian Library, Oxford), 128, f. 35; *MSS. of Mrs. Stopford-Sackville* (H.M.C. Reports), i. 4, 8–10, 12–19; Doble, C. E., editor, *Correspondence of Henry, Earl of Clarendon, and James, Earl of Abingdon, chiefly relating to the Monmouth Insurrection (1683–1685)* (Oxford Historical Society Publications, xxxii, *Collectanea*, Oxford, 1896), iii. 264–6; Davis, J., *History of the Second Queen's Royal Regiment, now the Queen's (Royal West Surrey) Regiment* (6 vols., London, 1887–1906), ii. 23–7, 48; Dalton, *English Army Lists*, ii. 3; Fitzroy, Sir Almaric, *Henry, Duke of Grafton, 1663–1690* (London, 1921), p. 39; *MSS. of the Duke of Buccleuch and Queensberry at Drumlanrig Castle* (H.M.C. Reports), ii. 82–3.

[2] Page, M., *The Battle of Sedgemoor* (Bridgwater, 1930), p. 18: 'Major Oglethorpe, a blustering cavalryman, whose adventures that night were humorous'; pp. 20–1, 28–31: the rebels 'passed, in fact, under Oglethorpe's nose' and 'it is clear that the Major was not watching at all, and we may safely assume that he was asleep on the hill'; pp. 37, 44, 49–51: Oglethorpe

the rebels at Keynsham[1] he was lauded by his superior, the Earl of Feversham, and the Earl of Clarendon, although modern authorities have been more critical of his tactics in this prelude to Sedgemoor, maintaining that he blundered into the enemy and was exceedingly fortunate in his escape. The fact remains that, after Sedgemoor, he allowed Monmouth's men to outflank him and temporarily at least to escape.[2] Be that as it may, James II, in sending Feversham on July 6 commissions of Major General for Churchill and MacKay, and Brigadier General for Sackville and Kirke, sent 'a blank Commission of Colonell . . . for Oglethorpe, if you think fitt to give it to him'.[3] Feversham, being a crafty courtier as well as a capable commander, realized fully the situation, and Oglethorpe, 'the one officer who was least responsible

'could still do nothing right'; pp. 62–5, 67, 76–9: 'our unblushing colonel'; Taylor, Frank, *The Wars of Marlborough, 1702–1709* (2 vols., Oxford, 1921), ii. 405–31: Oglethorpe at Keynsham was 'careless', and after Sedgemoor 'a courageous but incompetent officer, . . . almost hopelessly incompetent'; Oldmixon, *History of England*, pp. 704–5: Echard called Oglethorpe 'an insolent Bravo', and Oldmixon himself compared Oglethorpe and his fellow officers with the notorious Judge Jeffreys; Wolseley, General Viscount, K. P., *The Life of John Churchill, Duke of Marlborough, to the Accession of Queen Anne* (2 vols., London, 1894), i. 297–8, 322–4. The most moderate summation of criticism—and the most recent—is by Churchill, Winston S., *Marlborough: His Life and Times* (4 vols., London, 1933–5), i. 217–18.

[1] London *Gazette*, June 29, 1685, p. 1.

[2] London *Gazette*, July 2, 1685, p. 1; July 9, 1685, p. 1; Lord Dunblane to the Earl of Danby, no place, June 27, 1685, Add. MSS. (British Museum), 28050, Darnley Papers, f. 46; Baron de Wassenaer Duvenvoirde, Arnout van Citters, and Everard van Weede, Dutch Embassadors Extraordinary in England, to the States General, London, July 10, 1685, Add. MSS. (British Museum), 34507, Mackintosh Collections, xxi, Dutch Political Correspondence relating to England, 1685–8, i, f. 44; *MSS. of the Marquis of Ormonde*, New Series (H.M.C. Reports), vii. 343–4; Carte MSS. (Bodleian Library, Oxford), xl, f. 420; lxii, f. 611; Willcock, John, 'The Cipher in Monmouth's Diary', *English Historical Review*, xx. 731; Parke, Edmund, *An Historical Record of the Royal Regiment of Horse Guards* (2nd ed., London, 1847), pp. 33–42; Kennett, *Complete History of England*, iii. 432; Ralph, *History of England*, i. 878, 881.

[3] State Papers, Domestic (P.R.O.), James II, vol. ii, Inland Letters relating to the Duke of Monmouth's Rebellion, June 13–July 21, 1685, p. 55: Earl of Sunderland, Secretary of State (for James II) to the Earl of Feversham, Whitehall, July 6, 1685.

for it' in the eyes of his critics,[1] instead of being dismissed for 'incompetence and carelessness', was detailed to carry the good news of victory to his sovereign who, in the words of a contemporary, 'knighted Oglethorpe by the Queen's bed syde after hee had told all hee could in her hearing'.[2] Secure in this honour, in which Macaulay a century and a half later concurred,[3] Sir Theophilus could well afford to overlook the sneers of Sir John Bramston and John, Lord Churchill, who enviously wrote to the Earl of Clarendon that, 'as to the taking caire of the men and all other things that is my duty, I am shure nobody can be more careful then I am; and as for my obedience, I am shure Mr. Oglethorp is not more dutyfull then I am; . . . I see plainly that the troble is mine, and that the honor will be anothers'.[4] And one can well understand the pride with which the new knight wrote to his French friend, the Marshal de Duras, concerning his own part in ensuring victory for James II of England.[5]

Theophilus Oglethorpe was now somewhat of a popular hero, and he reaped a rich harvest from his labours. In November 1685 he took his seat in Parliament where he served on committees with such distinguished colleagues

[1] Edwards, H. J., and Edwards, E. A., *A Short Life of Marlborough* (London, 1926), pp. 48–50.
[2] Newton, Lady, *The House of Lyme* (London, 1917), pp. 335–6; Luttrell, *Brief Relation*, i. 349, 352; *The Autobiography of Sir John Bramston, K.B.* (Camden Society Publications, Old Series, xxxii, London, 1845), p. 185; *MSS. of the Duke of Rutland* (H.M.C. Reports, xii, Appendix, part v), ii. 90–2. Anne Oglethorpe told Thomas Carte that her father 'was knighted by the King himself in the Queen's bed chamber under a banner, when he arrived at Court with the news of the victory'. Thomas Carte to John Anstis, Garter Knight, London, Oct. 6, 1737, Carte MSS. (Bodleian Library, Oxford), ccxxxiv, f. 48. For Oglethorpe's account of the battle see Add. MSS. (British Museum), 18979, Fairfax Correspondence, f. 300. See also Add. MSS. 38012, Letters relating to Monmouth's Rebellion, f. 31 and verso.
[3] Macaulay, T. B., Lord, *History of England* (10th ed., 5 vols., London, 1854–61), i. 597–8, 610.
[4] John, Lord Churchill, to the Earl of Clarendon, 'Gomerton, Jully 4th, 1685', Singer, S. W., editor, *Correspondence of Henry Hyde, Earl of Clarendon* (2 vols., London, 1828), i. 141.
[5] Cosnac, Comte de, and Bertrand, A., editors, *Mémoires du Marquis de Sourches* (13 vols., Paris, 1882–93; index volume, Chartres, 1912), i. 271–3.

as Charles and Sidney Godolphin, Captain George and Sir Winston Churchill, Sir Dudley and Sir Henry North, Sir Christopher Wren, William Blathwayte, Thomas Fairfax, the Earl of Middleton, and Samuel Pepys. It was in this session, on November 16, 1685, that Oglethorpe heard Pepys present the cause of the English Navy and joined that great administrator in advocating a training period for seasoning recruits, affirming that 'new troops are not so good as old, and more subject to disorders, but will be less so, when they are longer under discipline. The King of France never sends Troops to his Army till they have been two or three years on foot in a garrison'.[1] But his interests were wider than merely the support of military and naval budgets on the floor of the House, for the honours had come in abundance not to him alone. To Ellen, of course, had fallen the title of Lady Oglethorpe and gradual establishment as a royal *confidante* in the King's *entourage*,[2] while Theophilus was made a King's Equerry and Colonel of the King's Holland Regiment of Foot, comprising six hundred men. In addition he received from the Scottish Parliament the forfeited estate of Gordon of Earlstoun, and in 1687 from James II that of Reginald Tucker, attainted for treason. But the greatest royal boon fell to the happy couple in November 1685, when a plot of ground, 200 by 135 feet, in St. James's Park, where the Laundry House stood, was deeded over by royal warrant to Lady Oglethorpe for thirty-one years

[1] Grey, *Debates of the House of Commons, 1667 to 1694*, viii. 367, 373–9; Cobbett, William, editor, *The Parliamentary History of England, 1066–1803* (36 vols., London, 1806–20), iv. 1346, 1382; *The Several Debates of the House of Commons, Pro & Contra., from November 9 to November 20, 1685* (no place, no date), p. 30; Chandler, Richard, editor, *The History and Proceedings of the House of Commons from the Restoration to the Present Time* (14 vols., London, 1742–4), ii. 191; *Commons Journals*, ix. 723, 729, 731, 733, 736, 740–1, 759. There are copies of Theophilus Oglethorpe's remarks in the following British Museum MSS.: Harleian MSS., 1236, p. 12; Harleian MSS., 6801, f. 276 verso; Sloane MSS., 1470, f. 68; and a shorthand version in Sloane MSS., 3082, f. 14 verso.

[2] M. de Bonrepans to the Marquis de Seignelay, London, Jan. 31, 1686, Baschet's Paris Transcripts, P.R.O. Bundle 163, f. 34 (French Archives, vol. 157, f. 42 ff.).

at the nominal annual rental of ten shillings, so that she might there erect Godolphin House. Henceforth the Oglethorpes were assured of the King's favour and when Sir Theophilus, as 'Keeper of the Walk called New Lodge in Cranborne within Windsor Forest', sought repairs to the lodge, his royal patron sent no less an authority on architecture than the Master of the King's Works, Sir Christopher Wren, the immortal creator of St. Paul's Cathedral and the Sheldonian Theatre, Oxford. The Oglethorpes were prospering, nor can it be said that they were at all reticent in seeking and employing varied means of amassing a fortune. Theophilus engaged in such diverse enterprises as his old coal-mine; the barter of army offices, wherein he received 260 guineas for the right to be agent to his regiment; the salvaging of a wreck near Hispaniola, an activity which from 1683 to 1689 had become a principal concern of Charles II and James II; and the arrangement of a financial compact with the King himself; while Lady Eleanor lent money to the King and then calmly sent her millinery and travelling expenses to the royal treasury which promptly paid them; and the climax came in 1688 when the King, at the latter's request, presented to Sir Theophilus a lease for an estate of 1,197 acres at Staughton Magna in Huntingdonshire.[1]

[1] MSS. English History (Bodleian Library, Oxford), b. 11, f. 66; b. 93, pp. 29, 37, 45, 53, 57, 161: Payments for Services to Charles II and James II from the Accounts of the Office of the Treasurer of the Exchequer; b. 102, pp. 2, 4; Fanny Oglethorpe to the Duke of Mar, Paris, Dec. 23, 1717, The King's Collection of Stuart MSS. at Windsor Castle; Add. MSS. (British Museum), 10118, First draft of a History of King James II, By Joseph Johnston, Prior of the English Benedictines at Paris, f. 167 (p. 255); A.O. 1 (Declared Accounts from the Audit Office), Bundle 2479, Roll 276 (P.R.O.), Account of Sir Christopher Wren for work at Windsor Castle, 1686–8; E. 351 (Declared Accounts from the Pipe Office): 3453 (P.R.O.). Works and Buildings. Windsor Castle, 1686–8; Works, 6:40 (P.R.O.), Accounts, St. James's. Repairs to Coll. Oglethorpe's lodgings, February 1687; 6:112, Warrants for Windsor Castle, 1687: Oglethorpe's New Lodge reported as 'very ruinous and in grave want of reparations'; Wren's estimate was £374 13s. See also *Calendar of Treasury Books*, viii. 1685–1689, pp. 326, 443, 504, 788, 923–4, 1052, 1229, 1273, 1280–1, 1443, 1597, 1794, 1796–7, 2050, 2067–8; *MSS. of the Duke of Rutland* (H.M.C. Reports, xii, Appendix,

Such regal liberality demanded strong proof of reciprocal loyalty, and 1685 offered the Oglethorpes ample opportunities which they handsomely met. James II, attaining the zenith of his power after Monmouth's defeat, attempted to force England back to Catholicism. The climax came when he sought to compel the Fellows of Magdalen College, Oxford, to elect, as their President, Anthony Farmer, a Catholic of no qualifications whatsoever; and he followed this by a trial of seven bishops for sedition because they refused to order the reading of the Declaration of Indulgence in the churches. The King lost both tests, but the revolution was not an assured event until the birth, on June 10, 1688, of a son who, in the succession, would precede James's two Protestant daughters, Mary, wife of William of Orange, and Anne, wife of Prince George of Denmark. Because of the known physical condition of both King and Queen, together with the early deaths of their other children, a rumour soon spread concerning a substitution of some other child for the express purpose of securing for the Stuarts and Catholicism the throne—a rumour which attained such magni-

---

part v), ii. 92; *Portland MSS.* (H.M.C. Reports), ii. 157-8; S.P. 44 (State Papers, Domestic, Entry Books, P.R.O.): 164, Military Commissions, 1679–87, pp. 240, 272; W.O. 25 (War Office, Commission Books, P.R.O.): 2, 1685, p. 14; Index 5448 (War Office Records, P.R.O.), p. 186 r., Succession of Regimental Colonels: The Buffs, October 25, 1685; Dalton, *English Army Lists,* ii. 58; Dalton, *The Scots Army,* ii. 119, note 2; Davis, *History of the Second Queen's Royal Regiment,* ii. 37; Scott, *The British Army,* iii. 229, 505–6; Knight, Captain H. R., *Historical Records of the Buffs, East Kent Regiment, Third Foot, Formerly Designated The Holland Regiment and Prince George of Denmark's Regiment* (1 vol. only published, London, 1905), p. 242; Fountainhall, Lord, *Chronological Notes of Scottish Affairs, from 1680 till 1701* (Edinburgh, 1822), p. 173; Grant, J., editor, *Seafield Correspondence from 1685 to 1708* (Scottish History Society, Edinburgh, 1912), p. 27; Sheppard, E., *Memorials of St. James's Palace* (2 vols., London, 1894), i. 51; Elliot, H. F., *Life of Sidney, Earl of Godolphin* (London, 1888), p. 198 note; Toynbee, *Reminiscences written by Mr. Horace Walpole in 1788,* p. 125 note; *MSS. of Mrs. Wentworth* (H.M.C. Reports), p. 395; *House of Lords MSS.* (H.M.C. Reports, xiii, Appendix, part v), 1691, p. 432; *Commons Journals,* xiii. 437-9; Karraker, C. H., 'Spanish Treasure, Casual Revenue of the Crown', *Journal of Modern History,* v. 301-18; Karraker, C. H., *The Hispaniola Treasure* (Philadelphia, 1934).

tude that King James took prompt steps to disavow such a story. Of the two persons chiefly affected by such a birth, Mary received the news in Holland by regular messenger, but to Anne, who at the time was with her husband at Bath, the King, in the words of Johann Philipp von Hoffmann, the Imperial Minister to England,

without losing a moment, . . . sent Colonel Oglethorpe with an autograph letter. . . . It was noticeable that the King said to the Colonel, it were not enough to receive the letter, but he had also to give him a visible evidence; at which words he took his hand and led him to the room of the Queen;

whereupon Sir Theophilus proceeded on his mission to Bath.[1]

After delivering his message to Princess Anne, Oglethorpe, with his regiment, which had been at Hounslow Heath in June and July, was sent on August 7 to occupy its autumn quarters at Shearness.[2] Here in September he received a letter from the Earl of Sunderland, conveying to him the royal desire that Oglethorpe stand for re-election to Parliament in Morpeth, the Earl adding that 'He desires you will loose no time in doing what shall be

---

[1] Report to Emperor Leopold I by Johann Philipp von Hoffmann, Imperial Minister to England, London, June 1/11, 1688. Haus-, Hof-, und Staats-Archiv. Wien, Österreich (hereinafter cited as Austrian Archives), Ministry of Foreign Affairs, England, vol. 34. The royal choice of Oglethorpe as bearer of the news to Princess Anne and Prince George of Denmark at Bath was a delicate compliment and seems to have been due to the fact that Oglethorpe's regiment was known not only as 'The Holland Regiment', but also as 'Prince George of Denmark's Regiment'. Knight, *Historical Records of the Buffs, East Kent Regiment, Third Foot, Formerly Designated The Holland Regiment and Prince George of Denmark's Regiment*. Oglethorpe had been with his regiment at York in April 1688. Sir J. Reresby to William Blathwayt, York, April 18, 1688, Add. MSS. (British Museum), 9735, Southwell Papers, f. 30; May 2, 1688, f. 32.

[2] W.O. 5 (War Office, Out-Letters: Marching Orders, P.R.O.): 3, pp. 148, 178–9; Report to William III by Jacob Van Leeuwen, Secretary to Hans Willem Bentinck, first Count of Portland, September, 1688, Japikse, N., editor, *Correspondentie van Willem III en van Hans Willem Bentinck, eersten Graf van Portland* (in progress, 's-Gravenhage, Holland, 1927——), i, *Correspondence in the Archives of Welbeck Abbey, England* (2 vols., 1927–8). ii. 610.

necessary—in order to your Election'.[1] But William of Orange—the husband of the Princess to whom Oglethorpe had *not* been sent with the royal message—now relieved Sir Theophilus of the obligations entailed in a political campaign by drawing him into a military campaign.

If the service rendered at the birth of the Prince of Wales seems slight, there is no question of Oglethorpe's position or importance in the Revolution of 1688. The birth of the heir to the throne of June 10 had led seven patriotic Protestants to invite their sovereign's son-in-law, William of Orange, to cross the Channel and save England. William accepted and the 'Glorious Revolution' had begun. What struggle there was, was brief. On November 5 William landed at Torbay. Six days later James commissioned Oglethorpe Brigadier over all the Foot Regiments,[2] and as such he commanded at a skirmish on November 20 near Amesbury. Four days later Oglethorpe routed the King out of bed at Warminster in the dead of night in order to encourage his despondent sovereign![3] At the same time Lady Oglethorpe, who as Lady-in-Waiting to Louise, Duchess of Portsmouth, had become a *confidante*—a spy, if you will—for the King, arranged at her home a meeting between James II and the Marquis of Halifax, whereat the last Stuart King of England made

---

[1] Earl of Sunderland to Sir Theophilus Oglethorpe, Windsor, Sept. 15, 1688, S.P. 44 (State Papers, Domestic, Entry Books, P.R.O.): 56, 1679-1688, p. 438; Add. MSS. (British Museum), 30192, Extracts out of the Secretary of State's Books, f. 120; Earl of Sunderland to the Duke of Newcastle, Windsor, September 13, 1688, Add. MSS. 34516, Mackintosh Collections, xxx, Extracts relating to English History, f. 50.

[2] W.O. 25 (War Office, Commission Books, P.R.O.): 4, 1685-1692, p. 94; Knight, *Historical Records of the Buffs*, pp. 251, 257-9, 263-4, 271, 277, 528-9; Davis, *History of the Second Queen's Royal Regiment*, ii. 73-6; Dalton, *English Army Lists*, ii. 200; Dalton, *The Scots Army*, ii. 119 note. For the range of Oglethorpe's influence at this time see *MSS. of the Earl of Dartmouth* (H.M.C. Reports), i. 135, 161.

[3] At 4.30 a.m. on Nov. 25, 1688, the Earl of Middleton at Andover wrote to Lord Preston that 'Coll. Oglethorpe desires he may not be named in the *Gazette* upon this occasion'. Was this modesty or strategy? See Add. MSS. (British Museum), 30192, f. 136 verso; *MSS. of Sir F. Graham, Bart.* (H.M.C. Reports), p. 418.

a futile effort to secure the latter's aid.[1] But it was all to no avail. On December 9 James sent his Queen and infant son to France; on December 19 his invading son-in-law was in London; and during the night of December 22–3 James II was allowed to escape to France. Eight years later a Captain John Scott, who seemed to be a spy for William III at the Jacobite retreat at Saint-Germain, reported that he had learned that King James, on his hasty departure from England that night of December 22, 1688, had entrusted his royal seal to Lady Oglethorpe, who was to deliver it to the Archbishop of Canterbury as a token of James's pledge to preserve the Protestant religion. The Archbishop refusing to accept it, Lady Oglethorpe personally had carried it to James in France.[2]

The conflict was ended and, as the year came to its close, the Earl of Feversham, Sir John Lanier, Sir John Fenwick, and Sir Theophilus Oglethorpe, pursuant to instructions from their exiled monarch, dismissed their men and forwarded to the victorious invader a signed communication to that effect.[3] William interpreted this as complete surrender and endeavoured to engage Oglethorpe in his service, but that stubborn loyalist would have nothing to do with the victor. Fortuitous circumstance might compel him to cease resistance, but nothing could compel him to welcome or join the enemy. His loyalty to the Stuarts cost him not only his regiment, which was given to Charles Churchill, brother of the newly created Earl of Marlborough,[4] but also his profes-

---

[1] Pinto, V. de Sola, *Sir Charles Sedley, 1639–1701* (London, 1927), p. 353; Toynbee, *Reminiscences written by Mr. Horace Walpole in 1788*, p. 125; Foxcroft, H. C., *Life and Letters of Sir George Savile, Bart., First Marquis of Halifax* (2 vols., London, 1898), ii. 2.

[2] *MSS. of the Duke of Buccleuch and Queensberry* (H.M.C. Reports), ii, part i, p. 292. For the general narrative of the Jacobite movement at this time, see Petrie, *The Jacobite Movement*, pp. 63–103.

[3] Mackintosh, Sir James, *History of the Revolution in England in 1688* (London, 1834), p. 522; Clarke, J. S., *Life of James the Second* (2 vols., London, 1816), ii. 249–50 note.

[4] Major William Churchill, a decade later, claimed that the Holland Regiment, when it came into Charles Churchill's hands, had been left over

sion, for the 'Glorious Revolution' was to him a *débâcle*. Refusing, unlike Marlborough, to serve against his King, he now retired to his manor of Westbrook in Godalming, Surrey, which he had purchased in July 1688.[1] As Colonel of the Holland Regiment of 780 men, Sir Theophilus Oglethorpe had proudly unfurled as his standard a flag described as 'black, in the centre, very large, covering fully half the space, the "Sun in Splendour" '.[2] But the Colonel's sun had set. The Stuarts had fled. What was to become of the Oglethorpes?

When James II had ordered his soldiers to cease their resistance against William of Orange, he had expressed the hope that

> you will still have the same fidelyty to mee, and tho I doe not expect you to expose your selves by resisting a foraine army and a poysoned Nation, yett I hope youre former principles will keep youre selves free from associations, and such pernitious things.[3]

How fully the Oglethorpes obeyed their master's wishes is evident, throughout the succeeding decades, in the Jacobite labours of both Theophilus and his spouse, the latter's efforts continuing without surcease into the fourth

---

five hundred pounds in debt by Oglethorpe, *MSS. of the Marquess Townshend* (H.M.C. Reports, xi, Appendix, part iv), p. 201. See also Oldmixon, *History of England during the Reigns of the Royal House of Stuart*, p. 761; Ralph, *History of England*, ii. 11 note i; Scott, *The British Army*, iii. 230; Arthur, *Story of the Household Cavalry*, i. 226; Wolseley, *Life of John Churchill, Duke of Marlborough*, i. 332.

[1] Echard, L., *History of England from the Restoration of King Charles the Second to the Conclusion of the Reign of King James the Second* (3 vols., London, 1718), iii. 950; Malden, H. E., editor, *Victoria County History of Surrey* (4 vols. and index, London, 1902–14), iii. 36–7.

[2] For the description of Oglethorpe's regimental flag see Knight, *Historical Record of the Buffs*, p. 259. For the number of men in his command, see Add. MSS. (British Museum), 34517, Mackintosh Collections on English History, xxxi, Extracts from Viscount Preston's Papers, f. 68 verso: An addition to Ambassador Arnout van Citter's letter to the States General of the Netherlands, London, Nov. 19, 1688.

[3] King James II to the Earl of Feversham, Whitehall, Dec. 10, 1688, *Supplementary Report on the MSS. of the Duke of Hamilton* (H.M.C. Reports), p. 113; Clarke, *Life of James the Second*, ii. 250.

decade of the eighteenth century. If it be that James Oglethorpe was to inherit the military zeal and, later, the parliamentary tradition from his father, then is it likewise true that he owed an equal share of his intense loyalty to the Crown, together with his staunch moral courage and high purpose, to his mother. Eleanor Wall Oglethorpe's career, since that day when she came as a simple Irish girl to the court of Charles II, had been such that the mere prohibitions of a Protestant intruder like William of Orange would hardly hinder her in maintaining the old doctrines with unswerving loyalty.[1] She, therefore, as much as her husband, was a guiding spirit in the Jacobite movement and her ardent defence thereof utterly amazed and disgusted her distinguished friend, Dean Jonathan Swift, in whose censorious eyes she seemed 'so cunning a devil'.[2]

Thus it was that Theophilus Oglethorpe's quiet retirement to Godalming in Surrey proved to be merely a screen for the tireless activities of his wife and himself. So well did the Oglethorpes maintain their loyalty to the Stuart cause that, within four months after the flight of James II, Minister Hoffmann was reporting to Emperor Leopold that Sir Theophilus was to be found in the north of England, fomenting insurrection in league with Lord Preston, Lord Griffin, and that arch-conspirator, Sir John Fenwick.[3] The new administration, it is true, took measures

---

[1] Grey, *Debates of the House of Commons*, ix. 181; Foxcroft, *Life and Letters of Sir George Savile*, ii. 2, 27 note, 53–69 note; Toynbee, *Reminiscences written by Mr. Horace Walpole in 1788*, p. 125 and note.

[2] Scott, Temple, editor, *The Prose Works of Jonathan Swift* (12 vols., London, 1897–1908), ii. *The Journal to Stella*, p. 299.

[3] Report of Minister von Hoffmann to Emperor Leopold I, London, March 14, 1689, Austrian Archives, Ministry of Foreign Affairs, England, vol. 34; Add. MSS. (British Museum), 10118, First Draft of a History of King James II by Joseph Johnston, Prior of the English Benedictines at Paris, f. 212 verso (p. 344); Luttrell, *Brief Relation*, i. 509. In the directions for Jacobite embarkation in France for Ireland, March 12, 1689, there occurs this line: 'Sur le "Neptune": Mr. Oglethorpe'. Gilbert, J. T., editor, *A Jacobite Narrative of the War in Ireland, 1689–1691* (Dublin, 1892), p. 316.

to secure these men[1] and check any uprising, even to the extent of arresting seven Irishmen who, as one diarist put it, were merely 'suspected to designe for the North to meete Oglethorpe';[2] but this particular Jacobite, at least, seems to have led a charmed life for, despite a search of his house at Godalming, the issuance of a warrant, and the lodging of gravely incriminatory information with the authorities concerning his unquestioned associations, he escaped arrest, thereby arousing the healthy hostility of King William himself.[3]

On June 1, 1689, Lady Oglethorpe gave birth to their fifth child and third son, James, who was baptized the next day at Saint James's Church, Piccadilly,[4] but neither her infant nor her husband's perils seem to have made Lady Oglethorpe in any wise more cautious. In the middle of February 1690, she and Lady Conway left London for Ireland, then a hot-bed of Jacobite intrigue. Fully aware of their departure and intended destination, Whitehall calmly allowed them to proceed as far as Chester where they were arrested and found to be in possession of what the warrant for arrest termed 'traitorous and seditious papers', containing plans for the proper welcome of James II on his return.[5] King William had urged the

[1] Earl of Shrewsbury to Colonel Heyford, Whitehall, April 25, 1689, Add. MSS. (British Museum), 30192, Extracts out of the Secretary of State's Books, f. 148.
[2] Hewitson, A., editor, *Diary of Thomas Bellingham, 1688–1690* (Preston, 1908), p. 58.
[3] As early as Dec. 18, 1688, Roger Kenyon had informed the Earl of Derby that 'a guard is sett upon the Earl of Feversham and Collonel Oglethorpe about some words of the Earl of Essex's death'. *MSS. of Lord Kenyon* (H.M.C. Reports, xiv, Appendix, part iv), p. 211. See also *Calendar of State Papers, Domestic*, William and Mary, 1689–1690, pp. 11, 71, 77; *MSS. of S. H. Le Fleming* (H.M.C. Reports, xii, Appendix, part vii), p. 261.
[4] Baptismal Register of Saint James's Church, Piccadilly, 1685–99.
[5] The Dutch Minister to England, Arnout van Citters, reporting her arrest at Chester, called Lady Oglethorpe 'een seer schrandere en intriguánte dame, soo men wil': 'a very clever lady, much inclined to intrigue, so they say'. Arnout van Citters to the States General, Westminster, March 14, 1690, Add. MSS. (British Museum), 17677 KK, State Correspondence between England and the Netherlands, f. 54 verso. For the details of the pursuit and arrest see letters of the Earl of Shrewsbury to Sir John Morgan

Earl of Macclesfield to 'use all possible means for seizing and securing the said lady Oglethorpe' on the crafty theory that her husband, in that event, might the more easily be taken.[1] Thus it was not because of her infant son, but in order to facilitate the capture of her husband that Lady Oglethorpe in March was discharged on good security not to leave the kingdom, and permitted—yea, urged— to return to Godalming.[2] But all to no avail, and in the early summer of 1690 Sir William Lockhart and Lord Ross of Scotland reported, in William's absence in Ireland, to Queen Mary, through her secretary, Abel Tassin D'Allone, that yet another Jacobite plot was brewing in the North among a group of officers, but that they 'remembered none of their names but Oglethorp'.[3] The *tempo* of life now increased. On May 9 that strong Stuart supporter, William Penn, had escaped from prison and fled to Scotland;[4] on May 30 Theophilus Oglethorpe's name appeared in a general proclamation against Jacobite conspirators;[5] on June 15 his infant son, one year old, was buried at Saint James's Church, Piccadilly, in London;[6] on July 10 the capture of Oglethorpe and another was

and the Earl of Macclesfield, Whitehall, Feb. 18–27, 1690, Add. MSS. 30192, Extracts out of the Secretary of State's Books, ff. 165–9; *Calendar of State Papers, Domestic*, William and Mary, 1689–1690, pp. 465–6; Luttrell, *Brief Relation*, ii. 18.

[1] *Calendar of State Papers, Domestic*, William and Mary, 1689–1690, pp. 470, 483.

[2] Earl of Shrewsbury to Sir John Morgan, Whitehall, March 1, 1690, Add. MSS. (British Museum), 30192, Extracts out of the Secretary of State's Books, f. 171; *Calendar of State Papers, Domestic*, William and Mary, 1689–1690, pp. 486–7, 512.

[3] Melville, W. L., editor, *The Leven and Melville Papers, 1689–1691* (Bannatyne Club, Edinburgh, 1843), p. 485. For further light on Abel Tassin D'Allone, a French Protestant refugee who in 1680 became secretary to Mary, Princess of Orange, and continued in 1688 as secretary to Queen Mary of England, see Agnew, D. C. A., *Protestant Exiles from France* (3rd ed., 2 vols., privately printed, no place, 1886), ii. 207.

[4] *MSS. of the late Allan George Finch* (H.M.C. Reports), ii. 278.

[5] Francesco Terriesi to the Secretary of State, Florence, London, Aug. 1, 1690, Add. MSS. (British Museum), 25380, Despatches of the Florentine Minister to England, xxiii, f. 238.

[6] Burial Register of Saint James's Church, Piccadilly, 1685–99.

soon expected;[1] on the 11th he with others was said to be 'at Powis house, where I fere it will be difficult to take them';[2] and on July 14 Queen Mary as Regent, aroused by the Ferguson Plot in Edinburgh, issued another proclamation, this time for the apprehension, on a charge of high treason, of seventeen conspirators including the Earl of Lichfield, son-in-law of Charles II; the Earl of Ailesbury, Charles's loyal friend; Lord Preston, Charles's representative at Paris; John Ashton; William Penn, Esquire, a Quaker whom Charles had bound to the Stuart cause with the gift of Pennsylvania—and Sir Theophilus Oglethorpe.[3] Despite his wife's continued conspiracies in Hyde Park, and although Preston and Ashton were taken and executed, Oglethorpe again eluded arrest, while Penn, by promptly giving himself up to the authorities, so enchanted them that they permitted him to hide in silence between periodic arrests, staged largely for effect, until his departure for Philadelphia in 1699.[4]

For the remainder of 1690 Oglethorpe eluded the royal officials so successfully that the charges against him seem to have been dropped, for in the first three months of 1691 he moved freely about the community. Now and then his capture was rumoured but, while to many the wish was undoubtedly father to the thought, his good fortune continued and seemingly emboldened him. When in April a conflagration in the palace sent Queen Mary

[1] *MSS. of the late Allan George Finch* (H.M.C. Reports), ii. 353. See also Add. MSS. (British Museum), 10118, First Draft of a History of King James II, by Joseph Johnston, Prior of the English Benedictines at Paris, f. 257 verso (p. 434).
[2] *MSS. of the late Allan George Finch* (H.M.C. Reports), ii. 354.
[3] London *Gazette*, July 21, 1690, p. 1; *Calendar of State Papers, Domestic*, William and Mary, 1690–1691, p. 65; Smollett, T., *History of England* (3rd ed., 15 vols., London, 1759), viii. 388.
[4] *MSS. of the late Allan George Finch* (H.M.C. Reports), ii. 377, 391–2, 439–40; Campana de Cavelli, Marquise, *Les Derniers Stuarts à Saint-Germain en Laye* (2 vols., Paris, 1871) i. 54–5; Grew, E. and M. S., *The English Court in Exile* (London, 1911), p. 257; Kennett, *Complete History of England*, iii. 603; Oldmixon, *History of England*, p. 51; Ralph, *History of England*, ii. 227. See also Gilbert, *A Jacobite Narrative*, p. 122.

scurrying forth *en déshabillé,* Narcissus Luttrell observed that

some persons, as sir John Fenwick, sir Theophilus Oglethorpe, and others, behaving themselves indecently as her majestie past by, looking her in the face and cocking their hats, are ordered to forbear those places, and the gates are to be kept more strict for the future.[1]

The King had been tolerant, but Oglethorpe had here insulted the Queen and henceforth the pursuit was to be redoubled in scope and intensity of effort.

On April 15 Viscount Sydney at Whitehall issued blanket orders to the Justice of the Peace of Westminster to proceed against a group including Oglethorpe; the next day Sir Theophilus, unperturbed, calmly challenged Sir Henry Goodrick to a duel whence both escaped, only the messenger being arrested; and on the 27th Lord Lexington commenced proceedings to acquire the estate in St. James's Park which James II had deeded over to Lady Oglethorpe for a term of thirty-one years in those happy, care-free, golden days of 1685.[2] At last on May 30, 1691, Theophilus Oglethorpe was captured, but the punishment was light. Hailed before a Justice of the Peace, he merely paid a fine of forty shillings for refusing to take the Oaths of Allegiance to William and Mary![3] For the next two months there was silence. On August 6 they said: 'Oglethorpe is taken and put in Newgate'; but again they erred.[4] Within a fortnight thereafter he had quietly come to London that he might present his children

---

[1] Luttrell, *Brief Relation*, ii. 204; Birch MSS. (British Museum), 4466, Diary of Mr. Sampson, p. 43; Strickland, *Lives of the Queens of England*, vii. 328.

[2] Viscount Sydney to the Justices of the Peace of Westminster, Whitehall, April 15, 1691, Add. MSS. (British Museum), 30192, Extracts out of the Secretary of State's Books, f. 184; *Calendar of State Papers, Domestic,* William and Mary, 1690–1691, pp. 336, 349; Luttrell, *Brief Relation,* ii. 212.

[3] James Vernon to Lord Wharton, London, May 30, 1691, Carte MSS. (Bodleian Library, Oxford), lxxix, f. 350 verso; News-letter, August 6, 1691, Carte MSS. lxxvi, f. 115.

[4] Sir William Hamilton of Whitelaw to William, Earl of Annandale, Aug. 6, 1691, Fraser, Sir W., *The Annandale Family Book of the Johnstones, Earls and Marquises of Annandale* (2 vols., Edinburgh, 1894), i. 53.

to old Dr. Sancroft, the retiring Archbishop of Canterbury, for his blessing. In a marvellously modern manner, a reporter for one of the London news-letters of that day interviewed Sir Theophilus on the prospects of Jacobitism, and the latter, with his thoughts on the disastrous Battle of the Boyne, fought the summer before, grimly admitted that 'he had always counted on Ireland, so that at present he found little on which to arouse hope'.[1] So the months passed and he continued to elude the authorities who were now no longer in doubt as to his sentiments. In December the disclosures of one William Fuller exposed to Parliament a new Jacobite plot, wherein a number of old Stuart adherents, including Oglethorpe, were implicated but, to the surprise of many, in Edward Harley's concise phrase, 'the discovery did not produce the fervour in the House which might have been expected'. Oglethorpe remained a free man.[2]

For a few months the active Jacobite found rest, but in May 1692 the officers of the Crown, intent on preserving William and Mary's throne, again issued warrants for the arrest of leading Jacobites including, of course, Theophilus Oglethorpe, who again eluded them, this time by flight to his master's court at Saint-Germain in France. In Luttrell's curt report, 'the messengers have searched for Sir Theophilus Oglethorp, but could not find him'.[3] This might have satisfied King William, but Mary now took a hand in the affair. She had not forgotten how Theophilus Oglethorpe had insulted her at the palace gates the year before, nor had she forgotten how, at a Jacobite meeting in Hyde Park during August 1690, Lady Oglethorpe had violently inveighed against her.[4] On June 30, 1692, the

[1] News-letter, London, Aug. 11/21, 1691, *MSS. of the Earl of Denbigh* (H.M.C. Reports, viii, Appendix, part i), p. 566 a.
[2] *Portland MSS.* (H.M.C. Reports), iii, *Harley Letters*, i. 485; Ailesbury, *Memoirs*, i. 273; *MSS. of the Earl of Denbigh* (H.M.C. Reports), p. 210.
[3] Luttrell, *Brief Relation*, ii. 441, 448, 462; Smollett, *History of England*, viii. 445; Ferguson, J., *Robert Ferguson, the Plotter* (Edinburgh, 1887), p. 295.
[4] Waterson, N. M., *Mary II, Queen of England, 1689–1694* (Durham, North Carolina, 1928), p. 75.

Earl of Nottingham at Whitehall informed Lord Chief Justice Holt that 'the Queen desires you to take bail of Sir Theophilus Oglethorpe, to appear the first day of next term at the King's Bench, being bound in £3,000 with two sureties each in £1,000'.[1] Two days later Oglethorpe surrendered and was admitted to bail,[2] but Mary and her minions failed to hold their man, a lapse quite explicable in the light of what had transpired at that very time. When James II made his gesture of return in 1692 which ended so ingloriously in the defeat of his French naval allies at Cape La Hogue, he had sent over, as advance agent, Sir James Montgomery who, through indiscretions, was captured and imprisoned by King William's men. Theophilus Oglethorpe, however, had bribed the guards and, in Ailesbury's terse phrases, had 'hurried away Sir James, and as the former told me himself, that he was resolved to make him away if he had resisted in the least; with this expression, "Dead men tell no tales" '.[3] No wonder that Oglethorpe's name graced the list of proscribed fugitives in December 1692![4]

Although thus listed as a dangerous character, Sir Theophilus seems to have been successful in remaining hidden at Godalming where he and his wife, in September 1693, welcomed twins, Sutton, who died seven weeks after birth, and Louisa Mary, who will be heard of later as Molly.[5] Inactive during most of this year, both Ogle-

---

[1] *Calendar of State Papers, Domestic*, William and Mary, 1691–1692, p. 343.
[2] News-letter, dated, Whitehall, July 11, 1692, Add. MSS. (British Museum), 34096, News-letters sent to Sir W. D. Colt, British Envoy to Hanover, 1692–3, f. 44 verso.
[3] Ailesbury, *Memoirs*, i. 308.
[4] *Calendar of State Papers, Domestic*, William and Mary, 1691–1692, pp. 542–3; Kennett, *Complete History of England*, iii. 639; Oldmixon, *History of England*, p. 73; Ralph, *History of England*, ii. 348; Dumont, J., and Basnage, H., *Lettres historiques: Contenant ce qui se passe de plus important en Europe, Janvier, 1692–Décembre, 1736* (90 vols., The Hague, 1692–1736), i. 660.
[5] Sutton was buried Nov. 25, 1693, Burial Register of Godalming Parish Church; Shield, *The Loyal Oglethorpes*, p. 41; Shield, A., and Lang, A., 'Queen Oglethorpe', *Blackwood's Edinburgh Magazine*, clxiii (Edinburgh, Feb. 1898), 199–200; Lang, A., *Historical Mysteries* (London, 1904), p. 217.

thorpe and William Penn, nevertheless, managed to send to Saint-Germain assurances of their steadfast loyalty to James II, and the copy-book of letters by the Earl of Middleton, James's Secretary of State for England at Saint-Germain, bears eloquent testimony in its various cipher lists to the importance throughout the next three years of both Theophilus and Lady Oglethorpe. They might be in hiding and temporarily *hors de combat* but, if their bodies were inactive, their minds were continually at work. Thus it was that on December 29, 1693, a Captain Williamson, one of the exile's numerous messengers, in reporting to James II his conferences with Clarendon, Ailesbury, Ferguson, Penn, and other Jacobites in Britain, could declare that

Chevalier Oglethorpe hopes Your Majesty will make your invasion in Spring at the latest with 30,000 men, a force sufficient to overcome your enemies and protect your friends. In order to conduct Your Majesty in all safety to Whitehall, that number of troops will be restored to the Fleet and the Army for duty. That disposed of, nothing is lacking but a superior force able to unite itself.[1]

Penn having expressed similar sentiments in favour of an expeditionary force of 30,000 men, James pondered the advisability of yet another attempt at a Stuart restoration and found that direct consultation with one or two English Jacobites might be of value. In February 1694, therefore, Luttrell noted that 'Sir Theophilus Oglethorp is gone for France'[2] where, it was reported, he 'was at St. Germain's with the King incognito, seen by none but those with whom he was to meet'.[3] Here, while Theophilus

[1] Report in French on Affairs in England by Captain Williamson to King James II, Saint-Germain-en-Laye, Dec. 29, 1693, Carte MSS. (Bodleian Library, Oxford), clxxxi, ff. 532–3 verso. For ciphers see Carte MSS., clxxxi, f. 572 and verso; cclvi, copy-book of letters of the Earl of Middleton, Saint-Germain, April 19, 1693–March 28, 1695, ff. 6, 11; and Parnell, Arthur, 'James Macpherson and the Nairne Papers', *English Historical Review*, xlv (April 1897), 259–60.

[2] Luttrell, *Brief Relation*, iii. 269; Strickland, *Lives of the Queens of England*, viii. 17–18.

[3] *MSS. of the Duke of Buccleuch and Queensberry* (H.M.C. Reports), ii,

portrayed to the exiled monarch the situation in England, Lady Oglethorpe, who had accompanied him, made it a point to discuss matters with James's Secretary of State for England, the Earl of Middleton, whom even as Dean Swift she impressed as being 'very intriguing and cunning'.[1]

The death of Queen Mary on December 28, 1694, brought fresh hope to the Jacobites for William's right to the throne had lain largely in her Stuart ancestry. Not without courage, Sir Theophilus Oglethorpe and William Penn again advocated a French invasion of England to hasten the restoration of James II, and at least the former shortly thereafter attended 'a meeting at a tavern in Holbourn', held with other Jacobites to plan for that event.[2] At the same time Lady Oglethorpe's brother from Tipperary, Matthew Wall, became involved in the ensuing complications as a spy for both sides with conscientious scruples or loyalty towards neither. For the next five years his activities were to prove millstones about the necks of James Vernon, William's aide at Whitehall, and Matthew Prior at The Hague, the latter being led to exclaim: 'I look upon Wall to be one of the greatest villains I ever yet spoke with.'[3] Whether it was Wall's machinations or William's more rigid enforcement, on his wife's death, of loyalty to the *de facto* government, and the consequent closing in of the royal officials upon the various Jacobites

---

part i, p. 296. It is surprising that not one of the Oglethorpes is mentioned in the list of Jacobites at the quasi-court of Saint-Germain printed by Professor Dulon. Dulon, J., *Jacques II Stuart: Sa Famille et les Jacobites à Saint-Germain-en-Laye* (Saint-Germain, 1897), pp. 65–152. See also de Beaumont, G. du Bosq., *La Cour des Stuarts à Saint-Germain-en-Laye, 1689–1718* (2nd ed., Paris, 1912).

[1] Macpherson, J., *Secret History of Great Britain* (2 vols., London, 1776), i. 484; ii. 675.

[2] Dalrymple, Sir John, *Memoirs of Great Britain and Ireland* (2nd ed., 2 vols., London, 1771–3), i, part ii, pp. 69, 237; *MSS. of the Marquess of Downshire* (H.M.C. Reports), i, part i, pp. 479–80, 487.

[3] *MSS. of the Marquis of Bath* (H.M.C. Reports), iii, *Prior Papers*, pp. 36–7, 39–40, 43, 46–7, 72–3, 344–5, 352, 354, 359, 365–6, 368, 372; *MSS. of the Duke of Buccleuch and Queensberry* (H.M.C. Reports), ii, part i, pp. 192, 196–8, 200, 204; Wickham Legg, L. G., *Matthew Prior* (Cambridge, 1921), pp. 77, 101, 292, 296, 307, 311.

still in England, Theophilus Oglethorpe again found discretion the better part of valour, and on June 8, 1695, a writer in a London news-letter reported that 'I know not what truth there is in it, but it makes a great deal of Noise that Sr. Theophilus Oglethorp is gone for France'.[1] The rumour proved to be fact, but this Jacobite had gone to Saint-Germain not only for safety but to present for the third time the plea of English Jacobites that James again attempt a restoration. Twice had it failed. This time it might succeed.

Reassured by his loyal followers in England, James II now sponsored the Jacobite attempt of 1696. He did not invade the homeland himself, but his henchmen attempted the next best thing, the elimination of William III! The secret mission to England of the Duke of Berwick, the exile's son by Arabella Churchill, strangely coincided with Sir George Barclay's scheme for murdering the King of England, so that the Duke was involved in the general conspiracy together with Sir Theophilus and Lady Oglethorpe. The latter in this case, it is true, did little, for in February 1696 she had given birth to another daughter, Frances Charlotte,[2] who will appear again as Fanny Oglethorpe; but Sir Theophilus was a marked man. On February 22 King William issued a proclamation for the arrest of Berwick, Sir George Barclay, Sir Theophilus Oglethorpe, and twenty-five others as traitors in a conspiracy, and offered a reward of one thousand pounds for each man captured and brought to justice. After his visit to James of June 1695, Oglethorpe had made periodic excursions to England where he was when the royal proclamation and 750 warrants of arrest were issued. There was no alternative to flight and Sir Theophilus hastened to Saint-Germain where the crowning blow of Fate awaited him.[3]

---

[1] News-letter, Whitehall, June 8, 1695, Carte MSS. (Bodleian Library, Oxford), ccxxxix, f. 12.

[2] Shield, 'The Loyal Oglethorpes', *The Royalist*, ix. 41.

[3] *MSS. of the Marquess of Downshire* (H.M.C. Reports), i, part ii, p. 622;

When James II had set up his exiled court at Saint-Germain in 1688, there had gradually appeared a cleavage among the Jacobites, the Catholics gathering under the Duke of Melfort, later Secretary of State for Scotland, and the Protestants under the Earl of Middleton, Secretary of State for England. Surrounded and dominated by the Catholicism of his wife, Mary of Modena, his host, Louis XIV, his adviser, Father Petre, and the representatives of the Hierarchy, James had become engulfed in the Catholic programme and was persuaded to rid his court of all Protestants, no matter how loyal to the Jacobite cause they had been.[1] By March 1696 Middleton had concluded that Saint-Germain, next to the Bastille, was 'the dreadfullest place in France'.[2] He was soon to find himself not alone in that opinion. Theophilus Oglethorpe had loyally followed his King even when it meant oblivion for himself. He often aided Catholic James, but he refused, in such loyalty to his temporal sovereign, to forsake the faith of his Yorkshire fathers. Following the example of William Penn who submitted to William III in 1694, Theophilus Oglethorpe, after twenty years of service to the Stuarts, ruefully returned to Godalming and in the late fall of 1696 took the oath of loyalty to William III.[3]

Calendar of State Papers, Domestic, William III, 1696, pp. 110–12; Grimblot, P., editor, *Letters of William III and Louis XIV* (2 vols., London, 1848), i. 165 note, 171 note; *MSS. of the late Reginald Rawdon Hastings* (H.M.C. Reports), ii. 259; Blackmore, Sir Richard, *A True and Impartial History of the Conspiracy against the Person and Government of King William III . . . In the Year 1695* (London, 1723), p. 153; Strickland, *Lives of the Queens of England*, viii. 59. See also the London *Post Boy*, March 26, 1696, pp. 1–2. Two decades later Lord Townshend received a letter, signed 'J. H.', wherein the writer observed that the anti-Jacobite measures of the Hanoverians in 1715 recalled the Jacobite endeavours of 1690–6, particularly Theophilus Oglethorpe's connexion with Fenwick's activities in 1695–6. J. H. to Lord Townshend, St. James's Street, London, Oct. 5, 1715, S.P. 35 (State Papers, Domestic, George I, P.R.O.): 4, no. 44.

[1] Parnell, 'James Macpherson and the Nairne Papers', *English Historical Review*, xlv. 255–6.

[2] Middleton to Caryll, Calais, March 21, 1696, Carte MSS. (Bodleian Library, Oxford), ccviii, f. 267. See also Carte MSS., lxxix, f. 578 verso.

[3] London *Flying Post*, Nov. 12, 1696, p. 1. In his biography of Marlborough Mr. Winston Churchill stresses the point that most of the leaders

In the words of a contemporary, he 'was so unkindly used, that he was very glad to get home to Old England again, where, 'tis expected, he will Plot no more'.[1] The prediction proved to be correct. Two modern Jacobite historians have branded Sir Theophilus Oglethorpe as 'a busy but trimming Jacobite';[2] but they forget that it was James's violent Catholicism and gross ingratitude which threw his supporter into the camp of William III!

While Oglethorpe was being dismissed so abruptly by his sovereign in France, William and his agents were industriously combing England and holding countless examinations and trials of suspected Jacobites, in which the name of Theophilus Oglethorpe was prominently mentioned. On his return the squire of Westbrook wisely offered immediate surrender on bail. If Theophilus Oglethorpe could repent, William—to whom, in Professor Trevelyan's trenchant phrase, 'personal resentments were nothing when the common cause was at stake'[3]—could forgive and, sensing this opportunity to gain a convert, with true regal magnanimity allowed Lady Oglethorpe's plea that her husband be not required to undergo the imprisonment ordained for such as he had been, going so far as to offer his former opponent a passport to any foreign country, except those of William's enemies. Perhaps because of the Order of the King in Council, of April 30, 1696, directing the Justices of the Peace of

of the Revolution also maintained relations with James II at Saint-Germain. This position was accepted by the historian of the British Army, Sir John Fortescue (London *Observer*, Oct. 8, 1933, p. 5). It is therefore of paramount importance and of the greatest credit to Theophilus Oglethorpe to note that when in 1696 he took the oath of loyalty to William III he kept it inviolate.

[1] [Macky, John], *A View of the Court of St. Germain, from the Year 1690, to 95, with an Account of the Entertainment Protestants meet with there. Directed to the Malcontent Protestants of England* (London, 1696), p. 14. For a contemporary approval of retirement from Jacobitism, such as that of Theophilus Oglethorpe, see *Simeon and Levi : Or Jacobite Villany and French Treachery, Hand in Hand. By a Person of Quality* (London, 1696), p. 23.
[2] Shield, A., and Lang, A., *The King Over the Water* (London, 1907), p. 43.
[3] Trevelyan, G. M., *England under Queen Anne : Blenheim* (London, 1930), p. 143.

Middlesex to transmit a list of 'such French-Papists who are not Naturalized or made Denizens',[1] Oglethorpe, during May and June, had toyed with the idea of going to the Continent to campaign in the army of the Emperor, but, as the months passed, that plan was dropped. In September Sir John Fenwick, fighting for his life in a trial for high treason, vainly attempted to save himself by incriminating Oglethorpe in a meeting 'at the Fountain in the Hay Market' with Sackville and himself;[2] but this was of slight concern to one of whom William had decreed: 'There is nothing alleged against him.'[3]

Something far more important than an abortive attempt at a Jacobite restoration, the condemnation of Sir John Fenwick, and the campaigns of Emperor Leopold I, now distracted the attention of Sir Theophilus and Lady Oglethorpe during the late fall and early winter of 1696. This was the impending advent of their ninth and last child, a fifth son, James Edward Oglethorpe, the child of his father's later years, whose birth was to dim still further the lustre of Jacobitism for his father, if not his mother, and make 1696 for Sir Theophilus truly an *annus mirabilis*.

[1] Add. MSS. (British Museum), 39923, Jacobite and other Letters, &c., f. 15.

[2] Add. MSS. (British Museum), 33251, Sir John Fenwick's Information taken by Mr. Vernon, Sept. 23, 1696, f. 17 verso. For further light on the Fenwick case see *Commons Journals*, xi. 579; Nicholson, T. C., and Turberville, A. S., *Charles Talbot, Duke of Shrewsbury* (Cambridge, 1930), pp. 108–30; Ballard, Colin, *The Great Earl of Peterborough* (London, 1929), pp. 76–90.

[3] *MSS. of the Marquess of Downshire* (H.M.C. Reports), i. 664; *MSS. of the Duke of Buccleuch and Queensberry* (H.M.C. Reports), ii, part i, pp. 320, 337, 364, 367, 410–13.

CHAPTER II

A JACOBITE YOUTH

SUCH then was the heritage of James Edward Oglethorpe who was born in London on December 22, 1696, and christened the following day at St. Martin-in-the-Fields[1] by its former Vicar, the Reverend Doctor Thomas Tenison, sometime Chaplain to Charles II, recently Bishop of Lincoln, and now Archbishop of Canterbury.[2]

Every account to date of his first twenty years has been largely an essay in controversy beginning with the confusion of his birth date with that of the infant James who died in 1690.[3] The early years of James Edward Oglethorpe are somewhat veiled in mystery, the sole indication of his upbringing during the first decade lying in his father's few remaining years under William III and his mother's unquenchable Jacobitism which quite made up for her husband's defection from the cause.[4] The infant was reared in London where lay his father's affairs and his mother's proclivities.

Sir Theophilus Oglethorpe—William had allowed him to retain the title bestowed by James II—set about his recovery in good earnest and by 1698 had risen to the dignity of a Magistrate and Deputy Lieutenant for Surrey,[5]

[1] Baptismal Register of St. Martin-in-the-Fields, London, See also Rawlinson MSS. (Bodleian Library, Oxford) H (Letters), 92, f. 609; and *Notes and Queries*, 3rd series, xii (1867), 68–9.

[2] On Dr. Tenison see Carte MSS. (Bodleian Library, Oxford), lxxvi, f. 593; and McMaster, J., *A Short History of the Royal Parish of St. Martin-in-the-Fields, London, W.C.* (London, 1916), pp. 161, 172.

[3] For the theory of identity with James, born 1689, see Bogart, W. S., 'The Mystery of Oglethorpe's Birthday', *Magazine of American History*, ii. 108–13; and *Collections of the Georgia Historical Society*, vii, part ii, pp. 12, 41–51.

[4] The general facts of Jacobite history in this chapter are based on Petrie, *The Jacobite Movement*, pp. 104–54.

[5] Bean, *The Parliamentary Representation of the Six Northern Counties of England*, p. 561. At this time Oglethorpe must have been in comfortable circumstances, for his money-lending is noted in *Calendar of State Papers, Domestic*, William III, 1697, pp. 54, 103.

but his ambition went farther. Like his parliamentary colleague of 1685, Samuel Pepys, Oglethorpe had been overshadowed by the Revolution of 1688; but, while Pepys, in the words of a recent biographer, 'was destined to suffer a final political eclipse',[1] the latter now determined to win a seat in one of William's Parliaments. In 1698 a new law was enacted, providing for the registration, arrest, or exile of undesirable Jacobites, in which category Secretary James Vernon had promptly placed the Oglethorpes.[2] But Theophilus confounded his adversaries by prompt submission, followed by announcement of his candidacy for Parliament in the borough of Haslemere, Surrey.

In July 1698 Haslemere sent him as their representative to Westminster,[3] where the victory of so recent a Jacobite caused consternation and led to a not unnatural appeal of protest by his defeated rival, George Rodney Bridge, charging Oglethorpe with bribery. On February 1, 1699, the Committee of Privileges of the House of Commons heard the petition against his election and voted Bridge's appeal 'vexatious and frivolous', in which decision the House, by a mere majority of fifteen, 154 to 139, a week later concurred.[4] Despite certain hostility to him as a quondam Jacobite—which in 1699 was expressed by a political satire urging him to bring in a bill for the proclamation of the (Jacobite) Prince of Wales[5]—the new Member for Haslemere soon took his proper place in the House. For three years he supported

[1] Tanner, J. R., *Mr. Pepys: An Introduction to the Diary together with a Sketch of his Later Life* (London, 1925), pp. 263, 267.
[2] Carte MSS. (Bodleian Library, Oxford), cx, f. 240 and verso; *MSS. of the Marquis of Bath* (H.M.C. Reports), iii. 188.
[3] London *Gazette*, July 28, 1698, p. 2; *Post Boy*, July 30, 1698, p. 2; Cobbett, *Parliamentary History*, iv. 1186.
[4] R. Yard to Lord Ambassador Williamson, Whitehall, Feb. 3, 1699. *Calendar of State Papers, Domestic*, William III, 1699, p. 42; Luttrell, *Brief Relation*, iv. 443, 478, 481; *Commons Journals*, xii. 349–50, 469, 491, 494–5; Carte MSS. (Bodleian Library, Oxford), cx, f. 179 verso; cxxix, ff. 436 verso, 437.
[5] *A Political Satire. Portland MSS.* (H.M.C. Reports), viii, *Harley Letters*, vi. 63.

A JACOBITE YOUTH 49

the policies of William III and performed his share of committee work on such varied questions as the woollen trade with Germany, the militia, the manufacture of glass, the settlement of estates and the naturalization of foreigners, Oglethorpe's two major interests; and ultimately he attained to the important committee on privileges and elections. An incursion into the field of colonial administration was followed by consideration of the public debt and national credit; and Sir Theophilus Oglethorpe's parliamentary career was crowned by his sympathetic attitude of forbearance towards the Men of Kent in their historic exposition of the right of petition to, and criticism of, a British Parliament.[1] He had been re-elected in January 1701 to the fifth Parliament of William III,[2] but, on his defeat in November of that year, retired, having achieved a moderate degree of popularity among his colleagues.[3]

[1] Cobbett, *Parliamentary History of England*, v. 1186, 1228, 1326; Appendix, no. xvii, *History of the Kentish Petition*, pp. clxxix–clxxx; no. xviii, *Jura Populi Anglicani*, pp. ccxxv–ccxxvi; *Commons Journals*, x. 150, 743, 804, 825, 837; xii. 462, 484, 523, 527, 530–2, 535, 540, 553, 557, 611, 625, 631, 641, 658, 672; xiii. 2, 7–8, 47, 134, 230, 280, 285, 297, 302, 308, 326, 339, 466, 481, 500, 533, 551, 573, 588–9, 634; Stock, Leo F., editor, *Proceedings and Debates of the British Parliaments respecting North America* (in progress, Washington, 1924——), ii. 363, 413; Carte MSS. (Bodleian Library, Oxford), cxxix, ff. 436 verso, 437; cx, ff. 178 verso, 179; Swanton, E. W., and Woods, P., editors, *Bygone Haslemere* (London, 1914), pp. 188–9; Smith, J. E., *The Parliamentary Representation of Surrey from 1290 to 1924* (London, 1927), pp. 28, 92–3; Oldmixon, *History of England*, pp. 698–9; Stanhope, Earl, *History of England, 1701–1713* (4th ed., 2 vols., London, 1872), i. 25–7.

[2] London *Post Man*, Jan. 7, 1701, p. 2; *Flying Post*, Jan. 7, 1701, p. 2; *Post Boy*, Jan. 9, 1701, p. 2; Cobbett, *Parliamentary History*, iv. 1228.

[3] *A List of One Unanimous Club of Members of the Late Parliament, November 11, 1701, that met at the Vine-Tavern in Long-Acre* (London, 1701) contained among the names of those to be opposed as pro-French and Jacobite, that of Sir Theophilus Oglethorpe for Haslemere, Surrey. For a rebuttal see *An Answer to the Black List; or the Vine-Tavern Queries* (London, 1701), among signatures to which is that of Theophilus Oglethorpe. As publisher of *A List of One Unanimous Club*, Tristram Savage was subsequently fined 20 marks and pilloried at the Old Bailey. London *Flying Post*, May 23, 1702, p. 2. See also Swanton and Woods, *Bygone Haslemere*, pp. 188–9. For the election of Nov. 1701 see the London *English Post*, Nov. 26, 1701, p. 2; *Gazette*, Nov. 27, 1701, p. 2; *Post Man*, Nov. 27, 1701, p. 2; *Post Boy*, Nov. 27, 1701, p. 2; *Flying Post*, Nov. 27, 1701, p. 2; Cobbett, *Parliamentary History*, iv. 1326.

James Edward Oglethorpe was little more than four years old when, on April 10, 1702, amid the national mourning attendant upon the death of William III, his own father died at the age of fifty-one, leaving Lady Eleanor Oglethorpe to rear seven children, but releasing her from any further domestic restraint on her ardent Jacobite activities.[1] For the next decade, therefore, James Edward is engulfed in the careers of his brothers and sisters, and the Jacobitism of his mother, wherein she made the most of her opportunities.

When James II, just before his death on September 16, 1701, had sought to write once more to his daughter, soon to be Queen Anne, he had entrusted that letter to his devoted follower, Lady Oglethorpe, and her daughter, Anne Henrietta![2] Thus, while her husband and, as will later appear, her two elder sons were gaining political preferments in England, Lady Eleanor, to whom parliamentary attendance and living in London was a boon, paid particular attention to gaining similar distinctions from the pseudo-court at Saint-Germain, as well as deriving what benefit she could from her associations with Marlborough. This was most apparent in the career of her eldest son, Lewis.

Upon the defeat of Sir Theophilus in the fall of 1701 the seat for Haslemere had gone to a county rival, but the dissolution of William's sixth Parliament in July 1702 had led to another election wherein, on a double return of a disputed ballot, Lewis, barely within the proper age limit of majority, was chosen. Taking his seat in October, Lewis during the next year and a half successfully defended his right to it as of age and served on various committees, including that on privileges, but, compared with his father's record, Lewis Oglethorpe's term in

---

[1] Theophilus Oglethorpe died in St. James's Street, Westminster, and was buried, April 14, 1702, at the north side of the altar in St. James's Church, Piccadilly. Burial Register of St. James's Church, Piccadilly, 1699–1723; *Register* of the College of Arms, 4 D 14, p. 69.

[2] Haile, Martin, *James Francis Edward: The Old Chevalier* (London, 1907), p. 140. See also Strickland, *Lives of the Queens of England*, vi. 260,

Parliament was of extremely mediocre merit. His greatest claim to doubtful fame lay in his challenge of, and subsequent duel with, Arthur Onslow for some remark made in debate. Although Onslow was advanced in years, his youthful opponent was disarmed and somewhat discredited.[1] Whether or not this episode was a cause for his action, Marlborough had made Lewis Oglethorpe his aide (at a bounty cost of thirty pounds!) and young Lewis in January 1704 forsook his career in Parliament and his post as Deputy Lieutenant for Surrey to campaign with his idol on the Continent where, at the taking of Donauwörth, just prior to the battle of Schellenberg, in July, six weeks before Blenheim, Lady Eleanor Oglethorpe's first-born received a leg wound from which he died at The Hague on October 30, 1704.[2]

Despite her Jacobite political activity, Eleanor Wall Oglethorpe was essentially the mother, and all the agony of suspense and the instinctive fears of a mother's heart for the safety on the battle-field of her first-born son are exposed in her pathetic note of September 8, 1704, written from Godalming to John Ellis, Under-Secretary of State:

I must entreat you, to do me the favour, to Let me know, if you have heard any thing, of my son. I have not had one word

[1] Add. MSS. (British Museum), 15661, Returns to Parliament, 1702–10, f. 42; London *Gazette*, July 23, 1702, p. 2; *Post Man*, July 23, 1702, p. 2; *Post Boy*, July 23, 1702, p. 1; *Flying Post*, July 23, 1702, p. 2; *Daily Courant*, July 23, 1702, p. 1; *Commons Journals*, xiv. 6, 8, 26–7, 34, 79, 85, 105, 129, 138, 211, 284, 286, 297; Cobbett, *Parliamentary History*, vi. 44; Swanton and Woods, *Bygone Haslemere*, pp. 189–90; Smith, *Parliamentary Representation of Surrey*, p. 93; Carte MSS. (Bodleian Library, Oxford), cxxix, ff. 436 verso, 437; cx, ff. 178 verso, 179; *MSS. of the Earl of Onslow* (H.M.C. Reports, xiv, Appendix, part ix), p. 490; Bray, William, editor, *Memoirs illustrative of the Life and Writings of John Evelyn, comprising his Diary from the Year, 1641, to 1705–6, and a Selection from his familiar Letters* (2 vols., London, 1818), ii. 79. For his admission to the House see also the London *Gazette*, Oct. 22, 1702, p. 1; and *Daily Courant*, Oct. 20, 1702, p. 1.

[2] *Calendar of State Papers, Domestic*, Anne, 1702–1703, p. 393; Cobbett, *Parliamentary History*, vi. 44; Luttrell, *Brief Relation*, v. 233, 256, 410; Dalton, *English Army Lists*, v, part ii, pp. 2, 7; *MSS. of the Earl of Cowper* (H.M.C. Reports, xii, Appendix, part iii), iii, *Coke MSS.*, pp. 43, 46; *Register* of the College of Arms, 4 D 14, p. 68.

from him, since the fifth of August, which makes me very uneasy, and I am sure, you know as—much, as any body does, and there fore I beg of you, for God sake, to Let me know how it is with him, I am prepared for the worst, gods will be done, and pardon this Liberty to

S[r]
your most humble servant
E. Oglethorpe.[1]

Bereft of her husband and eldest son, Lady Eleanor now besought Marlborough's influence to provide a post for her second son, Theophilus, junior, who had wasted a golden opportunity for success in India. Sent out in 1700 for training in colonial and commercial administration, the young man had been placed under his father's good friend, Thomas Pitt, the successor of Elihu Yale as Governor of Fort Saint George at Madras.[2] Theophilus made an excellent impression, Pitt writing to his father in 1701 that 'he will make a very hope full man for he wants not parts nor a hearty application to busyness'.[3] But, although Pitt 'us'd him as my own Child'[4] and made all allowance for the temptations and vagaries of youth, Theophilus, junior, fell from grace. In accordance with the customs of the East India Company, he was sent on the usual commercial mission to China in 1704 but succumbed to evil associations, piled up debts which Pitt at first generously paid, and early in 1705 was sent home in disgrace.[5] Now that he was the head of the family his

[1] Lady Eleanor Wall Oglethorpe to John Ellis, Under-Secretary of State, Godalming, Sept. 8, 1704, Add. MSS. (British Museum), 28892, Ellis Papers, f. 282.

[2] Elihu Yale became the benefactor of Yale University in the American colony of Connecticut. See Dalton, C. N., *Life of Thomas Pitt* (Cambridge, 1915), chaps. vii–viii.

[3] Thomas Pitt to Sir Theophilus Oglethorpe, Fort Saint George, India, Oct. 10, 1701, Add. MSS. (British Museum), 22844, Letter Book of Thomas Pitt, Sept.–Nov. 1701, f. 68 and verso.

[4] Thomas Pitt to Thomas Wooley, Secretary of the East India Company in London, Fort Saint George, India, September 27, 1702, Add. MSS. (British Museum), 22845, Letter Book of Thomas Pitt, Jan.–Oct. 1702, f. 28.

[5] For the whole tragic tale of fine family friendship, generous references, and sad failure, see Thomas Pitt to Sir Henry Johnson, Fort Saint George,

mother had needlessly feared a hasty marriage in India,[1] and on his return she promptly appealed to Marlborough who in September 1705 wrote from his camp at Walsbergen, offering to provide a post in the Guards for the son of his Jacobite confederate.[2] Nothing seems to have come of it, however, for in May 1708 Theophilus Oglethorpe, junior, succeeded to the parliamentary seat once held by his father and older brother.[3]

If Lewis Oglethorpe as a parliamentarian was rather a nonentity, Theophilus was not much more active. In the Third Parliament of Queen Anne, better known as the Second Parliament of Great Britain, the third Oglethorpe to represent Haslemere duly attained to the committee on privileges, and considered, among other subjects, cruisers and convoys, insolvent debtors, Windsor deanery (which Owen Oglethorpe had held a century and a half before), and the usual routine settlements of estates. This rather drab and monotonous existence was enlivened in 1710 by the danger of defeat in the Haslemere elections, a danger so great that Lady Oglethorpe felt impelled to implore, in a most appealing letter, the political aid and influence of Robert Harley. Her audacity proved vain for that personage disdained to reply, and Theophilus fought his campaign alone.[4] Despite Harley's rebuff, the son of Lady Eleanor was successful,[5] even against charges of bribery, and he received his due share of committee assignments. Having served on the com-

India, Oct. 17, 1701, Add. MSS. (British Museum), 22186, Johnson Papers, f. 130; Add. MSS. 22845-22852, Pitt Letter Books and Correspondence, 1701-1705; 22844, ff. 20, 40, 45-6, 49; 22845, ff. 24 verso, 26, 28, 70 verso; 22847, ff. 25-6, 67-71, 87-8; 22848, ff. 47, 49 verso, 88, 113; 22849, ff. 3-4, 11-12, 14 verso, 31-2, 135; 22852, ff. 6, 55, 57, 61-3, 84, 151.

[1] Theophilus Oglethorpe, junior, to Thomas Woolley, Fort Saint George, India, Feb. 14, 1704. India Office Archives, Home Letter Series, Miscellaneous, vol. 257, p. 13.

[2] Murray, Sir George, editor, *Letters and Dispatches of John Churchill, 1st Duke of Marlborough, 1702-1712* (5 vols., London, 1845), ii. 268.

[3] London *Gazette*, May 10, 1708, p. 1; *Daily Courant*, May 7, 1708, p. 2.

[4] *Portland MSS*. (H.M.C. Reports), iv, *Harley Letters*, ii. 590-1, 600, 610.

[5] London *Daily Courant*, Oct. 7, 1710, p. 1; *Evening Post*, Oct. 7, 1710, p. 2.

mittee to arrange accommodations for the trial of Henry Sacheverell, and having assisted Robert Walpole, the Chancellor of the Exchequer, Arthur Onslow, later Speaker of the House, and General Stanhope in drawing up the address to Queen Anne, asking her to send Marlborough to Holland for the negotiations leading to peace in Europe, Oglethorpe was now recognized by regular committee appointments until 1713 when he was finally defeated for re-election. Even in this his faithful and energetic mother had entered a petition of error bearing his forged signature, but he had already left England for the Continent, never to return.[1]

If success did not crown Eleanor Wall Oglethorpe's labours in behalf of her sons, her greatest achievement lay in her successful determination to place her daughters in France whereby the Oglethorpe family remained in constant contact with the Jacobites at Saint-Germain. After 1688, under the pressure of the exiled monarch's Catholic advisers, this Jacobite zealot had taken her young daughters to the court of James II, where Anne Henrietta and Eleanor, the elder pair, were reared as Catholics. Anne in 1704 returned to England without a pass and, being

[1] Theophilus Oglethorpe's committee assignments during the years, 1710–13, included such varied problems as privileges and elections, plantations, the address to the Queen, the auditing of public accounts, numerous estates, claims against the African and Indian Company in Scotland, army debts, Irish yarn, Scottish linen manufacture, Irish forfeitures, the Thames fisheries, the price and size of bread, duties on East Indian goods, the regulation of brokers, the naturalization of foreigners, and army abuses including arrearages in pay. See the *Commons Journals*, xvi. 25, 81–2, 109, 137, 145, 159, 164, 171–5, 182–3, 210, 234, 308, 314, 325, 337–8, 356, 370, 372, 375–6, 397–8, 401, 403, 421–3, 429, 443, 481–2, 502, 508, 510, 521, 528, 537, 539, 541, 547, 555, 573, 578, 585, 587, 593, 600, 603, 613, 619, 643, 657, 663, 679, 682, 691; xvii. 2, 33, 35, 38, 54, 70, 94, 112, 118, 124, 145, 147, 166, 279, 296, 305, 354, 373, 385, 402–3, 417, 420, 443, 445, 458, 462, 464, 475, 481, 483; Stock, *Proceedings and Debates of the British Parliaments respecting North America*, iii. 239, 285; Cobbett, *Parliamentary History*, vi. 747, 920; Carte MSS. (Bodleian Library, Oxford), cxxix, ff. 436 verso, 437; Add. MSS. (British Museum), 15661, Returns to Parliament, 1702–1710, f. 129; *Portland MSS.* (H.M.C. Reports), iv, *Harley Papers*, ii. 590–1, 600, 610; Swanton and Woods, *Bygone Haslemere*, p. 190; Smith, *Parliamentary Representation of Surrey*, p. 93; Oldmixon, *History of England*, p. 441.

arrested, gained her release only by the intervention and protection of Robert Harley, the future Earl of Oxford, who now became profoundly interested in her, rumour even having it that he and Lord Treasurer Godolphin were rivals for her favours.[1] Not content with this experience, she again found herself in trouble when in England during 1707, a year of great importance to all the feminine Oglethorpes. This time she was indicted before the Queen's Bench Court in London for 'perverting a young woman to the Romish faith and sending her to France'. Frances Shaftoe had been called to Godalming in 1699 to aid in preparing the outfit which young Theophilus was to take with him to India and, in the words of a modern Jacobite commentator, 'had heard too many secrets', so that Anne and Eleanor, on their return to France in 1700, had taken her along, 'virtually a prisoner'.[2] This charge of 'trepanning' Frances Shaftoe formed the justification for the latter's tale concerning the substitution of that first James Oglethorpe, the infant, for the Pretender in 1688, a narrative which appeared in print at this time and proved somewhat embarrassing to the family, despite the incontrovertible fact that the Pretender had been born in June 1688, and the Oglethorpe not until June 1689![3] The offence of 'trepanning', with conversion to

[1] For Anne Oglethorpe's relations with Harley and Godolphin see 'The Impartial Secret History of Arlus, Fortunatus and Adolphus, Ministers of State', in Add. MSS. (British Museum), 9122, Coxe Papers, f. 196; Boyer, A., *History of the Life and Reign of Queen Anne* (London, 1722), p. 127; Oldmixon, *History of England*, p. 331; and Cartwright, J. J., editor, *The Wentworth Papers* (London, 1883), p. 215.
[2] Shield, 'The Loyal Oglethorpes', *The Royalist*, ix. 42.
[3] For the Shaftoe case see particularly Shaftoe, Frances, *An Account of Her Being Eleven Months in Sir Theophilus Oglethorpe's Family* (1st ed., London, 1707; 2nd ed., London, 1745); Shaftoe, Frances, *More Memoirs; or, the Pretender What He Really Pretends to be* (London, 1713); and a Memoir on Anne Oglethorpe's visit to Robert Harley to effect a peace with France, in the Carte MSS. (Bodleian Library, Oxford), ccxl, Miscellaneous Papers of Thomas Carte, f. 223. See also the London *Observator*, x, March 25, 1711, pp. 1–2; April 4, 1711, pp. 1–2; xi, March 8, 1712, p. 1. In 'An Hue and Cry after the Pretender By Jack Catch, Esq.', James Stuart is always called 'alias Oglethorp', Add. MSS. (British Museum), 33954, Historical Tracts, ff. 31–2.

Catholicism as implied in the Shaftoe narrative bordered on high treason, and the oldest Oglethorpe daughter was discharged only on direct orders from Queen Anne who doubtless had given ear to Lady Oglethorpe's maternal importunities through the mediacy of Lady Marlborough.[1]

But if Anne had caused her mother much anxiety, Eleanor in 1707 made her happy by contracting a brilliant marriage with Eugène-Marie de Béthisy, Marquis de Mézières of Picardy, who, although her senior by thirty years and a pock-marked hunchback, had compiled an outstanding military record, rising from Cornet of Cavalry in 1674 to Marshal in 1704 and Governor of Amiens in 1706. This alliance was more esteemed by Lady Oglethorpe than by the French aristocracy whose criticism of the Marquis's choice of a 'young English girl who is not particularly noble'[2] did not, however, prevent his promotion to Lieutenant-General in 1710.[3]

By 1710, then, Lady Oglethorpe had given ample proof of her executive ability and had fully justified the opinion

---

[1] Luttrell, *Brief Relation*, vi. 166, 175, 182; Ruvigny and Raineval, Marquis of, *The Jacobite Peerage* (Edinburgh, 1904), pp. 137–8; Haile, *James Francis Edward: the Old Chevalier*, p. 140; Lart, C. E., *Jacobite Extracts from the Parochial Registers of St. Germain-en-Laye* (2 vols., London, 1910–12), i. viii–xii; *Portland MSS.* (H.M.C. Reports), iv, *Harley Letters*, ii. 284, 317, 378, 402, 417; ix. 220.

[2] Conches, F. de, editor, *Journal du Marquis de Dangeau* (19 vols., Paris, 1854–60), xi. 317. For the date of the wedding, March 5, 1707, see the *Register* of the College of Arms, 4 D 14, p. 72.

[3] For light on the Marquis de Mézières see Conches, *Journal du Marquis de Dangeau*, iii. 195, 318, 327; iv. 12, 377, 387, 391; v. 342; viii. 469; ix. 70; x. 165; xi. 21, 112, 119, 121, 124, 127; xiii. 130, 273; xvi. 470; Cosnac and Bertrand, *Mémoires du Marquis de Sourches*, iii. 282, 379, 395, 413–14; iv. 271, 280; v. 91; vi. 187; ix. 108; x. 9, 23, 91, 94, 97, 278; xii. 182, 193, 273; xiii. 46, 378–9; Boislisle, A. de, editor, *Mémoires de Saint-Simon* (41 vols., Paris, 1879–1928), xiv. 319, 321. By 1721 the Marquis de Mézières was a director of the historic French *Compagnie des Indes*. Barbier, E. J. F., *Journal Historique et Anecdotique du Règne de Louis XV* (4 vols., Paris, 1847–56), i. 69. The author has been unable to ascertain whether or not the Marquis de Mézières was a relative of the Athanase de Mézières who, although a Frenchman, established Spanish rule on the Louisiana-Texas frontier, 1768–80. See Bolton, H. E., editor, *Athanase de Mézières and the Louisiana-Texas Frontier, 1768–1780* (2 vols., Cleveland, Ohio, 1914).

of her expressed by Dean Jonathan Swift, with whom she now became friendly. In 1711 she spent some time with Queen Anne at Windsor Castle and became sufficiently intimate to lend her sovereign £200, which sum was repaid in 1714.¹ During September and October 1711, Lady Oglethorpe acted as matchmaker and *cicerone* for Swift in the royal *entourage* at Windsor and, from November to January 1712, continued as such in London, remaining in Swift's circle throughout the year, and continuing the friendship in 1714.²

Having lost her husband and eldest son, and having seen Theophilus, junior, elected to Parliament, Fanny and Molly now settled with Anne at James's court of Saint-Germain, and Eleanor well and suitably married to a French nobleman, Lady Eleanor, with her characteristic tenacity, stubbornness, will-power—call it what you may—now directed her unflagging efforts towards advancing the interests of her youngest son, James Edward Oglethorpe.

While the early years are lost in the careers of his brothers and sisters, James Oglethorpe did record, in a letter written in his retirement, his impressions of the great men of his youth:

> Even from my childhood I made it my business to see all the great men of my time from Lewis the 14th and Victor Amadeus, two kings, and the truly great Prince Eugene down to the poor spirited coviteous Duke of Marlborough, and good King John of Portigal.³

Except for this single letter of reminiscence and a later anecdote that, 'in the reign of Queen Anne, . . . together with the Duke of Rutland and several others of consider-

---
¹ *Portland MSS.* (H.M.C. Reports), v, *Harley Letters*, iii. 481.
² Although an Irishman, Dean Swift, like the Oglethorpes, had a Yorkshire heritage, so that he would naturally appeal in a dual sense to Lady Eleanor from Tipperary. Scott, *Works of Jonathan Swift*, ii. *Journal to Stella*, pp. 251, 253–4, 256, 279, 283, 299, 326; v. 482; Ball, F. E., editor, *Correspondence of Jonathan Swift* (6 vols., London, 1910–14), i. 354–5, 385.
³ James Oglethorpe to Field-Marshal Keith, Rotterdam, Holland, May 3, 1756, *MSS. of Lord Elphinstone* (H.M.C. Reports, viii), p. 229 *a*.

able rank', he frequently indulged in archery in and about London,[1] James Oglethorpe, unlike either his father's colleague, Samuel Pepys, or his own friend of half a century hence, James Boswell, left no diary or journal from which to reconstruct the picture of his childhood.

When then his mother turned her ministering zeal to her youngest offspring, it meant that James, now in his early teens, was to have his life for the next decade inextricably interwoven with his mother's Jacobite career. Determined, despite the fate of Lewis, on a military career for James, the loyal matriarch once more appealed to Marlborough. James Oglethorpe's name appears in the manuscript Army List for 1709 as an Ensign in Her Majesty's First Regiment of Foot Guards,[2] but there is no record anywhere of a Commission having been issued to that effect.[3] By 1712, however, he was definitely recorded as having offered five horses for the campaign in Flanders, and on November 21, 1713, despite the fact that Marlborough was then out of favour with Queen Anne, Lady Eleanor's youngest son was formally commissioned at Windsor to be Lieutenant unassigned and rank as Captain of Foot. One month later this probationary rank was raised to a definite Lieutenancy in the First Regiment of Foot Guards, but the military tendency now gave way, temporarily at least, to the academic.[4]

[1] Add. MSS. (British Museum), 29791, W. Latham's Anecdotes of Archery, f. 28 (p. 55).

[2] War Office Records (P.R.O.), Index 5429, Manuscript Army List for 1709, p. 16 b.

[3] See W.O. 25 (Commission Books): 9, 1708–10; W.O. 25:122. Notification Book, 1708–10; S.P. 44 (State Papers, Domestic, Entry Books): 172–175. Military Commissions, 1704–1714; MS. Calendar of State Papers, Domestic (P.R.O.), Anne, 1702–1713. The possession by a youth of a military commission in the eighteenth century was, of course, no index to an active military career.

[4] W.O. Index 5430, Manuscript Army List for 1715, p. 30 c; W.O. 25:12, Commission Book, 1713–14, p. 7; W.O. 25:125, Notification Book, 1713–14, p. 22; S.P. 44 (State Papers, Domestic, Entry Books): 175, p. 363. See also Dalton, *English Army Lists*, vi. 51, 53, 391; Dalton, Charles, *George the First's Army, 1714–1727* (2 vols., London, 1910–12), i. 126–7 and note 12; Hamil-

At an indeterminate date about this time the youth, following the precedent of his elder brothers, who had been there in 1698,[1] entered Eton College.[2] Far from the Eton of Warre, of Cornish, Arthur Benson and Percy Lubbock, the Eton to which Lewis, Theophilus, and James Oglethorpe went in the dawn of the eighteenth century was a strange composite of political patronage, high social rank, and fair intellect. From the meagre records of that generation, it is evident that the boys were there in the Provostship of Henry Godolphin, a brother of Sidney, Earl of Godolphin, who, as Lord High Treasurer under Queen Anne, had been interested, so 'twas said, in Anne Oglethorpe.[3] Nothing, however, is known of the academic activities of James Oglethorpe who remained here while his mother continued her Jacobite machinations despite a warning from Marlborough that both he and she were suspected of a plot against the court.[4]

ton, Sir F. W., *Origin and History of the First Grenadier Guards* (3 vols., London, 1874), ii. 49–64; iii. 443. In the *Byng Papers* is a letter to Captain Camocke, dated Malta, Dec. 19, 1712, and signed either 'J.' or 'T.' Oglethorpe. It expresses a Jacobite point of view. Although it seems impossible for James Oglethorpe to have been at Malta at the time, while Theophilus, junior, *might* have been there, the editor of the *Byng Papers* is convinced the signature is 'J. Oglethorpe.' Tunstall, W. C. B., editor, *The Byng Papers* (3 vols., Navy Record Society, London, 1930–2), iii. 57–8.

[1] A List by Thomas Rawlinson of some of his contemporaries at Oxford, who were Eton men, includes Lewis Oglethorpe and Theophilus Oglethorpe, junior. Rawlinson MSS. (Bodleian Library, Oxford), D, dcccxii, f. 444. See also Rawlinson MSS., B, cclxv, f. 19 *b*; *Etoniana, Ancient and Modern* (London, 1865), pp. 59–60; Austen-Leigh, R. A., *Eton College Lists, 1678–1790* (Eton, 1907), pp. xxix–xxx, 258.

[2] Rawlinson MSS. (Bodleian Library, Oxford), J. 4°. vi, f. 34.

[3] Lyte, H. C. Maxwell, *History of Eton College* (4th ed., London, 1911), pp. 277–80.

[4] Duke of Marlborough to Lady Oglethorpe, London, July 4, 1713, *MSS. of the Duke of Marlborough* (H.M.C. Reports, viii, Appendix, part i), p. 14 *a*. In Packet E 46 of the Manuscripts of the Duke of Marlborough at Blenheim Castle there lies a letter of Lady Oglethorpe to the Duchess. H.M.C. Reports, viii, Appendix, part i, p. 57. Unfortunately these documents are not available for use. For an undated, anonymous communication as to the secret activities of 'Madame Oglethorp at her house in Little Ridder Street', see S.P. 35 (State Papers, Domestic, George I, P.R.O.): 66, No. 115.

Her Jacobitism now led to one of the most significant events in the life of James Edward Oglethorpe.

Early in 1714 Lady Oglethorpe determined to give her Eton son the advantages of a university education by sending him to Oxford. University College was the natural goal for Yorkshiremen and their descendants but, if Merton, Christ Church, Exeter, and Wadham were known to betray Whig sympathies, it was the more certain that Jacobitism still reigned supreme at Corpus Christi College, where Lewis Oglethorpe had matriculated upon leaving Eton in 1698. Lady Eleanor therefore sought the aid of her ally, the Non-juring Bishop, George Hickes,[1] who on January 12, 1714, not long before the recipient's death, wrote thus to the politically powerful Dr. Thomas Turner,[2] President of the College and brother of the Jacobite Bishop Turner:

Yesterday my Lady Ogilthorp did me the favour to give me a visit with her son yet a scholar at Eaton-school. He is a very ingenious, understanding, and well-bred youth in the 17th year of his age. I found by her Lad[yshi]ps discourses at last, that the chief end of her visit was to let you know by me how desirous she was to have him, as his eldest brother formerly was, a fellow commoner of your College, under your inspection. She makes it her earnest request to you y^t [that] you would keep a place void for him and saith [that] she had written for that purpose to Mr. Perrot, but seemed troubled [that] she had had no answer from him, and therefore I pray you to send an answer to her by him, or me, or immediately to herself, if you are acquainted with her.[3]

[1] For further light on George Hickes and the Non-jurors see Broxap, Henry, *The Later Non-Jurors* (Cambridge, 1924), chaps. i–ii; Overton, J. H., *The Non-Jurors* (London, 1902); Lathbury, Thomas, *History of the Non-Jurors* (London, 1843).

[2] Dr. Thomas Turner had been one of the few Fellows of Oxford Colleges who in 1689 refused to take the oath of allegiance to William and Mary, Mallet, Sir Charles E., *History of the University of Oxford* (3 vols., London, 1924–7), iii. 4, note. As to President Turner's political power see *Portland MSS.* (H.M.C. Reports), vii, *Harley Letters*, v, *Stratford Letters*, pp. 1–200, *passim*.

[3] Rawlinson MSS. (Bodleian Library, Oxford), H (Letters), xcii, f. 609; J. folio, xxix, f. 365 verso; xxx, f. 138 verso; J. 4°, vi, f. 34.

A JACOBITE YOUTH 61

Such a request from such a source could not be denied, and James Oglethorpe entered Corpus Christi College, Oxford, on July 3, 1714.[1] Five days later he matriculated in the University, paying, as the son of a knight, a fee of one pound as over against the half-crown to five shillings required of commoners.[2] This university connexion was in full accord with family heritage for—despite their Yorkshire habitation, whence around 1600 William Oglethorpe had slipped down the east coast to Sidney Sussex, and John, as a Fellow, to Trinity College, Cambridge[3]—the Oglethorpes were Oxonians by tradition and instinct, having sent their sons thither throughout four generations which included a President of Magdalen College and a Vice-Chancellor of the University.[4]

Thus it was that early in July 1714 a post-chaise, probably the *Worcester Fly*, clattered along the London road to the west, bearing, among other travellers, a young gentleman named James Edward Oglethorpe, late of Eton, and now eagerly awaiting his first view of the spires of Oxford; past the verdant countryside, over Shotover Hill and across the Plain to Magdalen Bridge, the ancient gateway of a small town set amid green fields through which the gentle Isis wound its pleasant, timeless course; rumbling up the arching High Street, whence turned off other arteries of traffic scarcely more than cow-paths;

[1] Buttery Books of Corpus Christi College, Oxford, 1714–17; Fowler, Thomas, *History of Corpus Christi College, with Lists of its Members* (Oxford Historical Society Publications, Oxford, 1893), pp. 260, 275, 440.

[2] *Registrum Matriculationum*, 1713–14, The Archives of the University of Oxford; *Subscription Register*, 1694–1714, p. 333, July 8, 1714, Archives of the University of Oxford; Mallet, *History of the University of Oxford*, iii. 10 note; Foster, *Alumni Oxonienses, Early Series, 1500–1714*, iii. 1086.

[3] Venn and Venn, *Alumni Cantabrigienses*, iii. 277; Venn and Venn, *Book of Matriculations at Cambridge*, p. 498; Ball, W. W. R., and Venn, J. A., editors, *Admissions to Trinity College, Cambridge* (5 vols., London, 1911–26), ii. 252.

[4] Boase, *Register of the University of Oxford*, i. 137, 239; ii, part ii, pp. 98–100. It is interesting to note that in 1718 Oglethorpe Hall in Bramham, Yorkshire, passed into the hands of a Samuel Waddington whose descendant and namesake in 1865 was a B.A. of Brasenose College, Oxford. Forshaw, C. F., editor, *Yorkshire Notes and Queries*, i (Bedford, 1905), 105.

ending at the Mitre or, if the coachman be properly persuaded, driving up with a flourish to Bear Lane where the precious cargo was duly deposited at the gate of Corpus Christi College. We know not whether Oglethorpe, at seventeen, merited J. R. Green's description of the public schoolman, . . . strutting about town for a week or two before entrance, courting his schoolfellows' envy with his 'new suit of drugget, his pair of prim ruffles, his new bob-wig, and brazen-hilted sword', swaggering at coffee-houses and giving himself a scholar's airs at the bookshops.

Nor do we know definitely what he studied. The educational system of Oglethorpe's Oxford was somewhat in a state of coma. Few colleges had libraries, and the Bodleian was conducted in a wretched manner. Academic emphasis was laid on the Trivials: Logic, a major art at Oxford; Rhetoric, officially neglected but practically available; and Grammar. Mathematics, so warmly received at scientific Cambridge, was still a novelty in the home of the Classics. Casuistry had supplanted metaphysics, for Locke was yet to win university recognition; and canon law was still as important as the common law. History, politics, and geography were well regarded, but modern languages were neglected for the oriental studies required for Biblical criticism; while in medicine some theory but no practice was taught, so that Oxford, with dissection forbidden, languished far behind Leyden of Holland in surgery and anatomy.[1]

If we know not what Oglethorpe studied, neither are we certain that the future advocate of temperance here succumbed to the more riotous social customs of the period. Although Oxford at this time had more really poor boys than later, Oglethorpe never suffered the privation and misery and years of sacrifice endured by his

[1] Green, J. R., *Studies in Oxford History, chiefly in the Eighteenth Century* (Oxford Historical Society Publications, Oxford, 1901), pp. 46-83, 121-69; Godley, A. D., *Oxford in the Eighteenth Century* (New York and London, 1908), pp. 34, 172-5; Wordsworth, Christopher, *Scholae Academicae: Some Account of the Studies at the English Universities in the Eighteenth Century* (Cambridge, 1877), pp. 3, 5-6, 25, 83-5, 87-90, 120-4, 127, 135-53, 162-85.

friend of later years, Samuel Johnson of Pembroke. There is no evidence as to where he went after classes had followed an early rising: whether to the coffee-house, tavern, or gaming-room, or along the limpid Cherwell; nor know we whom he toasted as the belle of the town or with whom he flirted in Merton Walk. We do know that at Oxford the scholars rose early, dined at ten or eleven, supped at five or six. Drinking, as both an art and a sport, bowls, fives, and cock-fighting abounded, and in 1716 attention had to be called to the visiting of taverns by those *in statu pupillari*. Music was just beginning to attract interest, but the drama flourished. The ladies thought a man who breakfasted on toasts and ale a very vulgar fellow, but the native damsels were not averse to 'varsity men as husbands! The relations between town and gown were such, in fact, that students were often in need of warning and protection against hasty marriages, out of their station, with charming lasses of Oxford town.[1]

James Oglethorpe had come to Oxford in momentous days for college, university, and nation. He was a member of a college 'than which', in old Thomas Hearne's opinion, 'he could not have pick'd out a better in the whole University'.[2] Turner, it is true, had died before Oglethorpe arrived and Basil Kennett, his successor, did not long survive, but, under Mather as well, Corpus changed not its Jacobite convictions, and Oglethorpe found here congenial associates in Theophilus Leigh, grand-uncle of Jane Austen, the novelist, and later Master of Balliol for sixty years; John Burton, expounder of Locke's philosophy; John Rawlinson, and Thomas Randolph, Mather's successor as President of Corpus.[3]

[1] Green, *Studies in Oxford History*, pp. 38–45; Wordsworth, Christopher, *Social Life at the English Universities in the Eighteenth Century* (Cambridge, 1874), pp. 89, 93–5, 97, 123–7, 178–83, 200–1, 298, 350, 362–76, 436.
[2] Doble, C. E., Rannie, D. W., *et al.*, editors, *Remarks and Collections of Thomas Hearne* (hereinafter cited as *Hearne's Diaries*, 11 vols., Oxford Historical Society Publications, Oxford, 1884–1921), i. 130.
[3] Fowler, *History of Corpus Christi College*, pp. 261–76, 282; Doble, Rannie, *et al.*, *Hearne's Diaries*, iv. 357–8; v. 2, 7, 9, 11, 15, 21, 59.

Two weeks after Oglethorpe's matriculation at Corpus, Gloucester Hall had become Worcester College and, during his undergraduate days, the University Press began printing in the Clarendon Building whither it had been transferred from the Sheldonian Theatre, while Queen's College completed and opened its new buildings, and All Souls laid the foundation for the Codrington Library. The most important university event, however, was the death on November 1, 1714, of Dr. John Radcliffe, like Oglethorpe's forebears a Yorkshireman, concerning whose wealth and benefactions Hearne noted: 'He died worth about an hundred and fourty Thousand Pounds. He hath given fourty thousand Pounds to the University for building an additional Library to the Bodlejan Library, & to furnish it with books & provide for the Librarian', in addition to a bequest of five thousand pounds to his own University College.[1] But college and university occurrences paled into insignificance in comparison with the myriad events of national importance, the echoes of which penetrated the ivy-clad walls of Oxford and made the deepest impression on at least one young member of Corpus Christi College.[2]

The son of Lady Eleanor Wall Oglethorpe had come to the Jacobite college of the Jacobite stronghold of England in the dawn of the Rising of 1715. Within a month after James Oglethorpe's matriculation at Oxford, Robert Harley, Earl of Oxford, had retired as Lord High Treasurer, and Queen Anne herself was dead. Not the least affected by the sudden turn in events was the university city. Although John Wesley saw Oxford 'paved with the skulls of Jacobites', the deep, abiding faith remained, and the university did only the bare minimum necessary to

---

[1] Doble, Rannie, *et al.*, *Hearne's Diaries*, iv. 424. For Dr. Radcliffe's will see *Some Memoirs of the Life of John Radcliffe, M.D.* (2nd ed., London, 1715), pp. 101–6.

[2] For the Oxford of this period see Doble, Rannie, *et al.*, *Hearne's Diaries*, iv. 254–5, 383; v. 96, 110–11, 239–40; *Portland MSS.* (H.M.C. Reports), vii. *Harley Letters*, v, *Stratford Letters*, pp. 206–7; Mallet, *History of the University of Oxford*, iii. 1–101, *passim*.

A JACOBITE YOUTH

save its face in celebrating the proclamation of George I, nor was the situation at his coronation any better. The climax came in 1715 when news came to Oxford of the Rising in Scotland. With all about him bespeaking the great cause, James Oglethorpe would not have been true to his heritage or environment had he not followed, with that keen fervour which belongs to youth and high ideals, the trend of events in the north. With Atterbury succeeding John Locke at Christ Church and Oxford's men of letters, in Green's phrase, 'Jacobites to a man', it was but natural that young Oglethorpe should have joined the demonstration in Cornmarket which had marked the death of Anne. But more and worse was to come. The first anniversary since his accession of King George's birthday, May 28, 1715, gave the Jacobites of Oxford their golden opportunity to proclaim their faith by celebrating, the next day, the birthday of Charles II! The pro-Hanoverian Constitution Club had held a meeting at the King's Head on George's birthday. A riot had ensued. The combination of circumstances the next day proved too much and the Jacobites swarmed over Oxford. A fortnight later, the marking of the Pretender's birthday on June 10, led to further disorders which reached their climax in a town-and-gown conflict with the Hanoverian representatives on August 28 and 29. It is difficult not to believe that the healthy, exuberant son of brave Theophilus and ardent Eleanor Oglethorpe participated with glee in these Jacobite revels. And the probability that he at all times manifested his staunch Jacobitism, despite the collapse of the Rising in the North, is enhanced by the course of his career after the 'Fifteen.[1]

[1] London *Flying Post*, September 1, 1715, pp. 1-2; *St. James's Evening Post*, Sept. 1, 1715, p. 239; Pimlott, J. A. R., 'The English Jacobites under the Hanoverian Kings', Unpublished Stanhope Prize Essay in History, Oxford University, 1930, pp. 45-7; Mallet, *History of the University of Oxford*, iii. 38-43; Doble, Rannie, et al., *Hearne's Diaries*, iv. 387-9, 399, 417-18; v. 61-2, 64-6; Green, *Studies in Oxford History*, pp. 46-83, 121-69; Godley, *Oxford in the Eighteenth Century*, pp. 224, 231, 237-46; Quiller-Couch, L. M., *Reminiscences of Oxford by Oxford Men, 1559-1850* (Oxford Historical Society

Despite the salubrious Jacobite atmosphere of Corpus and Oxford, Oglethorpe did not remain long in residence, although, by his mother's statement on the family history in the *Register* of the College of Arms, he was still at Corpus in April 1716.[1] In the words of President Fowler, Oglethorpe's is an early instance, probably the first in Corpus in the case of a non-foundationer, of 'keeping the name on the books' during a prolonged period of non-residence. His name first disappears on May 3, 1717; it was re-entered on June 25, 1719, and finally disappears on October 20, 1727.

As will be seen, this accords well with his foreign activities in 1717 and also with his economic status, for his re-entry in 1719 follows within a year his succession to Westbrook and the family fortune.

For the greater part of the time after re-entering his name he does not battel, wrote the President of Corpus, and he seems never to have proceeded to the Degree of B.A., but when he had for some years been Member for Haslemere, and had already obtained considerable reputation for his philanthropic efforts on behalf of imprisoned debtors, he was specially created M.A. on July 31, 1731.[2]

Professor Trevelyan, describing, in a memoir of his distinguished father, the latter's years at Trinity College, Cambridge, has well averred that 'all his life long he felt towards Trinity as an Athenian towards Athens'.[3] While this could hardly be said of one who spent as little time at Corpus as did Oglethorpe, it is not exaggeration to assert that his interest in his old college never waned, and in 1772 he presented to it what is now a cherished

Publications, Oxford, 1892), pp. 68–96; *Portland MSS.* (H.M.C. Reports), v, *Harley Letters*, iii. 498.

[1] *Register* of the College of Arms, 4 D 14, p. 69.
[2] *Registrum Convocationis* (Archives of the University of Oxford), Bc. 32, 1730–41, f. 11 recto; *A Catalogue of All Graduates in Divinity, Law, and Physick; and of all Masters of Arts and Doctors of Musick, who have regularly proceeded or been created in the University of Oxford, Between October 10, 1659, and October 10, 1770* (Oxford, 1772), p. 258; Fowler, *History of Corpus Christi College*, pp. 275–6, 440.
[3] Trevelyan, G. M., *Sir George Otto Trevelyan: a Memoir* (London, 1932), p. 30.

memento, two beautifully illuminated volumes of the *French History of the Bible*, which originally had been executed at the order of Francis I of France.[1] Notwithstanding the Jacobite tendencies of the Foot Guards, Oglethorpe's commission therein of 1713 was renewed on January 7, 1715, by the Hanoverian George I who assigned him to the first troop of Guards under Marlborough, now returned to power as commander-in-chief; but the *Wanderlust* had enthralled him and, preferring possible action abroad to inertia at home, James Oglethorpe resigned from the British Army on November 23, 1715.[2] As his family had for some years been living as much in France as at Godalming, the young Oxonian ex-army officer some time in 1716 migrated to Paris where, at the Academy, he became a fellow student with the future Field-Marshal James Keith.[3] But the desire for action was still strong within him, and the campaign of Prince Eugene of Savoy against the Turks gave him his opportunity. Early in 1717 he eluded the French embargo on foreign service[4] and joined the Prince's *entourage* as his aide-de-camp. Here, as Boswell relates it, he received his first lesson in diplomacy in an encounter at the table with a Prince of Württemberg.[5] The

---

[1] Gutch, *Anthony à Wood's History and Antiquities of the Colleges of Oxford*, Appendix, p. 279; personal information from the late President Percy S. Allen of Corpus Christi College.

[2] W.O. 25 (War Office: Commission Books): 13, Commission Book, 1714–16, p. 24; W.O. 25:126, Notification Book, 1714–17, p. 22; S.P. 44 (State Papers, Domestic, Entry Books): 176, Military Commissions, 1714–17, p. 345; Dalton, *English Army Lists*, vi. 53; Dalton, *George the First's Army*, i. 127, note 12; Doran, J., *London in the Jacobite Times* (2 vols., London, 1877), i. 50.

[3] James Oglethorpe to Field-Marshal Keith (no place), Dec. 9, 1755, *MSS. of Lord Elphinstone* (H.M.C. Reports), p. 229 a; Keith, Field-Marshal James, *Memoir, 1714–1734* (Spalding Club Publications, Edinburgh, 1843), p. 33; Stephen, Leslie, and Lee, Sir Sidney, editors, *Dictionary of National Biography* (63 vols., London, 1885–1900; Oxford reissue, 21 vols., Oxford, 1920), x. 1212.

[4] The Duke of Mar to James III, Paris, April 8, 1717. *The King's Collection of Stuart Papers* (H.M.C. Reports), iv. 171.

[5] The Prince of Württemberg was either Alexander or Frederick. Campbell, J., *The Military History of Prince Eugene* (2 vols., London, 1736–7), ii. 228–32.

latter having cleverly filliped some wine from his glass into Oglethorpe's face, the young Briton, with an engaging and disarming smile, exclaimed: 'That's a good joke, but we do it much better in England', at that moment flinging an entire glassful of wine into the astonished royal countenance, to the great amusement and admiration of the company.[1] In this environment he spent the next six months, and by his military capabilities achieved merited distinction and the approval of his superiors. To the great pride of his sisters he mounted the trenches in the famous battle of Belgrade on August 3, 1717, which he described to his sister Fanny as 'very bloody and sharp', and wherein he was unharmed although 'his servant that was next to him is killed'.[2] With this Austrian victory, his account of which was to fascinate Dr. Johnson over fifty years later,[3] the war soon came to a close, leaving James Oglethorpe with a deservedly high military reputation, remarkable for a young man of twenty.

Although he had been reared on Jacobite precepts and in a distinctly Jacobite environment, young Oglethorpe's continental army career might have nullified the effect thereof, had not his mother and sisters again taken him in hand. In order then to understand the Jacobite activities of James Oglethorpe's young manhood, it is necessary to revert for a moment to the progress of the Oglethorpe family. Neither her own business affairs[4] nor Eleanor's marriage, nor Marlborough's compulsory retirement, nor yet the increasing stability of the *de facto* government

---

[1] Hill, George Birkbeck, editor, *Boswell's Life of Johnson* (6 vols., Oxford, 1887; revised edition by L. F. Powell, 6 vols., Oxford, 1934–5: all citations will be to the revised edition), ii. 180–1.

[2] Fanny Oglethorpe to the Duke of Mar, Paris, Aug. 27, 1717. *The King's Collection of Stuart Papers* (H.M.C. Reports), iv. 534; Fanny Oglethorpe to the Duke of Mar, Paris, Aug. 28, 1717. *The King's Collection of Stuart Papers*, iv. 539–40. For contemporary evidence of the severe losses in this battle see all English newspapers of Aug. 1717, especially the London *Post Man*, Aug. 29, 1717, p. 1.

[3] Hill, *Boswell's Life of Johnson* (Powell revision), ii. 181.

[4] For an example of Lady Oglethorpe's estate affairs see Add. MSS. (British Museum), 31143, Strafford Papers, ff. 506–7.

under Queen Anne and George I had checked, in the slightest degree, the Jacobite ardour of Lady Oglethorpe. Although Anne had made frequent trips to England in the cause during the first decade of the new century—the last of which in 1710 had been to lay the ground-work for the Treaty of Utrecht[1]—the centre of activities was still the quasi-court of James III at Saint-Germain where Anne and Fanny, still unmarried, basked in the royal favour while plotting assiduously with their sister, Eleanor, Marquise de Mézières. The Union with Scotland in 1707, the overthrow of the Tories in 1710, the dismissal of Marlborough at the close of 1711, and the death of Queen Anne in 1714, had all served to keep alive the Jacobite flame. And not the least factor in upholding the zeal and faith of the Oglethorpes was the annual pension of two thousand francs which the Marquis de Mézières and François de Salignac de la Mothe Fénelon, the brilliant *littérateur*, obtained from Louis XIV for Lady Oglethorpe's third daughter, Fanny, in 1713, two years before the donor and Fénelon died.[2] The sudden death of Queen Anne had found James's cohorts quite unprepared,[3] but the accession of George I led to a great counter-movement of Jacobites in France, including an invasion of Scotland, in which Anne and Fanny became liaison officers, so to speak, between the Stuart court circle in France and the confederates at home, chief among whom were Lady Eleanor Wall Oglethorpe, ardent as ever, and her fourth daughter, Mary, better known as Molly.

Despite an appointment as aide-de-camp to the Duke of Ormonde in the Flanders campaign of 1712–13, which led to his choice as bearer of the army funds in July, just before his defeat in the parliamentary elections,[4] Theophilus

---

[1] Carte MSS. (Bodleian Library, Oxford), ccxii, f. 36 verso; ccxl, ff. 223 and verso; Shield and Lang, *The King Over the Water*, pp. 153-4, 164.
[2] Fénelon, François de Salignac de la Mothe, *Correspondance* (11 vols., Paris, 1827–9), iii. 200–2; iv. 331, 347, 360–2, 371–2; Conches, *Journal du Marquis de Dangeau*, xv. 360; Boislisle, *Mémoires de Saint-Simon*, xiv. 320.
[3] *Portland MSS.* (H.M.C. Reports), v, *Harley Letters*, iii. 498.
[4] Theophilus Oglethorpe, junior, to Henry Watkins, Secretary to the

Oglethorpe, since Lewis's death head of the family, was heavily interested in the Jacobite cause. Upon learning of his defeat at Haslemere he remained on the Continent, never to return, and soon became an aide in the retinue of the Earl of Peterborough, who in 1696 had been a fellow conspirator with the elder Theophilus Oglethorpe,[1] and who now was Queen Anne's ambassador to the Duke of Savoy, newly created King of Sicily, at Palermo. In this party, also, as chaplain, was George Berkeley, who was to gain renown as theologian, philosopher, and colonial philanthropist.[2] The sudden death of the Queen, the next summer, recalled Peterborough, with whom Berkeley also returned to his cloister in Ireland, but Theophilus Oglethorpe, after wandering on the Continent from Ghent and Bruges to Messina, began a vain attempt to gain recognition as Jacobite representative at the court of the King of Sicily.[3]

Due largely to Lady Oglethorpe's contacts at court and in London,[4] Molly, on December 16, 1714, was proposed as a Maid of Honour to the Princess of Wales, a suggestion which evoked much sarcastic comment, whereupon

British Commanders in Flanders, Bruges, Aug. 8, 1713, Add. MSS. (British Museum), 33273, Letters to Henry Watkins, 1702–14, ff. 226–7; London *Flying Post*, May 27, 1712, p. 1; *Post Boy*, July 21, 1713, p. 1; Aug. 27, 1713, p. 1; *Daily Courant*, Aug. 27, 1713, p. 2; *Gazette*, Sept. 5, 1713, p. 2. See also Eleanor Oglethorpe de Mézières to Henry Watkins [no place], July 15, 1712. Add. MSS. 38852, Hodgkin Papers, vii, ff. 175–6. A certain Thomas Woodcock later claimed that in 1713, after serving for ten years in the First Regiment of Guards, he had been unjustly deprived of his commission by the Duke of Ormonde, who had given it to 'Mr. Oglethorpe'. Cust, Lady Elizabeth, *Records of the Cust Family, 1479–1700* (London, 1898), p. 436, note.

[1] Peterborough, Charles, Earl of (pseudonym, Matthew Smith), *Memoirs of Secret Service* (London, 1699), *passim*.

[2] Jaegle, E., editor, *Correspondance de Madame, Duchess d'Orleans* (3 vols., Paris, 1890), ii. 200; *MSS. of the Earl of Egmont* (H.M.C. Reports, vii. Appendix, part i), p. 239; Ballard, C., *The Great Earl of Peterborough* (London, 1929), pp. 76–90, 262–3; Hone, J. M., and Rossi, M. M., *Bishop Berkeley: His Life, Writings, and Philosophy* (London, 1931), pp. 94–6.

[3] *Portland MSS.* (H.M.C. Reports), v, *Harley Letters*, iii. 442, 481–2.

[4] Here she renewed her friendship with Dean Swift. *MSS. of the Earl of Dartmouth* (H.M.C. Reports, xi, Appendix, part v), i. 317.

Molly passed out of the picture.[1] By this time James III was ready for his attempt on Scotland which earned him only an exile in Italy, but the 'Fifteen found Anne, Eleanor, and Fanny—whom the Jacobite and French circles in Paris called 'the nymphs'—ready at the villa in the Bois de Boulogne to do their part in the peculiar diplomatic negotiations with Bolingbroke, who noted especially Fanny's important status with the pro-Jacobite French Ministry.[2]

Although, in the Stuart Papers, the evidences of blind, unwavering loyalty on the part of the Oglethorpes often border on the pathetic, the family had, for some time, conceived the idea that their joint labours deserved regal recognition. Whether or not the Dukedom given by James III in 1715 to the Earl of Mar was but an added incentive, they had gathered their evidence in meticulous fashion. As early as 1707 Theophilus Oglethorpe, junior, had approached Ralph Thoresby, the Yorkshire antiquarian, for the family pedigree and 'a true blazoning of the coat armory' of the Oglethorpes of Oglethorpe.[3] In 1714 Lady Eleanor and her daughter, Anne Henrietta, proceeded to engage Robert Dale at the College of Arms and, through him, Thomas Hearne, the Oxford historian, to compile, from the Dodsworth manuscripts and other sources, the family record. For three years the search continued, and by the autumn of 1717 the three sisters

[1] Cowper, Mary, Countess, *Diary* (London, 1864), pp. 32-3.
[2] D'Iberville to Torcy, London, July 18, 1715, Add. MSS. (British Museum), 34498, Mackintosh Collection, xii, Extracts of Diplomatic Correspondence in the Foreign Office, Paris, xi, f. 157, verso; Mallet, D., editor, *Works of Henry St. John, Viscount Bolingbroke* (3rd ed., 8 vols., London, 1809), i. 53, 101; Sichel, Walter, *Bolingbroke and his Times* (2 vols., London, 1901), i. 341; ii. 30; Roome, H. D., *James Edward, the Old Pretender* (Oxford, 1904), p. 68; Coxe, William, *Memoirs of the Life and Administration of Sir Robert Walpole, Earl of Orford* (3 vols., London, 1798), ii. 343; Haile, *James Francis Edward, the old Chevalier*, p. 219, note; Petrie, *The Jacobite Movement*, pp. 141-7.
[3] Theophilus Oglethorpe, junior, to Ralph Thoresby, Westbrook Place, Godalming, June 27, 1707, Lancaster, *Letters addressed to Ralph Thoresby*, pp. 150-1; see also pp. 244-7; Hunter, J., editor, *Diary of Ralph Thoresby* (2 vols. in 1, London, 1830), ii. 213, 219.

in France were ready for the attempt.[1] Basing their claims in general on six centuries of family loyalty to the Crown, and in particular on James II's desire at Bothwell Brigg to make Colonel Theophilus Oglethorpe, senior, a baronet—which, Fanny charged, jealous rivals had prevented—they now asked James III to confer some distinction, preferably a baronetcy, upon Theophilus, junior, with remainder to James Edward Oglethorpe who, for this purpose, was regarded as his brother's son.[2] At this same time David Nairne, Secretary to James III, was reminding Cardinal Gualterio that the loyalty of the Oglethorpe family deserved suitable recognition and urged the Cardinal to be attentive to Theophilus when the latter came to Rome.[3] It was natural, therefore, that the Pretender should welcome the petition of the Oglethorpe ladies to which he acceded on December 20, 1717, creating Theophilus Baron Oglethorpe of Oglethorpe, with remainders to his direct heirs or to his brother, James.[4] James Oglethorpe, at the age of twenty-one, thus became an embryonic recipient of one of the few Jacobite peerages of this period other than the Dukedom bestowed upon the loyal Earl of Mar, a fact which of itself

[1] See the 'Statement by Lady Eleanor Oglethorp' of April 21, 1716, in the *Register* of the College of Arms, 4 D 14, pp. 68–9. There is more detail on this episode in the original Hearne letters and diaries in the Bodleian Library than in the printed edition. See Rawlinson MSS. (Bodleian Library, Oxford), H (Letters), iv, ff. 102–10; xiv, ff. 93, 95, 97; xvi, f. 31; xix, ff. 28–9; K (Hearne Diaries), li, p. 156; lvi, p. 21; lvii, p. 106; lxxvii, p. 206; Doble, Rannie, *et al.*, *Hearne's Diaries*, iv. 410, 413; v. 59, 61, 66, 70, 315, 331, 353, 355, 370; vi. 13, 30, 145.

[2] Fanny Oglethorpe to the Duke of Mar, Paris, Nov. 24, 1717. *The King's Collection of Stuart Papers* (H.M.C. Reports), v. 229–32; Fanny Oglethorpe to the Duke of Mar, Paris, Dec. 23, 1717. An unpublished letter, written after James III had approved the request. The King's Collection of Stuart Papers at Windsor Castle.

[3] David Nairne, Secretary to James III, to Cardinal Gualterio, Urbino, Sept. 20, 1717, Add. MSS. (British Museum), 31260, Papers of Cardinal Gualterio: Letters of David Nairne, Secretary to the Pretender, ii (1717), ff. 159 and verso.

[4] James III to his Attorney- or Solicitor-General of England, Urbino, Italy, Dec. 20, 1717, *The King's Collection of Stuart Papers* (H.M.C. Reports), v. xxvii–xxviii. 289.

A JACOBITE YOUTH

indicates the high position of the Oglethorpe connexion in Jacobite history.[1]

With the close of the campaign against the Turks James Oglethorpe decided to return to his sisters in Paris by way of Turin, Italy, where his brother, Theophilus, then was. On October 15, 1717, the British representative at Venice reported to the Secretary of State this interesting bit of news:

On Monday last, Mr. Oglethorp an English Gent came to see me, He said, He was come from making ye Camp[ai]g^{ne} in Hungarie, where he had seen Mr. pitt, He told me what had passt there, I desired him to dine to me, and asked him when he thought to be in Engl[an]^d, He said after he had seen Italie, I told him it was a bad season to see the Cuntrey, if he had not seen it before, but He might possibilie meet a namesake of his at Turin. He said nothing to this, but was desireous to know ye business of Sardinia, I told him y^t [that] if ye Spaniards had success, ye Emp[ero]r would march troups into Italie, under ye command of C[oun]^t G^o Starenbergh. He told me y^t [that] prince Eugene would endeavour all he could to have y^t [that] command, I said, pr[ince] Eugene could not be evrie where, But I believe, He is the same Oglethorp y^t [that] has been at Turin, and is now returning.[2]

Mr. Cunningham, however, was wrong in confusing James with his elder brother, through whom, at Turin, he met the Duke of Mar. The Jacobites now saw a use for 'Jamie', concerning whom his sister, Fanny, wrote that 'the truth is that he is a very good youth and has a true foundation of honest principles'.[3] As he was shortly to leave for England to settle his errant brother's domestic affairs, the Paris group conceived the idea of making James Edward Oglethorpe a Stuart messenger. In December

---

[1] Ruvigny and Raineval, Marquis of, *The Jacobite Peerage*, pp. 136–7; *Notes and Queries*, Series III, ix. 71–2.

[2] S.P. 99 (State Papers, Foreign: Venice): 61 (P.R.O.) Despatches of Alexander Cunningham, British Representative at Venice, to the Secretaries of State, 1715–17. A. Cunningham to the Secretary of State, Venice, Oct. 15, 1717.

[3] Fanny Oglethorpe to the Duke of Mar, Paris, Nov. 24, 1717, *The King's Collection of Stuart Papers* (H.M.C. Reports), v. 232.

1717, however, he decided to go to Rome where his brother then was. The Jacobite stamp was rapidly but thoroughly being applied. 'He intends', wrote Fanny to Mar, who was then with James III in exile at Urbino, 'to ask to kiss our Master's hand. I suppose he'll address himself to you. He is charmed with your goodness to him at T[urin].'[1] Mar had often asked about 'Jamie', which highly pleased Theophilus who, waiting in Rome until his brother's arrival in January 1718, added his own approval to that of Fanny: 'I am very well satisfied with him and love him the more, because I see he is entirely affectionate to the King and that the Germans have not in the least prevailed on him.'[2] Exactly one month later Theophilus joyously reported that 'my brother is gone hence to pay his duty to his Majesty, being pushed by the natural zeal that belongs to the family'.[3] James's visit to court was a success for, in Mar's words, the Pretender 'was well pleased with him, and I believe Jamie no less with him'.[4] On his return to Paris, James paused in Rome to send Mar his thanks for the civilities that had been showered on him, and to assure the Duke how sensible he was and always would be of the Stuart King's kindness to him.

By this time the young man was strongly and surely identified with the cause. Theophilus, having failed to gain recognition from the King of Sicily as Jacobite envoy, largely because of what Nairne called his 'imprudent zeal',[5] now turned towards Naples where he almost fell into the clutches of the British Navy, but escaped to

[1] Fanny Oglethorpe to the Duke of Mar, Paris, Dec. 14, 1717, *The King's Collection of Stuart Papers* (H.M.C. Reports), v. 276.
[2] Theophilus Oglethorpe to the Duke of Mar, Rome, Jan. 22, 1718, *The King's Collection of Stuart Papers* (H.M.C. Reports), v. 401.
[3] Theophilus Oglethorpe to the Duke of Mar, Rome, Feb. 12, 1718, *The King's Collection of Stuart Papers* (H.M.C. Reports), v. 459.
[4] The Duke of Mar to Fanny Oglethorpe, Urbino, Feb. 19, 1718, *The King's Collection of Stuart Papers* (H.M.C. Reports), v. 494.
[5] David Nairne to Cardinal Gualterio, Urbino, Oct. 10, 1717, Add. MSS. (British Museum), 31260, Papers of Cardinal Gualterio: Letters of David Nairne, ii (1717), ff. 180, verso, 181.

A JACOBITE YOUTH

Malta; while James rejoined his sisters in France preparatory to the long-delayed return to England. Anne Oglethorpe now tendered to her sovereign her thanks for 'your particular marks of favour to my brother, James, till God enables him to acknowledge them by his services';[1] and her sisters proposed to Mar that, as James was soon returning to England, he would 'execute any orders you may have for him with the zeal and attachment which he and the rest of the family have for all orders coming from the master and you'.[2] Thus it was that in September 1718, while preparations were being completed for the abortive attempt of 1719, Fanny Oglethorpe could inform Mar that 'Jimmy is here and going home, very sensible of the goodness *the King* had for him, which he'll never forget'.[3] The inoculation of Jacobite virus was presumably a success.[4]

Although the young man had succumbed in the Jacobite atmosphere of Saint-Germain, Urbino, and Rome, there appeared, however, no guarantee that, returned to the pleasant haunts of Surrey, he would remain true to the cause. The situation in 1719 had altered materially from that of 1716 when 'Jamie' had come, fresh from Oxford, to join his family, then in the full flush of triumph at the quasi-court of James III. The years had not dealt kindly with their idol and, whether justified or not, the Old Pretender had allowed some of his resentment to fall upon the loyal Oglethorpes. The requirements of the Treaty of Utrecht and his own fatal expedition to Scotland

---

[1] Anne Oglethorpe to James III, Paris, April 5, 1718, *The King's Collection of Stuart Papers* (H.M.C. Reports), vi. 260.

[2] Fanny Oglethorpe to the Duke of Mar, France, Aug. 15, 1718; The Marquise de Mézières to the Duke of Mar, Paris, Aug. 29, 1718, *The King's Collection of Stuart Papers* (H.M.C. Reports), vii. 157-8, 215.

[3] Fanny Oglethorpe to the Duke of Mar, France, Sept. 19, 1718, *The King's Collection of Stuart Papers* (H.M.C. Reports), vii. 299.

[4] For various facts in this and the preceding paragraph see David Nairne to Cardinal Gualterio, Urbino, Dec. 26, 1717, Add. MSS. (British Museum), 31261, Papers of Cardinal Gualterio: Letters of David Nairne, ii (1717), f. 261; and *The King's Collection of Stuart Papers* (H.M.C. Reports), v. 231, 284, 351, 383, 466, 512; vi. 138; vii. 198.

in the 'Fifteen had led the hitherto friendly French to banish James III from the realm, even from Avignon, whence he found a haven successively in Bar-le-Duc,[1] Urbino and, finally, Rome. The Queen Mother, however, had been permitted to remain at Saint-Germain with the Oglethorpe ladies clustered about her until her death in 1718, when this group was dispersed. James III's visit to Spain in 1719 was but a last hope, and failure was the portion of the Stuarts and Earl-Marischal Keith, who was assisted by his brother, James, but not by the latter's comrade of Paris student days, James Oglethorpe. With the marriage of James III to Clementina Sobieski of Poland and the disastrous close of the 'Nineteen, the movement languished for two decades and the Oglethorpe influence perceptibly declined. The family must look elsewhere for recognition and sustenance.[2]

The court having left Saint-Germain, Fanny Oglethorpe, in 1718, was living with her sister, the Marquise de Mézières, in Paris where she profited greatly from the financial manipulations of John Law in his South Sea Bubble and Mississippi scheme. Selling her holdings before the crash came, Fanny—whom Thackeray so cruelly maligned in his *Henry Esmond*—in December 1719, married Jean François de Bellegarde, Marquis des Marches of Piedmont, son of the Marquis d'Autremont, Ambassador to France from the King of Sicily; and her dowry was eight hundred thousand livres! The de Mézières family had likewise profited greatly from Law's operations so that, after her husband's death in 1721, Eleanor Oglethorpe de Mézières retired to a home in the country where she emulated her mother in devoting her time to marrying off her seven children and hatching further Jacobite plots. How well she succeeded in the

---

[1] There is no mention of the Oglethorpes at Bar-le-Duc in Wolff, H. W., 'The Pretender at Bar-le-Duc', *Blackwood's Edinburgh Magazine*, clvi (1894), 226–46.
[2] Petrie, *The Jacobite Movement*, pp. 150–4.

former endeavour is indicated by the marriage of one daughter, Henrietta Eugénie, to Claude-Lamoral, Prince de Ligne of Luxembourg, and by her own achievement in 1722 in persuading James III to give her a sum of money for another daughter's marriage to Charles de Rohan, Prince Montaubon, in Ailesbury's esteem, 'one of the chief quality of France';[1] while her labours in the propagation of Jacobitism will receive due consideration in a discussion of the 'Forty-five. It is sufficient to note that, by October 1719, James III had become heartily weary of the self-justificatory communications with which the Oglethorpes continually bombarded him. In Turin, the next April, Theophilus Oglethorpe, according to a contemporary, was ordered by the King of Sardinia 'not to appear at Court, but forthwith to depart the Country: and accordingly he went away the next Day'[2] to Paris where he continued to plague the Stuarts, the Earl of Strafford, and Cardinal Gualterio until he finally died in 1737. Anne Oglethorpe, for her services in the cause, was created Countess of Oglethorpe in 1722 and later returned to Godalming where she made a home for her brother, James; but Molly, after waiting another decade, in 1733 married the Marquis de Bersompierre, a retired soldier of forty-seven, who had been with James III at Bar-le-Duc in 1713. Her husband died within a year of their marriage, and Molly closed her career in a minor post at the Court of Spain. In the light of these facts and the total absence of any references to the Oglethorpes in either the Nairne or Gualterio Manuscripts after 1721,[3] the letters of Cardinal Alberoni to the Duke of

[1] Ailesbury, *Memoirs*, ii. 669. For the financial arrangements of the marriage see Glover, J. H., *The Stuart Papers* (London, 1847), p. 180; appendix, pp. 143–5. For Law's operations see Bourgeois, Émile, *La Diplomatie Secrète au XVIIIe Siècle: Ses Debuts* (3 vols., Paris, no date), iii, book ii, chap. ii, 'La Guerre contre Law', pp. 177–210.

[2] Boyer, A., *The Political State of Great Britain* (60 vols., London, 1711–40), xix. 447.

[3] Add. MSS. (British Museum), 20241–20583; 31244–31267, Papers of Cardinal Gualterio; Stowe MSS. (British Museum), 250, Hanover State Papers: Jacobite Correspondence, 1722.

Ormonde in 1718–19,[1] and the letters of Queen Mary of Modena,[2] it is not strange that henceforth no mention is made in the Stuart Papers of James Edward Oglethorpe.[3]

In his volume on *The English in America*, J. A. Doyle has asserted that, while Theophilus Oglethorpe, junior, and Anne had 'drifted farther into Jacobitism than their father, . . . the support given by James Oglethorpe to the fallen cause was of a soberer type, and after the Hanoverian accession he enlisted himself among the followers of Windham. The outward conduct and policy of Oglethorpe reflected the more rational and reputable side of

[1] MSS. French (Bodleian Library, Oxford), e. 20.

[2] MSS. Additional (Bodleian Library, Oxford), c. 106–107, Stuart MSS.

[3] The last reference to the Oglethorpes in the printed calendar volumes of the Stuart Papers is in vol. viii, still in manuscript form at the Public Record Office: James III to the Duke of Mar, Montefiascone, Italy, Oct. 15, 1719. The narrative of this summary paragraph on the subsequent career of the Oglethorpes has been compiled from the following sources: Stowe MSS. (British Museum), 232: Hanover State Papers: Jacobite Correspondence, 1717–1719, f. 35, verso; Theophilus Oglethorpe to Cardinal Gualterio, Various letters, Paris, July 26, 1720; June 21, 1721; Sept. 8, 1721; Sept. 16, 1721, Add. MSS. (British Museum), 20310, Papers of Cardinal Gualterio, ff. 275, 296, 299–300; Theophilus Oglethorpe to the Earl of Strafford, Various letters, Paris, July 13, 1720–Jan. 24, 1722, Add. MSS. (British Museum), 31140, Strafford Papers: Political Correspondence, viii (1718–1765), ff. 56–8, 62, 76, 80–1, 124, 126, 131; Patrick Guthrie to Strafford, London, Jan. 30, 1729; Strafford to Guthrie, London, Nov. 5, 1729; Guthrie to Strafford, Paris, Feb. 7, 1730, Add. MSS. 31140, Strafford Papers: Political Correspondence, viii (1718–1765), ff. 175, 227–30, verso, 256; Toynbee, Mrs. Paget, editor, *Les Lettres de la Marquise du Deffand à Horace Walpole (1776–1780)* (3 vols., London, 1912), i. 304–5; Conches, *Journal du Marquis de Dangeau*, xviii. 17, 167; Boislisle, *Mémoires de Saint-Simon*, xiv. 319–21; xxxvii. 181–2; *The Letters of Francis Atterbury, Bishop of Rochester* (London, 1847), p. 180; appendix, pp. 143–5; Shield and Lang, 'Queen Oglethorpe', *Blackwood's Edinburgh Magazine*, clxiii (1898), 196–206; Lang, *Historical Mysteries*, pp. 229–30; Shield and Lang, *The King Over the Water*, p. 213; Shield, 'The Loyal Oglethorpes', *The Royalist*, ix. 43–5; Ruvigny and Raineval, Marquis of, *The Jacobite Peerage*, pp. 137–8; Oldmixon, *History of England*, p. 695; Dickson, W. K., editor, *The Jacobite Attempt of 1719: Letters of James Butler, Second Duke of Ormonde, relating to Cardinal Alberoni's Project for the Invasion of Great Britain on behalf of the Stuarts, and to the Landing of a Spanish Expedition in Scotland* (Scottish History Society Publications, Edinburgh, 1895), pp. 159, 267.

Jacobitism.'[1] This statement is true only in its summation. James Oglethorpe's greatest services to the Jacobite cause and the period when he was most heavily immersed therein, came after George I had ascended the throne of England, and the evidence that has been presented indicates the strength of the Jacobite influence to which the youth was exposed in his formative years as well as the spread among *all* the Oglethorpes of the Jacobite 'drift', and stamps as all the more remarkable the later 'rational' attitude of James Oglethorpe in the subsequent years of the Hanoverian era.

By 1719, then, the young veteran had returned to England where he succeeded his errant brother as incumbent of the family estate at Westbrook, Godalming, and, according to President Fowler, re-entered his name on the books of Corpus Christi College, Oxford.[2] Whether or not he returned to Oxford for a term or two, James Oglethorpe became in the widest sense the Squire of Westbrook. Owing to disagreements, even with the clergy, Theophilus Oglethorpe, junior, had been none too popular,[3] but James seems to have taken a prompt and keen interest in local affairs.[4] Despite the seemingly auspicious

[1] Doyle, J. A., *The English in America: The Colonies under the House of Hanover* (London, 1907), p. 416.

[2] Fowler, *History of Corpus Christi College*, pp. 275–6.

[3] *MSS. of W. M. Molyneaux, Esq.* (H.M.C. Reports, vii, Appendix, part i), p. 680.

[4] In 1729 'Mr. James Oglethorpe of Westbrook, a prominent citizen', gave one guinea towards repairing the market-house, and in 1749 'General Oglethorpe' again subscribed a guinea, this time towards the fund for repairing the communal fire engines and purchasing leather buckets. Nevill, R., 'The Corporation of Godalming', *Collections of the Surrey Archaeological Society*, xix (London, 1906), 118–19.

In Nov. 1754, Dr. Richard Pococke, Bishop, successively of Meath and of Ossory, noted in his Travel Diary a visit to Godalming, Surrey, where was 'General Oglethorpe's where there is a vineyard, out of which they make a wine like Rhenish. And I was informed that there are in the house some good drawings of Albani's which serve for hangings. . . . The Oglethorpe family are buryed here, originally of Yorkshire they are descended from Ligulp of the time of Ed. Confess^r.' Add. MSS. (British Museum), 23000, The Travel Diaries of Dr. Richard Pococke, ff. 81–2; Cartwright, J. J., editor, *The Travels through England of Dr. Richard Pococke, successively Bishop of Meath*

inoculation, he took no further part in the ebb and flow of Jacobite fortune. Here, then, at Westbrook he remained in innocuous desuetude for the next two years or more until in the spring of 1722, at the age of twenty-five, he emerged from his rural retreat to become a candidate for Parliament.

and of Ossory, during 1750, 1751, and Later Years (Camden Society Publications, New Series, 2 vols., London, 1888–9), ii. 163–4.

On September 17, 1781, Dr. Michael Lort wrote to Horace Walpole that, in returning from a visit to Hampshire, 'near Godalmin I went to see a house of General Oglethorpes, built soon after the restoration which has now all the furniture remaining Statu quo as then put into it'. Dr. Michael Lort to Horace Walpole, Lambeth Palace, London, September 17, 1781, Add. MSS. (British Museum), 12527, f. 60.

And as late as June 24, 1791, Gilbert White, the Selbourne naturalist, noted in his *Journal* a visit to Godalming: 'This place was for many years inhabited by General Oglethorpe. The house is now under a general repair being with its grounds the property of Mr. Godbold, a quack Doctor.' Johnson, Walter, editor, *Journals of Gilbert White* (London, 1931), p. 385.

The house to-day in 1935 still stands as the Meath Home for Incurables.

CHAPTER III
THE MEMBER FOR HASLEMERE TO 1743

WHEN James Oglethorpe made the momentous decision which was to bring him into national prominence as a Member of Parliament, he little realized what such a course meant. From his first candidacy he faced the virulent opposition of the Whig oligarchy. There lies among the manuscripts of the Marquess Townshend, at that time Secretary of State, a list of election returns up to March 28, 1722, wherein James Oglethorpe and Peter Burrell were noted as elected opposition members for Haslemere, the poll being reported as Oglethorpe, 46; Burrell, 45; More Molyneaux, 25; and Lord Blundell, 24. The two defeated candidates and their sponsors, the Ministry, declared this result false, but their joint petition of contest to Parliament, presented on October 18, 1722, was quietly withdrawn in February of the next year, and Oglethorpe and Burrell began a long tenure in the House of Commons.[1]

Unfortunately for Oglethorpe the campaign had been anything but temperate, so that the London *Daily Journal* of March 27 was able to regale its readers with the information that, in a chance meeting of Oglethorpe, Captain Onslow, and Mr. Sharp of the opposition on the streets of Haslemere, 'Mr. Oglethorpe drew his Sword there on Mr. Sharp (Secretary to the present Bishop of London) and wounded him in the Belly: Which Insult being resented by Capt. Onslow, Mr. Oglethorpe and he

[1] London *Daily Post*, March 29, 1722, p. 1; *Daily Journal*, March 29, 1722, p. 1; *Post Boy*, March 29, 1722, p. 1; *Evening Post*, March 29, 1722, p. 1; *Gazette*, March 31, 1722, p. 1; *Weekly Journal*, March 31, 1722, p. 2198; *Freeholder*, April 4, 1722, p. 72; *Flying Post*, April 7, 1722, p. 2; *MSS. of the Marquess Townshend* (H.M.C. Reports), pp. 136–7; *Commons Journals*, xx. 18, 125; Swanton and Woods, *Bygone Haslemere*, pp. 191–3; Smith, *Parliamentary Representation of Surrey*, p. 93. For the list of controverted election returns in 1722–3 see the London *Evening Post*, Jan. 19, 1723, p. 1. The London *Daily Courant* announced the election of Blundell and Molyneaux, March 29, 1722, p. 2.

Drew, and in the Re-encounter both being slightly wounded, the Captain disarmed Mr. Oglethorpe without pushing his Resentment so far as the Provocation deserved'.[1]

James Oglethorpe would not have been an Oglethorpe had he allowed this brief report to go unchallenged, and he promptly sent this heated reply:

London, March 29, 1722.
To the Author of the *Daily Journal*.

Sir, An untarnish'd Reputation is dearer to every honest Man than Life, and printing Lies without the Author's Name, is like Stabbing in the Dark; News-Writers, in whose Power it is to blacken the most spotless Character, should have very good Authority before they publish Things prejudicial to any one's Reputation, since the Injury they do thereby is almost irreparable, Men being more willing to believe the Scandal, than the Recantation. I am lead into these Reflections from the falseness of the Article from Haslemere, publish'd in your Paper of Tuesday last, and must desire you, in Justice to me, to publish the following true Account of what happen'd there.

On Sunday the 25th, after Evening Service, Captain Onslow and Mr. Sharpe, meeting Mr. Burrell and Mr. Oglethorpe in the Market-Place at Haslemere, Mr. Oglethorpe tax'd Mr. Sharpe with some Stories that he had rais'd. Mr. Sharpe giving him a warm Answer, Mr. Oglethorpe corrected him for it; Captain Onslow stepping in between, Mr. Sharpe drew his Sword, on which Mr. Oglethorpe, Captain Onslow, and Mr. Burrell also drew. In the Scuffle Mr. Oglethorpe wounded Mr. Sharpe in the Belly, and Captain Onslow in the Thigh. Mr. Burrell beating down Mr. Oglethorpe's Thrusts, of which Captain Onslow taking advantage, seiz'd on the Blade of Mr. Oglethorpe's Sword with his Left Hand, and said, your Life is in my Power. Mr. Oglethorpe answer'd, do your worst, and struggling, tore his Sword thro' the Captain's Hand which is very much disabled. The Mob being gathered no more happen'd; Mr. Oglethorpe (who was not wounded) bound up Captain Onslow's Wounds and sent for a Surgeon to him.

---

[1] London *Daily Journal*, Mar. 27, 1722, p. 2; *Applebee's Original Weekly Journal*, Mar. 31, 1722, p. 2332.

These are Facts; for the Truth of which I appeal to Captain Onslow himself.

I am, SIR,

JAMES OGLETHORPE.[1]

Inasmuch as no contradiction of this narrative by Onslow ever appeared, this account may be accepted as correct. The use of a sword for other than military reasons was not a rarity in the Oglethorpe family where James found excellent precedent in his father, who had killed his man in 1679, and his brother, Lewis, who had fought a duel almost two decades back. But, again unfortunately for James Oglethorpe, this little episode of *opéra-bouffe*, melodramatics and German *Studenten-Corps* slicing, was followed by something infinitely worse, wherein James Oglethorpe had no one with whom he might share the blame. Within less than a month after his election, he seems to have celebrated his victory not wisely but too well, for on April 25, 1722, the London *Daily Journal* (not probably without diabolical enjoyment at the discomfiture of its erstwhile critic) recorded this unhappy tale:

Yesterday Morning about 6 of the Clock James Oglethorpe, Esq., lately chosen at Haslemere in Surrey a Representative for the new Parliament, had the misfortune to go into a Night-House of evil Repute, without Temple-Bar (being overcome with Wine), where mixing with a promiscuous Company of Hackney-Coachmen, Shoe-Blackers, and Linkmen, Mr. Oglethorpe missed a piece of Gold, and charging a Link Fellow with having taken it from him, high Words arose, and the Linkman struck Mr. Oglethorpe several Blows with his Link, who resenting such usage drew his Sword and gave the Fellow a mortal Wound in the Breast, for which he was seiz'd and carried before Mr. Justice Street, who committed him to the Gate-House.[2]

As the linkman died, Oglethorpe was placed in the custody of a constable.[3] This time there was no denial. How long James Oglethorpe remained in durance vile

[1] London *Daily Journal*, Mar. 30, 1722, p. 1.
[2] Ibid., April 25, 1722, p. 1.
[3] London *Postmaster*, May 4, 1722, p. 3.

we know not, for the sequel is unrecorded, but it seems clear that in this particular case, either a plea of self-defence worked wonders, or the punishment did not fit the crime, for on October 9, 1722, James Oglethorpe took his seat at Westminster as Member for Haslemere, and became, under Sir William Windham, an Hanoverian Tory colleague of the great leaders of the Whig ascendancy,[1] despite one authority's contention that 'a constitutional Jacobite came to be an anomaly, almost a contradiction in terms'.[2] As the latest historian of the Tory Party has shown, the Revolution of 1688 had effected the decline of the Tories due to their Jacobite adhesion, with the result that, after the First Parliament of Queen Anne in 1702, and still more upon the ministerial revolution of 1710, the Whigs had attained an impregnable supremacy which not even a party scandal could destroy.[3] The leadership of Robert Walpole, as John Morley had pointed out, rose above the South Sea Bubble; discomfited the Jacobites who, encouraged by the popular discontent engendered by that affair, had planned a Stuart restoration; and created the great imperial movements of the eighteenth century.[4]

To such an Hanoverian House of Commons came James Oglethorpe with a goodly heritage, despite his past Jacobite record, but he created his own position on the vital issues of the day, for, while his father and two brothers had served long and well in the arduous and monotonous tasks of committee work, there exists little evidence that any of the three had exhibited that gift of eloquence which on the floor of Parliament earns the

---

[1] Hervey, John, Lord, *Memoirs of the Reign of George II* (Croker ed., 2 vols., London, 1848), i. 1–29.

[2] Petrie, *The Jacobite Movement*, p. 167.

[3] Feiling, K. G., *A History of the Tory Party, 1640–1714* (Oxford, 1924), pp. 480–1 ff.

[4] Morley, John, *Walpole* (Twelve English Statesmen Series, London, 1919), chaps. iii–iv. See also Brisco, Norris A., *The Economic Policy of Robert Walpole* (Columbia University Studies in History, Economics, and Public Law, xxvii, New York, 1907); and Realey, C. B., *The Early Opposition to Sir Robert Walpole, 1720–1727* (Philadelphia, 1931).

greatest reward: the swaying of opinion as manifest in a victorious vote. James Oglethorpe's parliamentary activities, hitherto overshadowed in history by his subsequent career, fall into four categories: his struggles for re-election; his famed efforts on behalf of imprisoned debtors; the wide range of subjects with which he dealt in his committee assignments; and, more particularly, his less widely known but especially significant views on problems of vital national or imperial import.

Under existing conditions and during the contest for his seat by his late opponents, James Oglethorpe, Tory son and brother of Jacobite loyalists, naturally took no part in debate until April 6, 1723, over a month after the petition of contest against him had been withdrawn, when, by a strange turn of fate, the Commons were debating the punishment to be meted out to Dr. Francis Atterbury, revolutionary Jacobite Bishop of Rochester, who from 1710 to 1713 had been an unpopular autocrat as Dean of Christ Church, Oxford.[1] The birth in 1720 of Charles Edward, 'the Young Pretender', had stimulated the Jacobites to renewed efforts towards arousing the English in 1721, the only result of which was the impeachment of Atterbury for complicity in this restoration plot. Walpole had uncovered his sentiments early in 1722 but had refrained from arresting him until August, and it was not until April, 1723, when a victim had to be found, of whom to set an example, that this harmless old cleric was made the object of a bill which evoked from Oglethorpe his maiden effort on the floor of the House.[2] Exhibiting most markedly the 'soberer type' of support for the Jacobite cause, the new Member for Haslemere strongly opposed the proposed banishment of the Bishop. Deprecating the powers of the Pretender whom, a bare five years before, he had wellnigh worshipped, but who

[1] *Portland MSS.* (H.M.C. Reports), vii, *Harley Papers*, v, *Stratford Letters*, p. 140; Mallet, *History of the University of Oxford*, iii. 9–10.
[2] Beeching, H. C., *Francis Atterbury* (London, 1909), pp. 263–80, 283, 289, 300–3; Doran, *London in the Jacobite Times*, i. 410–39, particularly p. 413; Petrie, *The Jacobite Movement*, pp. 161, 170–2.

now, he declared, 'it was plain . . . had none but a company of silly fellows about him', Oglethorpe opposed the punishment of Atterbury on the grounds of expediency, fearing that,

if the bishop, who was allowed to be a man of great parts, should be banished, he might be solicited and tempted to go to Rome, and there be in a capacity to do more mischief by his advice, than if he was suffered to stay in England under the watchful eye of those in power.[1]

As Oldmixon affirmed, 'it was not likely that such reasoning as this should hinder the passing of the bill';[2] his appeal failed; the measure was approved; Atterbury was banished; and, except for routine committee assignments, and his unopposed re-election on August 18, 1727,[3] no more was heard of Oglethorpe in Parliament for the next six years.

Probably the most tedious parliamentary obligation was that of committee work, wherein a member such as Oglethorpe spent long hours on divers subjects, often preparing the bills, a task sometimes followed by the honour of carrying the adopted measure to the House of Lords for its approval. In the six years following his first election and his solitary speech, Oglethorpe found himself on committees for such varied matters as Edinburgh city revenues, fines due to lords of manors, the regulation of journeyman shoemakers, the herring fishery industry, the rebuilding of the Church of St. Martin-in-the-Fields,

---

[1] Cobbett, *Parliamentary History*, viii. 216; Chandler, *History and Proceedings of the House of Commons*, vi. 308. Andrew Lang and Alice Shield rather unkindly, and without any authoritative references, suggest that, upon Anne Oglethorpe's departure to Paris in 1723, 'it was probably to conceal their conspiracies that the Oglethorpe home at Godalming was . . . protected by the sudden and unpopular closing of a right-of-way by her brother, the squire, who that year spoke for Atterbury in the House of Commons'. Shield and Lang, *The King over the Water*, p. 366.

[2] Oldmixon, *History of England*, p. 740.

[3] London *Gazette*, Aug. 19, 1727, p. 7; *Daily Post*, Aug. 21, 1727, p. 1; *Daily Courant*, Aug. 21, 1727, p. 1; *Daily Journal*, Aug. 21, 1727, p. 1; *Whitehall Evening-Post*, Aug. 22, 1727, p. 2; *Parker's Penny Post*, Aug. 23, 1727, p. 3; *Weekly Journal*, Aug. 26, 1727, p. 3.

where he had been baptized three decades before, numerous enclosure movements, the improvement of roads in all parts of Britain, the settlement of estates, the qualifications of certain individuals for office, the regulation of the Thames watermen, prohibitory legislation concerning the reckless stocking of gunpowder by dealers, the improved navigability of various rivers, Fulham Bridge, the art of brick-making, the dyeing trade, the problem of the Parish and Rector of Saint John, Clerkenwell, the relief of British subjects in Tuscany and of the poor in Gloucester, debts arising out of the South Sea Bubble, the high price of coal, the Medway oyster fisheries, the regulation, both of merchant seamen and of attorneys and solicitors, Guy's Charities, whence sprang the modern Guy's Hospital, and, what was a traditional and favourite interest of the Oglethorpes, the naturalization of foreigners. Although, strangely enough in the light of his later career, he was not placed on the committee to consider the bill for exporting European salt to Pennsylvania, his membership on four major committees in particular was to prove of great subsequent value. These were the committee on privileges and elections, the most important in point of honour and repute; the committees on 'the better paving and cleaning streets of Westminster City', and on the water supply of London, for which he helped to draw up the bill, wherein he gained municipal experience; and the committee on the relief of insolvent debtors, the work of which aroused in him the humanitarian instinct.[1]

It was the humanitarian spell which in 1728 and 1729 led to two important expressions by him, the one in print,

[1] *Commons Journals*, xx. 86, 132–4, 161, 194, 225, 262, 273, 288, 295, 303, 322, 328, 358, 369, 372–4, 382, 385–8, 408, 418, 428, 433, 439, 463, 465–6, 468, 471, 553, 571, 585, 594, 619, 650, 653, 655, 665, 738, 743, 769, 775–6, 792, 795, 799, 813, 817–18, 851, 858; xxi. 21, 37, 57, 59, 65, 73, 75, 82, 94, 114, 134, 140, 146, 148, 154, 160–1, 169, 179, 186, 209–10, 229, 232, 235–6, 239, 243, 245–6, 264, 271, 284, 303, 307, 312–13, 324–5, 345, 350; *MSS. of the Earl of Egmont; Diary of John Percival, First Earl of Egmont* (hereinafter cited as *Egmont Diary*, H.M.C. Reports, 3 vols., London, 1920–3), iii. 330–1; Chandler, *History and Proceedings of the House of Commons*, vi. 337.

the other in action as a Member of Parliament. From the earliest times, the history and welfare of Britain has been bound up with the sea, and even in the days of Marlborough and her greatest generals, before and since, the right arm of the Services has been the Navy. The colleague of James Oglethorpe's father, Samuel Pepys, is recognized as the great genius in the creation of Britain's post-restoration naval supremacy, but it was James Oglethorpe in 1728, not the Samuel Pepys of 1685, who called attention to the rights and welfare of that Navy's personnel. The plight of the ordinary seaman, made worse by the necessitous use of the press-gang and the complete lack of any means of petition for redress, evoked a few isolated and ineffective protests between 1693 and 1725 which have been clearly described by Oglethorpe's most recent biographer.[1] A new and unbearable epidemic of press-gang activities in 1727 led to the quasi-anonymous publication the next year of a fifty-two page protest, entitled *The Sailor's Advocate*.[2] Advertised as 'composed by most respectable members of the Opposition', it is now definitely accredited to James Oglethorpe who attacked the notorious system of impressment as a violation of Magna Carta and the Petition of Right.[3] This protest has properly been adjudged to have been 'restrained and sincere, and forms a crushing indictment of the conditions of the period'.[4] It cannot be said that Oglethorpe's protest was effective, but *The Sailor's Advocate* will be heard of again in the course of his life, and this effort on behalf of the Mariners of England is but the first of a series of humanitarian movements by the Member for Haslemere.

If James Oglethorpe's first championship of the oppressed was not a great success, his second attempt unquestionably was. For nigh seven years, as has been

[1] Church, L. F., *Oglethorpe: A Study of Philanthropy in England and Georgia* (London, 1932), pp. 25–7.
[2] [Oglethorpe, James], *The Sailor's Advocate* (London, 1728); Church, *Oglethorpe*, p. 27.
[3] Ibid. p. 28.
[4] Ibid. p. 30.

seen, he served his parliamentary apprenticeship in committee work and, when the opportunity came, he was ready. Important as were his other assignments, they all yield place to his chairmanship of the committee appointed on February 25, 1729, to inquire 'into the State of the Gaols of this Kingdom'.

The inquiry which was to bring Oglethorpe into national prominence was the result of the state of the times. The England of Oglethorpe's earlier years still retained the restoration viewpoint on morals. As Lecky declared, 'of the active reforming and philanthropic spirit which became so conspicuous in the reign of George III, we find scarcely any traces'.[1] One of the worst problems of the period was the legal status of debtors. The authority on English Law has shown how the early legal systems made the obligation of the debtor personal in such an extremely literal sense that the body of the debtor could be seized by the creditor. Modes of legal procedure gradually changed, but this provision was a vital source of relief and survived throughout the years. As a result of this policy, asserts Professor Holdsworth, 'constraint of the debtor's person thus became in England a more general method of execution than in many other countries of Europe', and so 'was entirely unregulated. The results can be read in the pages of Dickens'.[2] Because of this system the prisons became overcrowded, and this led naturally to malpractices of prison officials who were more likely to favour rich creditors than poor debtors. Sidney and Beatrice Webb have described in searing phrases the despotic powers of privileged keepers and jailers whose emoluments issued therefrom and who made the most of their vicious opportunities.[3] The idea

[1] Lecky, W. E. H., *A History of England in the Eighteenth Century* (8 vols., London, 1878), i. 498–9.
[2] Holdsworth, Sir W. S., *A History of English Law* (3rd ed., 9 vols., London, 1922), viii. 229–45.
[3] Webb, Sidney, and Webb, Beatrice, *English Prisons under Local Government* (London, 1922), pp. 1–12, 21–8; Webb, Sidney, and Webb, Beatrice, *English Local Government; English Poor Law History; Part I. The Old Poor Law*

of an investigation was nothing new: numerous acts for the relief of debtors had been passed in the latter part of the seventeenth century, but they had proved singularly ineffectual. As early as 1698 the abuses in the Fleet Prison had been brought to the attention of Parliament, and these two questions, debtors and jail conditions, were to loom as spectres before Britain during the first quarter of the eighteenth century. A certain tendency towards investigation and correction ran like a thread throughout this period, but no one acted.[1]

This system of sanctioning the incarceration of an individual, often in a foul dungeon and solely at the behest of his creditors, had led to the imprisonment of an architect named Robert Castell who, unable to pay the fees with which jailers mulcted their unfortunate charges, was confined in a house where prevailed small-pox, from which he subsequently died.[2] One of Castell's closer friends had been James Oglethorpe who, but for this event, so Lecky asserts, 'would probably have remained an undistinguished Member of Parliament'. Be that as it may, 'this incident directed the attention of Oglethorpe to the management of the prisons'.[3] Convinced that his friend's death was due to existent penal conditions, Oglethorpe began a movement for reform. Pressing for an investigation, he succeeded in obtaining, on February 25, 1729, the appointment by the House of Commons of a committee with himself as chairman to institute a parlia-

(London, 1927), pp. 149–313; Marshall, Dorothy, *The English Poor in the Eighteenth Century* (London, 1926), pp. 1–14; Leonard, E. M., *The Early History of English Poor Relief* (Cambridge, 1900), pp. 220–1 and notes; Lipson, E., *The Economic History of England; III. The Age of Mercantilism* (London, 1931), chap. vi, especially pp. 455–79.

[1] *MSS. of J. Eliot Hodgkin* (H.M.C. Reports, xv, Appendix, part ii), pp. 341–4; *Commons Journals*, xii. 235, 407, 465–6, 491, 515, 684, 687; xiii. 6–7, 50, 57–61, 92–3, 117, 122, 138, 141–2, 145–6, 158–9, 168, 228, 235, 247, 269, 408, 424, 592–3, 615, 624, 795–7, 826–8, 834, 859; xiv. 12, 43, 45, 60; xvi. 443, 445, 455–6, 458, 461–3, 470–1, 483.

[2] For an interesting prison diary, May 1728 to Sept. 1729 see MSS. Rawlinson (Bodleian Library, Oxford), D. 34, 'A Journal of My Life while in the Marshalsea, Southwark, by a Musician'.

[2] Lecky, *History of England*, i. 500.

THE FLEET PRISON COMMITTEE

from the painting by WILLIAM HOGARTH, 1729, in the National Portrait Gallery

mentary inquiry into 'the State of the Gaols of this Kingdom'. Although the committee included some of the most distinguished members of the Lower House, such as the Chancellor of the Exchequer, the Master of the Rolls, General Wade, William Windham, Colonel Onslow, Watkyn Williams Winn, James Vernon, and Lord Percival, Oglethorpe was the guiding genius and at all times the dominant force which sought and obtained full authority to examine all 'persons, papers, and records'. Unsupported by the press, probably due to the prohibition on printing parliamentary debates,[1] the committee began its inquiry with the Fleet Prison, a relic of the Court of Star Chamber. Throughout the spring of 1729 the investigators examined numerous imprisoned debtors who, for their testimony prejudicial to their respective jailers, were often cast into chains. The report of March 20 on the Fleet Prison and its maladministration by Warden Thomas Bambridge, together with Oglethorpe's preliminary report of May 14 on the Marshalsea and Westminster Prisons, with a supplementary survey of the Fleet Prison, indicated such assiduity on the part of the committee that the jailers, judges, and minor officials thus exposed began to execrate the investigators.[2] Although Oglethorpe informed a colleague that 'I was not very willing to revive the Committee, because I knew the ill will the Administration bore it; and the weight of the judges and Court would be against us',[3] the investigation was nevertheless renewed on February 21, 1730, by a committee of twenty-one men, because, in its chairman's words, it 'was neces-

[1] Not a word concerning the committee appears in the London press of 1729, except a list of members in the London *Journal*, July 5, 1729, p. 2. On March 29, 1729, the London *Universal Spectator* noted the arrest of the malefactors, but on June 28 affirmed that there was no news owing to the great cloak of secrecy cast over the affair. London *Universal Spectator*, March 29, 1729, p. 3; June 28, 1729, p. 2.

[2] The magnitude of the investigation is indicated by Oglethorpe's request to Sir Robert Walpole in May 1729 of an appropriation of £700 for clerk hire and other expenses. *Calendar of Treasury Books and Papers*, i. 1729–30, pp. 67, 71.

[3] *Egmont Diary* (H.M.C. Reports), i. 46.

sary for our reputations, being vilified for proceeding so zealously last year'.[1]

Throughout this second investigation Oglethorpe and the committee, in the words of the London press, 'with great Humanity and Diligence went through every part' of the King's Bench Prison in Southwark and the Marshalsea, during late February and early March of 1730, and 'took an exact Account of even the most nauseous, dark and dismal Parts thereof'.[2] This phase of the investigation, which was concluded in May,[3] was marked by an episode which indicated that the corrupt holders of monopolies and sinecures would go to any extreme to annul the investigation, even to the point of making it appear that Sir Robert Eyre, Knight, Lord Chief Justice and a Privy Councillor, had tampered with witnesses in Newgate Jail! But Oglethorpe was undaunted and carried the affair to its logical conclusion.[4]

As a result of these investigations, James Oglethorpe presented to the House of Commons three reports in which he charged the respective jailers and their deputies with the sale of offices, breaches of trust, enormous extortions, oppression, intimidation, gross brutalities, and the highest crimes and misdemeanours. His first report, that of 1729 on the Fleet Prison, has been characterized by Sidney and Beatrice Webb as 'one of the most horrifying of prison documents',[5] and forever inscribed on the roll of infamy the name of Thomas Bambridge who, as warden

[1] *Egmont Diary* (H.M.C. Reports), i. 46.
[2] London *Daily Post*, Feb. 23, 1730, p. 1; *Evening Post*, Feb. 24, 1730, p. 1; *Grub-Street Journal*, Feb. 26, 1730, p. 2; *Country Journal, or the Craftsman*, Feb. 28, 1730, p. 2; *Weekly Journal*, Feb. 28, 1730, p. 2; *Daily Courant*, March 6, 1730, p. 2. The press seems again to have become articulate!
[3] In May 1730 Oglethorpe asked Walpole for an additional £400. *Calendar of Treasury Books and Papers*, i. 366.
[4] *Commons Journals*, xxi. 237, 247, 254, 274–82, 307, 310–11, 316–17, 324–6, 328–30, 336, 345, 347–8, 350–2, 355–6, 362, 366–7, 374, 376–87, 444, 453, 468, 480, 488, 513, 567–8, 575–85; Stowe MSS. (British Museum), 373, Minutes of the Commons' Committee on Gaols, 1730, f. 6 verso; *Egmont Diary* (H.M.C. Reports), i. 46, 49–53, 55, 57, 78, 90, 95.
[5] Webb and Webb, *English Prisons under Local Government*, p. 26.

of that prison, was convicted by overwhelming evidence of his manifold offences. In measured phrases Oglethorpe asserted that Bambridge 'hath not regarded or complied with' the official regulations,

but hath exercised an unwarrantable and arbitrary Power, not only in extorting exorbitant Fees, but in oppressing Prisoners for Debt, by loading them with Irons, worse than if the Star-Chamber was still subsisting, and contrary to the great Charter, the Foundation of the Liberty of the Subject, and in Defiance and Contempt thereof, as well as of other good Laws of this Kingdom.[1]

The second report, on the Marshalsea Prison, yielded surprisingly similar evidence with emphasis on the torture of prisoners and loathsome sanitary conditions, and with William Acton exposed in the unenviable role of chief culprit. In his last report, after citing a long succession of evils, including the attempted bribery, Oglethorpe uttered this dire prophecy: 'If this be law, all England may be made one extended prison.'[2] Having presented its evidence, the committee made four major recommendations: the abolition of fees, gifts, presents, or any gratuities whatsoever, from jailers to judges, clerks, and servants; increased appropriations for the King's Bench Prison; revision and improvement in means of recovery of debts and damages upon escape of prisoners; and more stringent regulations for the King's Bench Prison.[3] Oglethorpe had done his work thoroughly in compiling and presenting the reports. As Henry Bruce has so aptly phrased it, 'these reports lie before me now, in sixty or seventy of the dim and stained pages of Cobbett's old Parliamentary History. They are not exhilarating reading. Here are a score of cases as bad as Castell's; here are some cases much worse. The yellow pages, like the leaves in Dante's dolorous wood, seem to cry out with

[1] *Commons Journals*, xxi. 274.   [2] Ibid. 578.
[3] For the reports see ibid. 274-83, 376-87, 576-85; *Journals of the House of Lords*, xxiii. 404-34, *passim*; and Cobbett, *Parliamentary History*, viii. 706-53, 803-26.

strong agony as one touches them';[1] and Robert Wright has justly affirmed of them that therein 'those who delight in sensational reading will—if facts can yield them as much pleasure as fiction—find much thrilling matter'.[2]

Largely as a result of Oglethorpe's impassioned zeal, the House of Commons unanimously voted the prosecution of Thomas Bambridge and John Huggins of the Fleet Prison, and William Acton and John Darby of the Marshalsea, together with a strict revision of the penal system. Oglethorpe had taken the lead, had pressed the issue, and had assembled and presented the evidence needed to convince his colleagues. But candour and equity demand that due tribute be paid to those colleagues who exhibited their enlightened interest by unanimously approving the reform programme on May 12, 1730. Action now rested with the government, which proceeded to state trials of the principal miscreants. The reports of these trials are far from edifying reading, and the result, a general acquittal of the defendants on all charges, nullifies to a great extent the value of reading the time-worn pages: in the words of the editor,

> it is remarkable that, though the prosecutions against Mr. Huggins, Mr. Bambridge, etc., were ordered by his majesty, on an Address from the House of Commons, and conducted by some of the greatest men at the bar, yet they got off—all being acquitted.[3]

After the trials commenced, Oglethorpe spoke but once; yet here again he manifested his strong sense of justice and obedience to the spirit, as well as to the letter, of the law. Acton of the Marshalsea, having been acquitted of a charge of murder, asked for his discharge, a plea which

---

[1] Bruce, Henry, *Life of General Oglethorpe* (New York, 1890), p. 47.

[2] Wright, Robert, *A Memoir of General James Oglethorpe* (London, 1867), p. 29. For an interesting criticism of Oglethorpe's committee for factional, political purposes, see Namier, L. B., *England in the Age of the American Revolution* (London, 1930), pp. 216–17.

[3] Cobbett, W., Howell, T. B., and Howell, T. J., editors, *A Complete Collection of State Trials* (33 vols. and index, London, 1809–1828), xvii. 616–17.

the Crown Attorney refused to support. Acton's lawyer then asked Oglethorpe, who had attended all the trials, for his consent to a discharge. In noble phrases the latter explained that, as he was not the person to decide this issue, he must decline to do so but, he continued,

were I prosecutor, I should desire the prisoner might be released; not that I think him innocent, but that every Englishman, let him be never so unjustly acquitted, hath, by the Habeas Corpus Act, on his acquittal, a right to be discharged.[1]

The decisions were thus eminently unsatisfactory, but the worst abuses of the *ancien régime* had been exterminated, and England was the better for Oglethorpe's labours which, declared one biographer, although 'too soon forgotten, were universally applauded at the time'.[2] Chief among contemporary tributes were a eulogy by the Reverend Samuel Wesley, junior, on *The Prisons Open'd*, wherein he sang:

> Yet Britain cease thy Captives' Woes to mourn,
> To break their Chains, see Oglethorpe was born![3]

and that by James Thomson, the poet, who, in his study of *The Seasons—Winter*, lauded with joy

> the glorious band
> Who, touched with human woe, redressive searched
> Into the horrors of the gloomy jail.[4]

Even though the goal had not been fully achieved, a task left for completion by John Howard half a century later, this episode in his parliamentary term was pregnant with consequences for Oglethorpe's future career.[5]

The prominence of this particular question in the history of eighteenth-century England has heavily over-

---

[1] Ibid., 562–3.
[2] Wright, *Memoir of General James Oglethorpe*, p. 23.
[3] Wesley, Samuel, junior, *Poems* (London, 1736), pp. 173–91.
[4] Thomson, James, *The Seasons—Winter* (Gilfillan ed., 2 vols., London, 1853), i. 144, lines 359–62.
[5] It is noteworthy that there is not one line on Oglethorpe's parliamentary career in the entire Rawlinson Correspondence: MSS. Rawlinson (Bodleian Library, Oxford), H (Letters), vols. 29–34.

shadowed the balance of Oglethorpe's career in the House, his committee assignments and, more especially, his part in debate on the vital issues of the day. With the conclusion of the prison inquiry, his merit received due recognition in numerous committee appointments,[1] and when in February 1732 the Commons elected twenty men to the committee on the Charitable Corporation, Oglethorpe received the eighth highest vote, an eloquent testimonial to his ability, industry, and popularity.[2] But his strength during these years lay not so much in his

---

[1] During the decade 1730–40 Oglethorpe served on the important committees on privileges and elections, and on the address to the King; and on the committee which considered a single bill to 'revive the laws . . . relating to the importation of foreign brandy, and other waters and spirits; for importation of Cochineal; to continue several acts, for preventing frauds in the Customs, for encouragement of the Silk manufacturers of this kingdom, for making copper ore, of the British Plantations, an enumerated commodity, and for suppressing of Piracy'. Other problems which claimed his attention included the relief of debtors and the poor, roads, navigation of inland waterways, the maintenance of certain parish rectors, the importing of salt into the American colonies, the price and size of bread, the proper language of legal proceedings, the regulation of the Charitable Corporation, of brokers in London, of pilots at sea, and of transportation of merchandise by carriage on the highway, the settlement of innumerable estates, the growth of coffee in the plantations, the manufacture of hats in Britain, the purity of drugs, the manufacture of cloth in Yorkshire and linen elsewhere, the copyright of printed books, the 'better regulating the night watch in St. James's Parish and St. George's, Hanover Square, Westminster City', the importation of iron from America and of rice from the Carolinas, the naturalization of foreigners, the regulation of Thames watermen, the 'more effectual securing the payment of rents, and to prevent the frauds of tenants', Lamb's creation of an engine to make 'organzine silk', and the affairs of the Royal African Company of England. *Commons Journals*, xxi. 351–2, 354, 366, 376, 397, 417, 436, 438, 446, 453, 459, 461–2, 465, 474, 487–8, 503, 522, 524, 539, 550, 559, 562, 589–90, 592, 610, 612, 621, 631, 635, 640, 643, 648, 653, 656, 658, 667, 684, 696, 702, 706, 710–12, 715, 719, 726–7, 734–5, 742, 745, 750, 756–7, 759, 777, 782, 788, 790, 792, 795–7, 800, 804, 806, 809–10, 813, 817, 824, 828–9, 832, 837, 840, 842, 846–8, 851, 856, 862, 874, 877, 887, 896, 898, 900, 908, 912–13, 930–3, 941; xxii. 326, 329, 364, 399–400, 402, 407–8, 411, 417, 433, 438, 451, 455, 469, 475, 478, 485–6, 493, 782, 791–2, 794, 796, 804, 820, 835, 858, 878, 884; xxiii. 15, 23, 27, 43, 70, 102, 139, 142. For Oglethorpe's position in Parliament see also Add. MSS. (British Museum), 31140, Strafford Papers, ff. 175–6, 230, 256; Add. MSS. 31149, Strafford Papers, f. 415.

[2] *Commons Journals*, xxi. 795–6.

diligent committee work as in his speeches. No longer the parliamentary novice, tainted with Jacobite ancestry, he now evinced an interest in national and imperial affairs which, to almost as great a degree as the penal problem, were to influence his future career.

In the same session as that which authorized the prison investigation, Oglethorpe, whose objection to alcohol, in Austin Dobson's words, 'stopped at "firewater" ',[1] expressed his approval of temperance by proposing a further duty on importations 'as well to discourage the pernicious use of spirits, such as gin, etc., as encourage the drinking malt liquors'.[2] Oglethorpe held his seat in Parliament at a crucial time both in domestic and European affairs. Not only did he attack royal extravagance in opposing a grant of £115,000 to cover arrears in the King's civil list,[3] but he opposed the government on the question of British participation in settling the peace of Europe.[4] The general situation, however, became so critical that in 1730 he began a persistent advocacy of military preparedness. On a bill for further troops, Oglethorpe, noted Egmont, 'on this occasion voted for the Court, though a very obstinate Tory, and gave for reason, that he believed we should go into a war with the Emperor, and therefore thought it necessary to have an army', especially, as he put it, 'while things stand as they do in Europe'. As to the army's nationality, he decried the hiring of Hessians, declaring that 'he had rather see an army of Englishmen than foreigners among us'. He preferred, moreover, that English and Irish troops, in lieu of Hessians, be sent to the Continent, where they would behave as well as the Germans, would thus gain experience, and would serve to introduce English goods on the Continent, thereby aiding English trade. At home he condemned the sad state of affairs, proclaimed the right of petition at all

---

[1] Dobson, *A Paladin of Philanthropy*, p. 14, note.
[2] *Egmont Diary*, iii. 344.
[3] Cobbett, *Parliamentary History of England*, viii. 706; *Egmont Diary*, iii. 343.
[4] *Egmont Diary*, iii. 345–6.

times, and demanded reduction of the Sinking Fund 'which he thought was grown so great that it might prove prejudicial to the kingdom's safety, and absolutely undo it if it fell into the hands of a bad Ministry'.[1]

By 1731 the European situation led him to reiterate his views on the Army. Although continuing his staunch advocacy of preparedness, Oglethorpe also continued his implacable opposition to the perennial hire of Hessian troops—a favourite Hanoverian practice—on the grounds that it entailed spending British money to uphold their sovereign's dynasty in Germany.[2] It was during the course of this year that his strong sense of right was expressed in the debate on the Pension Bill which he favoured. Answering an opponent who had inveighed against 'wicked and desperate opposition', Oglethorpe asserted that 'none who speak for liberty can do it wickedly and desperately', emphatically adding, in answer to threats of defeat in future elections, that 'men who discharge their consciences faithfully will be little solicitous of being again in Parliament'.[3] In addition to this, he opposed the abolition of duties on Irish yarn[4] and, because it prevented him from leaving any of his estate to the Catholic children of his sister, the Marquise de Mézières, strongly protested against the Naturalization Bill.[5] In all this, although opposing the administration, the Member for Haslemere firmly proclaimed the legitimacy of the Hanoverian dynasty. In a debate wherein emphatic affirmative references had been made to a possible parliamentary limitation of the royal authority, it was freely admitted that Oglethorpe, 'who was never a Courtier, said that he *trembled to hear the King's Title thus drawn into the question*'.[6]

---

[1] *Egmont Diary*, i. 12–13, 26, 35, 63, 68, 73.
[2] Ibid. 125–6; *MSS. of the Earl of Carlisle* (H.M.C. Reports, xv, Appendix, part vi), pp. 81–2; Parkinson, R., editor, *The Private Journal and Literary Remains of John Byrom* (4 vols., Chatham Society Publications, Manchester, 1854–7), ii. 481.
[3] *Egmont Diary*, i. 134, 140.   [4] Ibid. 175, 177.
[5] Ibid. 186–7.
[6] *Gentleman's Magazine* (300 vols., London, 1731–1907), i. 278.

With the opening of Parliament in January 1732 there arose an international complication. Britain had become involved in numerous treaties and conventions with continental powers for whom she spent money often without just cause or adequate protection. Petitions now came in from seaport merchants, complaining of Spanish depredations upon their West Indian commerce. At the same time the King, in his speech from the throne, proclaimed the general tranquillity of Europe and the confirmation of the Pragmatic Sanction in the Treaty of Vienna. It was quite manifest that Walpole was attempting to quell discontent at home and cover administration blunders by directing attention to his continental diplomacy. Much as he disliked opposing the reply to the King, 'for our King ought to be respected, and if we dislike anything it is the Ministry we must level our resentment at', Oglethorpe felt compelled to withhold his approval of a reply which embodied expressions implying blind acquiescence in every ministerial measure.[1] He now renewed his attacks on the disarmament policy of the administration, demanding 'full and complete satisfaction for the many depredations committed by the Spaniards', and expressing a desire 'to see more care taken in arming the country and disciplining our militia'. Thus staunchly advocating preparedness, he doubted the immediate importance of the Pragmatic Sanction as compared with 'many other things which at present relate more nearly to the honour and interest of this nation', chief of which, naturally, was the national defence. Turning to foreign affairs, he expressed his pleasure 'that we are not now so closely united with France as we formerly were; for I have generally observed, that when two Dogs are in a leash together, the stronger generally runs away with the weaker; and I am afraid this was something of the Case between France and us'; and he publicly manifested for the first time his interest in the oppressed Protestants of Salzburg in Austria. This group comprised Lutherans, now immortalized in

[1] *Egmont Diary*, i. 215; Smollett, *History of England*, ii. 503.

Goethe's *Hermann und Dorothea*, who were driven hither and thither in Central Europe by the persecutions of Archbishop Leopold Anton of Salzburg, persecutions which ultimately led thirty thousand of them to seek safety in England and Holland. Their plight, so well described by Carlyle, now revived in Oglethorpe that humanitarian impulse which had been prominent in *The Sailor's Advocate* and the late prison inquiry.[1]

James Oglethorpe had now placed himself on record as a mild High Tory, an opponent of both royal extravagance and Walpole's autocratic mismanagement in domestic affairs, a guiding spirit in the prison inquiries, a protagonist of anti-continental isolation, of national defence, and of the backbone of that defence—the British tar; and he had shown himself an ardent advocate for the spiritually oppressed. He now emulated his father, Sir Theophilus, in exhibiting no less an interest in the mercantile and imperial spheres of British polity. Late in January 1732, a bill 'for the better securing and encouraging the trade of his Majesty's Sugar Colonies in America' came before the House. In strict accordance with the contemporary colonial policy of the mercantile system, this measure gave preference to the West Indian insular colonies by prohibiting commerce between the French islands and the British colonies on the North American mainland. This aroused the opposition of many members of the Commons, some from their purely personal and selfish interest in the continental colonies, others like Oglethorpe from their wider view of affairs. Almost two centuries before Lord Balfour, at the Imperial Conference of 1926, proclaimed that, in the British Commonwealth

---

[1] Cobbett, *Parliamentary History of England*, viii. 875–6; Chandler, *History and Proceedings of the House of Commons*, vii. 96–7; Strobel, P. A., *The Salzburgers and their Descendants* (Baltimore, Maryland, 1855), pp. 25–43; Linn, C. A., 'The Georgia Colony of Salzburgers' (unpublished doctoral dissertation at Hartford Theological Seminary, Hartford, Connecticut, 1931), pp. 1–39; Spiers, E. B., 'The Salzburgers', *English Historical Review*, v. 665–90; Carlyle, Thomas, *Frederick the Great* (10 vols., London, no date), iii. 123–43.

of Nations, 'all are on an equality', James Oglethorpe—in phrases which presage the principles of the great Chatham, of Edmund Burke, of Benjamin Franklin and Thomas Jefferson, phrases which proclaim at once the unity of the Empire and the equality of all its citizens, wherever situate—Oglethorpe expounded the doctrine that, 'in all cases that come before this House, where there seems to be a clashing of interests between one set of people and another, we ought to have no regard to the particular interest of any country or set of people; the good of the whole is what we ought only to have under our consideration: our colonies are all a part of our own dominions; the people in every one of them are our own people, and we ought to shew an equal respect to all'.[1]

This sentiment he amplified upon the second reading of the bill in February. Professor Coupland has asserted that Adam Smith's 'opening of the long battle against Mercantilism ... was the immediate sequel and result of the American Revolution'.[2] But over a quarter of a century before Smith's *Wealth of Nations*, Oglethorpe, in February 1732, had expounded a novel colonial polity. Agreeing that 'our sugar colonies are of great consequence to us' and that 'we ought not to leave them under any hardships or under any distress'—for 'let it never be said of a British House of Commons that the distress of any of their fellow-subjects was pointed out to them, and they neglected to do what was in their power for their relief'—Oglethorpe countered with a word of caution that 'our other colonies in that part of the world ought also to be considered', and listed the products of those parts 'which contribute not a little towards preserving the general balance of trade in our favour'. Convinced that some

---

[1] Cobbett, *Parliamentary History of England*, viii. 920.
[2] Coupland, R., *The American Revolution and the British Empire* (London, 1930), pp. 53–5, 72, 76, 162–3, 178, 268, 276, 307–16; Stephen, Leslie, *History of English Thought in the Eighteenth Century* (2nd ed., 2 vols., London, 1881), ii. 289–301, 315–26; Fay, C. R., *Imperial Economy* (Oxford, 1934), chap. i, *America in the Old Empire*.

relief should be given the sugar colonies, he nevertheless maintained that 'we ought not to encourage or raise one colony upon the destruction or detriment of another; much less ought we to grant a favour to any subject, or to any particular set of people, which may prove to be against the public good of the nation in general'.[1] In short, he craved imperial preference, not isolated protection. Had George III and Lord North abided by these judgements, Oglethorpe himself might never have greeted John Adams as the first Minister of the United States to the Court of St. James's! But, as Wright has so neatly phrased it, 'as usual he was in the minority; for the Commons had still to pass through more than a century of strife ere they were compelled to give way to the Free Trade principles which he so long anticipated'.[2] Again the consequences were far-reaching, for Oglethorpe had shown no insular attitude towards imperial problems, but a far-sighted, cosmopolitan viewpoint which, as in all his parliamentary remarks, betokened a comprehensive grasp of the problems that might lie before him.

At the same time that the Sugar Colonies Bill was under consideration, a private petition came before the House which gave Oglethorpe an opportunity to encourage manufacture and industry. Thirty years before the Industrial Revolution was to begin its momentous transition in the manufacturing life of Great Britain, Sir Thomas Lamb, or Lombe, had received a patent on a machine known as a 'silk engine'. Owing to financial and technical handicaps but recently overcome, he now presented a petition to Parliament, craving an extension of the patent. Despite strong opposition thereto, Oglethorpe urged its renewal as the device was a proven success and the profit on this operation was fully fifty per cent. which, he said 'is all clear money got to the nation [and] all clear gain to us, because it is added by the labour and industry of our own

---

[1] Cobbett, *Parliamentary History of England*, viii. 1000–1; Chandler, *History and Proceedings of the House of Commons*, vii. 135–6, 217–19.

[2] Wright, *Memoir of General James Oglethorpe*, p. 136.

people'. Exhibiting a logic equal to his economic theory, Oglethorpe concluded that, 'since this gain can be made only by the means of this engine, we must grant that this gentleman has, at his own hazard and charge, brought home a very useful and profitable branch of trade to his own country for which he certainly deserves a recompense'.[1] To his interest in domestic public economy, freedom of conscience and worship, national defence, foreign commerce, and imperial policy, Oglethorpe now added a strong approval of the budding mechanical revolution in industry. He was rapidly becoming the well-rounded Member of Parliament.

Even as he had advocated protection of the rich industrial entrepreneur's investments, so Oglethorpe now spoke to protect the life savings of the small investor. In the last days of 1731 the Charitable Corporation, a huge company for advancing money at low rates to the poor, suddenly collapsed. Founded in 1707 with a capital modestly limited to £30,000, it had expanded under the guidance of leading financiers so that by 1731 its capital had risen to £600,000. The disappearance, in October of that year, of both the cashier and warehouse-keeper alarmed the proprietors who, demanding an investigation, found but £30,000 on hand. The shareholders, many of whom were thus reduced to poverty, petitioned the Commons for redress. Despite the extremely embarrassing fact that Sir Robert Sutton, a cousin, was one of the culprits, Oglethorpe, 'whose ears', as Wright justly claimed, 'were ever open to the cry of the oppressed',[2] seconded the motion for an investigation and was elected to the Committee of twenty-one members of the House.[3]

[1] Cobbett, *Parliamentary History of England*, viii. 924–5, 927–8; Chandler, *History and Proceedings of the House of Commons*, vii. 140–1, 144. On Aug. 14, 1735, Oglethorpe and Lamb presented a sample of this silk product to the Queen for the machine proved to be a great success. *Egmont Diary*, ii. 191. For a contemporary expression of approval of the machine by a mill worker who helped to make the sample given to the Queen see Hutton, William, *Life of William Hutton* (London, 1841), pp. 5, 7–8, 119–20.
[2] Wright, *Memoir of General James Oglethorpe*, p. 41.
[3] *Egmont Diary*, i. 219; *MSS. of the Earl of Carlisle* (H.M.C. Reports), p. 89.

In the ensuing debate, in which it was hinted that redress might be avoided by the use of legal technicalities, he strongly denounced those members who, on such slight technicalities, would have refused even to receive the petition of the unfortunates. Expressing his approval of the fundamental principles underlying such a corporation, whether called charitable or not, for 'the design was . . . in itself good and useful', he asserted that 'the better the design was, the more those persons deserved to be punished, who by their frauds have disappointed the people of reaping the benefit which might have accrued by an honest and faithful execution of so good an undertaking'. He was therefore 'persuaded that this Petition will be received in a manner deserving of the unhappy case of the sufferers, and of the justice of this House'.[1]

Turning now to constitutional questions, he opposed an amendment to the Qualification Bill, whereby Members of Parliament must swear to their qualifications, not at the time and place of their election, but at the Speaker's table. He not only opposed it 'as being contrary to the ancient constitution of England', but he reverted to the representative idea in Athenian democracy when he avowed that 'he wished there were no qualifications at all, but that the country might send up who they pleased, good sense and loyalty not being confined to fortune or estates, but to parts and education', for 'such members as would swear falsely at their elections would do the same before the Speaker'.[2] The quondam Jacobite was boldly presaging the reform bill liberal of the nineteenth century.

In addition to asserting his attitude on these measures, Oglethorpe likened Sir Robert Walpole's programme to Joseph's oppressions in Egypt, opposed a salt tax, and

[1] Cobbett, *Parliamentary History of England*, viii. 939–40; Chandler, *History and Proceedings of the House of Commons*, vii. 154–5; *Egmont Diary*, i. 185, 256, 275. For further light on the Charitable Corporation see Nicholls, Sir George, *A History of the English Poor Law* (new ed., 3 vols., London, 1904), ii. 23–4.
[2] *Egmont Diary*, i. 244–6.

also a conversion scheme of the South Sea Company because, as he put it, it would 'give occasion for much stock-jobbing', and strongly attacked a clause in the so-called Hat Bill providing that persons acquitted in the colonies might be tried again in England for the original offence. Although supporting the claims of sufferers from the Charitable Corporation *débâcle*, even to the point of advocating penalties for the guilty officials, Oglethorpe permitted family loyalty to supplant discretion, if not honour, in joining Sir Robert Sutton's brother as the only two Members to oppose Sir Robert's punishment for complicity in that affair.[1] This, the sole unworthy act of Oglethorpe's parliamentary career, brought the major portion of that career to a close. Other plans in June 1732, and at intervals later on, drew him away from England so that, despite retention of his seat in Parliament, his long absences dimmed his influence and during the later period he spoke but little.

In April 1734, while still overseas, Oglethorpe faced a contest for re-election which proved so critical that the Speaker of the House informed the Earl of Egmont, according to the latter's diary, that 'he had great difficulty to secure Mr. Oglethorpe's election at Haslemere, but, cost what it would, he would do it though he disobliged many friends thereby'.[2] The Speaker's influence prevailed and on April 25, despite his absence from England, James Oglethorpe was returned by his constituency.[3]

[1] *MSS. of the Earl of Carlisle* (H.M.C. Reports), pp. 89, 102; *Egmont Diary*, i. 248, 256, 261, 263, 266, 271.

[2] *Egmont Diary*, ii. 62; Nichols, John, *Literary Anecdotes of the Eighteenth Century* (9 vols., London, 1812), ii. 20, note; Smith, *Parliamentary Representation of Surrey*, p. 93.

[3] London *Gazette*, April 23, 1734, p. 4; *Daily Courant*, April 29, 1734, p. 2; *Daily Journal*, April 29, 1734, p. 1; *Grub-Street Journal*, May 2, 1734, p. 2; *Country Journal, or, the Craftsman*, May 4, 1734, p. 2; *Journal*, May 4, 1734, p. 2; *Universal Spectator*, May 4, 1734, p. 2; *Weekly Journal*, May 4, 1734, p. 3. For the methods used to ensure victory in parliamentary campaigns during this period see Morgan, W. T., 'An Eighteenth-Century Election in England', *Political Science Quarterly*, xxxvii. 585–604; and Williams, Basil, 'The Duke of Newcastle and the Election of 1734', *English Historical Review*, xii. 448.

By June he was back in England but Parliament, having been dissolved, did not convene again until January 1735, when the author of *The Sailor's Advocate* participated in the debate on the number of seamen desired for the current year. The Master of the Rolls, craving economy, had asked a reduction from 30,000 to 20,000. Oglethorpe, fighting successfully for the larger number, observed caustically 'that as to the expense, if 'twas necessary and we could not afford it, we must cease to be a nation; and that if we had a less Naval Force in the West Indies, and a quarrel with France, all our plantations would soon fall a prey to them; which would sink the value of all the lands in the nation 20 per cent.'[1] The colonial economist here justified his doctrine of preparedness. On other matters in this session he supported the administration 'for the first time', as one witness noted, on the reply to the King's speech, and again on the bill for limiting the number of officials to sit in the Commons.[2] At the end of that same year Oglethorpe again left England, and for over a year his voice was not heard in the House of Commons.[3]

Returning in January 1737 Oglethorpe immediately took his seat in Parliament where, except for an unsuccessful opposition to a scheme for the reduction of interest on the national debt,[4] his sole speech of importance during this session dealt with the Porteous affair, or Edinburgh riots, so fully described by Scott in his *Heart of Midlothian*. Here he opposed the administration's bill of punishment not merely on the grounds of expediency, but more especi-

---

[1] *MSS. of the Earl of Carlisle* (H.M.C. Reports), p. 150; Cobbett, *Parliamentary History of England*, ix. 691, 720.

[2] *MSS. of the Earl of Carlisle* (H.M.C. Reports), p. 147; Cobbett, *Parliamentary History of England*, ix. 677, 967–8; Chandler, *History and Proceedings of the House of Commons*, viii. 22, 101. See also Archives du Ministère des Affaires Étrangères, Paris, Correspondance Politique, Angleterre, vol. 390 ff. 205–22; and Mantoux, P., *Notes sur les Comptes rendus des séances du Parlement anglais au XVIIIe siècle conservées aux Archives du Ministère des Affaires Étrangères* (Paris, 1906), p. 102.

[3] *Egmont Diary*, ii. 200–1, 203, 209, 212.

[4] Cobbett, *Parliamentary History of England*, x. 62–155.

ally as being entirely too severe for, as he said, it was 'neither calculated to punish those who were negligent in suppressing that late riot, nor for preventing the like in time to come; and I could wish that gentlemen would fall upon some other means for answering both these ends'.[1] Having thus expressed his views in March 1737 he remained silent until May of 1738 when he left England for an absence of five years.

While he was thus occupied in distant climes, there came the third and most painful contest for re-election in February 1741, when his candidacy encountered opposition in the person of young Lord Percival, son of his close associate, the Earl of Egmont. When the youth impetuously claimed that his supporters 'had 43 sure votes and the whole number are but 69', Egmont, according to his diary, 'told him I was very sorry for it because he would fling out Col. Oglethorpe, for whom I profest friendship. He replied, he for that reason had not acquainted me with it: that he had offered to join with Col. Oglethorpe, but his friends refused, and after all, it was as good he should be elected as another, for they had been hawking the borough, and if he had not stood, another would, for the Colonel's managers, who are two attorneys, had received the money given at former elections, and divided nothing to the electors but sunk it in their own pockets. That he agreed for a sum, but no purchase, no pay.'[2] Heedless of his father's friendship, young Percival proceeded to campaign at Haslemere where, as he fondly believed, he made a marked impression. On his return he claimed that he was opposing, not Oglethorpe, but his colleague, Peter Burrell, at which time a compromise offer was made and rejected, but with the nullification in May of the Westminster elections in London, due to fraud, Percival was there chosen in the December re-balloting,

[1] Ibid. 247, 307; Chandler, *History and Proceedings of the House of Commons*, viii. 401, 454, 479, 507.

[2] *Egmont Diary*, iii. 188. For Percival's own excuse for entering the campaign see a biography of his son: Trehearne, Philip, *The Right Honourable Spencer Perceval* (London, 1909), pp. 15-16.

thus yielding Haslemere to Oglethorpe.[1] Interesting light is shed on contemporary campaign expenses by a prevalent rumour that Percival was proclaiming that Oglethorpe had paid him £800 to retire from the Haslemere contest. In Egmont's own words, his son's opposition 'was very unlucky' in the opinion of Oglethorpe's friends, 'for it cost Mr. Oglethorpe £1200 and £900 of it more than it needed have done if my son had not molested him'.[2] Thus for a second time, despite his absence, Oglethorpe retained his parliamentary seat, which he again occupied upon his final return to England in October 1743.

During Oglethorpe's absence, Robert Walpole, whom he had always bitterly opposed, fell from power in 1742. Soon afterwards, however, Henry Pelham acquired a stronger hold than even Walpole had maintained. With the Whigs in absolute control and devoid of the internal strife which had marked much of the Walpole regime, few dared to oppose the administration. Among these 'die-hards' was Oglethorpe who, although hailed by a contemporary as 'a gentleman of unblemished character, brave, generous, and humane',[3] was nevertheless consigned by Horace Walpole to a niche among 'the sad refuse of all the last oppositions'.[4] Burdened with inordinate garrulity and an 'exceedingly shrill voice, which could be heard in the lobby when he was speaking in the House',[5] Oglethorpe was no longer able to hold the attention of his colleagues.[6] Horace Walpole, who as late as 1751 was uncertain whether the Member for Hasle-

---

[1] *Egmont Diary*, iii. 190–4, 219–20, 234; London *Daily Gazetteer*, May 4, 1741, p. 4; *Daily Post*, May 5, 1741, p. 1; *Evening Post*, May 5, 1741, p. 2; *Gazette*, May 30, 1741, p. 1; Smith, *Parliamentary Representation of Surrey*, p. 93; Swanton and Woods, *Bygone Haslemere*, p. 195.
[2] *Egmont Diary*, iii. 244.
[3] Smollett, *History of England*, ii. 503.
[4] Walpole, Horace, *Memories of the Last Ten Years of the Reign of George the Second* (2 vols., London, 1822), i. 190.
[5] Nichols, *Literary Anecdotes of the Eighteenth Century*, ii. 21, note.
[6] Walpole, *Memories of the Last Ten Years of the Reign of George the Second*, i. 121.

mere was a Whig or a Jacobite, was, however, 'very certain that he was a troublesome and tiresome speaker, though even that was now and then tempered with sense'.[1] Oglethorpe thus became a rather passive opponent during his last decade in Parliament despite Sir Charles Hanbury-Williams's assertion to Henry Fox that Pelham's do-nothing attitude would be maintained by Pelham's own cane, Thomas Winnington's look, and Oglethorpe's 'very long sword'.[2]

But if, after 1743, Oglethorpe was largely a passive opponent of the administration, he had, during the first two decades of his tenure, expressed intelligent and timely opinions on a wide range of important subjects. When Leslie Stephen wrote his admirable *History of English Thought in the Eighteenth Century*, he might well have included a consideration of Oglethorpe's political philosophy as a superb specimen of far-sighted, independent, and liberal thinking by one whose spirit ran half a century and more ahead of his age. It is evident from this survey of his parliamentary career to 1743 that, as early as 1730, James Oglethorpe had established a reputation both as a leader among the opposition and as a humanitarian interested in eleemosynary activities. It was but natural, therefore, that he should assume a major part in a new movement which was to unite within itself the two great interests in his public career: Philanthropy and the Welfare of the Empire. This movement was the founding of Georgia.

[1] Ibid. 98.
[2] Ilchester, Earl of, and Mrs. Langford-Brooke, *Life of Sir Charles Hanbury-Williams* (London, 1928), p. 87.

CHAPTER IV

THE ORIGINS OF THE GEORGIA MOVEMENT

THE Georgia project grew out of the alliance of two major groups of forces. The first group was composed of the force of ideals as manifested in philanthropy and the expression of religious tolerance and freedom, ideals which, one authority contends, have influenced the progress of America more even than 'the economic man'.[1] The second group was the material and practical. Its chief attributes were those of which J. A. Doyle wrote when he asserted that, 'if the eighteenth century was the age of Addison and Horace Walpole, it was in a far more abiding sense the age of Chatham and Wolfe and Clive':[2] the forces of expansion and empire, together with the zeal for trade and imperial economy, expressed in its highest form in the doctrine of mercantilism, and the natural concomitant, the military theory of a southern outpost as a buffer state for the American colonies.

The prison inquiry, it is true, had eradicated many great evils, but no provision had been made for 'the miserable wretches . . . let out of Gaol' by the Act of 1729, people who, as Oglethorpe told his friend, Percival, were 'starving about the town for want of employment'.[3] To remedy this situation by relieving London of its surplus unemployed, Oglethorpe conceived the idea of sending a hundred or more of these people, as Percival's diary records, to 'the West Indies',[4] meaning America.[5]

No matter how high the ideal, such a programme

---

[1] Adams, E. D., *The Power of Ideals in American History* (New Haven, Connecticut, 1913), pp. xii–xiii.
[2] Doyle, *The English in America: The Colonies under the House of Hanover*, p. 418.
[3] *Egmont Diary*, i. 45. For the parliamentary consideration of this debtor problem see *Commons Journals*, xvi. 445, 455–6, 458, 461–3, 467, 470–1, 483.
[4] *Egmont Diary*, i. 90.
[5] Crane, Verner W., 'The Philanthropists and the Genesis of Georgia', *American Historical Review*, xxvii. 66, note.

THE ORIGINS OF THE GEORGIA MOVEMENT

needed material resources, and the money for this project came from two direct gifts and, later, from another, collateral, source. A haberdasher named King had recently died, having entrusted his estate of some £15,000 for charitable purposes to three trustees, two of whom were gentlemen over seventy years of age, the third King's heir. The latter desiring to convert it illegally, the two elders retained Oglethorpe to aid them in the fulfilment of their duties. A lawsuit resulted, which Oglethorpe won. The heir contested the verdict, but the Lord Chancellor handed down a sustaining decision. Anxious to be relieved of their responsibilities, the two remaining trustees now proposed to add this estate to some other fund for meritorious purposes. As a reward for winning their case for them, Oglethorpe was given a grant of £5,000 for his enterprise, to be added to such other sums as he could provide.[1] In accordance with the terms of this grant he now sought further funds and soon found another important source.

The Reverend Thomas Bray, founder of both the Society for the Promotion of Christian Knowledge and the Society for the Propagation of the Gospel in Foreign Parts, and quondam missionary to Maryland, was interested in numerous philanthropies, among which were the relief of poor families, chiefly by means of a colonial settlement, the creation of parochial libraries in Great Britain, and the Christian education of West Indian negroes.[2] For this

---

[1] *Egmont Diary*, i. 44–6; Roberts, R. A., 'The Birth of an American State: Georgia: An Effort of Philanthropy and Protestant Propaganda', *Transactions of the Royal Historical Society*, 4th series, vi (London, 1923), 24–5; Crane, V. W., *The Southern Frontier* (Durham, North Carolina, 1928), chap. xiii.

[2] There is a volume of Bray's memorials in Sion College Library, London. For his life and work see Stephen and Lee, *Dictionary of National Biography*, vi. 240; Todd, H. J., editor, *The Life and Designs of the Reverend Thomas Bray, D.D.* (2nd ed., revised, London, 1808), pp. 1–39; Pennington, E. L., *The Reverend Thomas Bray* (Church Historical Society Publications, vii, Philadelphia, 1934), chaps. ii–iii, v–vii; Tiffany, C. C., *A History of the Protestant Episcopal Church in the United States of America* (New York, 1895), pp. 65–70, 278–9; and McConnell, S. D., *History of the American Episcopal Church* (New York, 1890), pp. 96–112.

last purpose he had acquired a bequest of £900 from his friend, M. Abel Tassin D'Allone, who, as secretary to Queen Mary in those memorable years from 1689 to her death in 1694, had been so hostile to the Jacobite Oglethorpes.[1] In 1723 ill health made the cleric anxious for the perpetuation of these benevolences so that he organized the Associates of Dr. Bray. In 1729, just before his death, he chose as his trustees, largely at Oglethorpe's suggestion, John Viscount Percival, later Earl of Egmont, who had been Oglethorpe's colleague on the prison committee, James Vernon, and Thomas Coram. Through their common interest in imprisoned debtors, Oglethorpe had also met Dr. Stephen Hales, the illustrious scientist. Here then was his opportunity! As none of the trustees but Coram proved to be at all interested in either the Christian education of negroes or the spread of parochial libraries in Britain, Oglethorpe now added the King legacy to Bray's fund from the D'Allone bequest. On Bray's death in February 1730, Oglethorpe was made a trustee of his estate, and by December of that year, the D'Allone trusteeship having been converted, the programme awaited merely parliamentary aid for its successful inception.[2] Each step in James Oglethorpe's parliamentary career had thus contributed to the evolution of this design but, even as this philanthropic project was maturing in his fertile mind, the course of events in distant climes as well as in Westminster had created the comple-

[1] Abel Tassin D'Allone was a French Huguenot refugee to Holland where he successively became secretary to Queen Mary, both before and after her accession to the English throne, secretary for Dutch affairs to William III, 1698–1702, and finally secretary to Grand Pensionary Heinsius of Holland. Agnew, *Protestant Exiles from France*, ii. 207–10. See also Todd, *Life and Designs of the Reverend Thomas Bray, D.D.*, pp. 40–1; and Pennington, *The Reverend Thomas Bray*, pp. 43–4.

[2] *Egmont Diary*, i. 99, 119–20; Ford, W. C., editor, 'Letters of Thomas Coram', *Proceedings of the Massachusetts Historical Society*, lvi (Boston, 1923), 20–1; Clark-Kennedy, A. E., *Stephen Hales, D.D., F.R.S.* (Cambridge, England, 1931), pp. 118–19, 131–45, 170–88; Pennington, *The Reverend Thomas Bray*, pp. 44–6; Todd, *The Life and Designs of the Reverend Thomas Bray, D.D.*, pp. 41–50, 57; Crane, *The Southern Frontier*, chap. xiii.

THE ORIGINS OF THE GEORGIA MOVEMENT

mentary situation which made possible the fulfilment of Oglethorpe's dreams.[1]

At the opening of the eighteenth century there lay on the eastern coast of North America a slender chain of British colonies, extending from Massachusetts in the north to Carolina in the south. Although internally cemented by the Restoration conquest of New York from the Dutch and the expulsion of the Swedes from the Delaware, these colonies faced, on their frontiers, not only the Indians but also the colonists and claims of other European nations. Carolina, the southern border, lay unprotected against depredatory raids of both the Indians and the hostile Spaniard, for nigh two centuries ensconced in Florida; while farther to the west La Salle and d'Iberville had established in Louisiana the lower point of a French crescent which, rising with the aid of Le Moyne de Bienville and La Mothe Cadillac through the Mississippi and Ohio river basins, constituted an impenetrable barrier to the westward expansion of the British colonies that was not broken until Wolfe and Amherst met Montcalm on the Plains of Abraham in 1759 and a young Virginian by the name of George Washington helped to win the Ohio Valley.

By force of arms the Spaniard had conquered and, by force of religion, had held the 'Golden Isles', and during the seventeenth century had penetrated the Marshes of Glyn through Guale to the Savannah River so that even old Charles Town was at times in danger. The expansion of Carolina, chiefly due to the Indian trade, led to the ultimate collapse of the Spanish missions in Guale and the inception of the continued conflict of the next century. Despite the growing importance of the Mississippi question with France, the Spaniard remained the major

[1] 'To commence the history of Georgia with the colony under Oglethorp, would be extremely like beginning the history of New-England, jumping over all the early voyages and other transactions which led to its settlement.' Drake, S. G., 'The Early History of Georgia and Sir Alexander Cuming's Embassy to the Cherokees', *The New England Historical and Genealogical Register* (Boston, 1847——, in progress), xxvi. 261.

problem in the Atlantic lowlands with the Chickesaw and other Creek Indians holding the vital balance of power.[1] The Yamassee Indian War in 1715–16 made it quite manifest that Carolina needed the protection of a buffer state on its southern border as well as a determination of boundaries in a debatable territory wherein the English eventually established Fort King George on the Altamaha River.[2] In 1717 Sir Robert Montgomery, son of a Nova Scotian baronet who with others had failed in an earlier attempt to colonize southern Carolina, issued a prospectus entitled *A Discourse concerning the designed establishment of a New Colony to the South of Carolina, the most delightful country in the Universe*. Herein he proposed the creation of 'the Margravate of Azilia' between the Savannah and the Altamaha rivers, the chief purpose of which, according to the American authority on colonial history, was 'that it would be a barrier against the Spanish and Indians'.[3] At the same time it was proposed that the Carolina proprietors should surrender their rights to the Crown, a suggestion which, however, was declined. In the keen analysis of a Georgia historian, the Margravate of Azilia 'was magnificent upon the map, but was impracticable in reality', so that the proposals, 'though garnished with the most glowing descriptions, . . . were issued in vain';[4] Montgomery's programme failed; Azilia, in a modern historian's curt phrase, 'went up in rhetoric';[5] and the southern frontier of Carolina continued unprotected. The erection in 1721 by Colonel John Barnwell of Fort King George on the Altamaha, denoting English occupancy of

[1] Coulter, E. M., *A Short History of Georgia* (Chapel Hill, North Carolina, 1933), chap. i; Crane, *The Southern Frontier*, chaps. i–vi; Macleod, W. C., *The American Indian Frontier* (New York, 1928), pp. 67–99.

[2] Bolton, H. E., and Marshall, T. M., *The Colonization of North America, 1492–1783* (New York, 1922), p. 315; Bolton, H. E., and Ross, M., *The Debatable Land* (Berkeley, California, 1925), pp. 63–9; Crane, *The Southern Frontier*, chaps. vii, x; Macleod, *The American Indian Frontier*, pp. 253–70.

[3] Osgood, H. L., *The American Colonies in the Eighteenth Century* (4 vols., New York, 1924), ii. 365.

[4] Stevens, W. B., *History of Georgia* (2 vols., New York, 1847), i. 59.

[5] Bolton and Ross, *The Debatable Land*, p. 71.

THE ORIGINS OF THE GEORGIA MOVEMENT

Guale, naturally aroused the Spaniards. To the English, then, throughout this period, Port Royal, Fort King George, and the Altamaha River became the southern outposts of Carolina. In 1730, a year after the transition to a crown colony, when the province was divided into North and South Carolina, Sir Alexander Cuming[1] succeeded in nullifying a rising French influence among the Cherokee Indians, who now formally acknowledged English supremacy, and Jean Pierre Pury, a Swiss, established a South Carolina outpost at Purysburg; but the Spanish peril remained and the British Government continued to seek a sound programme of simultaneous colonial expansion and defence.[2]

While the Colonial Office was seeking a *modus operandi*, Oglethorpe had completed his plans with Percival. By April 1, 1730, having determined on America as the site for his colony, Oglethorpe was so charged with enthusiasm for the cause that for three full hours he held Percival enthralled with his efforts to send the 'colony of poor and honest industrious debtors to the West Indies' on the grant from the King estate which, despite subsequent attempts to nullify this movement, was ultimately paid over to Oglethorpe. By June 26 he had chosen Carolina, and on July 1 the decision was made to use all available funds from the various estates. Oglethorpe now proposed to unite the trustees for the D'Allone estate to those for the King estate, to which plan the Lord Chancellor and Percival consented. But one item was still lacking. The project needed a patent or charter.[3]

In the archives at the Public Record Office there lies a 'List of business for the Privy Council session on

---

[1] Thirty-four years later, in 1764, Cuming, in his 'Autobiographical Memoir', affirmed that, in this interval, 'three blazing Stars have appeared in different parts of the World; for in this light we may consider General Oglethorpe from England, King Theodore of Corseca, and the Persian Monarch from the rising of the Sun', Thomas Kouli Kan. Add. MSS. (British Museum), 39855, Autobiographical Memoir of Sir Alexander Cuming, 1764, ff. 5–6.

[2] Crane, *The Southern Frontier*, chap. x.   [3] *Egmont Diary*, i. 90, 98–9.

November 19, 1728', the third item of which was a 'Petition of Lord Percival and others for a Grant of Land in South Carolina for Settling a Charitable Colony'.[1] Whether Oglethorpe was one of the 'others' we know not, for there is no mention of this move, two years before the Georgia petition, in any records of the Privy Council or, in fact, anywhere else.[2] And so the first mention of an actual attempt to secure the Georgia charter is found in Percival's diary notation of July 30, 1730, to the effect that 'we agreed on a petition to the King and Council for obtaining a grant of lands on the southwest of Carolina for settling poor persons of London, and having ordered it to be engrossed fair, we signed it, all who were present, and the other Associates were to be spoke also to sign it before delivered'.[3] On September 17 this petition for a charter was presented to the Privy Council where, in committee and through reference to the Board of Trade, it languished for well over a year.[4] During this long period of suspense, Oglethorpe's faith in both the King and the Whig oligarchy never faltered, although he and Percival were compelled to use all their political skill in extracting from a reluctant Walpole a satisfactory document. What with securing the favour of the Board of Trade; personal scruples 'whether the acceptance of the government of the colony we are sending to Georgia doth not vacate our seats in Parliament',[5] which Oglethorpe proposed to overcome by a qualifying Act; the

[1] S.P. 36 (State Papers, Domestic: George II, P.R.O.): 9, 1728, f. 47.

[2] P.C. 2:90, Privy Council Register, 1727–1729, pp. 386–91; Grant, W. L., and Munro, J., editors, *Acts of the Privy Council of England: Colonial Series* (6 vols., London, 1908–12), iii. 1720–1745, pp. 180–210.

[3] *Egmont Diary*, i. 99.

[4] For the attitude and procedure of the Privy Council see Grant and Munro, *Acts of the Privy Council of England: Colonial Series*, iii. 299–305; *Journal of the Commissioners for Trade and Plantations*, vi. 165, 167–70, 175, 259–60; P.C. 2:91. Privy Council Register, 1729–1732, pp. 318–21; *MSS. of the Marquess Townshend* (H.M.C. Reports), p. 258: Among the papers relating to the American Plantations in the Townshend MSS. at Raynham Hall, Norfolk, is 'An Account of the Several Steps taken by the Privy Council upon granting the Georgia Charter'.

[5] *Egmont Diary*, i. 129.

necessity of securing Lord Carteret's approval as the last of the Carolina proprietors; and, finally, the effort of obtaining Walpole's promise both to secure the passage of an enabling Act of Parliament, and to allow the project a share of the proceeds of the current state lottery—with all this it was little wonder that by June 17, 1731, Oglethorpe was dissatisfied with the first draft of the charter as submitted by the Attorney-General who, in Percival's words,

has constituted a new election of Councillors every three years which we apprehend is to take the power out of our hands and put it into new ones, who may convert the scheme into a job. He has also put the Militia of the intended colony into the single hand of the Governor of Carolina, whereby he at his pleasure may distress our people.[1]

In addition, this first draft gave the King financial benefits of such a nature as to make the project unattractive to others. In September 1731 the leaders therefore presented their objections to the Attorney-General, emphasizing their desire 'to be independent of the Governor of Carolina', and opposing 'a rotation of Common Council men' to prevent possible corruption.[2] By November Oglethorpe was hopeful of gaining the consent of the committee of the Privy Council, but the two leaders now found that, despite their successful plea for revision of the charter, the Whig bureaucracy was delaying its release. On January 26, 1732, the King 'put the fiat to our Carolina charter'[3] and the next day appeared an Order in Council authorizing the preparation of the final draft of the charter for the royal signature,[4] but now the Duke of Newcastle, as Secretary of State for the Colonies, held up its delivery, to the deep disgust of the trustees, some of whom wanted to resign. Walpole now blamed the

[1] Ibid. 193. [2] Ibid. 204.
[3] Ibid. 218; London *Evening Post*, Feb. 5, 1732, p. 1.
[4] C.O. 5:21, Orders in Council, 1728–1754, f. 15; P.C. 2:91, Privy Council Register, 1729–1732, pp. 571–2; Grant and Munro, *Acts of the Privy Council of England: Colonial Series*, iii. 305.

King for holding it back because he objected to granting the trustees the right to name militia officers. This worried Percival who was not relieved by Horace Walpole's explanations. But the King had not rejected; he had merely delayed. On April 21, 1732, he signed the charter, but not until the end of May did it finally pass the bureaux to be promulgated on June 20, 1732.[1]

To James Oglethorpe and nineteen associates, most of whom had been on the prison investigation committee with him, was granted the status of 'Trustees for establishing the colony of Georgia in America'. The motives for such a grant were here listed as threefold: In the first place, domestic unemployment.

Many of our poor subjects, if they had means to defray their charges of passage, . . . would be glad to settle in any of our provinces in America where by cultivating the lands, at present waste and desolate, they might . . . gain a comfortable subsistence for themselves and families.

In the second place, the King, while discoursing philanthropically, was thinking imperially, so that he hoped 'they might not only gain a comfortable subsistence for themselves and families, but also strengthen our colonies and increase the trade, navigation, and wealth of these our realms'. Finally he gave heed not only to imperial expansion but also to imperial defence, and sanctioned the project of a buffer state for South Carolina because 'our provinces in North America have been frequently ravaged by Indian enemies; more especially that of South Carolina' which, having been previously laid waste, 'will in the case of a new war be exposed to the like calamities; inasmuch as their whole southern frontier continueth unsettled, and lieth open to the said savages'. To this score of Englishmen the King therefore granted, for only twenty-one years, however, full rights of government by a common council of twenty-four, nine of whom, including Percival and Oglethorpe, were named by the King,

[1] *Egmont Diary*, i. 120–64, 209, 218, 220, 223, 226–7, 232, 235, 260, 277–8, 282; *Journal of the Commissioners for Trade and Plantations*, vi. 313–14, 316.

THE ORIGINS OF THE GEORGIA MOVEMENT 119

the others to be chosen by the nine already named. The territory bestowed was that of the defunct Margravate of Azilia, extending from the Savannah River on the north to the Altamaha on the south, and from the Atlantic to the Pacific. In the terse phrase of one historian, 'what cared King George that the grant cut a wide swath through Florida, Louisiana, and Texas? Or that, incidentally, it included Albuquerque, Socorro, and other New Mexico settlements?'[1] In accordance with the prevailing English tenets, the charter ordained that, always excepting Roman Catholics,[2] 'forever hereafter there shall be a liberty of conscience allowed in the worship of God'. After providing for colonial defence in which the Governor of South Carolina was to command the Georgian militia, the charter closed with the provision for Georgia's reversion to the Crown at the end of twenty-one years.[3] As the American authority on this subject has shown, 'the granting of such a charter was in a measure a reversion to type';[4] that is, to the old idea of ultimate royal control; and the essence of the scheme is to be found in the reply of the Board of Trustees to a rich contractor, who wanted to settle with his servants in Georgia in 1733, when they decreed that 'the design of our charter was in settling our Colony to provide for the necessitous poor of our country, and not to make men of substance richer'.[5]

The charter having been granted, the Trustees at once began to function, and the record of weekly meetings of

[1] Bolton and Ross, *The Debatable Land*, p. 71.
[2] See Hughes, Thomas, S.J., *History of the Society of Jesus in North America* (2 vols., London, 1907–17), ii. 191–2.
[3] For the charter see Colonial Office Records (P.R.O.), Colonies General (hereinafter cited as C.O. 324): 49, Entry Books, 1714–1781, Commissions, etc., pp. 87–116; C.O. 5:681; and Candler, A. D., editor, *The Colonial Records of the State of Georgia* (hereinafter cited as *Col. Rec. Ga.*, in progress, Atlanta, Georgia, 1904——), i. 11–26. For a recent criticism of the Georgia charter see Keith, A. Berriedale, *Constitutional History of the First British Empire* (Oxford, 1930), pp. 170–1.
[4] McCain, J. R., *Georgia as a Proprietary Province: The Execution of a Trust* (Boston, 1917), pp. 24–5.
[5] *Egmont Diary*, i. 370. See also Crane, 'The Philanthropists and the Genesis of Georgia', *American Historical Review*, xxvii. 65.

the Board, together with the faithful attention to obligations of the Common Council, as found in the journals of the respective bodies and the diary of John Percival, Earl of Egmont, is one of which that nobleman and Oglethorpe could well be proud. Having tendered their thanks to the Duke of Newcastle and all the officials who aided in 'passing the Charter', as well as to Lord Carteret who, giving up his one-eighth share of Carolina, now offered them excellent advice as to the procedure of colonization, the Trustees organized on July 20, 1732, by selecting Percival as President of the Colony. Percival, Oglethorpe, Dr. Samuel Hales 'the clergyman', James Vernon, and Captain Thomas Coram proved to be the nucleus of the Board which, despite the absence of eight Common Councilmen and two Trustees, promptly chose Benjamin Martyn as secretary without pay until the Corporation could afford a salary. Oglethorpe at once proposed an important suggestion 'for employing an ingenious person to reside in our colony, where he has already been, to search out medicinal plants and roots, and to make experiments of grain to be planted there, and to instruct the colony in agriculture', a plan which Percival and the others thought 'might be of great use both to the colony and to England'. What was equally important was Oglethorpe's report of pledges, towards supporting this programme, of £50 a year from Lord Petre and £20 annually from the Duke of Richmond and Oglethorpe's famed medical friend, Sir Hans Sloane.[1] By August 3, then, the Common Council was able to organize under its chairman, the Honourable Edward Digby.[2]

As this project, in the words of Austin Dobson, was to be one of 'assisted emigration',[3] particular attention was

[1] Colonial Office Records (P.R.O.), America (hereinafter cited as C.O. 5): 686, Journal of the Trustees, 1732–1737, pp. 1–3; Candler, *Col. Rec. Ga.* i. 65–9; *Egmont Diary*, i. 278, 282–3, 285–6, 289; London *Daily Post*, July 22, 1732, p. 1.

[2] C.O. 5:689, Minutes of the Common Council, 1732–1736, pp. 1–2; Candler, *Col. Rec. Ga.* ii. 3.

[3] Dobson, *A Paladin of Philanthropy*, p. 9.

paid to two problems: Proper publicity for the venture and the acquisition of adequate revenues, in both of which Oglethorpe played a major role. At the Council meeting of August 3, 1732, he was appointed publicity agent to advertise the project in all the newspapers and also to censor all undesirable articles relating thereunto.[1] In the words of Professor Osgood, 'by 1730 the newspaper and periodical press was well developed in England, and its influence was enlisted on behalf of Georgia to an extent which was never dreamed of in the case of any other colony';[2] so that, as Professor Crane shows, 'to a marked degree, the extraordinary vogue that Georgia enjoyed in those first years was the consequence of efficient "booming" by its promoters, and by their literary and journalistic friends. Promotion literature was, of course, no new *genre*, but the Trustees perfected its technique.'[3] Benjamin Martyn now prepared a brochure entitled *Some Account of the Designs of the Trustees for Establishing the Colony of Georgia in America*, wherein the Georgia movement was compared to the old Roman conception of colonization as 'among the noblest of their works'.[4] This was printed by order of the Trustees[5] and subsequently appeared in the public press.[6] In addition to his many other labours, Oglethorpe himself contributed *An Essay on Plantations*[7] and is generally credited with producing a prospectus entitled *A New and Accurate Account of the Provinces of South Carolina and Georgia*,[8] wherein, after

[1] C.O. 5:689, p. 2; Candler, *Col. Rec. Ga.* ii. 3.
[2] Osgood, *The American Colonies in the Eighteenth Century*, iii. 37.
[3] Crane, V. W., *The Promotion Literature of Georgia* (Cambridge, Massachusetts, 1925), p. 1.
[4] Sloane MSS. (British Museum), 3986, ff. 38–9, verso.
[5] *Egmont Diary*, i. 289.
[6] London *London Journal*, Aug. 5, 1732, p. 1; *Gentleman's Magazine*, ii. 893–4.
[7] It was printed by William Bowyer in 1732. Nichols, *Literary Anecdotes of the Eighteenth Century*, ii. 17.
[8] The only opponent of the view that Oglethorpe wrote this prospectus is Professor Verner Crane who holds that, as the 'Georgia publicity was not merely persistent, but of high grade', Benjamin Martyn was the probable author of *A New and Accurate Account*, Oglethorpe only paying for the printing

a description of the region, its natural advantages, and its inhabitants, he proclaimed the philanthropic purposes of the colony:

> The unfortunate will not be obliged to bind themselves to a long servitude, to pay for their passage, for they may be carried gratis into a land of liberty and plenty; where they immediately find themselves in possession of a competent estate, in a happier clime than they knew before, and they are unfortunate, indeed, if here they cannot forget their sorrows.[1]

Asserting that persons reduced to poverty were not wealth to the nation, but might be happy in Georgia and there become profitable to England, Oglethorpe placed such paupers within the design of the patent and drew a picture of the British Empire in terms of that of Rome, adding a sound economic argument for the prospective advantages of commerce and agriculture.[2] A nobler and more modest appeal than Montgomery's florid proclamation of over a decade before, Oglethorpe's *New and Accurate Account* merited a more successful issue.[3]

The greater the appeal of the prospect and the warmer its reception,[4] the more necessary became increased resources. The charter had created a corporation 'for the receiving, managing and disposing of the contributions of our loving subjects', but long before this formal royal authorization, Oglethorpe and Egmont had sought further funds to add to the King and D'Allone nuclei. Campaigning for subscriptions, large and small, had begun in

of this tract which, contends Professor Crane, was too scholarly a product to be accredited to James Oglethorpe (Crane, *Promotion Literature of Georgia*, pp. 9–12). The facts of Oglethorpe's heritage and academic career hardly substantiate this contention.

[1] A sharp indictment of the generally prevalent system of white indentured servants.

[2] The material or trade reason for Georgia is explained in Martyn, Benjamin, *Reasons for Establishing the Colony of Georgia, with Regard to the Trade of Great Britain*, . . . (London, 1733), reprinted in *Collections of the Georgia Historical Society*, i (Savannah, 1840), 203–38.

[3] For the text of *A New and Accurate Account* see *Collections of the Georgia Historical Society*, i. 42–78.

[4] 'No other American colony, surely, had so good a press, or so musical a chorus.' Crane, *Promotion Literature of Georgia*, p. 16.

July 1730, and Egmont diligently followed up all estate grants to charity; nor were the possibilities of a lottery overlooked. Basing his estimate on that of Captain Coram 'who knew the West Indies well', Percival deemed £12,000 a necessity, holding £10,000 to be an absolute minimum.[1] Despite their successes to date, the greatest stroke of good fortune was yet awaiting the promoters. In 1723 George Berkeley, an Irish churchman who had been Percival's friend since 1709 and who, as Chaplain, had been with Theophilus Oglethorpe, junior, in the Peterborough *entourage* to Sicily in 1714, informed Percival of his own project for a Christian college in 'the sea-girt Bermuda islands with their innocence and security' for 'the reformation of manners among the English in our western plantations and the propagation of the Gospel among the American savages'.[2] Proclaiming, in his *Verses on the Prospect of planting Arts and Learning in America*, his belief that 'Westward the Course of Empire takes its way', Berkeley hailed America as

In happy climes the seat of innocence
Where nature guides and virtue rules.[3]

Realization of his dream, however, depended on very substantial, material aid. Berkeley now received a subscription of £200 from Percival[4] and £3,000 from the estate of Mrs. Hester van Omry, which, as he had not even known the lady, proved a windfall.[5] Finally, on the promise of a government grant of £20,000, Berkeley went out to Bermuda in 1728 and laboured both there and in

[1] *Egmont Diary*, i. 260–1; Compston, H. F. B., *Thomas Coram, Churchman, Empire Builder and Philanthropist* (London, 1918), p. 64.
[2] Rand, Benjamin, editor, *Berkeley and Percival: The Correspondence of George Berkeley, afterwards Bishop of Cloyne, and Sir John Percival, afterwards Earl of Egmont* (Cambridge, England, 1914), pp. 32, 203. For Berkeley's career see pp. 19–20, 31–43, 130, 230, 269–79; Hone and Rossi, *Bishop Berkeley*, pp. 55–6, 77, 94–6, 130–66; Ballard, *The Great Earl of Peterborough*, pp. 262–3; *MSS. of the Earl of Egmont* (H.M.C. Reports), i. 237, 241–3.
[3] Smith, D. Nichol, editor, *The Oxford Book of Eighteenth Century Verse* (Oxford, 1926), pp. 219–20.
[4] *Portland MSS.* (H.M.C. Reports), vii, *Harley Letters*, v. 417.
[5] *MSS. of the Earl of Egmont* (H.M.C. Reports), pp. 241–4.

Rhode Island for the next three years, but as one church historian has so well said, 'to secure the grant was one thing, to secure the money quite another'.[1] Without it Berkeley could do nothing. As trustee for the D'Allone legacy to convert negroes, Percival had fondly hoped to use that fund to aid Berkeley's project, but was deterred by Oglethorpe who asserted that 'experience had shown that religion will not be propagated in the Indies by colleges'.[2] With the parliamentary grant for Berkeley as distant as ever, Percival, on December 23, 1730, at last informed the Irish clergyman of the Georgia project: 'Mr. Oglethorpe, a young gentleman of very public spirit and chairman of the late committee of jails, gave the first hint of this project last year, and has very diligently pursued it.'[3] This subsequently led Berkeley to return, deeply disappointed at the utter lack of support accorded to his venture.[4] Oglethorpe now concluded that his own project, 'being entirely calculated for a secular interest', held greater promise of governmental support than Berkeley's missionary idea,[5] with the result that on March 10, 1731, the Georgia enthusiasts proposed to ask the government for a share of the £20,000, as yet still unpaid to Berkeley.[6] Oglethorpe, therefore, wrote to the latter in Rhode Island, asking him to aid the Georgia project in view of his own inability to acquire the grant, and promising to return the support of the Georgia Trustees for Berkeley's future projects.[7] The missionary's reply was to return to England on October 30, 1731, and the next

---

[1] McConnell, *History of the American Episcopal Church*, p. 133. See also Tiffany, *History of the Protestant Episcopal Church in the United States*, pp. 282–6.
[2] *Egmont Diary*, i. 45.
[3] Percival to Berkeley, Bath, Dec. 23, 1730, Rand, *Berkeley and Percival*, pp. 269–72.
[4] Berkeley to Percival, Rhode Island, March 2, 1731, Rand, *Berkeley and Percival*, pp. 273–4.
[5] Rand, *Berkeley and Percival*, pp. 270 ff.; Crane, 'The Philanthropists and the Genesis of Georgia', *American Historical Review*, xxvii. 63–9.
[6] *Egmont Diary*, i. 157; Rand, *Berkeley and Percival*, p. 274.
[7] Oglethorpe to Berkeley, London, May 1731, Rand, *Berkeley and Percival*, pp. 275–9.

day repair to Percival's home where, during succeeding months, he and Oglethorpe at times 'sat from dinner till ten o'clock', engaged in lengthy conferences. The result of these meetings was complete acquiescence on the part of Berkeley and a motion in Parliament in May 1732 for a grant to the Georgia project of £10,000, the ultimate success of which move was aided by an uncommon amount of vagrancy in London at that time, a situation of which Oglethorpe took prompt advantage.[1] The granting of the charter in June opened the purses of the financial interests for, upon this royal recommendation, Governor Johnson of South Carolina sent £50; the directors of the Bank of England subscribed £300; the trustees of the late Earl of Thanet's charitable legacies, thanks to Percival's zeal, pledged a similar sum; and the officials of the East India Company gave £600; so that by September 14, 1732, over £2,000 had been harvested for the great cause.[2]

Having organized at their first meeting on July 20 and having secured both publicity and resources, the Trustees now turned to the question of the colonizing personnel. Oglethorpe had given the project such wide publicity that, when the charter grant opened the way for the first expedition to the colony, the Trustees received applications, not only from domestic paupers but also from Swiss emigrationists and the Salzburg Protestants whom Oglethorpe had so recently befriended on the floor of Parliament. Thus it was that in July 1732 the Trustees, although deeming the moment not yet propitious for departure, had selected the personnel of the first party, made up of ambitious English paupers, reputable, respectable, but unfortunate individuals, all of whom had their creditors'

[1] *Egmont Diary*, i. 207, 214, 272–4; Rand, *Berkeley and Percival*, pp. 43, 279.
[2] *Egmont Diary*, i. 292, 304; *Gentleman's Magazine*, ii. 975; Rand, Benjamin, *Berkeley's American Sojourn* (Cambridge, Massachusetts, 1932), pp. 52–7; Hone and Rossi, *Bishop Berkeley*, chaps. viii–ix. See also a very interesting letter from William Wise to Henry Newman, Secretary of the Society for the Propagation of the Gospel in Foreign Parts, London, April 14, 1733, Rawlinson MSS. (Bodleian Library, Oxford), D. 839, f. 155.

leave to go, and none of whom were deserting wives or families, when domestic circumstances permitted James Oglethorpe to make an offer to the Trustees which was to change the entire course of both his own life and the Georgia project.[1]

On June 19, 1732, Lady Eleanor Wall Oglethorpe, having attained the scriptural age of three score years and ten, had 'dy'd at her House in the Palace-Yard at Westminster'.[2] Although she had retained her sturdy Jacobite loyalties to the last, all was forgiven and forgotten in honour of the woman. When five days later she was buried in the grave of her husband and eldest son, Lewis, 'near the altar in St. James's Church', Piccadilly, the pall was supported by the Earl of Arran, Lords Muskerry, Kingsale, and Carpenter, and Sir Robert Sutton.[3] And the London newspapers, which, not unlike a large part of the modern press, paid far more attention to criminals than to Christians, spread themselves in an encomium of respectful tribute. Not only because she was the mother of James Oglethorpe, but essentially in her own right, Eleanor Wall Oglethorpe deserves to be remembered by this paragraph:

She died in the 70th year of her age, and was very conversant with state affairs in the end of King Charles the Second and King James's Reign, and was acquainted with the first springs and motives of the principal transactions of those and the succeeding times. At the Revolution Sir Theophilus, who was then Major General, Colonel of a Regiment, and Gentleman of the Horse, resigning his employments; she, tho' bred in all the gayety of a Court, was not only contented, but even pleased with the putting down their equipage, and living in the most

---

[1] *Egmont Diary*, i. 282–9, 298; *Gentleman's Magazine*, ii. 874.
[2] London *Evening Post*, June 20, 1732, p. 1; *Daily Courant*, June 21, 1732, p. 2; *Daily Journal*, June 21, 1732, p. 1; Boyer, *Political State of Great Britain*, xliii. 649; *Gentleman's Magazine*, ii. 827.
[3] London *Daily Courant*, June 26, 1732, p. 2; *Daily Journal*, June 26, 1732, p. 1; *Daily Post*, June 26, 1732, p. 1; *Evening Post*, June 27, 1732, p. 2; *London Journal*, July 1, 1732, p. 3. For the burial see Burial Register, 1732–1754, Saint James's, Piccadilly.

THE ORIGINS OF THE GEORGIA MOVEMENT 127

frugal and retired manner. She was severe to herself, human to others, and contemned all kind of delicacy and shew. She was a Woman of excellent memory and address, piercing wit, and solid judgment, and indefatigable in serving her friends. She had courage and learning superior to her sex: the latter of which she strove to conceal; and was far from being vain of the former, but used it as a support in the various accidents of life. To her last hour she kept her chearfulness, tho' three months bed-rid and dead on one side with the palsy. The very day before her death, tho' she knew she could not outlive the morrow, she in a pleasant and easy way rallied the Physician, spent the evening as usually in prayer, and died in a calm, christian, and heroic manner.[1]

Such a mother deserved the care and attention bestowed upon her by her youngest and dearest son, James, and the future of the Georgia movement would have been far different had it not been for her death on June 19, 1732. But even as the death of her husband thirty years before had freed her own Jacobite spirit from the restraints of a post-revolution parliamentarian's wife, so now her own demise left her distinguished son without any domestic encumbrance to check his future career. Whether or not inspired by Samuel Wesley's ode on this occasion,[2] James Oglethorpe in October, 1732, determined to cast his lot with the Georgia pioneers. This self-sacrificing offer on the part of one who was his mother's sole heir,[3] evoked the congratulations, not only of Percival and his colleagues among the Trustees, but also of Thomas Penn, Proprietor of Pennsylvania, Governor Robert Johnson of South Carolina, and Governor Jonathan Belcher of Massachusetts. Belcher, who had known Oglethorpe in London, avowed that 'I have a very great honour & esteem' for him to whom Massachusetts was much indebted for

---

[1] London *Grub-Street Journal*, June 29, 1732, p. 3; *Fog's Weekly Journal*, July 1, 1732, p. 2.
[2] *An Ode to James Oglethorpe, Esq., Written soon after the Death of the Lady Oglethorpe, His Mother*, Wesley, *Poems*, pp. 370–6. See also Add. MSS. (British Museum), 13942, Collection of Epitaphs, xxvii, ff. 166–9.
[3] Swanton and Woods, *Bygone Haslemere*, p. 193.

his support in Parliament, and was delighted that he was to make the journey to America.[1]

Attached to Oglethorpe's offer, however, was a proviso that the first band of emigrants should sail at once. To this Percival and many others were opposed on the grounds of unpreparedness, although the former rejoiced 'that Mr. Oglethorpe would go, for my great pain was that although we were ever so well prepared, it would be difficult to find a proper Governor, which post he has accepted of'. Oglethorpe, nevertheless, was adamant and by mid-October the Trustees, of whom but half remained interested, decided to send the party immediately.[2]

With this decision one phase of James Oglethorpe's life became a closed chapter and another was opened, the importance of which in the pages of history even James Oglethorpe could not have surmised. The quondam Jacobite had travelled far. The Atlantic and abiding fame lay before him.

---

[1] Smith, C. C., *et al.*, editors, 'The Belcher Papers', *Collections of the Massachusetts Historical Society*, 6th series, vi–vii (2 vols., Boston, 1893–4), i. 58, 112, 211; *Egmont Diary*, i. 293, 304; Jones, C. C., *History of Georgia* (2 vols., Boston, 1883), i. 115, 131.

[2] *Egmont Diary*, i. 293, 304; C.O. 5:686, pp. 25–6; Candler, *Col. Rec. Ga.* i. 79–80. For an interesting report of a lady's generous donation of clothing to hasten the departure see the London *Daily Post*, Nov. 11, 1732, p. 1.

CHAPTER V

GEORGIA: THE FIRST PHASE: ADMINISTRATION

THE Trustees having acceded to Oglethorpe's wishes for a speedy departure, every bureau at Whitehall was pressed into service to provide for the welfare of the wanderers, both on the high seas and in their future homeland. No transatlantic airman of the twentieth century ever received more attention and care than did the first colonists of Georgia: Percival, himself, asked the Admiralty to issue instructions to all ships of war on the Atlantic and American stations, bespeaking their assistance;[1] the Admiralty not only issued these orders, but gave Oglethorpe a general requisition on any ships he might call upon for aid;[2] the Privy Council sent explicit instructions for the proper welcome of the group to Governor Robert Johnson of South Carolina;[3] and the Duke of Newcastle, as Secretary of State for the Colonies, wrote in similar vein to all the English Governors in America.[4] At home the Trustees saw to it that the party included not only the Rev. Henry Herbert, D.D., son of the illustrious Lord Herbert of Cherbury, as chaplain, but also a surgeon, an apothecary, and a civil engineer; and, in Percival's own words, 'as for provision, medicines, tents,

[1] *Egmont Diary*, i. 296.
[2] Josiah Burchett, Secretary to the Lord Commissioners of the Admiralty, to Henry Newman, Secretary of the Society for the Propagation of the Gospel in Foreign Parts, Whitehall, Nov. 10, 1732; J. Burchett to James Oglethorpe, Whitehall, Nov. 10, 1732, Admiralty 2:465, Secretary's Letter Book, 1731–1732 (P.R.O.), p. 460.
[3] P.C. 2:92, Privy Council Register, 1732–1734, p. 59; Grant and Munro, *Acts of the Privy Council: Colonial Series*, iii. 305.
[4] C.O. 5:401, South Carolina, Instructions from the Board of Trade, 1730–1739, pp. 52–3; South Carolina Transcripts in the Department of Archives at Columbia, South Carolina (hereinafter cited as S.C. Rec.), i. 114–15; Benjamin Martyn to Governor Johnson, London, Oct. 18, 1732, C.O. 5:666, Letter Book of the Trustees, 1732–1738, pp. 1–2; C.O. 5:686, Journal of the Trustees, pp. 35, 38; Candler, *Col. Rec. Ga.* i. 80; C.O. 324:36, pp. 376–9; *Journal of the Commissioners for Trade and Plantations*, vi. 341.

arms, etc., nothing is wanting'.[1] Despite the seemingly disinterested silence of the press, the departure was to be in every respect auspicious.

On November 15, 1732, James Oglethorpe set out from London to drive to Gravesend; and so it came to pass that when, after many delays, the 200-ton frigate *Ann* set forth on November 17, in the quaint words of the *Gentleman's Magazine*, with 116 persons and '10 tons of Alderman Parson's best beer . . . for the service of the colony', James Oglethorpe was the accompanying Trustee 'to see them settled' in Georgia.[2]

For seven weeks the little band of emigrants braved the tempestuous seas of winter, all surviving but two infants, and on January 13, 1733, they arrived at Charles Town, South Carolina, where they were warmly welcomed by the Governor and the Speaker of the Commons House of Assembly who, with their fellow Carolinians, fully appreciated the value to themselves of Georgia as a buffer state.[3] As early as October 7, 1732, had the *South Carolina Gazette* proclaimed that 'we are very impatient here to know the Particulars of the Charter',[4] and that interest never abated, for throughout December and January the work of the Trustees received unusual space in this oldest of southern newspapers.[5] In the light of subsequent events and numerous misinterpretations and misunderstandings, it is therefore important to note that Governor Johnson had continually informed both the Duke of Newcastle and the Georgia Trustees that he was at all

---

[1] *Egmont Diary*, i. 296.
[2] London *Daily Journal*, Nov. 17, 1732, p. 1; Nov. 21, 1732, p. 1; *Evening Post*, Nov. 18, 1732, p. 1; London *Journal*, Nov. 18, 1732, p. 1; *Gentleman's Magazine*, ii. 1029, 1079–80; *Egmont Diary*, ii. 295.
[3] *Egmont Diary*, i. 304–5, 339, 364; C.O. 5:434 (no pagination), S.C. Journal of the Upper House, Jan. 12, 1733; S.C. Rec. v. 266–7, 346–7; London *Daily Courant*, March 2, 1733, p. 1; *Daily Journal*, March 2, 1733, p. 1; London *Journal*, March 3, 1733, p. 2; *Grub-Street Journal*, March 8, 1733, p. 2.
[4] Charles Town *South Carolina Gazette*, Oct. 7, 1732, p. 3.
[5] Ibid. Dec. 2, 1732, pp. 1–2; Dec. 9, 1732, pp. 1–2; Jan. 13, 1733, p. 4; Jan. 27, 1733, p. 3.

GEORGIA: THE FIRST PHASE: ADMINISTRATION 131

times anxious to aid the new-comers to the fullest extent,[1] and both the Upper House and the Commons House of Assembly of South Carolina approved a resolution that 'we are unanimously of opinion that all due countenance and encouragement ought to be given' to the Georgia movement.[2] But their aid was not confined to resolutions: it was profoundly practical. While the immigrants were still on the high seas, the South Carolina Assembly voted to provide Oglethorpe with 'boats to carry his people to their design'd settlement, 105 head of cattle, 25 hoggs, and a quantity of rice for provisions', and they allotted twenty rangers or colonial police to patrol the new settlement against Indians or Spaniards. And in Governor Johnson's concluding phrase, 'if anything more is necessary to further the success of this undertaking, I will do all in my power to forward it'.[3]

Thus it was that, after a brief stay in Charles Town, the pioneers, accompanied by Colonel William Bull and a body of rangers, proceeded to their southern wilderness where, on February 12, 1733, on a tract ceded by the Indians and lying on the banks of the Savannah River, ten miles from its mouth, they began to erect the town of that name.[4] The Trustees had decided on November 1, 1732, that a town named Savannah should be built as their first piece of work on a tract of 5,000 acres,[5] 'as near

[1] Governor Johnson to the Duke of Newcastle: Charles Town, Jan. 1733, C.O. 5:388, f. 61; S.C. Rec. xvi. 38.
[2] C.O. 5:433, S.C. Journal of the Commons House of Assembly, Jan. 18, 1733; S.C. Rec. i (part 2), 894–5, 1014–15, 1066–7; C.O. 5:434, S.C. Journal of the Council and Upper House, Jan. 12 and 26, 1733; S.C. Rec. v. 252, 346–9.
[3] Governor Johnson to the Duke of Newcastle, Charles Town, Jan. 1733, C.O. 5:388, f. 61; S.C. Rec. xvi. 38; C.O. 5:434; S.C. Rec. v. 381, 410, 444–6, 450–1, 466–8. See also Labaree, L. W., *Royal Government in America* (New Haven, Connecticut, 1930), p. 330.
[4] Charles Town *South Carolina Gazette*, March 31, 1733, p. 3.
[5] In 1885 Mr. William Harden of Savannah addressed the Georgia Historical Society on the origin of the plan for Savannah as found in Castell's *Villas of the Ancients, Illustrated* (London, 1728), the volume by the architect whose sufferings and death in a debtors' prison led to Oglethorpe's inquiry. *New England Historical and Genealogical Register*, xl. 127.

the Savannah', in Martyn's words, 'as conveniently they can, that they may be at a greater distance from the Spaniards'.[1] The Trustees had also ordained that Savannah should have a complete civil government, but this provision was waived for, in Percival's words, 'we were not particular in establishing the constitution because till we come to that the laws of England take place'.[2] Full powers in this as in other matters were assumed by Oglethorpe[3] for, in one historian's trenchant words, 'as so frequently the case in philanthropic enterprises, the recipients of the charity in Georgia were expected passively to take what was given, and Oliver Twists were not included in the calculations of Oglethorpe or the other trustees'.[4] For the next fifteen months Oglethorpe's activities were devoted to problems of administration: the beginnings of Savannah, conciliation of the neighbouring Indians, the details of domestic government including amicable relations with South Carolina, immigration from the Continent, the legal difficulties of tail male which was to prove sorely vexatious to prospective colonists,[5] and certain phases of what to-day would be called social service.

In creating the first municipality in the new colony, and laying it out in rigidly regular blocks, relieved only by squares, much on the old Margravate of Azilia plan, Oglethorpe achieved not the least of his many triumphs. Two of his letters to the Trustees, written in February 1733, paint the picture perfectly: While the colonists waited at Beaufort, South Carolina,

I went myself to view the Savannah River. I fixed upon a healthy Situation, about Ten Miles from the Sea. The River here forms an Half-moon, along the South side of which the

[1] Benjamin Martyn to Governor Johnson, London, Jan. 24, 1733, C.O. 5:666, pp. 3-4.
[2] *Egmont Diary*, i. 295.
[3] See C.O. 5:670, pp. 22 ff.; Candler, *Col. Rec. Ga.* xxxii. 22.
[4] McKinley, A. E., *The Suffrage Franchise in the Thirteen English Colonies in America* (Philadelphia, 1905), p. 163.
[5] *Egmont Diary*, i. 309.

GEORGIA: THE FIRST PHASE: ADMINISTRATION 133

Banks are about Forty Feet high, and on the Top a Flat, which they call a Bluff. The plain High ground extends into the Country Five or Six Miles, and along the River-side about a Mile. Ships that draw Twelve Feet Water can ride within Ten Yards of the Bank. Upon the River-side, in the Center of the Plain, I have laid out the Town, opposite to which is an Island of very rich Pasturage, which I think should be kept for the Trustees Cattle. The River is pretty wide, the Water fresh, and from the Key of the Town you see its whole Course to the Sea, with the Island of Tybee, which forms the Mouth of the River, for about Six Miles up into the Country. The Landskip is very agreeable, the Stream being wide, and bordered with high Woods on both Sides.[1]

Ten days later he added:

Our People are all in Perfect Health. I chose the Situation for the Town upon an high Ground. Forty Feet perpendicular above High-water Mark; the Soil dry and sandy, the Water of the River fresh; Springs coming out from the Sides of the Hills. I pitched upon this Place, not only for the Pleasantness of the Situation, but because from the above mentioned and other Signs, I thought it healthy; for it is sheltered from the Western and Southern Winds (the worst in this Country) by vast Woods of Pine-trees, many of which are an Hundred, and few under Seventy Feet high. There is no Morse on the Trees, tho' in most parts of Carolina they are covered with it, and it hangs down Two or Three Feet from them. The last and fullest Conviction of the Healthfulness of the Place was, that an Indian Nation, who knew the Nature of this Country, chose it for their Situation.[2]

But the proximity of the Indian proved far more vital to Oglethorpe's labours than merely to serve as a health certificate for the Savannah region.

[1] Oglethorpe to the Trustees, The Camp near Savannah, Feb. 10, 1733, C.O. 5:711, *An Account Showing the Progress of the Colony of Georgia in America from its First Establishment* (London, 1741), p. 16; Candler, *Col. Rec. Ga.* iii. 380; London *Evening Post*, April 24, 1733, p. 1.

[2] Oglethorpe to the Trustees, The Camp near Savannah, Feb. 20, 1733, C.O. 5:711, *An Account Showing the Progress of the Colony of Georgia*, pp. 16–17; Candler, *Col. Rec. Ga.* iii. 381. See also a letter, signed 'T.G.', in the London *Daily Courant*, July 9, 1733, p. 2; and the *Grub-Street Journal*, July 12, 1733, p. 3.

In his study of *American Colonial Government, 1696–1765*, Professor O. M. Dickerson has declared that 'the friendship of the southern Indians was cultivated even more assiduously than was that of the northern ones, and presents in large quantities were regularly given to the Indians on the borders of South Carolina and Georgia'.[1] In this work of pacification and proselyting, Oglethorpe did his full share. Within four months of his first arrival at Savannah, Oglethorpe, largely through the mediacy of Mary Musgrove, the half-breed wife of a white trader, was able to meet the neighbouring Yamacraws, a branch of the Creek Indians, whose chief, Tomochichi, was to be his strongest ally in the New World.[2] With him he concluded the vitally necessary convention whereby the natives not only surrendered the tract of land between the Savannah and Altamaha rivers, but also agreed to have no further communication with either the French or the Spaniards. Thus in the very beginning of the enterprise Oglethorpe effected a measure which proved of supreme value in protecting the colony from Indian attacks during the critical period of its early history. But it is also important to remember that it was due not only to his brilliant foresight but even more to his paternal kindliness, and the fact that 'he understands somewhat of their language', that Oglethorpe was able to win the affection of the Indians, who were so impressed that, in the words of Pastor Bolzius, they 'honour Mr. Oglethorpe as their Father, and ask his Advice in all their circumstances'.[3]

[1] Dickerson, O. M., *American Colonial Government, 1696–1765* (Cleveland, Ohio, 1912), p. 337.

[2] For an example of Tomochichi's loyalty see a letter from Savannah of June 25, 1733, printed in the London *Daily Courant*, Sept. 1, 1733, p. 2; *Daily Post*, Sept. 1, 1733, p. 1; *Grub-Street Journal*, Sept. 6, 1733, p. 3.

[3] Urlsperger, Samuel, editor, *Ausführliche Nachricht von den Saltzburgischen Emigranten, die sich in America niedergelassen haben* (3 vols. in 1, Halle, Germany, 1735), pp. 35, 84, 174–92; Charles Town *South Carolina Gazette*, June 2, 1733, pp. 2–3; Philadelphia *Pennsylvania Gazette*, July 5, 1733, pp. 2–3; *An Extract of the Journals of Mr. Commissary Von Reck, who conducted the First Transport of Saltzburgers to Georgia: and of the Reverend Mr. Bolzius, One of their Ministers* (S.P.C.K. London, 1734); Force, Peter, editor, *Tracts*

GEORGIA: THE FIRST PHASE: ADMINISTRATION

Shortly after he had achieved the pacification of the Indians, Oglethorpe paid a visit to Charles Town to cement relations with South Carolina. In a spirited address to the Assembly on June 9, he frankly recognized the triple threat of France, Spain, and the Indians, foretold his own early return to England, and besought South Carolina to watch over Georgia in his absence. At this time the Carolinian government gave a dinner, 'a very handsome entertainment', for Oglethorpe, who reciprocated with a ball where 'there was the greatest Appearance of People of Fashion, that has been known upon such an occasion'.[1] Although he set out for Georgia on June 10, a report had spread in the northern colonies that Oglethorpe, before sailing shortly for home, would visit New England. As a token of his repute in other sections the Massachusetts House of Representatives, remembering his parliamentary labours in their behalf, on June 19, 1733, empowered a committee to arrange a reception for him, 'that so the Government may express their grateful Sense of his good Services to the publick Interest of the Province'. Governor Jonathan Belcher, finding to his regret that 'there is no Money in the Publick Treasury to defray the Charge of the Reception and Entertainment of that Honourable Gentleman', offered him the Governor's mansion as a residence.[2] The next month the Legis-

---

and other Papers relating principally to the origin, settlement, and progress of the colonies in North America, from the discovery of the country to the year 1776 (4 vols., Washington, 1836–46), iv. 22; *Egmont Diary*, i. 364; ii. 69. For brief surveys of Oglethorpe's early Indian relations see Church, *Oglethorpe*, pp. 110–16; Macleod, *The American Indian Frontier*, p. 456; McCain, *Georgia as a Proprietary Province*, pp. 67–8; Greene, E. B., *Provincial America, 1690–1740* (The American Nation Series, vi, New York, 1905), p. 257; Coulter, E. M., 'Mary Musgrove, "Queen of the Creeks": A Chapter of Early Georgia Troubles', *Georgia Historical Quarterly*, xi. 1–30.

[1] Charles Town *South Carolina Gazette*, June 2, 1733, p. 4; July 14, 1733, pp. 1–2. The address was printed *in extenso* in the London *Daily Courant*, Sept. 7, 1733, pp. 1–2.

[2] C.O. 5:837, part iv, pp. 32, 34–5; *Journals of the House of Representatives of Massachusetts* (in progress, Boston, 1919——), xi. 245–9, 255, 280; xii. 13; C.O. 5:801, Minutes of the Massachusetts Council in Assembly, 1732–1735, pp. 22–3; Smith, 'The Belcher Papers', *Collections of the Massachusetts*

lature of 'Rhode Island and Providence Plantations' adopted a similar resolution to 'entertain him according to his quality',[1] but the entire project came to naught as a host of administrative duties forever prevented Oglethorpe from faring north of Charles Town.

The core of the problems in administration was the vital question of defence. The Indians had been pacified, but the Spaniard in Florida and, to a lesser degree, the Frenchman in Mississippi remained. The building of fortifications to protect Savannah, the creation of Fort Argyle as a southern outpost, and military activities on Saint Simon's Island, unauthorized by the Trustees, together with a rigorous training of the colonists in arms, constituted Oglethorpe's plan of defence in which he secured the hearty support of South Carolina.[2] But for this purpose the growth of the populace was equally important, and here Oglethorpe surpassed the English bureaucratic conception of colonies. As George Louis Beer showed in his survey of British colonial policy, official England opposed migration at this time so that the philanthropy was really that of Oglethorpe rather than of the government.[3] Except then for a party of 88 British subjects sent over by the Trustees in the summer of 1733,[4] Oglethorpe strove to build up Georgia with continental emigration. The art of the Amatis brothers of Savoy, Italy, in the culture of the silk-worm led Oglethorpe to find a place for them and their associates in an ill-faring project,[5] and only Georgia's rigid legal conception of

---

Historical Society, i. 273, 278, 283, 298, 390, 392, 501–2, 511; ii. 69–70; Charles Town *South Carolina Gazette*, Aug. 25, 1735, p. 3; Boston *New-England Weekly Journal*, June 25, 1733, p. 2; Sept. 3, 1733, p. 2; New York *Gazette*, July 9, 1733, p. 2.

[1] Bartlett, J. R., editor, *Records of the Colony of Rhode Island and Providence Plantations in New England* (10 vols., Providence, 1856–65), iv. 486.

[2] *Egmont Diary*, ii. 69.

[3] Beer, G. L., *British Colonial Policy, 1754–1765* (New York, 1907), pp. 133, note—134, note.

[4] *Egmont Diary*, i. 383–4.

[5] C.O. 5:689, pp. 32, 35–44; Candler, *Col. Rec. Ga.* ii. 20–3, 26–7; *Egmont Diary*, i. 309, 327, 336, 339–40, 344–7, 404; ii. 370; Hertz, G. B.,

GEORGIA: THE FIRST PHASE: ADMINISTRATION 137

inheritance by tail male prevented the migration of a group of French Vaudois Protestants after all arrangements for their departure had been made.[1] Nor was this haven of Georgia confined to Christians. Despite the prohibition of the Trustees who, when they learned the facts, strongly opposed Oglethorpe's course of action,[2] two groups of Jews came to Georgia in the summer of 1733, a number of German Jews of whom little is known, and the more illustrious body of 39 Sephardic or Portuguese Jews who, under the sound leadership of the Sheftall family and the liberal sympathy of Oglethorpe who gave them grants of land in the original division of Savannah, erected their Temple of Mickva Israel and became a potent factor in the life of the colony.[3] But far more numerous and, for Oglethorpe's immediate purpose, more important than either Savoyards or Vaudois or Jews were the Salzburger Lutherans.

There had been German Palatines in England as early as 1710,[4] but the great migrations from the Continent

'The English Silk Industry in the Eighteenth Century', *English Historical Review*, xxiv. 716.

[1] C.O. 5:689, pp. 81–2; Candler, *Col. Rec. Ga.* ii. 48; *Egmont Diary*, i. 463; ii. 42–3, 55, 75, 103–4, 106–7, 147, 184. Oglethorpe gave generous aid to the French Protestant (Huguenot) Church at Purysburg, South Carolina. Hirsch, A. H., *The Huguenots of Colonial South Carolina* (Durham, North Carolina, 1928), p. 82.

[2] 'The Trustees have heard with concern of the arrival of Forty Jews with a design to settle in Georgia. They hope they will meet with no sort of encouragement, and desire, Sir, you will use your best endeavours that the said Jews may be allowed no kind of settlement with any of the grantees, the Trustees being apprehensive they will be of prejudice to the Trade and Welfare of the Colony.' Benjamin Martyn to Oglethorpe, London, Oct. 18, 1733, C.O. 5:666, p. 41. See also C.O. 5:686, pp. 153–60; Candler, *Col. Rec. Ga.* i. 149–53. A month later, while grateful for the work of a Jewish physician in having saved many lives, the pious Trustees expressed the hope that Oglethorpe had rewarded him suitably, but with some gratuity other than 'in granting of lands'. Benjamin Martyn to Oglethorpe, London, Nov. 22, 1733, C.O. 5:666, p. 43.

[3] *Egmont Diary*, i. 440, 463; ii. 3, 55, 119, 375; Abrahams, E. H., *Some Notes on the Early History of the Sheftalls of Georgia* (Savannah, Georgia, 1909), pp. 1–6; Hühner, Leon, *The Jews of Georgia in Colonial Times* (New York, 1902), pp. 1–7.

[4] *Commons Journals*, xvi. 457; Stanhope, *History of England*, ii. 209–10.

in the name of spiritual freedom did not begin until October 1731, when Archbishop Leopold Anton of Salzburg decreed the expulsion of the Salzburger Lutherans, ten thousand of whom received a warm welcome from Frederick William I of Prussia in Regensburg and Halle, while others went to Holland and Sweden.[1] Although the Trustees had resolved not to tempt the Salzburgers to Georgia before they had first been banished from the Tyrol,[2] the welcoming gestures of the Protestant Princes of Germany caused them to invite these 41 Lutherans who, under Baron Georg Philip Friedrich von Reck,[3] Samuel Urlsperger, and Pastors John Martin Bolzius and Israel Christian Gronau of Halle, came over early in 1734, the first religious body to seek asylum in Georgia.[4] Sustained in a material sense by a portion of a parliamentary grant of £10,000,[5] the Salzburgers, according to unimpeachable and overwhelming evidence, placed all their faith in their 'oftbelobten Herr Oglethorpe', who earned their abiding devotion and gratitude by postponing his return to England in the spring of 1734 so that he might go to Charles Town to welcome these aliens in person and supply them, still on their boat, with bounteous provisions: 'A large quantity of fresh beef, two butts of wine, two tunn of spring water, cabbage,

[1] Linn, 'The Georgia Colony of Salzburgers,' pp. 24–39.

[2] The Georgia Trustees, however, according to the Earl of Harrington, Secretary at War, wanted the 'Popish part of the Magistracy of Auspurg' [Augsburg] to 'be induced' to let the Salzburgers go to Georgia. Earl of Harrington to Sir Thomas Robinson, British Ambassador at Vienna, Hampton Court, Oct. 8, 1733, Add. MSS. (British Museum), 23789, Original Letters to Sir Thomas Robinson as British Ambassador at Vienna, x. Aug.–Dec. 1733, f. 226.

[3] Baron von Reck was the son of the Hanoverian Minister to the Diet of Ratisbon, appointed by King George of England as Elector of Hanover.

[4] Add. MSS. (British Museum), 23789, Original Letters to Sir Thomas Robinson as British Ambassador at Vienna, x, ff. 228–33, 408; *Egmont Diary*, i. 302–3, 345, 463; Linn, 'The Georgia Colony of Salzburgers', pp. 40–70; Faust, A. B., *The German Element in the United States* (revised ed., 2 vols. in 1, New York, 1927), pp. 234–47.

[5] *Commons Journals*, xxii. 146, 151–2; C.O. 5:689, pp. 59, 78–9, 82–6; Candler, *Col. Rec. Ga.* ii. 35, 46, 48–50. There are no references whatsoever to Georgia in the *Lords Journals*, xxiii–xxvi. 1729–43.

turnips, radishes, fruit, &c., as a present from the Trustees to refresh the Salzburgers.'[1] And not the least among the examples of 'good will toward men' in these distant wilds was the ensuing kindness shown these Teutonic Lutherans by the Anglican rector and the Jews of Savannah.[2] Baron von Reck, as Commissary, with the practical aid of Oglethorpe,[3] soon established the town of Ebenezer, which unfortunately proved to be on barren soil in an unhealthy district, while Pastors Bolzius and Gronau, in their associations with those of diverse faiths, exhibited at all times the best principles of their preceptor, the great Halle Pietist, August Hermann Francke. Thus the Salzburgers during their first year in Georgia soon lent to the colony a certain vital stability of honest labour, military strength, and strong moral character.

The manner of inviting the Salzburgers and their importance in his defensive programme caused Oglethorpe to pay particular attention to all the colonists among whom he freely mingled, superintending their work, sharing their physical labours, caring for the sick, settling disputes, and maintaining discipline.[4] The enforcement of the law of tail male, the prohibition of negro slavery, and the almost communistic system of property rights led to a mild mutiny while Oglethorpe was in Charles Town, an uprising which was promptly quelled on his return.[5] But throughout there was a profound respect for his equity, for 'Herr Oglethorpe hält accurat

[1] 'Not enough praise can be showered on Oglethorpe for his plans.' Von Reck to Urlsperger, Dover, England, Jan. 8, 1734, Urlsperger, *Ausführliche Nachricht*, pp. 30–2, 79–80, 203, 207–8; Linn, 'The Georgia Colony of Salzburgers', pp. 62, 67; *Egmont Diary*, ii. 104; Charles Town *South Carolina Gazette*, March 23, 1734, p. 2; C.O. 5:686, p. 137; Candler, *Col. Rec. Ga.* i. 139–40; *Extracts of the Journals of Mr. Commissary Von Reck . . . and Reverend Mr. Bolzius*, Force, *Tracts*, iv. 8–9, 11, 26.

[2] Urlsperger, *Ausführliche Nachricht*, p. 82; Linn, 'The Georgia Colony of Salzburgers', pp. 67–9; Hühner, *The Jews of Georgia in Colonial Times*, pp. 11–12.

[3] Oglethorpe had done his work 'by the explorations of a General, rather than from the swivel chair of a Governor'. Linn, 'The Georgia Colony of Salzburgers', p. 72; Charles Town *South Carolina Gazette*, March 30, 1734, p. 2.

[4] Osgood, *The American Colonies in the Eighteenth Century*, i. 49.

[5] *Egmont Diary*, i. 440, 451.

über Recht und Gerechtigkeit';[1] and evidences of his interest in his people abound in the journals and letters of the two Lutheran leaders who recurrently recorded their gratitude for what Pastor Bolzius called Oglethorpe's 'Fatherly Care',[2] so that at times almost every other paragraph of the *Ausführliche Nachricht* contained an allusion to their hero.[3] When therefore in 1734 his imminent departure was rumoured, it was little wonder that von Reck recorded in his journal the sorrow of the Salzburgers at the prospect of losing one 'who had carefully watched over them as a good Shepherd does over his Flock, and who had had so tender a Care of them, both by Day and by Night; and they were afflicted, that the Fatigues and Difficulties of so long a Voyage left them very small Hopes of seeing Him again'.[4]

Oglethorpe's position in the colony during this first year has been a subject for conflicting opinions. Despite Percival's notation in his diary that he was to be 'Governor',[5] Professor Osgood has claimed that, 'on his first visit, Oglethorpe's relations to the colony were temporary and informal', with a reminder that 'he accompanied the expedition voluntarily, paying his own expenses and taking with him no distinctly official commission'.[6] While Dr. McKinley has admitted that 'it is difficult to define the authority as exercised' by him,[7] Dr. McCain has asserted that Oglethorpe was needed as an unofficial guiding hand, but was not expected to stay long in the colony. 'He was not a governor under the Trustees, but their Attorney to act in their stead' with powers limited

---

[1] Urlsperger, *Ausführliche Nachricht*, p. 91.
[2] *Extracts of the Journal of the Reverend Mr. Bolzius*, Force, *Tracts*, iv. 23.
[3] Urlsperger, *Ausführliche Nachricht*, pp. 84–91, 112–13, 174–8.
[4] *Extracts of the Journal of Mr. Commissary Von Reck*, Force, *Tracts*, iv. 13.
[5] *Egmont Diary*, i. 293.
[6] Osgood, *The American Colonies in the Eighteenth Century*, iii. 49. For a similar view as to 'informal government' in Georgia see Greene, E. B., *The Provincial Governor in the English Colonies of North America* (New York, 1907), p. 39.
[7] McKinley, *The Suffrage Franchise in the Thirteen English Colonies in America*, p. 164.

GEORGIA: THE FIRST PHASE: ADMINISTRATION 141

to specific matters.[1] In short, it seems, in the words of Professor Channing, that Oglethorpe, without due authorization, 'exercised paternal power over the settlers, acting as judge, lawgiver, and defender'.[2] Despite both these strictures on his assumption of broad prerogatives, James Oglethorpe's first period in Georgia, if judged by the comment of the press and the majority of colonists, was an unquestionable success. Within six weeks after his arrival, a South Carolina visitor, noting that he was using as a guide Sir Walter Raleigh's journal of over a century before, was inspired to this paean of praise in the Charles Town *Gazette*:

> Mr. Oglethorpe is indefatigable; takes a vast deal of Pains; his Fare is but indifferent, having little else, at present, but salt provisions; he's extreamly well beloved by all his People: The general Title they give him, is FATHER: If any of them is sick, he immediately visits them and takes a great deal of Care of them: If any Difference arises, he's the Person that decides it. ... He keeps a strict Discipline. ... In short, He has done a vast deal of Work for the Time; and, I think, his NAME justly deserves to be *Immortalized*.[3]

During the ensuing year this opinion was confirmed in a plenitude of evidence from the expressions of both Salzburgers and Indians; and in England the attitude of the press was indicated in this striking statement in *Hooker's Weekly Miscellany*:

> The Planting of Colonies is of such publick Utility, that we think we cannot do anything more acceptable, than to take Notice of all that occurs material on such Occasions. The new one in GEORGIA, carry'd on with so much Chearfulness and Ardour by the honourable Trustees appointed for that Purpose, claims our particular Attention; and we have therefore, from time to time, inserted such Accounts as have come to Hand in relation thereto.[4]

[1] McCain, *Georgia as a Proprietary Province*, pp. 63, 65.
[2] Channing, E., *A History of the United States* (7 vols., New York, 1904–32), ii. 363.
[3] Charles Town *South Carolina Gazette*, March 24, 1733, p. 3.
[4] London *Hooker's Weekly Miscellany*, Dec. 1, 1733, p. 3.

This journal reprinted the observations of the South Carolinian[1] and in 1734 the opinion from Savannah that 'I want Words to express what we owe to the indefatigable Care and Pains of Mr. *Oglethorpe*'.[2] The good esteem in which Oglethorpe was held in no wise diminished for when, early in 1734, Peter Gordon, a chief magistrate of Georgia, came to England for a surgical operation, Egmont noted in his diary that Gordon told the Trustees 'a great deal of Mr. Oglethorpe's indefatigable zeal in carrying on our affairs, conducting the building of the town, keeping peace, laying out lands, supplying the stores with provision, encouraging the fainthearted, etc.' Although Savannah already had forty houses for its population of over 400 souls, 'Mr. Oglethorpe still lay in the tent set up before the houses were built'. Above all, Gordon emphasized the fact that Oglethorpe was largely responsible for the friendship of the Indians, for the pure water supply of the colony, and for that crowning asset of a community: 'That when he came away, the people were healthy and orderly.'[3]

When, therefore, in March 1734 Oglethorpe departed for England, he left not only a group of soldiers and colonists, pitched amid the forests on the banks of the Savannah River, but a total of eleven communities, of which Savannah, the largest, containing half the population of Georgia, was a town neatly laid out with particular emphasis on gardens and with ample provision for streets, cemetery, church, houses, water supply, and the means of navigable communications with both other villages and the homeland.[4] Spending virtually all his time in the north, Oglethorpe had indeed created what

---

[1] London *Hooker's Weekly Miscellany*, June 2, 1733, p. 2.
[2] Ibid., Jan. 19, 1734, p. 2.   [3] *Egmont Diary*, ii. 36–7.
[4] Ibid., ii. 111–12. The Georgia of the first two years has been described by Francis Moore in *A New Voyage to Georgia* (London, 1735), reprinted in *Collections of the Georgia Historical Society*, ii. 37–60. For a good, impartial, contemporary account of Georgia see Oldmixon, J., *The British Empire in America* (2nd ed., 2 vols., London, 1741), i. 525–41. See also Wright, Richardson, *The Story of Gardening* (New York, 1934), p. 335.

Benjamin Martyn had envisioned: Savannah as 'the metropolis of the country'.[1]

While Oglethorpe had thus continued to labour in Georgia, even when at times ill—either from fever or from the effects of falling from his horse among some canes, three of which entered his body[2]—Percival, now become Earl of Egmont, had filled an equally important post at home. He it was who conceived, presented, and, at times, wellnigh fought for the annual petitions to Parliament seeking further grants of £10,000 and more in aid of the project; and even when Oglethorpe was available to lead the fight for more funds, it was Egmont's keen mind which planned how best to spend the proceeds![3] Throughout the history of the great emprise Egmont's diary reveals an abiding attention to the diverse domestic details of the trust which at all times equalled and often surpassed that of his colleague in the colony.[4]

Despite numerous private contributions, such as £50 from Governor Johnson of South Carolina and £100 with a shipload of bread and flour from Governor Thomas Penn of Pennsylvania,[5] the Trustees were harassed by a constant need of money which sorely worried Egmont and led to repeated, almost annual, requests to Walpole and the government for a grant of £10,000.[6] Coupled with this was the allied problem of meeting the numerous drafts which Oglethorpe drew on the Trustees without first advising them of his intentions. Although he was roundly scored for this 'negligence', the Trustees were

[1] Benjamin Martyn to Oglethorpe, London, June 13, 1733, C.O. 5:666, p. 29. As one of the Georgia colonists, William Bateman, duly emphasized to the Trustees in 1734: 'Philadelphia was 10 or 12 years before it could boast of such a Towne as Georgia is at Present'. William Bateman to the Trustees, Savannah, Sept. 3, 1734, C.O. 5:636, part i, f. 21 verso.
[2] *Egmont Diary*, i. 372, 451, 476.
[3] Ibid. ii. 166.
[4] Ibid. i–iii, *passim*.
[5] Ibid. i. 304, 372; Samuel Eveleigh to Oglethorpe, Charles Town, South Carolina, Aug. 21, 1734, C.O. 5:636, ff. 12–13; C.O. 5:686, pp. 50, 87–8; Candler, *Col. Rec. Ga.* i. 92, 114.
[6] *Egmont Diary*, i. 310, 364, 366, 372–4.

compelled to honour these drafts to prevent their going to protest which, Egmont was convinced, 'would have brought great scandal on our Colony'.[1] In addition to these financial problems, a serious situation now arose, caused, first, by an utter lack of interest on the part of numerous Trustees, and second, by complaints on the part of James Vernon, one of the most important Trustees, concerning 'the neglect Mr. Oglethorpe shows in not corresponding with us frequently, and thereby keeping us in great ignorance of his proceedings'.[2] The combined problems of weak finances, lack of interest by Trustees, and seeming negligence in Georgia by their leader, beckoned Oglethorpe to England in March 1734, a voyage which had been rumoured in July 1733.[3]

Although there was a sound, solid, substantial foundation of character and high purpose in James Oglethorpe, he also possessed the keen qualities of the showman, and so it is not particularly surprising that when, on March 23, 1734, he left Savannah in the man-of-war, *Aldborough*, and finally set out from Charles Town on May 7 to meet the complaints of his fellow Trustees in London, he took with him some samples of the finest native products of Georgia: Tomochichi, the ninety-year-old Chief of the Yamacraw Indians, his wife, his heir and grand-nephew, and five stalwarts of his tribe. The ostensible purpose of their visit was 'to learn English and the Christian religion and to confirm the peace' between Indians and Englishmen, but the novelty of their presence became a potent though sometimes mute factor in further parliamentary appropriations.[4]

On June 16, 1734, Oglethorpe arrived off the Isle of Wight, made a hasty visit to Godalming, and by the

---

[1] *Egmont Diary*, ii. 23, 29, 41.
[2] Ibid. 41, 55; Benjamin Martyn to Oglethorpe, London, March 25, 1734, C.O. 5:666, p. 49.
[3] *Egmont Diary*, i. 389; ii. 3. As early as June 15, 1733, Benjamin Martyn had asked Oglethorpe how long he expected to remain in Georgia. Benjamin Martyn to Oglethorpe, London, June 15, 1733, C.O. 5:666, p. 32.
[4] *Egmont Diary*, ii. 112–14, 117, 119–27.

evening of June 20 was in London, where the reaction to his appearance with the Indians was characterized by a 'grand entertainment' by the Trustees, 'and the Night concluded with Ringing of Bells, a Bonfire, and other Demonstrations of Joy and Gratitude'.[1] A superb set of apartments at the Georgia Office had been furnished for the Indians,[2] who during the next three months were fêted and lionized by the King, the Archbishop of Canterbury, and Sir Hans Sloane, escorted to Bartholomew Fair, to china shop and theatre, honoured with reviews in Hyde Park and taken sightseeing on an itinerary which reads like a Cook's Tour of London,[3] taken to Eton,[4] and, in one case at least, almost literally 'killed with kindness'. Not only were they shown historic England but they themselves were on display. A contemporary account of their presentation to the royal household at Kensington has been preserved, the narrative of which amply sustains Oglethorpe's faith in the tact and delicate finesse of these so-called savages who time and again impressed upon their hosts their own unfeigned esteem and affection for their mentor.[5] Tomochichi, whose courage weakened

[1] London *Daily Journal*, June 19, 1734, p. 1; June 20, 1734, p. 1; *Grub-Street Journal*, June 20, 1734, p. 2; *Weekly Journal*, June 22, 1734, p. 3; *Hooker's Weekly Miscellany*, June 22, 1734, p. 3; *Evening Post*, June 22, 1734, p. 2.
[2] London *London Journal*, June 22, 1734, p. 2; June 29, 1734, p. 2; *Daily Journal*, June 27, 1734, p. 2; Boston *Weekly News Letter*, Sept. 26, 1734, p. 1.
[3] Harman Verelst to Sir Hans Sloane, London, Oct. 1, 1734, Sloane MSS. (British Museum), 4053, f. 277; London *Daily Courant*, Aug. 11, 1734, p. 2; Aug. 20, 1734, p. 2; Sept. 1, 1734; Oct. 7, 1734, p. 2; Oct. 22, 1734, p. 2; *Daily Journal*, July 16, 1734, p. 2; July 24, 1734, p. 2; July 25, 1734, p. 1; Aug. 13, 1734, p. 1; *Evening Post*, Aug. 20, 1734, p. 2; *Hooker's Weekly Miscellany*, Aug. 10, 1734, p. 3; Oct. 26, 1734, p. 3; *Grub-Street Journal*, July 18, 1734, p. 2; Oct. 24, 1734, p. 2.
[4] London *London Journal*, Sept. 21, 1734, p. 3. For a Latin poem by Richard West on the visit of the Indians to Eton College see Toynbee, Paget, editor, *The Correspondence of Gray, Walpole, West and Ashton* (2 vols., Oxford, 1915), ii. 303–6.
[5] Alured Clarke to Viscountess Sundon, Kensington-Square, Aug. 3, 1734, Add. MSS. (British Museum), 20102, Letters received by Charlotte, Viscountess Sundon, i, ff. 116–17; Thomson, Mrs., editor, *Memoirs of Viscountess Sundon* (2 vols., London, 1847), ii. 264–7; London *London Journal*, July 20, 1734, p. 2; Aug. 3, 1734, p. 2; *Gentleman's Magazine*, iv. 329.

only before the 'Magick Lanthorn',[1] frankly told the Trustees that he would not have crossed the Atlantic 'but for the sake of Mr. Oglethorp, whom he could trust and had used them kindly';[2] when some of the Indians became ill in London, Oglethorpe sent his personal friend, the great physician, Sir Hans Sloane, to minister unto them;[3] and upon the death of one from smallpox, 'they went to Mr. Oglethorpe's in Surrey to dissipate their sorrow'.[4] It was therefore small wonder that on October 30, when they set out for Gravesend to board the *Prince of Wales* bound for Georgia, Tomochichi besought Oglethorpe to accompany them, affirming that he was very glad to return home, but to part with Oglethorpe 'was like the day of death'.[5]

But if the Indians proved to be the stellar attraction Oglethorpe himself was not forgotten, either by the King who pored over charts and maps with him,[6] or the Queen, interested in the silk products of the colony, or by press and public. Characterized as 'a Roman hero',[7] 'a Gentleman whose singular Services to his Country, by his indefatigable Pains in settling the new Colony of Georgia, will render him ever famous in English History',[8] Ogle-

[1] Boston *Weekly News Letter*, Nov. 8, 1734, p. 1.
[2] *Egmont Diary*, ii. 114; C.O. 5:686, pp. 195-6; Candler, *Col. Rec. Ga.* i. 177-8. [3] *Egmont Diary*, ii. 118.
[4] Ibid. ii. 120; London *Daily Journal*, Aug. 5, 1734, p. 1; Aug. 8, 1734, p. 1; *Daily Courant*, Aug. 8, 1734, p. 2; *Grub-Street Journal*, Aug. 8, 1734, p. 2; *Evening Post*, Aug. 10, 1734, p. 2; *London Journal*, Aug. 10, 1734, p. 2.
[5] *Egmont Diary*, ii. 126, 132; C.O. 5:686, pp. 207-8, 217; Candler, *Col. Rec. Ga.* i. 184-5. Tomochichi 'showed a great deal of tenderness' in his farewell to Oglethorpe. London *Evening Post*, Nov. 5, 1734, p. 3. Philip Thicknesse had a profound regard for Tomochichi, whose ethical qualities he considered far superior to those of many Christians. Thicknesse, Philip, *A Year's Journey Through France and Part of Spain* (3rd ed., 2 vols., London, 1789), i. 36-7. A modern commentator suggests that Tomochichi, although never in Ireland, must have kissed the Blarney Stone! Roberts, 'The Birth of an American State', *Transactions of the Royal Historical Society*, 4th series, vi. 45.
[6] London *Evening Post*, July 23, 1734, p. 2; *Grub-Street Journal*, July 25, 1734, p. 2; *London Journal*, July 27, 1734, p. 2.
[7] Boyer, *Political State of Great Britain*, xlviii. 19-20.
[8] London *Daily Courant*, June 19, 1734, p. 2.

THE GEORGIA COUNCIL

from the copy by A. E. DYER of W. VERELST's painting, now hanging in
Rhodes Memorial Hall, Atlanta, Georgia

GEORGIA: THE FIRST PHASE: ADMINISTRATION 147

thorpe was welcomed, in Professor Osgood's phrase, both now and again in 1737 'with odes and ascriptions not only from the pen of Pope and Thomson, but in terms of most extravagant eulogy from many an anonymous writer in the public prints',[1] much of which found its way into the *Gentleman's Magazine*.[2] At this time also the Trustees not only returned their thanks to him 'for the many and great Services he has done the Colony of Georgia',[3] but even launched a new ship of 250 tons 'which was called the *Oglethorpe*' at Rotherhithe,[4] while the Town Council of Inverness made him a burgess by proxy,[5] and his likeness graced a prize medal, proposed by Sylvanus Urban of the *Gentleman's Magazine*.[6] Professor McCain could thus well conclude that 'his one year of labors in Georgia had gained for him more consideration and honor than he could have won from decades of service in Parliament or from a whole life of mingling in the society of the times'.[7]

It was at this time also that Oglethorpe expanded his humanitarian interests to include the sons of Ham. On December 31, 1730, he had been elected to the Court of Assistants, or Directorate, of the Royal African Company for the next year, and on January 27, 1732, having qualified by the purchase of £1,000 worth of stock, was made

---

[1] Osgood, *The American Colonies in the Eighteenth Century*, iii. 37.

[2] e.g. iv. 505, 'To the Honourable James Oglethorpe. On His Return from Georgia.' For other poetry see Thomson, James, *Liberty*, part v, lines 638–46; Fitzgerald, Thomas, *Georgia: A Poem*, and an ode on Tomochichi; and Pope, *Imitations of Horace*. For Thomson and Pope see Nichols, *Literary Anecdotes of the Eighteenth Century*, ii. 23, note. In Austin Dobson's opinion, Pope's lines have 'done more to preserve the memory of the founder of Georgia than all the records of the Office at Westminster'. Dobson, *A Paladin of Philanthropy*, p. 17.

[3] C.O. 5:686, p. 192; Candler, *Col. Rec. Ga.* i. 175.

[4] London *Weekly Journal*, June 29, 1734, p. 2; *London Journal*, June 29, 1734, p. 2; *Grub-Street Journal*, July 4, 1734, p. 2; Boston *Weekly News Letter*, Sept. 26, 1734, p. 1.

[5] George Dunbar to Oglethorpe, Inverness, Sept. 20, 1735, C.O. 5:638, f. 38; Candler, *Col. Rec. Ga.* xxi. 20–1; Stevens, *History of Georgia*, i. 127.

[6] *Gentleman's Magazine*, v. 778. See also vi. 99.

[7] McCain, *Georgia as a Proprietary Province*, p. 71.

Deputy Governor. As a director Oglethorpe served on the finance committee and had some little correspondence with the Joar Factory in Gambia, Africa. Whether because of his opposition to negro slavery or for some other reason, Oglethorpe, on December 21, 1732, sold his stock and retired from active participation in company affairs, but in May 1733 became bondsman for a negro in a most interesting case. In 1730 Job ben Solomon, or Job Jalla, as he was generally known, had been seized in Gambia as a slave and taken to Maryland whence, in 1732, he escaped, only to be recaptured. Job Jalla now indited an Arabic epistle to his father in Africa which, passing into the hands of officials of the Royal African Company in London, ultimately came to Oglethorpe's attention. The latter sent it to Oxford University for translation, which yielded such a pitiful story of homesickness that Oglethorpe guaranteed all expenses to bring Job to London, where he arrived in April 1733. As a Mohammedan Job proved sufficiently expert in Arabic to win the warm praise of Sir Hans Sloane whom with others he served well until in July 1734, while Oglethorpe was in England, Job Jalla was returned to his Gambian home, laden with gifts from his English friends. If Oglethorpe was humane, his protégé was grateful and, through Francis Moore in 1735 and again in letters to Sir Hans Sloane in 1734 and 1737, showed that he never forgot.[1]

[1] T. 70 (Treasury Papers: Royal African Company, P.R.O.): 93, Minute Book of the Court of Assistants of the Royal African Company of England, xx, 1728–1735, pp. 119, 121–64, 168, 180, 189–90, 194–5, 200, 232, 243; T. 70:104, Minutes of the Committee of Seven, ii, 1727–1731, pp. 289–331; T. 70:182, Balances of Stock; T. 70: 215, Stock Journal, 1727–1751, pp. 55, 72, 84; T. 70:239, Cash Book, 1731–1741, pp. 17, 19; Job Solomon to Sir Hans Sloane, James Fort, Rio Gambia, Dec. 8, 1734; Sloane MSS. (British Museum), 4053, Original Letters to Sir Hans Sloane, f. 341; London *Daily Journal,* Jan. 20, 1731, p. 1; *Daily Post,* Jan. 20, 1731, p. 1; *Weekly Journal,* Jan. 23, 1731, p. 3; *Monthly Chronicle,* iv, no. 1, p. 5; Jalla, Job, *Memoirs* (London, 1734), pp. 423–5; Moore, Francis, *Travels into the Inland parts of Africa; containing a description of several nations for the space of 600 miles upon the river Gambia; with a particular account of Job Ben Solomon, a Pholey, who was in England in 1733, and known by the name of 'the African Prince'* (London, 1738), reprinted in Donnan, Elizabeth, editor, *Documents Illustra-*

But while this visit to England was replete with an exhibition of Indians, a manifestation of humanitarian instincts towards the Negro, and a shower of journalistic and literary bouquets, Oglethorpe's real mission was being performed, quietly but regularly and scrupulously, in the House of Commons and at the head-quarters of the Trustees in Old Palace Yard, Westminster. Not only did he present his financial statement[1] and organize a counter-propaganda to overcome the hostile reports on Georgia conditions spread by Thomas Lowndes[2] and criticism of the Salzburgers emanating from a discontented cleric named Fullerton; he did far more. On March 10, 1735, he personally presented to the House of Commons the annual appeal of the Trustees for an appropriation, stressing neither religion nor the support of the poor, nor yet the defence against the Spaniard, but the grave danger emanating from the French settlement at 'Moville', or Mobile on the Mississippi. He knew that King George was favourable to the Georgia enterprise and he had won the Queen by the presentation of a dress, made from thirty pounds of raw Georgia silk and woven by Sir Thomas Lamb on his new machines.[3] By emphasizing the fear of France, which held the government enthralled, Oglethorpe was able to gain a grant of £25,800 with which to build a chain of twenty forts. Urged to accept the governorship of South Carolina, he declined out of

tive of the History of the Slave Trade to America (in progress, Washington, 1930———), ii. 393–419, particularly 403, note—404, note, 415–16, 419, 423–7, 455. See also *MSS. of the Duke of Buccleuch and Queensberry* (H.M.C. Reports), i. 389; *Gentleman's Magazine*, i. 27; ii. 584; vi. 681; Nichols, *Literary Anecdotes of the Eighteenth Century*, v. 91; Harris, T. M., *Biographical Memorials of James Oglethorpe, Founder of the Colony of Georgia, in North America* (Boston, 1841), pp. 24–37; Bruce, *James Edward Oglethorpe*, pp. 132–8.

[1] C.O. 5:689, pp. 151–2; Candler, *Col. Rec. Ga.* ii. 115–17.

[2] *Journal of the Commissioners for Trade and Plantations*, vi. 347.

[3] London *Grub-Street Journal*, April 10, 1735, p. 2; *Hooker's Weekly Miscellany*, April 12, 1735, p. 3; Aug. 16, 1735, p. 3; *Evening Post*, Aug. 14, 1735, p. 2; *General Evening Post*, Sept. 2, 1735, p. 1. At the King's birthday reception on Oct. 30, 1735, the Queen wore her dress of Georgia silk which 'was universally acknowledg'd to excel that of any other Country'. London *Universal Spectator*, Nov. 1, 1735, p. 2.

regard for the incumbent, that great friend of Georgia, Robert Johnson, but he did accept the command of the joint militia[1] and was made commissioner for administering the act for maintaining peace with the Indians.[2]

Although some Trustees had retired from the Board and still more had become but passive members, Egmont by March 1733 had succeeded in securing the requisite number of Trustees, a representative body including the Earls of Shaftesbury, Tyrconnel and Derby, and Viscount Limerick.[3] Oglethorpe's return and the presence of the Indians had, temporarily at least, revived the falling attendance at the Trustees' meetings,[4] so that it was possible for the Board, largely at Oglethorpe's instigation, in April 1735 to enact the most vital three laws in the proprietary history of Georgia. While no prohibitionists as to good old English ale, the Trustees were strongly opposed to 'excessive Drinking of Rum', to which they ascribed most of the evils which ever beset the colony, and the letters of the Trustees to Oglethorpe and others in the colony during his first residence there plainly indicated their position.[5] In accordance then with both their views and his own as expressed in Parliament in 1730, Oglethorpe now renewed his adherence to temperance rather than total abstinence in supporting the law to prohibit the sale of rum in Georgia. In urging the enactment of the second law, that prohibiting negro slavery in the colony, James Oglethorpe, the Director and Deputy Governor of the Royal African Company and emancipator of Job Jalla, became a forerunner of Abraham Lincoln.[6] The third measure, for 'maintaining

[1] *Egmont Diary*, ii. 157-9, 162, 165-6, 168, 187, 191, 387.
[2] C.O. 5:689, pp. 205-6, 211; Candler, *Col. Rec. Ga.* ii. 120.
[3] *Egmont Diary*, i. 343; C.O. 5:689, pp. 38-41; Candler, *Col. Rec. Ga.* ii. 36-7. [4] *Egmont Diary*, ii. 112.
[5] Benjamin Martyn and Harman Verelst to Oglethorpe and others, London, Nov. 22, 1733, July 27, Oct. 28, 1734, May 15, 1735, C.O. 5:666, pp. 42-4, 61-6, 68-76, 104; C.O. 5:689, p. 80; Candler, *Col. Rec. Ga.* ii. 47; Charles Town *South Carolina Gazette*, Aug. 25, 1733, p. 1.
[6] The Trustees' preference for white servants, rather than negro slaves, was a matter of expediency and economics rather than ethics. See Benjamin

GEORGIA: THE FIRST PHASE: ADMINISTRATION 151

Peace with the Indians in the Province of Georgia', dealt with the Indians and South Carolina, and was the result of an anomalous situation, growing out of South Carolina's fear, not only of the Spaniard in Florida, but more so of the French at 'Moville', whose potent influence on the neighbouring Indians compelled the Carolinians to ask for a greater share of the Indian trade in sheer self-defence.[1] In order to meet this issue, Oglethorpe, in April 1735, advocated the last of the three new laws, one which regulated peaceful dealings with the Indians, providing for a system to license traders which was later to cause inter-colonial strife with South Carolina.[2] As Professor Osgood so well concluded, these three pieces of legislation as supported by Oglethorpe 'expressed to the full the idealism which animated him, but they were so far in advance of conditions at the time and place as to be unpractical and to serve mainly as subjects of controversy'.[3]

The rumblings of an imminent dispute with South Carolina, reports of insurrections in Georgia, complaints against Noble Jones, surveyor of the colony, and Thomas Causton, the storekeeper, together with personal matters, all served to hasten Oglethorpe's return to Georgia after a series of lengthy Trustees' meetings, wherein appro-

Martyn to Samuel Eveleigh, London, May 1, 1735, C.O. 5:666, p. 113. It is interesting to note, however, that white and Indian servitude remained a practice in Georgia after those forms had passed in the other colonies. Osgood, *The American Colonies in the Eighteenth Century*, ii. 486; Lauber, A. W., *Indian Slavery in Colonial Times within the Present Limits of the United States* (Columbia University Studies in History, Economics and Public Law, liv, New York, 1913), p. 108.

[1] Petition of the Assembly of South Carolina to the King, Charles Town, April 9, 1734, C.O. 5:363, ff. 91–6; C.O. 5:383, f. 13; S.C. Rec. xvi. ff. 388–401.

[2] C.O. 391 (Journal of the Board of Trade, P.R.O.): 44, ff. 20, 24, 26, 33; S.C. Rec. xvii, ff. 256, 277, 279. For these measures see the printed texts in C.O. 5:365, ff. 164–77; and in manuscript in C.O. 5:681; also Candler, *Col. Rec. Ga.* i. 31–55, 197–8. See also *Journal of the Commissioners for Trade and Plantations*, vii, 1735–1741, pp. 6–7, 9, 23; *Egmont Diary*, ii. 171; C.O. 5:689, p. 167; Candler, *Col. Rec. Ga.* ii. 96–7.

[3] Osgood, *The American Colonies in the Eighteenth Century*, iii. 49–50.

priations were budgeted, the number of various emigrant groups fixed, and the discovery of a new herb from Georgia—'the true balsam copivi and the Ipecacuanha root'—noted for a report to that inveterate collector, Sir Hans Sloane.[1] On September 25 Oglethorpe gave a farewell dinner to 'the Agents of the several British Colonies on the Continent of America' who were 'splendidly entertain'd at Pontack's';[2] on the twenty-ninth he took leave of the Queen;[3] and at 9 a.m. on October 14, 1735, after a visit to the mother country of a year and a half, which, however, could hardly be termed a holiday, James Oglethorpe set out from Westminster for Cowes to join the good ship, *Simmonds*, bound for his beloved Georgia.[4]

[1] *Egmont Diary*, ii. 164, 172, 183, 186, 200; James Oglethorpe to Sir Hans Sloane, Savannah, Sept. 19, 1733, Sloane MSS. (British Museum), 4053, f. 53.
[2] London *Daily Journal*, Sept. 27, 1735, p. 2.
[3] London *Daily Post*, Sept. 30, 1735, p. 1.
[4] *Egmont Diary*, ii. 200; London *Hooker's Weekly Miscellany*, Oct. 18, 1735, p. 3.

CHAPTER VI

GEORGIA: THE SECOND PHASE: RELIGION

At Cowes Oglethorpe found assembled the largest party ever to sail as a unit for Georgia, numbering 257 souls. As was so often the case, contrary winds prevented their departure throughout the remainder of October and well into November. On November 19 Oglethorpe to Verelst from 'Cows Road': 'I hope by the Blessing of God we shall be able to go thro' the Undertaking.'[1] But before a move could be made, three more weeks passed in delay which, according to Francis Moore, was 'tedious and expensive'.[2] On December 3, after a fever which had sent him to bed, Oglethorpe, in sheer desperation, avowed that 'I had rather have run the danger of my life at sea than have risqued the losing of the season of the year in Georgia and the sickness which may probably happen to the people by lying here. Some are already ill!' But his zeal to leave was continually thwarted by the refusal of the ship's captain to venture forth in unfavourable weather.[3] A week later the party, having embarked in two small vessels, had journeyed as far as the Needles whence Oglethorpe sent back a final message: 'God be praised we at last have got an Easterly Wind in the morning.'[4]

The tribulations of transatlantic travel two centuries ago have been recorded by Francis Moore and in the diaries of John Wesley, Benjamin Ingham, David Nitschmann, and John Andrew Dober. From the moment the

[1] Oglethorpe to Harman Verelst, 'Cows Road', Nov. 19, 1735, C.O. 5:638, ff. 92–3; *Collections of the Georgia Historical Society*, iii. 3.
[2] Moore, Francis, 'A Voyage to Georgia in 1735', *Collections of the Georgia Historical Society*, i (Savannah, 1840), 85–7.
[3] Oglethorpe to Verelst, Cowes, Dec. 3, 1735, C.O. 5:638, ff. 98–9; Candler, *Col. Rec. Ga.* xxi. 49–52; *Collections of the Georgia Historical Society*, iii. 5–7.
[4] Oglethorpe to Verelst, The Needles, Dec. 10, 1735, C.O. 5:638, f. 101; Candler, *Col. Rec. Ga.* xxi. 52–4; *Egmont Diary*, ii. 198, 200–9.

ships left Cowes the passage was most unpleasant. As Wesley's journal noted, 'the Waves of the Sea were mighty and raged horribly. They rose up to the Heavens above, and clave down to Hell beneath.'[1] Although himself still a convalescent from the fever which had confined him at Cowes,[2] Oglethorpe, as so many have testified, repeatedly watched through the long hours of the night at the side of some sick emigrant.[3] According to Ingham's journal, Oglethorpe

> himself went several times about the ship to comfort and encourage the people; and, indeed, he has never been wanting in this respect. He is a pattern of fatherly care and tender compassion, being always ready, night and day, to give up his own ease and convenience to serve the poorest body among the people. He seldom eats above once a day, and then he usually chooses salt provisions (though not so agreeable to his health), that he might give the fresh to the sick.

He insisted that Mrs. Welch, a prospective mother, be moved to his own cabin where he 'constantly supplied her with all the best things in the ship'. Despite the general belief that 'she'd die', Oglethorpe alone 'continued in hope', and she survived.[4] When the rude sailors wished to make sport of those passengers who never before had experienced the ministrations of King Neptune, Oglethorpe, in humanity towards the sick, forbade it, and when, owing to the scarcity of good water, the crew discriminated against certain poor emigrants, the great-hearted leader

---

[1] Curnock, *John Wesley's Journal*, i. 141. For confirmation of this from the Nitschmann and Dober diaries see Fries, Adelaide L., *The Moravians in Georgia, 1735–1740* (Raleigh, North Carolina, 1905), pp. 110–19.

[2] *Egmont Diary*, ii. 212; Curnock, *John Wesley's Journal*, i. 123–4, 133, 138; Fries, *The Moravians in Georgia*, p. 108; Oglethorpe to Verelst, Cowes, Dec. 3, 1735, C.O. 5:638, ff. 99–100; Candler, *Col. Rec. Ga.* xxi. 51.

[3] Moore, 'A Voyage to Georgia', *Collections of the Georgia Historical Society*, i. 88; Curnock, *John Wesley's Journal*, i. 132–8; Fries, *The Moravians in Georgia*, p. 102: Nitschmann's diary; *Gentleman's Magazine*, vi. 229.

[4] The Journal of Reverend Benjamin Ingham, Tyerman, L., *The Oxford Methodists* (New York, 1873), pp. 61–81, especially p. 72. See also Curnock, *John Wesley's Journal*, i. 132.

GEORGIA: THE SECOND PHASE: RELIGION 155

ordered all to be treated alike.[1] It was therefore little wonder that John Wesley was so impressed as to declare: 'We can't be sufficiently thankful to God for Mr. Oglethorpe's presence with us';[2] for this was but one of the reasons why the colonial records of Georgia abound in letters by the colonists eulogizing his vast humanity whether on surging seas or in the forest primeval.[3]

Despite the rigours of the crossing, the band of emigrants arrived safely at Savannah on February 6, 1736, 'to the Inexpressible joy of all the Inhabitants' who, like Thomas Causton, marvelled at 'the Repeated Success which Imediately attends Mr. Oglethorp's unwearied Endeavours'.[4] Their welcome included warm greetings from Lieutenant-Governor Broughton and both the Council and Assembly of South Carolina;[5] and it was with pardonable pride that Oglethorpe wrote home to the Trustees: 'God be praised all the people are in Health, nor has one passenger died at Sea.'[6] The next day an anonymous correspondent of the *Gentleman's Magazine* confirmed this, adding some strong commendation of Oglethorpe:

Tho' we had a long and very stormy passage, yet we arrived without the loss of a Soul out of any of our ships. . . . Mr. Oglethorpe, during the Passage, was extremely careful both of the Souls and Bodies under his care; but what surprizes me beyond Expression, is his abstemious and hard living, for, tho' even

[1] Nitschmann and Dober diaries, Fries, *The Moravians in Georgia*, pp. 112–13.
[2] Telford, J., editor, *The Letters of the Rev. John Wesley, A.M.* (8 vols., London, 1931), i. 193–4.
[3] C.O. 5:638–41, *passim*; Candler, *Col. Rec. Ga.* xxi–xxv, *passim*.
[4] Thomas Causton to the Trustees, Savannah, March 10, 1736, C.O. 5:638, f. 227; Candler, *Col. Rec. Ga.* xxi. 125.
[5] Lieutenant-Governor Thomas Broughton to Oglethorpe, Charles Town, Feb. 11, 1736, the Council of South Carolina to Oglethorpe, Charles Town, Feb. 11, 1736, the Assembly of South Carolina to Oglethorpe, Charles Town, Feb. 11, 1736, C.O. 5:638, ff. 146–7; Candler, *Col. Rec. Ga.* xxi. 85–8.
[6] Oglethorpe to the Trustees, On board the *Simmonds* in Tybee Road, Feb. 13, 1736. This letter is missing now in C.O. 5:638. For copies see Candler, *Col. Rec. Ga.* xxi. 448–53; *Collections of the Georgia Historical Society*, iii. 13.

Dainties are plentiful, he makes the least use of them, and goes thro' the Woods, wet or dry, as actively as any Indian; his Humanity so gains upon all here, that I have not words to express their regard and esteem for him.[1]

Equal to his humanity during the voyage was his industry at Savannah so that Sam Eveleigh, who, next to Governor Johnson, was probably Oglethorpe's most loyal supporter in South Carolina, could inform Harman Verelst that 'Mr. Oglethorpe all the while He was at Savanah Satt up Every Night till one or Two of the clock, and Yett was up before any on the Bluff at Leat at Sun riseing'.[2] Thus in a rapid, though thorough, tour of inspection, wherein he convinced a volunteer that in Georgia old clothes proved best for work, Oglethorpe found Savannah 'in good Order & much increased in Buildings', but he wrote to the Trustees that 'The People who come at their own charge live in a manner too expensive which will make sumptuary laws necessary for the Province'.[3] The colonists, having had some trouble with Thomas Causton, the storekeeper,[4] now expected Oglethorpe to tarry and set matters aright, but, despite this question and their manifest joy at his return, he did not linger at Savannah.

On September 26, 1735, the Trustees in London had resolved that Oglethorpe should establish a new town in the southern part of the colony for the dual purpose of expansion and defence,[5] and on November 1, 1735, the *South Carolina Gazette* had announced his imminent return

---

[1] *Gentleman's Magazine*, vi. 229.

[2] Sam Eveleigh to Harmon Verelst, South Carolina, March 24, 1736, C.O. 5:638, f. 213; Candler, *Col. Rec. Ga.* xxi. 114–18.

[3] Oglethorpe to the Trustees, On board the *Simmonds* in Tybee Road, Feb. 13, 1736. Missing in C.O. 5:638; Candler, *Col. Rec. Ga.* xxi. 448–53; *Collections of the Georgia Historical Society*, iii. 13.

[4] One colonist bluntly informed Oglethorpe that Georgia, under Causton's rule, was 'a very hell upon Earth'. E. Bland to Oglethorpe, Savannah, June 14, 1735, C.O. 5:637, f. 96 verso; Candler, *Col. Rec. Ga.* xx. 96. See also the complaint of Robert Parker, Nov. 9, 1736, Add. MSS. (British Museum), 19332, ff. 26–7; Rawlinson MSS. (Bodleian Library, Oxford), D. 916, f. 194.

[5] C.O. 5:686, p. 286; Candler, *Col. Rec. Ga.* i. 231; *Egmont Diary*, ii. 181.

GEORGIA: THE SECOND PHASE: RELIGION 157

'to compleat the setling the Colony of Georgia, and to put the Frontiers of South-Carolina into a Posture of Defence'.[1] As the most important frontier of South Carolina at this time was the southern frontier of Georgia against Spain, Oglethorpe, after a severe schedule of conferences which would have tired most men, proceeded south on February 14, 1736,[2] taking with him the Reverend Benjamin Ingham, whose journal records that trip by water through high waves 'so that every moment we were in jeopardy of our lives; and truly, if Mr. Oglethorpe had not roused up himself and struck life into the rowers, I do not know but most of us might here have made our exit'.[3] Intent on claiming the line of the Altamaha River for imperial reasons, despite the opposition of some Trustees at home,[4] Oglethorpe proceeded to lay out 'in a neat and regular method', according to Ingham,[5] the town of Frederica, named in honour of Prince Frederick of the royal family,[6] and situated on Saint Simon's island at the mouth of the 'wild Altama' of Goldsmith's *Deserted Village*.[7] Although its founder firmly believed that this settlement would be duly appreciated by the Spaniards as helping to keep 'pirates and other Banditti' from 'insulting' them,[8] this act proved pregnant with possibilities for the future of the colony for, in Professor Crane's retrospective phrase, Oglethorpe 'was carrying to completion the ideas of Barnwell, Nicholson, and the Board of Trade', first advanced a decade or more before.[9] But at this moment an issue of greater import was taking shape in Savannah.

[1] Charles Town *South Carolina Gazette*, Nov. 1, 1735, p. 2.
[2] Ibid., March 13, 1736, p. 2.
[3] Ingham's Journal, Tyerman, *The Oxford Methodists*, p. 76.
[4] Osgood, *The American Colonies in the Eighteenth Century*, iii. 50.
[5] Ingham's Journal, Tyerman, *The Oxford Methodists*, p. 78.
[6] *Egmont Diary*, ii. 185, 196.
[7] Dobson, *A Paladin of Philanthropy*, p. 13.
[8] Oglethorpe to Andrew Stone, secretary to the Duke of Newcastle, Frederica, March 16, 1736, C.O. 5:654, f. 38.
[9] Crane, *The Southern Frontier*, p. 251. For excellent reports on Georgia's defences against the Spaniard see Oglethorpe to the Trustees, Frederica, March 16, 1736, C.O. 5:638, ff. 185–6; Candler, *Col. Rec. Ga.* xxi. 103–5;

If the first period of Oglethorpe's Georgia career was noteworthy for pioneering problems in administration, the second was equally so in the sphere of religion. Centuries before, an Oglethorpe in Bramham Parish in the West Riding of Yorkshire had endowed a chantry light 'to have continuance forever' as a token of family piety,[1] and this trait had continued through succeeding generations; but James Oglethorpe never paraded his views on religion. What little is known of his personal faith is found in his labours for his fellow men, his reverent attitude towards the clergy,[2] his recurrent expressions of devout trust in, and deep gratitude to, the Almighty,[3] and the testimony of those about him. Although John Wesley often reproved him for being lax in attendance at prayer meetings and being uncommunicative on doctrinal religion, Oglethorpe always took it well so that Wesley stoutly affirmed that 'Oglethorpe was "right" ';[4] Francis Moore emphasized the fact that 'Mr. Oglethorpe showed no discountenance to any for being of different persuasions in religion';[5] and Pastor Bolzius confidently testified that 'I know Mr. Oglethorpe's fear of God, His fatherly mercy towards persecuted and Distressed people',[6] adding two weeks later that 'from what knowledge we have of Him, we conclude that He hath a great Esteem for God's holy Word and Sacraments, and a great Love for God's Servants and

---

Martyn, Benjamin, *An Account Showing the Progress of the Colony of Georgia*, C.O. 5:711, pp. 27–30; Candler, *Col. Rec. Ga.* iii. 387–8; Boyer, *The Political State of Britain*, lii. 35–40; Boston *Evening Post*, April 12, 1736, p. 2.

[1] *Certificates of Commissioners appointed to survey the Chantries, Guilds, Hospitals, etc. in the County of York* (Surtees Society Publications, xcii, Durham, 1895), p. 397.

[2] Oglethorpe to Pastor J. M. Bolzius, Frederica, March 16, 1736, C.O. 5:638, f. 237; Candler, *Col. Rec. Ga.* xxi. 132.

[3] Various letters by Oglethorpe to Harman Verelst, the Trustees, and Pastor Bolzius, C.O. 5:638, ff. 92–3, 98–9; Candler, *Col. Rec. Ga.* xxi. 51–3, 79; *Collections of the Georgia Historical Society*, iii. 3–13.

[4] Curnock, *John Wesley's Journal*, i. 114, 124, 128, 131–2, 136.

[5] Moore, 'A Voyage to Georgia', *Collections of the Georgia Historical Society*, i. 87.

[6] Pastor J. M. Bolzius to ——, Ebenezer, Feb. 28, 1736, C.O. 5:638, ff. 140–1; Candler, *Col. Rec. Ga.* xxi. 79.

Children, and wishes to see the Name of Christ glorified everywhere'.[1] James Oglethorpe's magnanimity towards Anglican and Nonconformist, Catholic and Protestant, Jew and Gentile, conclusively indicated his spirituality and his firm faith in Alexander Pope's

> Father of all, in every age
> In every clime adored,
> By Saint, by Savage, and by Sage,
> Jehovah, Jove, or Lord.

Religion had been accepted as a bulwark of the colony and the first buildings planned for Savannah had been a church and a home for the clergyman in charge;[2] but religion to most of those connected with the movement in London meant the Church of England. The attitude of the Trustees towards the Jews has been recorded and as early as November 30, 1732, Egmont had stressed the opposition to 'Papists for they would only be spies upon our colony to inform the French or Spaniards of the condition of the colony', in which view the Trustees concurred.[3] This strongly Anglican attitude was evident in Egmont's notation of Sunday, July 9, 1732, that he had gone to church and had 'communicated ... and taken a certificate thereof, it being necessary upon the passing our charter of Georgia'.[4] Moreover, a contributor to the London *Weekly Miscellany* had expressed the hope that 'a better Face of Religion will be preserv'd in Georgia than appears in many of our American Settlements'.[5] A large body of Anglicans had naturally grown up in Georgia, which fact, together with the nature of the colony, gave the Established Church its usual favoured position,[6] but the Reverend Henry Herbert, the first minister, had survived

---

[1] *Extracts of the Journal of the Reverend Mr. Bolzius*, Force, *Tracts*, iv. 26. See also Oglethorpe to Pastor Bolzius, Frederica, March 16, 1736, C.O. 5:638, f. 237; *Collections of the Georgia Historical Society*, iii. 23.
[2] *Egmont Diary*, i. 295, 304–5.   [3] Ibid. 299.   [4] Ibid. 284.
[5] London *Weekly Miscellany*, Aug. 11, 1733, reprinted in the *Gentleman's Magazine*, iii. 413–15.
[6] Cross, A. L., *The Anglican Episcopate and the American Colonies* (Harvard Historical Studies, ix, New York, 1902), pp. 52–112.

but three months, dying on June 15 of a fever while at sea on his return voyage to England.[1] His eager successor, the Reverend Samuel Quincy,[2] proved a severe burden on the Trustees, and in December, 1734, Harman Verelst had to inform him that they were 'surprised they have never, in all this time, heard from you of the state of your parish';[3] but Quincy failed to reply. Having in turn been Dissenter, Independent, Presbyterian, and Anglican, Quincy, in Egmont's opinion, appeared 'for a long time to be unfit for his employment'[4] for, in Dr. Tiffany's words, he 'had not . . . the stamina of a pioneer missionary'.[5] After a futile effort, Quincy fled precipitately to South Carolina,[6] but later in Savannah broke his silence, complaining, in a letter to the Honourable Edmund Quincy of Massachusetts, of conditions in Georgia and decrying the work of the Trustees,[7] while to the Society for the Propagation of the Gospel he used ill health as an excuse,[8] but later asked for another appointment in America![9] Quincy's desertion of his post necessitated itinerant efforts by Carolina clergy[10] and the situation

[1] *Egmont Diary*, i. 293–7; London *Hooker's Weekly Miscellany*, June 30, 1733, p. 4; *Grub-Street Journal*, Sept. 13, 1733, p. 3; Tiffany, *History of the Protestant Episcopal Church in the United States*, p. 250.
[2] See the S.P.G. Documents, Series A (Letters Received), xxiv. 73–4; and Journals and Minutes, v. 63–4, 73.
[3] Harman Verelst to Reverend Samuel Quincy, London, Dec. 13, 1734, C.O. 5:666, p. 80. [4] *Egmont Diary*, ii. 184.
[5] Tiffany, *History of the Protestant Episcopal Church in the United States*, p. 251. See also the *Egmont Diary*, i. 302–3; ii. 195.
[6] Osgood, *The American Colonies in the Eighteenth Century*, iii. 109. See also Pennington, E. L., 'The Reverend Samuel Quincy, S.P.G. Missionary', *Georgia Historical Quarterly*, xi. 157–65.
[7] The Reverend Samuel Quincy to the Honourable Edmund Quincy, Savannah, Oct. 23, 1735, *Collections of the Massachusetts Historical Society*, 2nd series, ii (Boston, 1814), 188–9.
[8] The Reverend Samuel Quincy to the Secretary of the S.P.G., Savannah, Georgia, June 15, 1735, S.P.G. Documents, Series A (Letters Received), xxvi. 135–6.
[9] The Reverend Samuel Quincy to the Secretary of the S.P.G., London, Dec. 17, 1736, Jan. 4, 1737, S.P.G. Documents, Series A, xxvi. 430–2. He wanted Saint George's Parish in South Carolina.
[10] Report by the Reverend Mr. Lewis of Saint Helen's, South Carolina, June 18, 1734, S.P.G. Journals and Minutes, vi. 188.

GEORGIA: THE SECOND PHASE: RELIGION 161

thus developed now gave rise to one of the most imposing episodes in the spiritual history of an American colony. On August 23, 1735, Harman Verelst, in the name of the Trustees, wrote to Nicholas Spence, the Secretary of the Society for the Promotion of Christian Knowledge, requesting that body to recommend a minister for Georgia.[1] Nothing came of this, but Oglethorpe, at the time in England, now stepped in and found the men he wanted. Through his old college mate at Corpus Christi, Oxford, Dr. John Burton, a Fellow thereof and a Trustee for Georgia, Oglethorpe made inquiries of Dr. Stephen Hales at Lincoln College, Oxford,[2] where he met three young theologians, pupils of Dr. West and guiding spirits in the Holy Club of Oxford: Charles Wesley, Scholar of Christ Church; his brother, John, Fellow of Lincoln; and Benjamin Ingham of Queen's College, like the Oglethorpes, a Yorkshireman.[3]

The father of the Wesleys, the Reverend Samuel Wesley, had been a good friend of James Oglethorpe, and in 1734, but six months before his death, had asked the latter to find a place in the colony for his widower son-in-law, the Reverend John Whitelamb.[4] Samuel Wesley, junior, the poet, had likewise been a friend of the Georgia colonist,[5] and the mother of the Wesley boys had been a staunch Jacobite,[6] so that there was every reason for an accord with Oglethorpe. John Wesley's hesitation to accept the challenge was overcome by his mother's ardent approval of the mission,[7] and the three young men agreed to accompany Oglethorpe to Georgia in order to minister

[1] Harman Verelst to Nicholas Spence, London, Aug. 23, 1735, C.O. 5:666, pp. 138–9.   [2] *Egmont Diary*, ii. 184.
[3] Ibid. 194; Tyerman, *The Oxford Methodists*, pp. 57–154.
[4] Tyerman, *The Oxford Methodists*, pp. 378–80; Mallet, *History of the University of Oxford*, iii. 111.
[5] Elton, Oliver, *A Survey of English Literature, 1730–1780* (2 vols., London, 1928), ii. 222.
[6] *The Jacobite*, i (Feilding, New Zealand, 1922), 1.
[7] Sweet, W. W., *Methodism in American History* (New York, 1933), pp. 31–2. The Georgia Trustees recommended John Wesley to the S.P.G. See S.P.G. Journal, vi. 305.

4201   Y

both to colonists and Indians.[1] Only the objections of his relatives prevented the sailing of a fourth missionary, Ingham's close friend, Matthew Salmon of Brasenose College, Oxford.[2]

Thus it was that Oglethorpe on that morning of October 14, 1735, left Westminster for Gravesend not alone, but accompanied by Ingham and the two Wesleys[3] who, despite the derision of Oxford,[4] set out in the *Simmonds*, bound for the New World with one great purpose, in John Wesley's words, 'to save our souls'[5] by preaching the Gospel to the heathen.[6] In March 1734 the Trustees, having been aroused by Oglethorpe's laxity in keeping them duly informed of the state of affairs in the colony, had proposed that he appoint a secretary,[7] and Charles Wesley now went out as Secretary for Indian Affairs,[8] while his brother and Ingham, making Savannah their head-quarters, planned to convert the Indians.[9] Throughout the rough voyage, John, while working hard to have Oglethorpe 'open his heart' for a definite profession of faith,[10] had been a perfect colleague in ministering

---

[1] Telford, *The Letters of the Rev. John Wesley, A.M.*, i. 187–8; *Gentleman's Magazine*, v. 617. See also Tyerman, L., *Life and Times of the Rev. John Wesley* (3 vols., London, 1870), i. 109–10; and Southey, Robert, *Life of Wesley* (2 vols., New York, 1874), i, chap. iii.

[2] Ingham's Journal, Tyerman, *The Oxford Methodists*, p. 65; Mallet, *History of the University of Oxford*, iii. 116.

[3] London *Grub-Street Journal*, Oct. 16, 1735, p. 3.

[4] Godley, *Oxford in the Eighteenth Century*, pp. 265–6; Mallet, *History of the University of Oxford*, iii. 104–21.

[5] Curnock, *John Wesley's Journal*, i. 109.

[6] *Egmont Diary*, ii. 194; Tyerman, *Life and Times of the Rev. John Wesley*, i. 115; Lee, Umphrey, *The Historical Backgrounds of Early Methodist Enthusiasm* (Columbia University Studies in History, Economics, and Public Law, cccxxxix, New York, 1931), pp. 123–4.

[7] Benjamin Martyn to Oglethorpe, London, March 25, 1734, C.O. 5:666, pp. 49–52.

[8] C.O. 5:689, p. 211; Candler, *Col. Rec. Ga.* ii. 123; *Egmont Diary*, ii. 195–6.

[9] C.O. 5:686, pp. 289–90, 301–2; Candler, *Col. Rec. Ga.* i. 234–5, 241; *Egmont Diary*, ii. 200; *Gentleman's Magazine*, v. 617.

[10] Curnock, *John Wesley's Journal*, i. 109–11, 114, 116, 124, 128, 131, 142, 157, 159, 191–2, 221.

to the sick,[1] and his first impressions of Georgia were distinctly favourable,[2] despite the prompt regression of Ingham who, possibly because he was 'too handsome for a man', as one writer has phrased it, became 'intoxicated with the Moravian vanity' and, marrying Lady Margaret Hastings, forsook the Wesleyan cause.[3] But the story of the Wesleys themselves in Georgia is not a pleasant one, despite Oglethorpe's sincere efforts to help them.

On March 9, 1736, Charles Wesley arrived in Frederica where, according to his own journal, 'Mr. Oglethorpe received me very kindly';[4] but his enthusiasm receded rapidly when he found himself merely his superior's private secretary, engaged, day after day, in writing letters. On March 16 he noted in his journal that 'I was wholly spent in writing letters for Mr. Oglethorpe. I would not spend six days more in the same manner for all Georgia';[5] and by March 24 he considered Oglethorpe 'the chief' of all his 'enemies'.[6] An open breach might have been averted had not the malevolent tongues of two Frederica women spread a tale of sin on Oglethorpe's part, which scandal they maliciously ascribed to Charles Wesley. Neither of the two men behaved rationally in the crisis and the breach was in no wise healed by the impetuous visit to Frederica of John Wesley who completely failed to comprehend the whole vile plot.[7] In May Charles Wesley suddenly returned to Savannah, and on July 25,

[1] John Wesley to the Rev. Dr. John Burton, On board the *Simmonds*, Jan. 20, 1736, Telford, *The Letters of the Rev. John Wesley, A.M.*, i. 193–4.
[2] John Wesley to Mrs. Samuel Wesley, Savannah, March 18, 1736, Telford, *The Letters of the Rev. John Wesley, A.M.*, i. 196.
[3] Ingham returned to the fold in 1756. Tyerman, *The Oxford Methodists*, pp. 103–23, 139–40; Mallet, *History of the University of Oxford*, iii. 115–16.
[4] Telford, J., editor, *The Journal of the Rev. Charles Wesley* (London, 1909–10), p. 7.
[5] Ibid., p. 11.
[6] Ibid., p. 17.
[7] Ibid., pp. 9–65; Telford, *The Letters of the Rev. John Wesley, A.M.*, i. 200; Curnock, *John Wesley's Journal*, i. 193; Telford, J., *Life of the Rev. Charles Wesley* (revised ed., London, 1900), pp. 49–52.

1736, within five months of his arrival in Georgia, his journal recorded this curt entry: 'I resigned.'[1] The next day he left with his brother for Charles Town, South Carolina, whence the younger missionary sailed for England on August 11, 1736.[2]

If feminine gossip and slander caused Charles Wesley's break with Oglethorpe, the advice of other men in an *affaire du cœur* put an end to his brother's labours in Georgia. His Indian mission having been forbidden for fear of French attacks,[3] John Wesley, as much as his brother, had served Oglethorpe with generous devotion as a secretary and even as messenger.[4] Finding, in a week's visit, 'so little either of the form or power of religion at Frederica, that I am sincerely glad I am removed from it',[5] John Wesley had become pastor of Christ Church, Savannah, where, as a High Church ritualist, he was sadly out of place on the frontier, than which, in the words of a church historian, 'no place more ill adapted to his rubrical rigor could have been found'. Thus 'the incessant attendance required by him at meetings and prayers and sermons tended inevitably to formalism and hypocrisy'; indeed, 'men declined so great a usurpation over their consciences', and Wesley 'quickly estranged his people by his malapropos zeal'.[6] In short, he forgot that in Georgia there were not only Anglicans, but other Protestants, Nonconformists, as well as Jews. Although prohibiting the Indian mission and seemingly too busy for regular

---

[1] Telford, *Journal of the Rev. Charles Wesley*, p. 66; Curnock, *John Wesley's Journal*, i. 213, 217-18.

[2] Curnock, *John Wesley's Journal*, i. 251; Telford, *The Letters of the Rev. John Wesley, A.M.*, i. 185. For a somewhat dramatic presentation of the Charles Wesley story see Hoole, Elijah, *Oglethorpe and the Wesleys in America* (London, 1863).

[3] McConnell, *History of the American Episcopal Church*, p. 162.

[4] Curnock, *John Wesley's Journal*, i. 156, 251-5.

[5] Telford, *The Letters of the Rev. John Wesley, A.M.*, i. 200.

[6] McConnell, *History of the American Episcopal Church*, p. 163; Tiffany, *History of the Protestant Episcopal Church in the United States*, pp. 251, 253. For a report by John Wesley on his work in Savannah, and an account of his services see S.P.G. Journals, vii. 261.

GEORGIA: THE SECOND PHASE: RELIGION 165

attendance at public prayers,[1] Oglethorpe aided John Wesley whenever he could, as in ordering Sunday to be set apart as a Holy Day. Thus when he was absent Oglethorpe was greatly missed by one who so sorely needed his support. On the other hand, Oglethorpe, when perplexed and dismayed by his various administrative problems, gained spiritual comfort from Wesley. The need and the aid were thus mutually reciprocal. With Charles Wesley's departure, John found that he 'had less and less prospect of doing good at Frederica',[2] and devoted his further attentions to Savannah whence he was soon able to inform Verelst and the Trustees that 'the Good I have found here has indeed been beyond my expectations'.[3] Here, however, the climax of his Georgian career was attained during Oglethorpe's absence in England in 1736–7, when John Wesley's mission was brought to an abortive conclusion by his unfortunate romance and the Hopkey-Williamson case which, his letters show, began early in 1736.[4] Among the congregation at Frederica was Mrs. Causton's niece, Sophia Hopkey, who was greatly coveted by a youth of evil repute. In her perplexity and despair the eighteen-year-old girl turned for spiritual comfort to the Rev. John Wesley, whose primary interest in her spiritual welfare and salvation from such a marriage evolved into a strong admiration for her on his own part. Although Oglethorpe himself did his best to advance the cleric's courtship[5] in an affair which has not unfairly been called 'painfully ludicrous',[6] Wesley, accepting the advice of his clerical colleagues not to marry, stoically forbore, but his journal plainly indicates his mental and spiritual torment.[7] For four months he struggled with his prob-

[1] Telford, *The Letters of the Rev. John Wesley, A.M.*, i. 200–1; Curnock, *John Wesley's Journal*, i. 211. [2] Curnock, *John Wesley's Journal*, i. 259.
[3] John Wesley to Harman Verelst, Savannah, Nov. 10, 1736, C.O. 5:639, f. 340; Candler, *Col. Rec. Ga.* xxi. 453–4.
[4] Telford, *The Letters of the Rev. John Wesley, A.M.*, i. 199; Curnock, *John Wesley's Journal*, i. 283–5. [5] Curnock, *John Wesley's Journal*, i. 286–7.
[6] Tyerman, *Life and Times of the Rev. John Wesley*, i. 146–7.
[7] Curnock, *John Wesley's Journal*, i. 313–28.

lem and had seemingly conquered himself when Mrs. Causton announced her niece's desire that he publish the banns of marriage between Sophia Hopkey and William Williamson, Causton's clerk. For days Wesley pondered over the course to pursue when suddenly Williamson took her to Purysburg, South Carolina, for the marriage. Unable to bear this with composure, the brooding cleric found in some technical offences, such as inattention to fasting and morning prayers, the excuse to repel the bride from the communion service, thereby exposing himself to Williamson's charge of defaming his wife, and an eventual warrant for arrest.[1] Deeming discretion the better part of valour, Wesley left Georgia early in December 1737 for Charles Town, whence on the twenty-second he sailed for England, whither the enraged bridegroom, Williamson, had promptly sent a complaint to the Trustees.[2]

The importance of this episode, as Egmont so clearly saw, was not the mere personal equation but the 'great misfortune to us [the Trustees] for nothing is more difficult than to find a minister to go to Georgia who has any virtue and reputation'.[3] Oglethorpe had done his best for John Wesley as the latter freely acknowledged to him:

I bless God that ever you was born. I acknowledge His exceeding mercy in casting me into your hands. I own your generous kindness all the time we were at sea. I am indebted to you for a thousand favours here. Though all men should revile you, yet will I not.[4]

But, as one church historian justly observes, 'it was well

[1] Telford, *The Letters of the Rev. John Wesley, A.M.*, i. 210–11, 223–6; Stephens, William, *A Journal of the Proceedings in Georgia, beginning October 20, 1737* (London, 1742), reprinted (hereinafter cited as *Stephens' Journal*) in Candler, *Col. Rec. Ga.* iv. 12–19, 24, 37–42.
[2] Curnock, *John Wesley's Journal*, i. 360–7, 376–408; Charles Town *South Carolina Gazette*, Jan. 5, 1738, p. 2; William Stephens to the Trustees, Savannah, Dec. 20, 1737, C.O. 5:640, ff. 25–30; Candler, *Col. Rec. Ga.* xxii, part i, pp. 32–41; Tyerman, *Life and Times of the Rev. John Wesley*, i. 143–65.
[3] *Egmont Diary*, ii. 451.
[4] John Wesley to James Oglethorpe, Savannah, Feb. 24, 1737, Tyerman, *Life and Times of the Rev. John Wesley*, i. 136.

GEORGIA: THE SECOND PHASE: RELIGION 167

for himself and the colony that his stay in Georgia was short'.[1] On February 1, 1738, he surprised both Oglethorpe and his brother, Charles, by presenting his version of colonial affairs to the Trustees,[2] as had Charles a year and a half before,[3] but John later admitted that 'all the time I was at Savannah I was thus beating the air'.[4] That their Georgia career was not a red-letter subject in the family annals is evident from the scant, almost curt, reference to it in the memoirs of Charles Wesley's son, Samuel, written in 1836.[5] Although John in 1738 painted a negative picture of Georgia to some prospective Swiss emigrants in Cologne,[6] he maintained his interest in the colony and the work there of the Church,[7] while Charles in London renewed his friendship with Oglethorpe to such an extent that he was invited to return to Georgia, a contingency which, perhaps fortunately, did not eventuate.[8] It seems clear that the similarity in the dogmatic character of both Oglethorpe and the Wesleys left much to be desired, but the former's kindliness is accentuated by John Wesley's everlasting efforts at conversion and spiritual preaching from embarkation at Cowes to his last day in Savannah.[9]

[1] Tiffany, *History of the Protestant Episcopal Church in the United States*, p. 254.
[2] Telford, *The Letters of the Rev. John Wesley, A.M.*, i. 365–6; Curnock, *John Wesley's Journal*, i. 435–8; *Egmont Diary*, ii. 466.
[3] *Egmont Diary*, ii. 312–15, 318.   [4] Curnock, *John Wesley's Journal*, ii. 62.
[5] The only allusions to the Georgia episode are these: 'My Uncle John ... entered at Lincoln College, Oxford, and afterwards accompanied General Oglethorpe with my Father to Georgia:—Thence he returned to England and commenced his preaching Labours throughout the Island' (f. 2 verso); and 'When my Unkle John went to Georgia with General Oglethorpe, my Father accompanied him thither. On his Return to England he went over to South Wales' (f. 8). Add. MSS. (British Museum), 27593, Reminiscences of Samuel Wesley, 1836.   [6] Curnock, *John Wesley's Journal*, ii. 62.
[7] Telford, *The Letters of the Rev. John Wesley, A.M.*, v. 156, 183–4, 210; vi. 171.
[8] Telford, *The Journal of the Rev. Charles Wesley*, pp. 110 ff., 137, 197; Telford, *The Letters of the Rev. John Wesley, A.M.*, i. 236; Curnock, *John Wesley's Journal*, i. 437–8.
[9] Curnock, *John Wesley's Journal*, i. 109, 111, 114, 116, 124, 128, 131, 142, 157, 159, 191–2, 271. For a concise, sympathetic account of the Wesleys in Georgia see Sweet, *Methodism in American History*, pp. 27–35.

In the words of Austin Dobson, 'the Wesleys, however, are but an episode in Georgian history',[1] and Oglethorpe —to whom 'the Day and Night together is not long enough to dispatch the number of trifling things that are here necessary'[2]—in this second period found other matters of importance to consider, including the continued selection of new types of immigrants; the problem of defence; the finances of the colony; and the seemingly minor question of maintaining friendly relations with the Indians, which, however, was to prove of paramount interest.

The factor of immigration was still closely related to that of religion in the type of continental Protestant refugee whom the Trustees welcomed to Georgia. A group of Anabaptists from Saxony had thought of going to the colony in 1733,[3] while only the law of male entail had prevented the visit of the Vaudois. The Salzburger Lutherans, as Captain George Dunbar reported, maintained their reputation as 'a pious, sober and industrious people',[4] despite their evident hardships on the barren soil about Ebenezer. The arrival of two more parties of Salzburgers, most of whom preferred the company of their comrades at Ebenezer to the lighter, but lonelier, labours at Frederica, led the elders to seek Oglethorpe's permission to move five miles farther on to what became New Ebenezer on Read Bluff in a more healthful environment.[5] This aroused the objection of both the Trustees and Oglethorpe. The former, through a letter to Pastor Bolzius from their secretary, Benjamin Martyn, expressed their surprise that von Reck 'should have cast a longing eye on the said Lands, and doubt not, Sir, that you informed him out of Scripture that he ought not to covet

---

[1] Dobson, *A Paladin of Philanthropy*, p. 21.
[2] Oglethorpe to the Trustees, Savannah, July 1, 1736, C.O. 5:638, f. 324; Candler, *Col. Rec. Ga.* xxi. 184.
[3] *Egmont Diary*, i. 476.
[4] Captain George Dunbar to Oglethorpe, Savannah, Jan. 23, 1735, C.O. 5:636, f. 154.
[5] Baron von Reck to Oglethorpe, Savannah, March 7, 1736, C.O. 5:638, ff. 232–3; Candler, *Col. Rec. Ga.* xxi. 127–31.

his Neighbour's Goods'.[1] Notwithstanding his many other duties, Oglethorpe, unable to understand why they were 'mightily discontented',[2] took the time to reason with the Salzburgers, finally yielding to their importunities in a decision which he was never to regret.[3] The move to New Ebenezer was rich in reward, for here the Lutherans continued the first Sunday School in Georgia, transplanted from the old site, and here they founded the first orphanage in the colony.

While it is true that there were neither Quakers nor Scotch-Irish in Georgia,[4] the Presbyterian faith appeared soon after Oglethorpe's return to the colony, when a body of one hundred and fifty Scottish Highlanders, largely survivors of the Jacobite Rising of 1715, came over in the *Prince of Wales* and founded New Inverness, now Darien, on the Altamaha, built a fort on St. Simon's Island, and subsequently proved so vital a military asset in defence against the Spaniard that Oglethorpe sometimes wore the plaid and tartan in compliment to these Highlanders.[5] But the outstanding body of pious pioneers in this second period, comparable with von Reck's Salzburgers during Oglethorpe's first visit to Georgia, proved to be none of these, but the forerunners of that small, saintly com-

[1] Benjamin Martyn to Pastor J. M. Bolzius, London, June 10, 1736, C.O. 5:666, p. 249.
[2] James Oglethorpe to the Trustees, Frederica, March 16, 1736, C.O. 5:638, f. 186; Candler, *Col. Rec. Ga.* xxi. 103–5.
[3] Urlsperger, Samuel, editor, *Erste Continuation der ausführlichen Nachricht von denen Saltzburgischen Emigranten, die sich in America niedergelassen haben* (Halle, 1738), *passim; Zweite Continuation* (Halle, 1739), pp. 685–93, 823; Linn, 'The Georgia Colony of Salzburgers,' pp. 82–105. See also Samuel Urlsperger to the Society for the Promotion of Christian Knowledge, Augsburg, Feb. 24, 1736, Rawlinson MSS. (Bodleian Library, Oxford), C. 743, f. 71.
[4] Jones, Rufus M., *The Quakers in the American Colonies* (New York, 1911), pp. 298, 300 note; Ford, Henry Jones, *The Scotch-Irish in America* (Princeton, New Jersey, 1915), *passim*.
[5] Sam Eveleigh to Harman Verelst, South Carolina, March 5, 1736, C.O. 5:638, f. 218; Candler, *Col. Rec. Ga.* xxi. 120–1; Charles Town *South Carolina Gazette*, March 20, 1736, pp. 2–3; Boston *Weekly News Letter*, April 8, 1736, pp. 3–4; *Egmont Diary*, ii. 202, 268; MacLean, J. P., *Settlements of Scotch Highlanders in America prior to the Peace of 1783* (Cleveland and Glasgow, 1900), pp. 146–50.

munion, variously known as the *Unitas Fratrum, Fratres Bohemiae*, or, in modern America, by the simple, yet illustrious, name of Moravians.

Originating in the fifteenth-century Bohemia of John Huss, the Unity of Brethren early in the sixteenth century were forced, like the later Salzburgers of the Tyrol, to flee to Protestant centres in Poland and Germany where, at Herrnhut in Saxony, they established their head-quarters. Personal security and freedom of worship for themselves did not, however, lull these hardy souls to rest 'on flowery beds of ease', but they organized a worldwide missionary movement which, in England, drew the attention of James Oglethorpe through his meeting with Nicholaus Ludwig, Count Zinzendorf. The Count had been in England for many years, having lost all his wealth by a sentence pronounced in October 1680,[1] and had been sympathetic to the Jacobites and a friend of Sir Theophilus Oglethorpe[2] and of Prince Eugene, James Oglethorpe's commander in his youthful military days.[3] A comradeship with James Oglethorpe, M.P. and imperial patriot, was thus a natural sequence. A former Lutheran, Zinzendorf in 1733 had petitioned the Trustees for a grant in Georgia to a band of exiled Schwenkfelders, an off-shoot of the Lutherans, in a document which showed his plans as well matured. Due to their request for financial aid, the appeal of the Schwenkfelders failed and they ultimately settled in the south-eastern counties of Pennsylvania, but Zinzendorf proved more successful when he sponsored the Herrnhut Moravians. Except for celibacy of the clergy, congregational purism, and the doctrine of works as over against Luther's justification by faith, there was little difference between the early Moravian and Lutheran positions, and Zinzendorf easily made the transition. After a direct conference with Oglethorpe in

---

[1] Carte MSS. (Bodleian Library, Oxford), civ, f. 32.

[2] *Letters of Francis Atterbury*, p. 283.

[3] John Drummond to the Earl of Oxford, Amsterdam, March 15, 1712, *Portland MSS*. (H.M.C. Reports), v, *Harley Letters*, iii. 149.

London early in 1735, the Moravians were accepted.[1] Oglethorpe did his full share in securing financial credit as well as cash contributions for their material welfare, while he also succeeded in obtaining for them the approval of Bishop Edmund Gibson, Anglican Bishop for the Plantations.[2] Thus it was that the first band of ten Moravians under August Gottlieb Spangenberg, like Zinzendorf a quondam Lutheran, landed in Georgia on April 8, 1735. For almost a year they laboured successfully as pioneers, making ready for the arrival of Bishop David Nitschmann who, as Missionary to the Indians, accompanied Oglethorpe and the Wesleys on the former's return to the colony in February 1736.[3] With Nitschmann came twenty-four members of his faith whom Egmont rather uncharitably dubbed 'a lot of enthusiasts . . . who take it in their head that everything which comes uppermost is the immediate impulse of the spirit of God',[4] but who won from Charles Wesley the reputation of being 'the most laborious, cheapest workers and best subjects in Georgia';[5] while Benjamin Ingham called them 'not only the most useful People in the Colony, But also they are certainly the holiest Society of Men in the whole World'.[6] The Moravians in turn regarded Oglethorpe as 'indeed our good friend, who cares for us like a father' even as he had promised, on boarding the *Simmonds* at Cowes.[7] Like Zinzendorf, Nitschmann had received a grant of land, and the sober, steady, industrious Brethren soon became

[1] C.O. 5:689, pp. 143–5; Candler, *Col. Rec. Ga.* ii. 81; Fries, *The Moravians in Georgia*, p. 50.

[2] Sykes, Norman, *Edmund Gibson, Bishop of London, 1669–1748* (Oxford, 1926), pp. 321–32.

[3] Zinzendorf had sought consecration as Bishop, but Bishop Jablonsky had refused him that honour, agreeing finally to consecrate Nitschmann as the first Bishop of the Renewed Moravian Church and also the first Colonial Bishop. Hutton, J. E., *A History of Moravian Missions* (London, 1923), p. 79. See also Osgood, *The American Colonies in the Eighteenth Century*, iii. 109.

[4] *Egmont Diary*, ii. 132–3, 140–1, 166.

[5] Ibid. 313, 333.

[6] Reverend Benjamin Ingham to Sir John Phillipps, Savannah, Sept. 15, 1736, C.O. 5:638, f. 404; Candler, *Col. Rec. Ga.* xxi. 221–3.

[7] Fries, *The Moravians in Georgia*, pp. 93, 102.

leaders in the colony.[1] Possibly the most vital factor in the life of the Moravians in Georgia and certainly one of the greatest reasons for Oglethorpe's success in handling the sundry sects was the close comradeship of the Church between John Wesley and Spangenberg in Georgia, and between Wesley and Zinzendorf in London. On his arrival in the colony Wesley had lived for a few weeks in the Moravian community and had attended their services. A very deep and genuine respect for each other was soon evident in both leaders.[2] The climax of Moravian history in this period came on March 10, 1736, when Bishop Nitschmann ordained Anton Seifert as pastor of the Savannah congregation in the first ordination service by a bishop in America. Soon after, Spangenberg and Nitschmann went to Pennsylvania, but the Moravians in Georgia continued to prosper.[3]

But while Oglethorpe had welcomed those of diverse faith to that freedom of worship which characterized his colony, he never lost sight of the major motive for increased immigration: colonial defence. Although Westminster was still so scared of the Mississippi French that the government had hardly examined Oglethorpe's seven sound reasons therefor, but had automatically granted his recurrent requests for further appropriations,[4] that danger had wellnigh passed, as had the fear of the Indian. The Spaniard alone remained forever hovering on the southern border to become the *bête noire* of the Georgians. Oglethorpe never forgot the Spaniard but, in truth, the Spaniard never gave him the opportunity to forget, for

[1] C.O. 5:689, p. 145; Candler, *Col. Rec. Ga.* ii. 82.
[2] e.g. Telford, *The Letters of the Rev. John Wesley, A.M.*, i. 194–6, 227–8.
[3] In addition to the references cited above, this narrative of the Moravians in Georgia owes much to these sources in the Archives of the Moravian Church at Moravian College for Men, Bethlehem, Pennsylvania: The Correspondence of August Gottlieb Spangenberg (in German); 'Beilage zum Bethlehemischen Diario, Dezember 13, 1747, von Reisen nach und von America, 1734–1747'; and particularly 'Kurzgefasster Aufsatz der Mährischen und Böhmischen Brüder . . . in den Nord Amerikanischen Colonien . . . 1732 bis 1741.'
[4] *Egmont Diary*, ii. 159, 245–6.

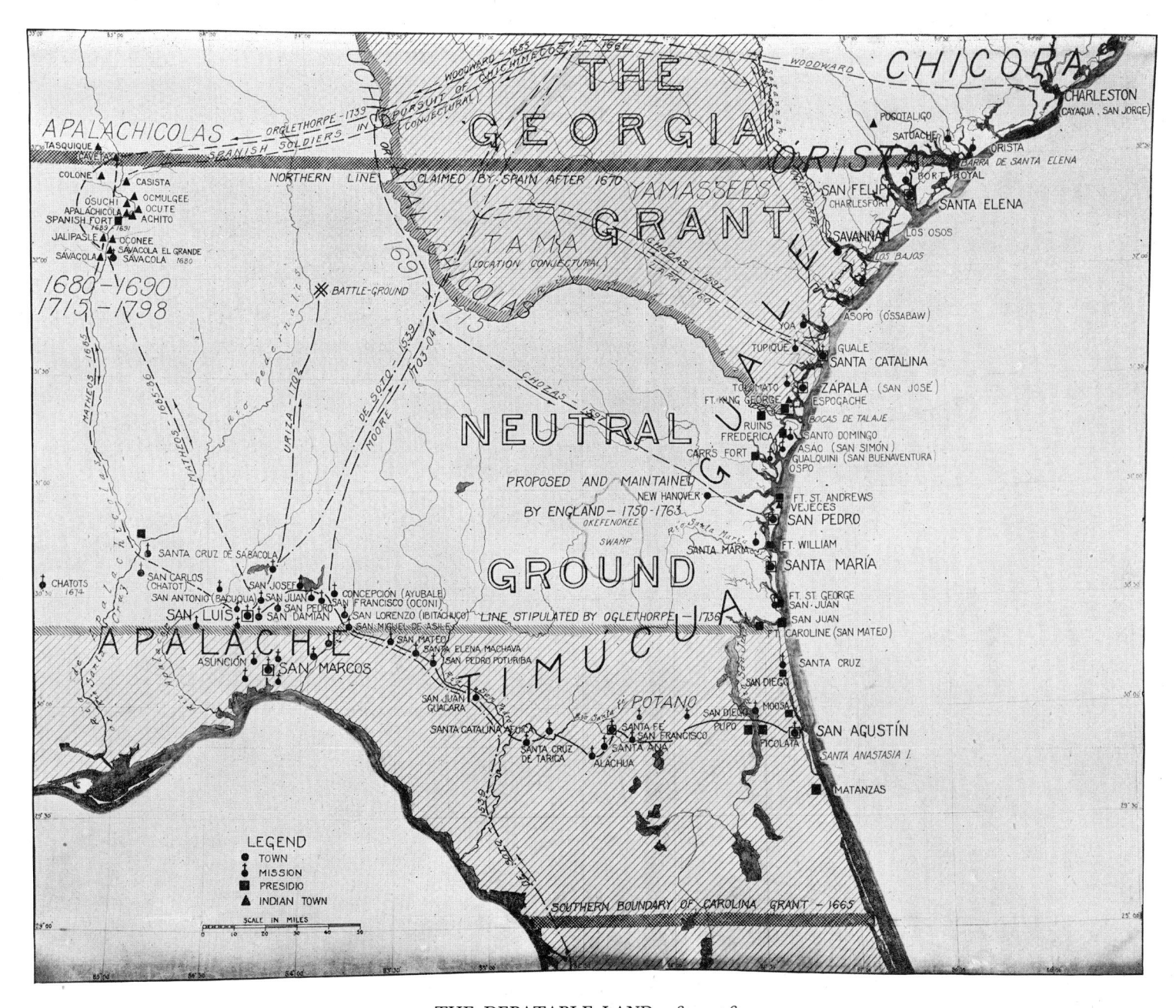

THE DEBATABLE LAND, 1670–1763

taken, by permission, from H. E. Bolton and M. Ross, *The Debatable Land* (University of California Press, 1925)

the diplomatic conflict was carried on not only between Savannah and Saint Augustine, through Havana, and to Madrid, but to London as well. As has been indicated, most of the territory comprising the royal grant of Georgia was unquestionably part of what Spain had won by right of religion and missions as much as by *force majeure*.[1] The encroachments of Englishmen from Charles Town and the subsequent withdrawal of Spanish outposts from Saint Catherine's to the Altamaha and still later to the Saint Mary's river in the seventeenth century, culminating in the further removal of Spanish control to the Saint John's river in 1702, had merely set the stage for what has been called 'a half decade of bluster and argument'.[2] With Georgia now boasting a population of over 1,200,[3] the founding of Frederica on the Altamaha, only thirty miles north of Saint Augustine, together with Oglethorpe's admitted efforts to make Fort Saint George on the Saint John's river (in what is now Florida) the southern outpost of Georgia,[4] proved to be the one spark needed to provoke a renewal of Spanish claims to all the territory south of the Carolinas.[5]

The proclamation of Spain's hostile attitude was no sudden change of mind, and Whitehall knew it. As early as 1730 Benjamin Keene, Arthur Stert, and John Goddard, the three British Commissioners to treat with the representatives of the King of Spain, had been instructed to guard Britain's rights arising out of the southern boundary of South Carolina;[6] and ever since Oglethorpe's arrival

---

[1] 'The Spaniards were unassailable' in their right to Georgia. Lanning, J. T., 'A Descriptive Catalogue of Some Legajos on Georgia in the Spanish Archives', *Georgia Historical Quarterly*, xiii. 416.
[2] Bolton, H. E., editor, *Arredondo's Historical Proof of Spain's Title to Georgia* (Berkeley, California, 1925), p. 4.   [3] *Egmont Diary*, ii. 251.
[4] Oglethorpe to Lieutenant-Governor Thomas Broughton, Frederica, March 28, 1736, C.O. 5:638, f. 224; Candler, xxi. 121-3.
[5] Oglethorpe's policy, in Spanish eyes, 'was adjusted solely to the plaudits contingent upon successful conquest'. Lanning, 'A Descriptive Catalogue of Some Legajos on Georgia in the Spanish Archives', *Georgia Historical Quarterly*, xiii. 419.
[6] Add. MSS. (British Museum), 33006, Newcastle Papers, ff. 298-303.

in Charles Town in 1733, a steady stream of reports on his imperial activities had gone back from Saint Augustine to Havana and thence to Madrid.[1] By 1734 the Spanish government, through their Minister in London, Don Tomás Geraldino, had begun what was to prove a lengthy and, in general, a vain series of official protests to the British government against Oglethorpe's incursions into Spanish Guale.[2] No action resulted therefrom until Oglethorpe's continued encroachments in 1736 could no longer be overlooked.

The Duke of Newcastle, as Secretary of State for the Colonies, tiring of his futile conversations with the adamant Geraldino in London, finally sent Captain Charles Dempsey as his representative to investigate the situation at first hand. In a fine letter to Dempsey of April 10, 1736, Oglethorpe, in expounding the English claim to the Debatable Land, reminded his fellow countryman that

the discovery of this countrey was made by Sebastian Cabbot who was fitted out by Henry 7th & 8th, and possession then taken in the name of the King of England, and that Sr Walter Raleigh and Sr Francis Drake did in the reign of Queen Elizabeth, upon the Spaniards settling there, take and burn the Fortress of Augustine and thereby maintained the English right, which

---

[1] Archivo de Indias, Estante 87, Cajón 1, legajo 1 (from photostat copies in possession of the Florida State Historical Society, hereinafter cited as A.I. 87-1-1), No. 8, Governor Don Antonio Benavides to Don José Patiño, Spanish Colonial Secretary, Saint Augustine, Feb. 3, 1733; No. 9, Benavides to Patiño, Saint Augustine, July 27, 1733; No. 10, Dionisio Martínez de la Vega to Patiño, Havana, Oct. 14, 1733; No. 12, Benavides to Patiño, Saint Augustine, April 6, 1734; No. 11, Benavides to Patiño, Saint Augustine, April 12, 1734; No. 15, Governor Don Francisco del Moral Sanchez to the Crown, Saint Augustine, March 5, 1735; No. 16, del Moral Sanchez to the Crown, Saint Augustine, April 2, 1735; No. 17, Conde del Montijo to Patiño, London, April 15, 1735; No. 18, del Moral Sanchez to the Crown, Saint Augustine, May 23, 1735. For instructions as to these reports see A.I. 87-1-1, No. 14, Official letter, no signature, to del Moral Sanchez, Madrid, Jan. 18, 1735.

[2] A.I. 87-1-1, No. 27, Instructions, unsigned, to Don Tomás Geraldino, San Lorenzo, Spain, Nov. 14, 1735; C.O. 5:686, pp. 334-5; Candler, *Col. Rec. Ga.* i. 260-1.

GEORGIA: THE SECOND PHASE: RELIGION 175

claim King Charles the second also supported by his Grant of these Countreys to the Lords Proprietors of Carolina, from which Lords Proprietors the King and Parliament five years since purchased the same.

In addition, Oglethorpe noted that the Treaty of Utrecht guaranteed the *status quo* at a time when Saint Augustine was besieged by the English who 'kept possession as far as the River St. John'. In any case, he concluded, the 'original proprietors' were the Indians, from whom this land had been duly purchased by the English.[1] This brief did not, however, check Dempsey's survey, and while he, in Prof. Bolton's neat phrase, 'darted back and forth between Georgia and Florida like a shuttle-cock',[2] Oglethorpe, as adamant in Georgia as Geraldino in London, insisted—with the aid of soldiers—on the Saint John's River as a boundary. On April 17 he sent to Newcastle the pledge that 'I cannot deliver up a foot of ground belonging to his Majesty, to a foreign Power without the breach of my allegiance to his Majesty. I will alive or dead keep possession of it till I have his Majesty's orders.'[3] An *impasse* naturally arose, and now Spain sent a representative to treat with Oglethorpe.[4]

Antonio de Arredondo, military engineer by profession and diplomat by appointment, was sent to Frederica in the summer of 1736 by the Spanish colonial authorities at Havana to secure the retreat of the English northward

[1] Oglethorpe to Captain Charles Dempsey, Frederica, April 10, 1736, C.O. 5:654, ff. 50–1. The Cabot-Drake-Charles II grant story was the standard English version. See also Add. MSS. (British Museum), 35909, Hardwicke Papers: Papers relating to America, ff. 78–9, 81.
[2] Bolton, *Arredondo's Historical Proof of Spain's Title to Georgia*, p. 73.
[3] Oglethorpe to Newcastle, Frederica, April 17, 1736, C.O. 5:654, ff. 60–1.
[4] For the major facts see the *Journal of the Commissioners for Trade and Plantations*, vii, 1735–41, pp. 128, 131–5; Bolton, *Arredondo's Historical Proof of Spain's Title to Georgia*, pp. vi, 1–5, 72–4. For the early Spanish settlements see Lowery, Woodbury, *Spanish Settlements within the Present Limits of the United States, 1513–1574* (New York, 1901–5); Johnson, J. G., 'The Spanish Period of Georgia and South Carolina, 1566–1702', *Bulletin of the University of Georgia* (Athens, Georgia, 1923); Parkman, F., *The Pioneers of France in the New World* (Champlain ed., 2 vols., Boston, 1897), i. 95, 153; ii. 39–41; Bolton and Ross, *The Debatable Land*, chaps. ii–iv.

beyond Port Royal, South Carolina! That Oglethorpe, while brazen towards the Spaniard, was deeply worried by the trend of affairs is evident from his correspondence with Lieutenant-Governor George Clarke of New York in May, and the Council of Virginia in July 1736 asking for aid in case of a Spanish attack on Georgia. Clarke was optimistic, but promised both Oglethorpe and the Duke of Newcastle that he would help in an emergency,[1] and on June 17 issued a proclamation of aid,[2] while the Council in Virginia kept its troops in readiness for any eventuality.[3] With such support behind him Oglethorpe was unaffected by the treachery of an English lieutenant, John Savy, who went to Cuba under the name of Miguel Wall to keep the Spaniards informed as to Georgia for 1,000 pesos a year.[4] Full of confidence, Oglethorpe could write a most courteous letter of welcome to the enemy and sent a sloop to Saint Augustine for Arredondo[5] whom he met at the end of August in a conference wherein the Spaniard demanded that his English opponent retire north to the Edisto River and Saint Helena Sound, north even of Port Royal, South Carolina, which was the farthest point of Spanish claims! Oglethorpe countered with a demand that Spain evacuate all of Florida north of 29° inasmuch as Sir Francis Drake, under orders of Queen Elizabeth, had once taken Saint Augustine.[6] It was obvious that the original demands of

---

[1] C.O. 5:1093, ff. 408–11; O'Callaghan, E. B., editor, *Documents relative to the Colonial History of the State of New York* (14 vols., Albany, New York, 1855–83), vi. 70–1.

[2] *New York Gazette*, July 5, 1736, p. 1.

[3] McIlwaine, H. R., editor, *Executive Journals of the Council of Colonial Virginia* (in progress, Richmond, Virginia, 1925——), iv. 376, 389.

[4] A.I. 87–1–1, No. 28, Fernando Triviño to Patiño, Paris, Jan. 30, 1736; Enclosure, Patiño to Triviño, Aranjuez, April 9, 1736; No. 30, Triviño to Patiño, Paris, April 23, 1736; No. 31, John Savy or Saby to a Spanish official, probably Patiño, Cadiz, June 8, 1736; No. 33, Royal order to Governor Guemes y Horcasitas of Cuba, Madrid, June 24, 1736; No. 35, Royal order to Guemes y Horcasitas, Madrid, June 28, 1736; No. 39, Guemes y Horcasitas to Patiño, Havana, July 24, 1736.

[5] A.I. 87–1–1, No. 48B, Oglethorpe to Antonio de Arredondo, Savannah, July 29, 1736; Frederica, Aug. 9, 1736.

[6] A.I. 87–1–1, No. 45, Oglethorpe to Arredondo, Georgia, Aug. 30, 1736;

both parties were equally ridiculous. After much talk Oglethorpe, on October 22, 1736, agreed to a treaty with Governor Francisco del Moral Sanchez, whereby each party undertook to control its own Indian allies and to refrain from molesting each other. Oglethorpe, warned by a letter of July 7 from Benjamin Martyn that the Trustees would not pay any expenses 'incurred beyond the Boundaries of the Province of Georgia' as 'they can authorize no Proceedings of yours out of the Province of Georgia',[1] now promised in the treaty with the Spaniards to evacuate Fort Saint George on the island at the mouth of the Saint John's river and retire to the northward, leaving the boundaries to be decided by the respective home governments.[2] Oglethorpe—for the moment—was satisfied, as was Sam Eveleigh, after Governor Johnson's death the former's most loyal supporter in South Carolina;[3] but poor del Moral Sanchez was recalled to Spain and hanged.[4]

While Oglethorpe had been struggling with the Spanish question an old domestic problem of administration had returned to plague him. One of the most important powers given to him on his first voyage had been to draw bills on the Trustees. It was as much his failure to send vouchers with these drafts as it was his failure to keep the

---

No. 46, Oglethorpe to Guemes y Horcasitas, Georgia, Aug. 30, 1736; 87–1–3, No. 1, Arredondo to the Governor of Havana, Saint Augustine, Aug. 31, 1736; Charles Town *South Carolina Gazette*, Sept. 18, 1736, p. 2; Oct. 9, 1736, p. 2. See also the Boston *Weekly News Letter*, Nov. 4, 1736, p. 2; Nov. 18, 1736, p. 2; *New England Weekly Journal*, Nov. 9, 1736, p. 2; *Evening Post*, Nov. 8, 1736, p. 2; Nov. 22, 1736, p. 2; New York *Gazette*, Nov. 15, 1736, p. 3.

[1] Benjamin Martyn to Oglethorpe, London, July 7, 1736, C.O. 5:666, p. 247.

[2] There is a copy of the treaty in Add. MSS. (British Museum), 32794, Newcastle Papers, ff. 255–60. See also Harris, J., *Navigantium atque Itinerantium Bibliotheca. Or a Complete Collection of Voyages and Travels* (2 vols., London, 1744–8), ii. 331–2.

[3] Sam Eveleigh to Harman Verelst, South Carolina, Oct. 13, 1736, C.O. 5:638, f. 383; Candler, *Col. Rec. Ga.* xxi. 211–12.

[4] *Egmont Diary*, ii. 410; iii. 141; Bolton, *Arredondo's Historical Proof of Spain's Title to Georgia*, p. 74.

Trustees informed of affairs that had led Vernon to make the charges which had drawn Oglethorpe back to England in 1734.[1] In his second visit to the colony he had been given the sole right to draw bills of credit on the Trustees,[2] but this time he created even a worse situation than before by sending bills to the Trustees for them to pay, instead of settling them in Georgia with the money he had taken with him.[3] Admittedly allowing his defensive military zeal to overcome his financial caution and paying little or no attention to the warnings of his colleagues, Oglethorpe during 1736 incurred such large expenses that the Trustees, some of whom like Egmont suspected him of having secret instructions from the King, in sheer desperation demanded that he submit his bills directly to the British government, and they proposed to abolish the individual drawing of bills, substituting therefor printed sola bills, in order to protect their credit with English merchants.[4]

But, while this was a crucial matter as to Oglethorpe's personal judgement and efficiency, the most important administrative problem of the period was one which affected the inter-colonial relations of Georgia with her sponsor, guide, and neighbour, South Carolina. A great American historian, in positing the existence of law in history, once proclaimed a law of interdependence.[5] South Carolina, finding this law to be true and interdependence to be a necessity, had been amazingly generous to her infant neighbour with large appropriations of money, and had fully appreciated the value of Georgia as a buffer, not only against Spain but against the French in Mississippi as well.[6] The death of Governor Robert Johnson in May

[1] *Egmont Diary*, ii. 29, 41.
[2] C.O. 5:689, pp. 193–4; Candler, *Col. Rec. Ga.* ii. 113–14.
[3] C.O. 5:690, p. 29; Candler, *Col. Rec. Ga.* ii. 168, 170.
[4] *Egmont Diary*, ii. 252–3, 268–95; Harman Verelst to Thomas Causton, London, June 18, 1736, C.O. 5:666, pp. 241–3.
[5] Cheyney, E. P., *Law in History and Other Essays* (New York, 1927), pp. 15–17.
[6] *Egmont Diary*, i. 389, 398; ii. 120, 185; C.O. 5:434. Journal of Council and Upper House, South Carolina; S.C. Records, vi. 2, 4.

1735 had opened the way for Oglethorpe to become Governor of South Carolina, but he had declined in order to hold his parliamentary seat at home.[1] When then in October 1735 Oglethorpe had returned to Georgia, he brought with him a letter from Newcastle to Lieutenant-Governor Thomas Broughton, Johnson's successor, wherein the Secretary of State for the Colonies emphasized the faith of the British government in Oglethorpe's understanding of conditions in Carolina and earnestly urged the Carolinians to consult him in all matters relating to their 'Safety, Defence, and Improvement'.[2]

Despite Oglethorpe's tact, trouble came through two of the three laws enacted by the Trustees during his visit to England in April 1735. The prohibition of negro slavery had entailed economic disadvantage only in Georgia, where it was highly unpopular,[3] but the other two laws led to strife with South Carolina. With the two colonies in much the same position as Canada and the United States during the prohibition era, the law excluding the rum trade led to such extensive rum-running and consequent attempts at enforcement that a Georgian of 1735 could write thus: 'Our strictness in relation to the Rum Trade is like to occasion some disputes with our neighbours of Carolina. Seizures and confiscations and arrests have been made.'[4] The corollary, moreover, was equally true, for there is a strangely American touch to the evidence adduced before the Trustees by a Scottish Highlander to the effect that, although 'great care was taken to prevent the introduction of rum', the people of

[1] W. Augustine to John Brownfield, Westbrook, Georgia, June 13, 1735, C.O. 5:637, part iii, f. 311.
[2] 'Mr. Oglethorpe, who will be upon the Spot, has so true a Knowledge of the nature and constitution of the Colony, & so much zeal & concern for the Interest of it, that Her Majesty is persuaded, he will be able to give you very usefull Lights, whenever you shall consult with him in Matters relating to the Safety, Defence & Improvement of Carolina.' Newcastle to Broughton, Whitehall, Oct. 10, 1735, C.O. 5:388, p. 67; C.O. 324:36, pp. 528–9.
[3] *Egmont Diary*, ii. 204–5.
[4] Letter from Georgia, *Gentleman's Magazine*, vi. 357. See also the *Egmont Diary*, ii. 286, 297.

Savannah 'still get at rum, notwithstanding all our care, by means of the Carolina boats, which in the night time land it in creeks unknown to the magistrates'.[1] The 'bootlegger' is not an original novelty of the twentieth century! But there was another law of Georgia far more damaging to the prosperity of South Carolina than that prohibiting rum. This was the law regulating trade with the Indians.

Until the creation of Georgia, South Carolina had naturally held a monopoly in the Indian trade, and even before Oglethorpe's return in 1735, when he had been appointed 'sole Commissioner to grant licences to trade to the Indians',[2] South Carolina, as Egmont put it, had 'grown extremely jealous'.[3] Although on February 18, 1735, they had obtained an opinion from their consultant Privy Councillor, Francis Fane, who found the laws to be to Carolina's advantage,[4] Oglethorpe's rigorous exforcement policy not only destroyed the Carolinian monopoly but, by restricting this important source of profit to Georgians, virtually ruined the neighbouring traders. Coupled with this was the continual fear of the Frenchman which, it must be admitted, affected the Carolinians far more than the Georgians.[5] In addition to those problems, Carolina felt its complaints justified when during 1735 and 1736 Captain Patrick MacKay, as the ranking enforcement officer for Georgia, stirred up resentment by his arbitrary rulings against Carolina traders.[6] A protracted correspondence with Oglethorpe ensued, the net result whereof was that his reply, stressing the prohibition

---

[1] *Egmont Diary*, ii. 268, 317.
[2] C.O. 5:689, pp. 205–6, 211; Candler, *Col. Rec. Ga.* ii. 120; *Egmont Diary*, ii. 195.
[3] *Egmont Diary*, ii. 199.   [4] C.O. 5:401, pp. 133–5.
[5] Message of Feb. 4, 1736, C.O. 5:437; S.C. Rec. ii. 141–9; vi. 180; viii. 138–54; viii (part ii), 2.
[6] C.O. 5:437; S.C. Rec. vi. 206–7; ix. 641–6; Alured Popple to Benjamin Martyn, London, Dec. 10, 1735, C.O. 5:365, f. 10; C.O. 5:401, pp. 167–8; S.C. Rec. xvii. 383–7, 396–407, 442–4; C.O. 5:686, p. 302; Candler, *Col. Rec. Ga.* i. 241–2; Broughton to the Trustees, Charles Town, Oct. 1735, C.O. 5:638, ff. 1–2; Candler, *Col. Rec. Ga.* xxi. 3–5; *Journal of the Commissioners for Trade and Plantations*, vii, 1735–41, pp. 78–9, 82.

GEORGIA: THE SECOND PHASE: RELIGION 181

act on rum, 'does not give that satisfaction' which was desired;[1] so that early in June 1736 it was reported that the Georgia leader would come to Charles Town for a conference.[2] In asking a legislative appropriation for his entertainment at public expense, Governor Broughton lauded Oglethorpe; the Assembly declared itself 'very sensible of his services' and, out of esteem for him, 'would be proud of shewing their regard';[3] while the Upper House agreed to the 'esteem'; but, to Broughton's disgust, both houses refused to make the appropriation.[4] Although Oglethorpe, preferring to continue the controversy by correspondence, did not come to Charles Town, a committee of the Upper House of South Carolina, in presenting a report on this perplexing and involved question of the Indian trade and relations with Georgia, plainly indicated its great faith in Oglethorpe's fairness and impartiality, and each communication from him was considered in a special session of the Upper House.[5] Despite this deference, Oglethorpe now made a move which, whether by accident or design, in no wise eased the situation. This was his conference with the Chickasaw Indians at Savannah on July 12 and 13, 1736.

On March 9, 1734, in explaining to the South Carolinians his financial inability to create further frontier garrisons for their protection, Oglethorpe had declared that 'at present he was so limited that he could not go into any expences farther than making Presents to the Indians', wherewith to assure their 'firm attachment' to the English cause.[6] Eighteen months later, on setting out for his second visit to Georgia, James Oglethorpe took with him a supply of presents for the Indians, costing over £400.[7] It is therefore not strange that the close

[1] C.O. 5:437; S.C. Rec. vi. 247–8.
[2] Charles Town *South Carolina Gazette*, June 5, 1736, p. 2.
[3] C.O. 5:437; S.C. Rec. vi, 255; C.O. 5:439; S.C. Rec. ix. 714–16.
[4] C.O. 5:437; S.C. Rec. vi. 256–7; C.O. 5:439; S.C. Rec. ix. 718–19.
[5] C.O. 5:437; S.C. Rec. vi. 288–94.
[6] C.O. 5:433; S.C. Rec. ii. 158–9.
[7] C.O. 5:689, p. 125; Candler, *Col. Rec. Ga.* ii. 71.

friend of Tomochichi should have held a two-day conference with the most important Indian nation between Carolina and the French; that he should have told them, 'I am a red man, an Indian, in my heart, that is why I love them'; that, when the Chickasaws reported the French propaganda against the quality of British ammunition, he calmly replied: 'Let some of your young men try, and see whether the powder we give you is good. Take the good and leave the bad'; and it is not strange that he taught them to throw back the French hand grenades, and to keep themselves in the open fields or behind trees.[1] In short, Oglethorpe's entire Indian policy was expressed in this sentence, written to the Trustees two weeks after the conference: 'If the French be allow'd to destroy our Indians, Nation by Nation in time of Peace, the Settlements must follow in the first of a Warr.'[2] The sounder the advice he gave, the closer Oglethorpe bound these Indians to himself and to Georgia; but all this contributed towards nullifying Carolinian prestige and influence among them.

The *London Journal* of October 26, 1734, in referring to the departure of the Salzburgers for Georgia observed that 'Many People are likewise gone, and more going daily to settle in Carolina, that Colony being well secured by that of Georgia'.[3] South Carolina seemed to have forgotten that fact and, despite her express desire that 'a harmony and good understanding may be preserved between the two Provinces',[4] a note of acrimony now crept into the discussion. Carolina on July 17, 1736, forwarded a long, formal petition to the King in Council[5]

[1] *MSS. of Marquess Townshend* (H.M.C. Reports), pp. 259–62. For an interesting sidelight on the Indian question see Bissel, Benjamin, *The American Indian in English Literature of the Eighteenth Century* (Yale Studies in English, lxviii, New Haven, Connecticut, 1925), pp. 39, 63.

[2] Oglethorpe to the Trustees, Savannah, July 26, 1736, C.O. 5:638, f. 351 verso; Candler, *Col. Rec. Ga.* xxi. 195–6.

[3] London *London Journal*, Oct. 26, 1734, pp. 2–3.

[4] C.O. 5:437; S.C. Rec. vi. 301–3, July 17, 1736.

[5] Grant and Munro, *Acts of the Privy Council: Colonial Series*, iii. 511–14; C.O. 5:437; S.C. Rec. xviii. 83–101.

and on August 6 Broughton bluntly avowed in a letter to the Board of Trade that, while he had presumed that the Trustees had agreed to an amicable arrangement, 'the conduct of the Gentlemen who are in the Exercise of Power at Georgia has given occasion for a further complaint of new and additional hardships', adding that the people of South Carolina 'apprehend it to be inconsistent with the Freedom of Englishmen to receive laws from the Trustees of Georgia made without their participation and consent.' As to the effect on the Indians, he concluded, not without logic and reason, that, 'if the Indians are provoked, they make no distinction amongst Englishmen; this Province must share with Georgia in the effects of their Revenge'.[1] South Carolina's previous complaints had proven to be in vain,[2] nor was the tense situation relieved by the Wesleys and Oglethorpe. John Wesley was definitely pro-Georgia,[3] while Charles, in a statement to the Trustees, berated the northern neighbours as 'utter enemies to Georgia' who were arousing both the Spaniards and Indians against the infant colony![4] But strongest of all was Oglethorpe's own letter to Newcastle, sent in July before Broughton's complaint had been written. Passing over the Spanish situation as a state of armed neutrality, Oglethorpe let go his sharpened quill at the South Carolinians, ever fearful of Bienville at Mobile:[5] In Charles Town, he affirmed, 'the People seem very unwilling to comply with any of his Majesty's Orders. I was a favourite with them when I was here before a Private man, but now they are angry, because I insist upon their paying Obedience to the King's Commands, particularly to that

---

[1] Broughton to the Board of Trade, Charles Town, Aug. 6, 1736, C.O. 5:365, ff. 139–47; S.C. Rec. xviii. 47–67; *Journal of the Commissioners for Trade and Plantations*, vii, 1735–41, pp. 153–4, 157–62.
[2] *Egmont Diary*, ii. 295–6.
[3] Telford, *The Letters of the Rev. John Wesley, A.M.*, i. 201–3.
[4] *Egmont Diary*, ii. 312, 318.
[5] For a complaint by Bienville against English encouragement of the Indians against the French, see Bienville to Oglethorpe, Mobile, Nov. 2, 1736, C.O. 5:639, f. 65; Candler, *Col. Rec. Ga.* xxi. 266–9.

maintaining the Peace with the Indians'. He excoriated the English merchants who were carrying on a clandestine trade with the French and Indians in total indifference to Indian defections to both French and Spaniards, because 'those merchants gain by it' in profiteering. Asserting that it was better to have the English regulate and punish their own traders than to allow the Indians to do it, Oglethorpe concluded thus: 'I thank God, there are enough honest and faithfull Subjects to his Majesty both here and in Carolina, to execute the King's Orders notwithstanding the Clamours of the Men, who can bear no kind of Government, but would rather assist Foreigners, to draw Slavery upon themselves and their Posterity, than they will obey Laws made by the best of Princes for their Benefit.'[1] Such language allowed of little or no compromise; the issue was joined; and South Carolina perforce appealed to Westminster.[2]

The storm now broke over Oglethorpe's head. All the complainants launched their thunderbolts at the central figure in the situation. Not only did Geraldino embarrass Newcastle and Walpole with his charges, but the Reverend Samuel Quincy, having been refused a bonus for his expenses and doubtful services in Georgia, was spreading the tale of the malcontents,[3] ably abetted by Philip Thicknesse, the former apothecary's assistant, who years later described himself as 'one of the first fools who went over with Oglethorpe'.[4] Rumours now spread that Ogle-

[1] Oglethorpe to Newcastle, Savannah, July, 1736, C.O. 5:383, ff. 29–30; S.C. Rec. xviii. 40–4.

[2] For the best secondary accounts of the South Carolina Controversy see McCrady, Edward, *The History of South Carolina under the Royal Government (1719–1776)* (New York, 1899), chaps. vii–xii; Smith, W. R., *South Carolina as a Royal Province* (New York, 1903), pp. 189–90, 193, 199, 218–19, 277; Hewart, Alexander, *An Historical Account of the Rise and Progress of the Colonies of South Carolina and Georgia* (2 vols., London, 1779), ii, chaps. vii–viii.

[3] *Egmont Diary*, ii. 294–5, 303–4.

[4] Philip Thicknesse to Lord Monboddo, London, March 18, 1789, *MSS. of Lord Monboddo* (H.M.C. Reports, iv, Appendix), p. 519; Thicknesse, Philip, *Memoirs* (2 vols., London, 1788), i. 21–37, 43–63; Nichols, *Literary Anecdotes of the Eighteenth Century*, ix. 257; Maxwell, Constantia, *The English Traveller in France, 1689–1815* (London, 1932), p. 105.

thorpe, having gained a monopoly, was privately trafficking in furs.[1] Because, in Egmont's plaintive words, they were 'kept so much in the dark' by his 'short, unsatisfactory accounts', and because 'it is not our duty or the intention of Parliament that we should support and defend Carolina with the money given us', the Trustees now became so incensed at Oglethorpe that they sent him a letter 'conceived in very strong terms, and expressing our uneasiness that we know nothing from him of the situation our affairs are in in Georgia, and so are incapacitated from answering to the complaints made against us from all quarters'.[2] Finally, the South Carolinians themselves, infuriated by the alleged machinations of one who had been commissioned to act as arbitrator between their colony and Georgia,[3] hurled at him the wild charge that he was 'no white man, but a subject of France who murdered all the English he could get'.[4]

This avalanche of official Spanish diplomatic complaint; censure by the Trustees; inane prattle of the discontented; gossip of the streets; and ridiculous revilements and calumnies of the Carolinians, marked the first real discord in Oglethorpe's colonial career. On September 13, 1736, Harman Verelst, in informing him of the relief felt by the Trustees that Spanish hostilities had been 'so providentially prevented', emphasized their concern over the South Carolina situation and hinted broadly at Oglethorpe's imminent return by asserting that, without him, the Trustees could obtain no more parliamentary appropriations.[5] A month later Verelst renewed this suggestion in the name of Egmont, Vernon, and the other Trustees who desired Oglethorpe's 'presence in England as early as may be, for the approaching session of Parliament; which is expected to meet about the middle of January next. For without your presence, they have no manner of

---

[1] *Egmont Diary*, ii. 307.   [2] Ibid. 289–93, 309.
[3] Ibid. 187.   [4] Ibid. 315.
[5] Harman Verelst to Oglethorpe, London, Sept. 13, 1736, C.O. 5:666, p. 264.

hopes of any further supply; and then Georgia will be in a melancholy state.'[1] This was tantamount to a command, and so in November 1736 Oglethorpe was summoned home by the three issues of paramount importance to those in authority: the plight of the Trustees, due to Oglethorpe's extravagance and neglect in correspondence; South Carolina's appeal to Westminster; and the vital necessity of organizing a stronger defence against the rising wrath of Spain.

On November 23, 1736, James Oglethorpe left Georgia in the ship, *Two Brothers*, still secure in the good wishes of his devoted followers, for whose safety and welfare he had spent fully seven of the last nine months in Frederica and the south.[2] The next day Verelst in London sent forth another missive in which he reported that the Trustees were complaining that they had heard nothing from Oglethorpe since June, observing that it was obviously impossible for them to meet the complaints of South Carolina without the reports of Oglethorpe and Causton, especially inasmuch as Charles Wesley, who had recently returned to England, had as yet failed to report to them. 'Upon the whole the Trustees cannot think they can carry on the settlement of Georgia, or apply again to Parliament with any success; unless you shall come over to answer the objections, and give an account of the progress already made, and justify the application of the sums heretofore granted.'[3] Fortunately for all concerned, Oglethorpe was already at sea when this letter went out to Georgia, but even here the poor man had no peace and quiet.

Crossing the Atlantic at possibly the worst time of the year, Oglethorpe sailed directly into fog and storm. Two stirring descriptions of the ship 'being drove' into Bristol

---

[1] Harman Verelst to Oglethorpe, London, Oct. 22, 1736, C.O. 5:666, pp. 268–9; C.O. 5:686, p. 336; Candler, *Col. Rec. Ga.* i. 261.

[2] Thomas Causton to the Trustees, Savannah, Nov. 26, 1736, C.O. 5:639, f. 20; Candler, *Col. Rec. Ga.* xxi. 270–5; Charles Town *South Carolina Gazette*, Oct. 23, 1736, p. 2.

[3] Harman Verelst to Oglethorpe, London, Nov. 24, 1736, C.O. 5:667, f. 1 verso.

Channel[1] have been recorded: a contemporary London journal noted that the vessel

was in a terrible Storm for several Hours on the Western Coast, so that the Hands on board were quite tired with working the Ship; and Mr. Oglethorp himself, Mr. Tanner, jun. of Haslemere, a Woman on board and the Master were oblig'd to work for several Hours, tho' it rain'd prodigiously hard all the time; and they at last, with great Difficulty, brought the Ship into Harbour.[2]

And Egmont, who probably had it directly from his friend, wrote in his diary that 'he had a narrow escape, being caught on the English coast in the late storm, and so thick a fog for nine days that they could not know where they were, and at last found themselves on breakers'. The crew, giving themselves up for lost, dropped their work 'so that Mr. Oglethorp and Mr. Tanner who came with him were obliged to jump out of bed in their shirts to pull the ropes'.[3] The weather indeed fully justified the fears of Anne Oglethorpe, awaiting her brother at Godalming, when on December 29, 1736, she wrote to her Oxonian friend, Thomas Carte: 'j expecte my brother eny day am under the utmost consarne at thise stormes ... butt hope god will protecte him for better times and that he will be soone here'.[4] Her prayer was answered, and on January 2, 1737, Oglethorpe, in Egmont's words, quite fortunately landed in safety 'at Ilfracombe in Wales',[5] to the great relief of his friends in Georgia who, as Causton later reported, 'are just now rejoycing round a Bonfire and I have given them a Barrell of Beer'.[6]

Proceeding immediately from Devon towards London,

---

[1] London *Evening Post*, Jan. 8, 1737, p. 1; *Grub-Street Journal*, Jan. 13, 1737, p. 2.
[2] London *Hooker's Weekly Miscellany*, Jan. 15, 1737, p. 3.
[3] *Egmont Diary*, ii. 325.
[4] Anne Oglethorpe to Thomas Carte, Godalming, Surrey, Dec. 29, 1736, Carte MSS. (Bodleian Library, Oxford), ccxxvii, f. 268.
[5] *Egmont Diary*, ii. 325.
[6] Thomas Causton to the Trustees, Savannah, March 8, 1737, C.O. 5:639, f. 222 verso; Candler, *Col. Rec. Ga.* xxi. 379.

Oglethorpe 'was handsomely entertained on the Road by several Persons of Distinction, who knew him and caressed him on his safe Return to England'.[1] On January 6 he arrived at Old Palace Yard;[2] the next day 'he waited on her Majesty, and met with a gracious Reception; and afterwards waited on the Right Hon. Sir Robert Walpole, at his House in Downing-Street, and also on the Trustees'.[3] It was evident that he meant to reassert himself! In December, while Oglethorpe was yet on the high seas, Charles Wesley had presented to the Trustees his long-delayed and none too favourable report on the state of affairs in Georgia,[4] so that the former now faced a sceptical audience. In a four-hour conference on January 9, Oglethorpe, who was 'in very good health and spirits',[5] convinced Egmont of his own impeccable conduct and the salutary condition of Georgia, emphasizing particularly the advantages to England of the agreement recently concluded with Governor del Moral Sanchez of Florida.[6] With honeyed words and a more equable balance-sheet than he had been able to exhibit on his previous visit, he next, on January 12, overcame the complaints of the Trustees in such a decisive manner that they gave him a unanimous vote of thanks![7] In ten days after landing at Ilfracombe Oglethorpe had disposed of the first problem and, with the Trustees mollified and reunited in the common cause, he could now with calm assurance face the two remaining issues: the dispute with South Carolina, and the protests of Spain.

The appeal of South Carolina took the form of a lengthy report 'on the proceedings of the people of Georgia', for-

---

[1] London *Gazetteer*, Jan. 8, 1737, p. 2; *Grub-Street Journal*, Jan. 13, 1737, p. 2.
[2] London *The Old Whig: Or, the Consistent Protestant*, Jan. 13, 1737, p. 3.
[3] London *Gazetteer*, Jan. 8, 1737, p. 2; Charles Town *South Carolina Gazette*, March 5, 1737, p. 2.
[4] *Egmont Diary*, ii. 312–17; C.O. 5:686, p. 343; Candler, *Col. Rec. Ga.* i. 265.
[5] *Egmont Diary*, ii. 325.   [6] Ibid. 325–7.
[7] C.O. 5:686, pp. 345–6; Candler, *Col. Rec. Ga.* i. 266–7; *Egmont Diary*, ii. 331; *Gentleman's Magazine*, vii. 58–9.

warded to England on December 15, 1736, while Oglethorpe was still *en route* home. In this document South Carolina fairly claimed priority in the district from the reign of Charles II, citing Oglethorpe's letter of February 15, 1736, in confirmation of it. Having previously held a monopoly of the entire Indian trade by treaty with the Indians themselves, South Carolina, while appreciating both the value of Georgia and its own obligations to the new buffer colony, was willing to share the trade but refused to be shut out entirely therefrom. Admitting that the Georgia Trustees had repudiated the conduct of Patrick Mackay, South Carolina, however, charged that 'he is still sheltered in Georgia, and no care has been taken that he should make reparation for the injury he has done'. The investigating committee of the South Carolina Assembly therefore offered two major complaints: (1) Against Oglethorpe's claim 'to confine the sole regulation of the Indian Trade to the Colony of Georgia'; (2) Against any negation of the free 'right of navigation in the River Savannah'. Asserting that the Trustees, through Oglethorpe, as late as July 1736 had admitted their lack of exclusive right thereto, the Carolinians charged that their own right 'to the Indian Trade is a matter of property which they claim under Laws made for Carolina by an Authority at least equal to that under which the Laws of Georgia are made'.[1] This question had greatly worried Egmont who, on Oglethorpe's safe return, thought it 'very fortunate that he is come before the hearing of the Carolina complaint against us, for his presence will clear up things which we were not so well instructed to speak to as we could wish'.[2] Whether deterred by Oglethorpe's presence or for some other reason, South Carolina in January 1737 postponed further action on its complaint[3] for so long and indefinite a period

[1] C.O. 5:439; S.C. Rec. x. 212–318.
[2] *Egmont Diary*, ii. 325.
[3] Alured Popple to Benjamin Martyn, Whitehall, Jan. 25, 1737, C.O. 5:401, ff. 197–8; S.C. Rec. xviii. 166–9; *Journal of the Commissioners for Trade and Plantations*, vii, 1735–41, pp. 157–60.

that Secretary Martyn, for the Trustees, finally had to ask for a hearing.[1] At last on May 19, 1737, Oglethorpe appeared at a meeting of the Lords Commissioners for Trade and Plantations and again on June 6 and 9. Throughout June the conferences and presentation of testimony and argument continued.[2] During July the question was under adjudication, and on July 28, 1737, the Attorney-General and Solicitor-General handed down a decision. Accepting Oglethorpe's proof of Carolina rum-running and illicit Indian trade without the requisite Georgia licences,[3] the judges ruled that the act excluded Carolinians from all trade with the Indians in Georgia.[4] The dispute was now compromised by an order of the Privy Council giving the South Carolinians trade rights under licences, and peace again reigned on the Edisto.[5] Two of Oglethorpe's three grave problems had been settled. The third, and to Oglethorpe the most important, remained.

Despite del Moral Sanchez's treaty with Oglethorpe—or perhaps because of it—Don Tomás Geraldino had not ceased to protest against the ruthless aggrandizement of the English below the Altamaha, penetrating even to the Saint John's River which was definitely in Spanish territory. On August 27, 1736, there issued from San Ildefonso a royal order, directing him to take due measures for the cessation of English excesses in Florida and containing as the sole alternative a definite threat of force.[6] Henceforth

---

[1] B. Martyn to the Lords of Trade, Georgia Office, London, Jan. 28, 1737, C.O. 5:365, f. 45; S.C. Rec. xviii. 182–4; Martyn to Popple, London, Jan. 28, 1737, C.O. 5:667, ff. 4, verso–5; *Journal of the Commissioners for Trade and Plantations*, vii, 1735–41, pp. 161–2, 165, 175, 177–9; C.O. 5:687, pp. 213, 215.

[2] *Journal of the Commissioners for Trade and Plantations*, vii, 1735–41, pp. 181–3, 189–93, 196–203; C.O. 5:401, pp. 219–21; S.C. Rec. xviii. 108–52; New York *Gazette*, Aug. 22, 1737, p. 3.

[3] *Egmont Diary*, ii. 333. See also Osgood, *The American Colonies in the Eighteenth Century*, iii. 397–9.

[4] C.O. 5:366, f. 60; S.C. Rec. xviii. 255–6; *Journal of the Commissioners for Trade and Plantations*, vii, 1735–41, pp. 208, 211, 213, 284.

[5] C.O. 5:366, ff. 83, 92; S.C. Rec. xix. 79–84, 96–8.

[6] A.I. 87–1–1, No. 44, Royal order to Geraldino, San Ildefonso, Aug. 27, 1736.

Geraldino plied Newcastle with a steady stream of protests and arguments, written and oral, only to find the Secretary of State for the Colonies quite adept at those dilatory tactics reserved by tradition as a Spanish characteristic. Don José Patiño, the Spanish Minister for Colonial Affairs, had sent him all the vital reports received in Madrid from del Moral Sanchez in Saint Augustine,[1] and on October 2 the Spanish representative in London presented his most powerful argument. Recalling Newcastle's assurances to Geraldino in September 1735 that Oglethorpe's second visit to Georgia would in no wise affect the existing Anglo-Spanish treaties or friendship as to Florida, the Spaniard emphasized del Moral Sanchez's 'mortification to see a Fortress, situated in the Territory belonging to His Majesty, eight Leagues distant from Saint Augustine, attacked' by Georgians on March 3, after which they themselves built a fort in Florida. Bluntly affirming that Oglethorpe's conduct was likely to snap the peace between the two powers, Geraldino repeated the geographical formulae which, according to Spain, determined the relative boundaries of Florida and Georgia, and concluded with the recurrent demand that Oglethorpe destroy the illegal fortifications and remain within the territorial precincts of Georgia.[2] On October 17 Geraldino, hearing nothing from Newcastle, saw the Prime Minister, Sir Robert Walpole, who at first merely repeated Newcastle's earlier assurances that the British government 'was not attempting to have the settlers of Georgia extend their boundaries beyond the limits to which this crown was permitted by treaties'. But Walpole promptly 'confessed . . . that Don Diego Oglethorpe had gone to some excess, from which he would be forced to desist'. Despite this assurance, Geraldino's 'apprehensions can have no alleviation in view of the dilatory

[1] A.I. 87–1–2, No. 1, Geraldino to Patiño, London, Sept. 13, 1736.
[2] S.P. 100 (State Papers Foreign: Foreign Ministers in England, P.R.O.): 58, Geraldino to Newcastle, London, Oct. 2, 1736. Also in Add. MSS. (British Museum), 32792, Newcastle Papers, vol. 107 (Diplomatic), f. 326. In French.

method which this government considers necessary',[1] a charge fully sustained by the contemporary correspondence between Newcastle in London, Benjamin Keene in Madrid, and Horace Walpole in Hanover.[2] The burden of proof now fell on poor Newcastle who neatly passed it on to the Trustees, who in turn righteously proclaimed their innocence and ignorance of any improper instructions to Oglethorpe, solemnly affirming that any such actions by their representative in Georgia were entirely contrary to the

inclinations and intentions of the board, and they are convinced that if the matter be more carefully examined, it will be closely evident that these reports are without foundation; and that none of the colonists of Georgia have made incursions into the dominion of the King of Spain nor molested his subjects, the Board having at all times kept within the limits prescribed by the Charter.[3]

The absence of Oglethorpe and Newcastle's unsatisfactory reply of November 25 obviously proved a handicap, and a rumour from Georgia, appearing in the *Gaceta de Madrid*, to the effect that new fortifications were being constructed,[4] in no wise eased the situation which rapidly approached the state of an *impasse*.

On January 25, 1737, James Oglethorpe, secretly hoping to obtain £20,000, calmly asked Parliament to grant him £30,000 for a proper defence of Georgia.[5] A few

[1] A.I. 87-1-2, No. 2, Geraldino to Patiño, London, Oct. 18, 1736; *Egmont Diary*, ii. 300-1. See also A.I. 87-1-1, No. 53, Geraldino to Patiño, London, Oct. 4, 1736; and No. 55, Geraldino to Patiño, London, Oct. 11, 1736.

[2] See Add. MSS. (British Museum), 32792, Newcastle Papers, f. 306, Newcastle to Keene, Whitehall, Sept. 23, 1736; f. 326, Geraldino to Newcastle, London, Oct. 2, 1736; Add. MSS., 9145, Coxe Papers, f. 48, Walpole to Keene, Hanover, Oct. 21, 1736; f. 60, Walpole to Keene, Hanover, Oct. 26, 1736; Add. MSS., 32793, Newcastle Papers, ff. 47-52, Walpole to Keene, Hanover, Oct. 21, 1736; ff. 71-4, Walpole to Keene, Hanover, Oct. 26, 1736; ff. 98-100, Walpole to Keene, Hanover, Nov. 2, 1736.

[3] S.P. 100:58, Newcastle to Geraldino, Whitehall, Nov. 25, 1736; Add. MSS. (British Museum), 32793, Newcastle Papers, f. 261. In French.

[4] A.I. 87-1-3, No. 4, Excerpt from the *Gaceta de Madrid*.

[5] *Egmont Diary*, ii. 334, 341. See also *Commons Journals*, xxii. 740, 779.

days later Geraldino made it a point to see him and question him categorically as to his activities in the Debatable Land. Oglethorpe tried to pacify him as to his intentions there by recalling the agreement with del Moral Sanchez,[1] but the Spanish Minister's report of the situation led Madrid to take stringent measures for the reinforcement of the troops at Saint Augustine.[2] The international situation had assumed a sable hue, the intensity of which was not relieved by Sir Robert Walpole's position in London.

Oglethorpe's parliamentary request for £30,000 had created a crisis for the Prime Minister who now sought the former's advice concerning the proper measures to be taken for the security of the American colonies. Oglethorpe gave it without stint. As Egmont so interestingly reported it, 'he spoke with great freedom to Sir Robert, who told him he was not used to have such things said to him. Mr. Oglethorpe replied, Yes, he was when he was plain Mr. Walpole; but now he was Sir Robert, and Chief Minister, he was surrounded by sycophants and flatterers who will not tell him the truth.' In this extraordinary conversation Oglethorpe emphasized his earnest desire to continue the project, but 'he would and must give it up if not supported by him [Walpole], for he had twice been overseas to carry on the Colony, and not only ventured his life and health, to the neglect of his own affairs, but actually spent 3,000*l* of his own money'. Georgia, he continued, 'was a national affair, and he did not pretend to be a Don Quixote for it, and suffer in his reputation, as he must do, if he continues his concern without public countenance'. Predicting that, if Walpole should drop Georgia, Spain would immediately acquire it and France could then attack the Carolinas and Virginia, Oglethorpe categorically asserted that 'there were but two ways of defending our Colonies from the French and Spaniards

[1] A.I. 87–1–2, No. 5, Geraldino to the Marquis of Torrenueva, London, Jan. 31, 1737. Patiño had died in November 1736.

[2] A.I. 87–1–2, No. 6, Torrenueva to Sebastian de la Quadra, Madrid, Feb. 6, 1737; A.I. 87–1–2, No. 7, Torrenueva to de la Quadra, Madrid, Feb. 9, 1737.

and their Indians, the one by forming a regular and warlike militia, the other by keeping a body of regular troops'. He therefore asked for the power to raise a local militia, which Walpole refused him. He then asked for an Inspector-General of Colonial Forces to co-ordinate all colonial militia, to which Walpole acceded, proposing him for the post. Oglethorpe was willing to assume the additional responsibility, but Walpole suddenly raised the question of his continued eligibility as a Member of Parliament, which in the former's opinion mattered little. The Prime Minister asked whether he would accept the Governorship of South Carolina, but this Oglethorpe declined, requesting only that Walpole dismiss those Carolina officials who were hostile to Georgia, a suggestion in which Sir Robert showed no interest whatsoever.[1]

The situation proving far from satisfactory to Oglethorpe, the month of February passed in silence and not until March 14 did Walpole agree to commission him General of the Forces of South Carolina and Georgia,[2] an act which went far to revive Carolina's friendship.[3] As Parliament now granted the £20,000 which he had expected,[4] Oglethorpe fully realized the strength of his own position and refused the commission as General of the Forces until he could obtain what he had originally sought, a regiment of 700 men, with himself as Colonel, wherewith to defend South Carolina and Georgia.[5] By April Walpole was striving desperately to obtain his acceptance of the Governorship of South Carolina whose people, admitting now their debt to Oglethorpe,[6] greatly desired him and his aid[7] but, as such procedure would automatically forfeit his seat in Parliament, the latter again declined to return in any capacity save that of military commander.[8] Since March London had been buzzing with all kinds of rumours concerning Spanish preparations in Cuba,[9] and both Newcastle and the Trus-

---

[1] *Egmont Diary*, ii. 339–41. [2] Ibid. 368.
[3] Ibid. 477. [4] Ibid. 349, 364–5, 370. [5] Ibid. 383.
[6] Ibid. 394. [7] Ibid. 374, 389. [8] Ibid. 401. [9] Ibid. 376.

tees had received dire warnings of impending dangers from Broughton in Charles Town.[1] In March Oglethorpe had sent to Newcastle a strong memorandum on preparedness[2] which had been duly criticized by that optimistic sailor, Sir Charles Wager,[3] but the continuance of the rumours led Walpole to reconsider matters, so that on June 19 Oglethorpe 'kissed hands'[4] for a commission as 'General and Commander in Chief of all and singular his Majesty's Forces employed and to be employed in his Majesty's provinces of South Carolina and Georgia in America; and likewise to be Captain of that Independent Company of Foot doing Duty in his Majesty's said Province of South Carolina'.[5]

But if rumours of Spanish preparations in distant Cuba had altered Walpole's mind once, the continued protests, oral and written, of Geraldino in London could make the Prime Minister change again. The smooth diplomatic replies of Newcastle in the late months of 1736 and even the guileless evasions of Oglethorpe himself in January 1737 had deceived neither the Spanish Minister to England nor the authorities in Madrid. On March 4 the Council of the Spanish King met in a full session to consider Oglethorpe's penetration of the Saint John's River country[6] and, although a small piece of paper attached

[1] Broughton to Newcastle, Charles Town, Feb. 6, 1737, C.O. 5:388, f. 141; S.C. Rec. xvi. 170–3; Broughton to the Trustees, Charles Town, Feb. 7, 1737, C.O. 5:639, f. 89; C.O. 5:687, p. 12.

[2] Memorandum from Oglethorpe to Newcastle, London, March 26, 1737, C.O. 5:654, ff. 101–2; Candler, *Col. Rec. Ga.* xxv, f. 101.

[3] Sir Charles Wager's Observations, April 7, 1737, C.O. 5:654, ff. 105–6; Candler, *Col. Rec. Ga.* xxv, f. 105.

[4] London *Grub-Street Journal*, June 23, 1737, p. 2; *Universal Spectator*, June 25, 1737, p. 2.

[5] London *Gazette*, July 5, 1737, p. 1; S.P. 44 (State Papers, Domestic. Entry Books, P.R.O.): 181, Military Commissions, 1730–9, p. 532; W.O: 25 (War Office): 19, Commission Books, 1735–40, pp. 55–6; W.O. 25:133, Notification Books, 1735–40, p. 45; C.O. 324: 37, ff. 36–7; C.O. 324:49, pp. 126–8; C.O. 5:366, f. 75; S.C. Rec. xviii, ff. 249–50; *Egmont Diary*, ii. 412, 417; Thomas Carte to John Anstis, London, Oct. 6, 1737, Carte MSS. (Bodleian Library, Oxford), ccxxxiv, f. 48.

[6] A.I. 58–1–25, No. 8, Deliberations of the Council relative to the English, Madrid, March 4, 1737.

to the report thereof notes that the council had no result, it is worthy of note that four days later Torrenueva, as Patiño's successor in the Colonial Office, sent to Geraldino explicit instructions from the King himself, that, as long as Oglethorpe remained in London, the Spanish Minister should 'contrive with the utmost cunning and activity to inquire into the plans, proposals, and petitions which he may present to the board of administrators of Carolina and New Georgia, and what these administrators and that ministry decide with regard to them'. In addition he was to keep a check on all munitions of war being shipped to Georgia.[1] In accordance with these instructions Geraldino on March 28 sent home a lengthy report concerning that fateful armistice between Oglethorpe and del Moral Sanchez, observing that the English signatory thereof had greatly over-emphasized its value as a means of maintaining peace and expressing unqualified criticisms of it as deleterious to Spanish interests.[2] As a result of Geraldino's warnings, the Madrid administration in April instructed the Governor of Havana to procure the 'extirpation of the English from the territories which they have usurped in his Majesty's dominions belonging to the provinces of Florida';[3] and even the Archbishop Viceroy of New Spain in Mexico was called on for aid, both military and financial.[4] Rumours as to both Spanish and English activity in the West Indies now flew thick and fast,[5] and plain evidence appeared of the treachery of an English-

---

[1] A.I. 87-1-2, No. 9, Torrenueva to Geraldino, Madrid, March 8, 1737.
[2] A.I. 87-1-2, No. 14, Geraldino to Torrenueva, London, March 28, 1737.
[3] A.I. 87-1-2, No. 18, Torrenueva to Governor Juan Francisco de Guemes y Horcasitas, Madrid, April 10, 1737; A.I. 87-1-3, No. 8, Madrid official to Horcasitas, Madrid, April 10, 1737. See also A.I. 87-1-3, No. 13, Torrenueva to Horcasitas, Madrid, April 27, 1737.
[4] A.I. 87-1-3, No. 9, Unsigned letter to the Archbishop Viceroy of New Spain, Madrid, April 10, 1737; No. 10, Unsigned letter, probably Torrenueva, to Don Juan de Vuarron y Eguiarreta, Archbishop Viceroy of Mexico, Madrid, April 10, 1737.
[5] A.I. 87-1-2, No. 19, Geraldino to Torrenueva, London, April 11, 1737; No. 39, Geraldino to Torrenueva, London, May 9, 1737.

man, John Savy, who in Havana became Miguel Wall.[1] While Geraldino continued his protests in London, Newcastle had instructed Benjamin Keene in Madrid to be equally observant of the Spanish trend of affairs and to emphasize at all times to the Spanish Court the fact that Oglethorpe's agreement with del Moral Sanchez at Saint Augustine had definitively removed any and all causes of complaint. It was, therefore, to be presumed that the English need have no fear of a Spanish attack on Georgia.[2] Throughout April Newcastle and Keene sought a frank and satisfactory statement of intentions from Spain, only to find that Madrid was subtly repudiating del Moral Sanchez's agreement with Oglethorpe of the previous October,[3] and, in fact, was recruiting and forwarding large reinforcements and stocks of munitions materials for war to Cuba.[4] On April 26 Newcastle begged Geraldino in London to have Spain check its rumoured war preparations in Cuba; on May 1, the Spaniard having as yet done nothing, Newcastle repeated the request and gave him a copy of the Oglethorpe-del Moral Sanchez agreement, 'notwithstanding that I [Geraldino] told him that neither one nor the other had had any power to do it'.[5] By May Keene had despaired of finding any way to prevent a Spanish attack on Georgia[6] and Newcastle, half

[1] A.I. 87-1-2, No. 19, Geraldino to Torrenueva, London, April 11, 1737; A.I. 87-1-3, No. 11, Unsigned letter, probably Torrenueva, to Horcasitas, Madrid, April 10, 1737.

[2] Newcastle to Benjamin Keene, Whitehall, March 24, 1737, Add. MSS. (British Museum), 32794, Newcastle Papers, ff. 242-7.

[3] Newcastle to Keene, Whitehall, April 7, 1737, Add. MSS. (British Museum), 32794, Newcastle Papers, ff. 330-2; Keene to Newcastle, Madrid, April 22, 1737, Add. MSS., 32794, Newcastle Papers, ff. 337-42.

[4] A.I. 87-1-3, No. 12, Unsigned letter, probably Torrenueva, to Horcasitas, Madrid, April 16, 1737; A.I. 87-1-2, No. 21, Geraldino to Torrenueva, London, April 18, 1737; A.I. 87-1-2, No. 41, Unsigned dispatch to the Viceroy Archbishop of Mexico, Madrid, May 13, 1737.

[5] A.I. 87-1-2, No. 28, Geraldino to Torrenueva, London, May 2, 1737, enclosing articles of armistice made between Oglethorpe and Governor d · Moral Sanchez.

[6] Keene to Newcastle, Casa del Monte, Spain, May 13, 1737, Add. MSS. (British Museum), 32795, f. 1.

dictatorial, half pleading, found his every effort checked in London,[1] where Geraldino, fully awake to his unique opportunity, joyously continued his protests.[2]

This situation continued throughout June and July, the English position remaining static,[3] while Geraldino gathered both courage and momentum. Oglethorpe's success in securing his regiment and his commission during June now led to the Spaniard's most vital stroke. He deliberately approached Sir Robert Walpole, the Prime Minister, and subsequently Newcastle and Horace Walpole in order to prevent Oglethorpe's prospective return to Georgia;[4] and when he found that impossible, he did the next best thing: continued protests and threats of reprisals,[5] culminating in a sharp note to Newcastle on August 8. In this the Spaniard flatly refused to believe or accept the Foreign Minister's denial of Oglethorpe's illegal operations in Florida, and bluntly reported that the King of Spain, while still relying on 'the Good Faith & Justice' of Britain's ruler, was looking for the reform in British methods, so greatly needed, but never produced.[6]

[1] Newcastle to Keene, Whitehall, May 5, 1737, Add. MSS. (British Museum), 32795, ff. 22–5.

[2] A.I. 87–1–2, No. 53, Geraldino to Sebastian de la Quadra, Spanish Secretary of State, London, May 23, 1737.

[3] Keene to Newcastle, Casa del Monte, Spain, June 3, 1737, Add. MSS. (British Museum), 32795, Newcastle Papers, f. 80; Keene to Newcastle, Casa del Monte, June 10, 1737, Add. MSS., 32795, ff. 90–1; Keene to Newcastle, Madrid, June 17, 1737, Add. MSS., 32795, ff. 94–6; Newcastle to Keene, Whitehall, June 23, 1737, Add. MSS., 32795 ff. 131–5; Keene to Newcastle, Madrid, July 1, 1737, Add. MSS., 32795, ff. 127–8; Keene to Newcastle, Madrid, July 22, 1737, Add. MSS., 32795, ff. 164–5.

[4] A.I. 87–1–2, No. 62, Geraldino to Torrenueva, London, June 13, 1737; No. 64, Geraldino to Torrenueva, London, June 20, 1737; No. 65, Geraldino to Torrenueva, London, June 27, 1737.

[5] A.I. 87–1–2, No. 69, Geraldino to Torrenueva, London, July 4, 1737; No. 70, Torrenueva to de la Quadra, Madrid, July 14, 1737; No. 71, Geraldino to Torrenueva, London, July 18, 1737; No. 72, Geraldino to Torrenueva, London, Aug. 1, 1737.

[6] S.P. 100 (State Papers, Foreign: Foreign Ministers in England, P.R.O.):59, Geraldino to Newcastle, London, Aug. 8, 1737; A.I. 87–1–2, No. 73, Geraldino to Torrenueva, London, Aug. 8, 1737, enclosing the note to Newcastle; Geraldino to Newcastle, in French, London, Aug. 8, 1737, Add. MSS. (British Museum), 32795, Newcastle Papers, f. 311.

This had the desired effect, for on August 10 Sir Robert Walpole, retracting his grant of less than two months before, requested Oglethorpe to disband his regiment in order to placate Spain.[1] At this Oglethorpe, supported by contemporary opinion,[2] 'fired and asked him what man he took him to be, and whether he thought he had no conscience, to be the instrument of carrying over 3,000 souls to Georgia, and then abandoning them to be destroyed by the Spaniards, for the consideration of a regiment. He also desired to know whether Georgia was to be given up, yea or nay? If so, it would be kind and just to let the Trustees know it at once, that we might write immediately over to the inhabitants to retire and save themselves in time.'[3] Whether it was due to Oglethorpe's blunt, derisive speech, or to a memorial for protection from the Trustees,[4] or yet to the fact that at this time the Georgian had been invited to hunt with the King himself,[5] Walpole capitulated[6] and, despite one more weak attempt to keep him at home as a parliamentary drudge,[7] James Oglethorpe, on August 25, 1737, was commissioned 'Colonel of the Regiment of Foot for the Defence of His Majesty's Plantations in America'.[8] He had beaten Walpole on every count, and, after a successful interview with King George, in September 1737, proceeded to recruit his regiment[9] which, in the words of Britain's army historian, 'was formed by the simple process of turning over the whole of the effective privates of the Twenty-fifth Foot' to his

---

[1] *Egmont Diary*, ii. 429.

[2] e.g. editorial in the London *Daily Post*, Aug. 23, 1737, reprinted in the *Gentleman's Magazine*, vii. 500; *Egmont Diary*, ii. 429.

[3] *Egmont Diary*, ii. 429.

[4] C.O. 5:687, pp. 35–6; Candler, *Col. Rec. Ga.* i. 296.

[5] *Egmont Diary*, ii. 430. For confirmation of this theory see Bolton and Ross, *The Debatable Land*, p. 76.

[6] *Egmont Diary*, ii. 429–30, 436.

[7] Ibid. 433–4.

[8] S.P. 44 (State Paper, Domestic, Entry Books, P.R.O.):181, Military Commissions, 1730–9, p. 370; W.O. 25:19, Commission Books, 1735–40, p. 73.

[9] *Egmont Diary*, ii. 433–4; *Gentleman's Magazine*, vii. 638.

command,[1] an action which aroused deep distrust among the Spaniards.[2]

Having, as he presumed, completely set at rest the Spanish complaints, Oglethorpe spent the next six months in recruiting his regiment, in attending the sessions of the House of Commons, and in pressing for an appropriation of almost £13,000 for that regiment of 684 men,[3] while in personal social intercourse he renewed his friendship with Charles Wesley.[4] In 1737 he had been made a Governor of Westminster Infirmary, in the welfare of which he now took a deep interest,[5] and early in 1738 he became a patron of literature by subscribing to the forthcoming edition of a poem, London, by an unknown author named Samuel Johnson.[6] But neither humanity nor the humanities could protect him from the ceaseless assaults of Spain, which by April 1738 led to one of the most brilliant examples of diplomatic evasion and sheer bluff in the annals of British imperialism.

The core of the Spanish protest had lain in two points: Oglethorpe's British Fort Saint George blocking the mouth of the Saint John's River in undeniably Spanish territory, and the Spanish claim of Georgia and much of Carolina to 33° 50′ by the seventh article of the Anglo-Spanish treaty of 1670. The latter question was promptly settled by a successful British reference to the text of the document in question,[7] but the former problem depended largely on the word of one witness—James Edward Oglethorpe. When on August 25 Walpole had capitulated to

---

[1] 'This incident marks the farthest limit to which the principle of separating Colonial and Imperial service was pushed by the War Office.' Fortescue, J. W., *History of the British Army* (13 vols., London, 1910–30), ii. 43.
[2] A.I. 86–6–5, No. 38, News report, Saint Augustine, Oct. 29, 1737.
[3] *Commons Journals*, xxiii. 12–13.
[4] Telford, *The Journal of the Rev. Charles Wesley*, pp. 110 ff.
[5] *Egmont Diary*, ii. 455, 458, 464.
[6] The volume appeared in May, 1738. Hill, *Boswell's Life of Johnson* (Powell revision), i. 118.
[7] Horace Walpole to Keene, The Hague, Sept. 3, 1737, Add. MSS. (British Museum), 32795, Newcastle Papers, ff. 250–1; Newcastle to Keene, Hampton Court, Sept. 12, 1737, Add. MSS., 32795, ff. 303–10.

the Georgian's demands, Newcastle decided it was time to answer Geraldino's communication of August 8,[1] and on September 2 he sent a lengthy and explicit denial of any English trespassing in Florida. In a total repudiation of Spain's territorial claims, he gave the assurance that the King of England would 'not permit any of his governors in America, nor any one else whomsoever, who acts by his authority, to invade or encroach on any part of the states belonging to his Catholic Majesty', and then observed that 'His Majesty is very greatly vexed that any umbrage should be taken' at any of Oglethorpe's activities: 'It doth not appear to the king that Mr. Oglethorpe, during the time he has been employed by the directors of the company of Georgia, has given the court of Spain any just cause for complaint' and the King reserved the right to employ whom he pleased.[2]

Throughout the remaining months of 1737 there was a surfeit of correspondence between Benjamin Keene in Madrid, Horace Walpole at The Hague, and Newcastle in London, which yields nothing of value.[3] At the same time Geraldino industriously reported to Torrenueva and suggested that, as the Oglethorpe-del Moral Sanchez convention of 1736 was void due to the impotency of both signatories to act legally, Newcastle's proposal of a boundary commission might prove feasible.[4] In September Geraldino reported Walpole as 'saying in confidence' that Ogle-

[1] A.I. 87–1–2, No. 79, Geraldino to Torrenueva, London, Aug. 29, 1737.

[2] S.P. 100 (State Papers, Foreign: Foreign Ministers in England, P.R.O.): 59, Newcastle to Geraldino, Hampton Court, Sept. 2, 1737; S.P. 104 (Foreign Entry Books):141, Spain, 1734–9, Newcastle to Geraldino, Hampton Court, Sept. 2, 1737; A.I. 87–1–2, No. 80, Newcastle to Geraldino, in French, Hampton Court, September 2, 1737; Add. MSS. (British Museum). 32795, Newcastle Papers, f. 315. See also Newcastle to Keene, Hampton Court, Sept. 12, 1737, Add. MSS., 32795, ff. 303–10.

[3] See Add. MSS. (British Museum), 32795, Newcastle Papers, ff. 324–8, 374–6; Add. MSS., 32796, ff. 11–13, 18, 26–30, 36–7, 45–8, 52–4, 59–61, 111–21, 129–35, 163–5, 174–5, 182–5, 190–1, 209–28, 234–43, 268–70, 272–3, 284–9, 295–8.

[4] A.I. 87–1–2, No. 80½, Geraldino to Torrenueva, London, Sept. 5, 1737; No. 81, Geraldino to Torrenueva, London, Sept. 19, 1737; No. 82, Geraldino to Torrenueva, London, Sept. 23, 1737.

thorpe 'will not be allowed to go' to Georgia 'and apparently the directors of Georgia so understand it'.[1] By October the fear of Oglethorpe's departure was greater and was magnified by news of his regiment.[2] Torrenueva promptly warned Horcasitas in Havana of the prospective situation,[3] while Geraldino sought what proved to be an embarrassing and disturbing interview with Walpole. The Prime Minister, in an irascible mood, passed the Spaniard on to Newcastle who, when asked as to Oglethorpe's regiment and Georgia, vigorously charged that 'the least movement disturbed' Geraldino and asked why he had not spoken to Walpole. The Spaniard, however, refusing to be the diplomatic football for these two Englishmen, stuck to his guns and courageously questioned the necessity for the regiment.[4] Late in November the convention plan to settle the boundaries of Georgia and Florida was again advanced as a substitute for the defunct agreement of October 1736,[5] largely as the result of a massive report on the English in Carolina and Georgia, compiled by the Conde del Montijo.[6] The year closed with a definite decision by the King of Spain to create such a commission.[7]

In January 1738 the rumours and prospect of a boundary commission again found Newcastle ever anxious to

[1] A.I. 87–1–2, No. 82, Geraldino to Torrenueva, London, Sept. 23, 1737.
[2] A.I. 87–1–2, No. 83, Geraldino to Torrenueva, London, Oct. 10, 1737, Enclosure: Torrenueva to Geraldino, rough draft, Madrid, Nov. 4, 1737.
[3] A.I. 87–1–3, No. 20, Torrenueva to Horcasitas, Madrid, Oct. 12, 1737; A.I. 87–1–2, No. 84, Torrenueva to Horcasitas, Memorandum of orders to the Governor of Havana, Madrid, Oct. 12, 1737.
[4] A.I. 87–1–2, No. 89, Geraldino to Torrenueva, London, Oct. 17, 1737.
[5] A.I. 87–1–2, No. 96, Torrenueva to Geraldino, Madrid, Nov. 28, 1737. This did not, however, weaken the warning instructions sent to del Moral Sanchez's successor in Florida, Governor Manuel de Montiano, A.I. 87–1–2, No. 98, Unsigned dispatch to Montiano, Madrid, Nov. 28, 1737. See also A.I. 87–1–2, No. 99, Unsigned letter, probably Torrenueva, to Horcasitas, Madrid, Nov. 28, 1737; and No. 100, Torrenueva to Horcasitas, Madrid, Nov. 28, 1737.
[6] A.I. 87–1–2, No. 92, Report by the Conde del Montijo, San Lorenzo, Nov. 9, 1737.
[7] A.I. 87–1–2, No. 104$\frac{1}{2}$, Torrenueva to Geraldino, Madrid, as of Nov. 28, 1737; sent Dec. 23, 1737.

placate Spain,[1] but he now asked Oglethorpe to suggest instructions for the Commissioners. While Don Manuel de Montiano was assuming the administration of Florida and reporting, to both Havana and Madrid, that Oglethorpe deemed Saint Augustine more important to England than all her other American possessions,[2] the forthright Colonel of the Georgia-Carolina Regiment on February 8 bluntly affirmed the 'clear and full Right' of Britain to Georgia, emphasizing the point that 'it is incumbent upon the Crown of Spain, if they claim the same, to make out and prove their Rights, and then His Majesty's Commissaries will be able to make proper Answers to those Proofs'. In short, 'as Plaintiffs therefore, it is their Business to show their Rights',[3] in which contention Oglethorpe was upheld by Minister Keene in Madrid.[4] But while the question of Spanish rights was easily arranged, the old problem of Oglethorpe's fort on the Saint John's River continued to make trouble.

Throughout January and February of 1738 the important topic of Spanish diplomatic correspondence had been the composition of the prospective British commission on the boundary,[5] but on March 17 Benjamin Keene reported to Newcastle that the Spaniards were insisting on the

[1] Newcastle to Keene, Whitehall, Jan. 26, 1738, Add. MSS. (British Museum), 32797, Newcastle Papers, ff. 37–8; Keene to Newcastle, Madrid, Feb. 24, 1783, Add. MSS., 32797, f. 93.

[2] Don Manuel de Montiano to the Governor-General of Cuba, No. 2, Saint Augustine, Florida, Nov. 11, 1737, *Collections of the Georgia Historical Society*, vii. (part i), 8–9; A.I. 86–6–5, No. 42, Montiano to the King of Spain, Saint Augustine, Dec. 19, 1737.

[3] Oglethorpe to Newcastle, London, Feb. 8, 1738, Add. MSS. (British Museum), 32797, Newcastle Papers, ff. 52–3.

[4] Keene to Newcastle, Madrid, Feb. 23, 1738, Add. MSS. (British Museum), 32797, Newcastle Papers, ff. 91–2.

[5] A.I. 87–1–2, No. 106, Geraldino to Torrenueva, London, Jan. 23, 1738; No. 107, Geraldino to Torrenueva, London, Jan. 30, 1738; A.I. 87–1–3, No. 23, Geraldino to Torrenueva, London, Feb. 6, 1738, Enclosed is draft of Torrenueva's reply of Feb. 24; No. 24, Torrenueva to de la Quadra, Buen Retiro, Feb. 8, 1738; No. 25, Torrenueva to de la Quadra, Buen Retiro, Feb. 16, 1738; A.I. 87–1–2, No. 109, Conde del Montijo to the King, Madrid, March 3, 1738; No. 110, Dispatch to de la Quadra, Buen Retiro, March 13, 1738.

demolition of Oglethorpe's fortifications in Spanish territory as a pre-requisite to any conference for boundary adjustments.[1] Despite del Moral Sanchez's report of the autumn of 1736[2] and Torrenueva's admission to Horcasitas on April 10, 1737, that Oglethorpe had abandoned the fort on the Saint John's River,[3] the Spanish demands of March 1738 implied the continued existence of Fort Saint George on the Saint John's River which Oglethorpe had agreed to evacuate in the negotiations with Arredondo and del Moral Sanchez in the autumn of 1736. The burden of proof in this matter now lay on the one man in England who knew the facts—James Oglethorpe. Well aware that none of his fellow Trustees had been to Georgia and that, on the other hand, none of his garrison from Fort Saint George were in England to disprove his words, and cognizant above all that—as Walpole was obviously ruthlessly willing to use Georgia as a pawn, if necessary, in the European game—on his own word depended the destiny of empire for Britain in the south, James Oglethorpe indulged in a gallant, magnificent, imperial evasion. Newcastle having asked him to name the forts 'in the Provinces under my Command, and what had been demolished', Oglethorpe mentioned a number before coming to 'Fort King George or Fort Saint George' which, he deliberately affirmed, still stood 'upon that Part of the Alatamaha nearest to the River which the Spaniards call St. Johns'. Deceiving Newcastle and the Trustees as to the individual identity of these two forts, one of which, Fort Saint George, was unquestionably in Spanish territory on the Saint John's River, Oglethorpe calmly justified as perfectly legal

---

[1] Keene to Newcastle, Madrid, March 17, 1738, Add. MSS. (British Museum), 32797, Newcastle Papers, ff. 166–71.

[2] A.I. 87–1–2, No. 19, Geraldino to Torrenueva, London, April 11, 1737, Enclosure No. 1, Governor del Moral Sanchez to the Conde del Montijo, Saint Augustine, [probably October] 14, 1736.

[3] A.I. 87–1–3, No. 8, Unsigned letter, probably Torrenueva, to Horcasitas, Madrid, April 10, 1737. See also A.I. 87–1–2, No. 99, Unsigned letter, probably Torrenueva, to Horcasitas, Madrid, Nov. 28, 1737; and No. 100, Torrenueva to Horcasitas, Madrid, Nov. 28, 1737.

and proper the British claim to all that portion of the Debatable Land between Fort King George on the Altamaha, north even of Frederica, and Fort Saint George at the mouth of the Saint John's, deep in Spanish Florida. In order to emphasize this, he blinded his audience to his own manœuvres by directing their dazed attention to the brilliance of English imperial history from the conquest of Saint Augustine by that gentleman buccaneer, Sir Francis Drake, through the various grants to the Proprietors of Carolina and the Trustees for Georgia, down to the instructions of 1735.[1] Oglethorpe had saved the colony for England from the clutches of Spain only to find himself in great danger of losing it for lack of interest on the part of the Trustees!

While the great game of European politics was being played behind the scenes, the Trustees, unaware of the international forces causing Walpole's variable attitude, had come to the rather obvious conclusion that the government was opposed to Oglethorpe's imminent return to Georgia 'as believing his head too full of schemes and that he may possibly by his warmth of temper run the Colony into an unnecessary quarrel with Spain'.[2] Oglethorpe throughout had been intent on advertising the colony and making large plans for it, but, before allowing him to depart, the Trustees imparted to him much good advice, struck numerous items from the budget, drew his attention to their ever-decreasing membership, and chided him for his own haphazard attendance at board meetings which they ascribed to his opposition to their new policy of retrenchments.[3] Having drawn recruits from various northern centres[4] Oglethorpe, on March 29, invited the

[1] Oglethorpe to Newcastle, London, April 2, 1738, C.O. 5:654, ff. 131-2; Add. MSS. (British Museum), 32797, Newcastle Papers, ff. 292-4.

[2] *Egmont Diary*, ii. 469. See also pp. 399 and 468.

[3] Ibid. 472-4. For resignations of Trustees see C.O. 5:687, pp. 60-1; Candler, *Col. Rec. Ga.* i. 310.

[4] On Jan. 14, 1738, 280 recruits for Oglethorpe's regiment were ordered to march from Birmingham to Woburn and Dunstable; on Feb. 7 they were to leave Dunstable for the duration of the local fair; in March they were to

Trustees to review the departing regiment the next day but, except for Egmont and three others, that group of worthies shunned both the review—the press said his troops 'made a handsome Appearance'[1]—and the 'very elegant dinner' which followed.[2] Despite his deep disappointment, Oglethorpe on May 1 tendered a farewell dinner to eleven Trustees and Common Councilmen at which James Vernon frankly told him 'he must look after the military affairs, and the Trustees would look after the civil'.[3] A week later, on May 8, King George II gave Oglethorpe special instructions carefully to 'avoid giving any just Cause of Offence or Jealousy to the Spaniards', but rather to 'maintain the strictest friendship'.[4] Three days later Oglethorpe left London[5] for Southampton where he arrived on the evening of May 16 and, in the words of a contemporary journal, the next morning 'at Six o'Clock saw his Regiment under Arms: They went through all their Exercise and Evolutions very much to the Satisfaction of the Spectators, of whom there was a great Number. They made a good Appearance, being finely armed, well cloathed, and strong middle-siz'd young Men. There are above twenty Gentlemen of good Families and Fortune that go as Volunteers, and carry Arms in the Regiment'.[6] Following this inspection which seemed almost a portent, Oglethorpe set out for Portsmouth and Georgia.[7] In every respect the most difficult period of his entire colonial career lay before him.

---

proceed via 'St. Albans, Barnet, Highgate, Hampstead, Wandsworth, Putney, Kingston, Two Cobhams, Ripley, Guildford, Godalmin, Farnham, Alton, Alresford, Winchester', to Southampton, W.O. 5 (War Office. Out-Letters: Marching Orders, P.R.O.): 33, 1737–40, pp. 11, 20, 29–30, 38, 53.

[1] London *Hooker's Weekly Miscellany*, April 7, 1738, p. 3.
[2] *Egmont Diary*, ii. 475. See also the London *Daily Gazetteer*, March 31, 1738, p. 2; April 3, 1738, p. 2; and the New York *Gazette*, Aug. 21, 1738, p. 2.
[3] *Egmont Diary*, ii. 482–3.   [4] C.O. 5:654, ff. 133–6.
[5] *Egmont Diary*, ii. 484–5. See also the New York *Gazette*, July 24, 1738, p. 4.
[6] London *Evening Post*, May 23, 1738, p. 1; *Hooker's Weekly Miscellany*, May 26, 1738, pp. 3–4: 'Country-News. Southampton, May 17, 1738.'
[7] London *Daily Gazetteer*, May 20, 1738, p. 2.

CHAPTER VII

GEORGIA: THE THIRD PHASE: IMPERIAL DEFENCE

As had been the case in his other voyages to America, Oglethorpe was delayed by unfavourable weather conditions from the middle of May to late June. Leaving Portsmouth in the *Blandford* on June 26,[1] Oglethorpe was checked in Plymouth Sound whence he sent two letters, recording his impatience to depart, one to Newcastle,[2] the other to the Trustees.[3] At last on July 5 the *Blandford* set out to sea with the man-of-war, *Hector*, and five transports, a convoy system which the Admiralty had generously and efficiently placed at the disposal of the Trustees for some time.[4] By July 18 they were at Madeira where Oglethorpe wrote to Newcastle with evident pride: 'There has been the greatest care taken of the troops on board, and though they are much crowded, yet we have lost (God be praised) but one man and one woman, who died at sea.'[5] By September 13 he could report that 'we have had a very happy Passage',[6] and on the nineteenth, when off Jekyll Island, he wrote to Sir Joseph Jekyll, for whom that isle was named, that 'we have had the finest Passage'.[7] The

[1] New York *Weekly Journal*, Aug. 28, 1738, p. 3.
[2] Oglethorpe to Newcastle, On board the *Blandford* at Plymouth, July 3, 1738, C.O. 5:654, f. 158.
[3] Oglethorpe to the Trustees, On board the *Blandford* at Plymouth, July 3, 1738, C.O. 5:654, f. 161.
[4] Admiralty 1:4108, Correspondence from the Duke of Newcastle, Secretary of State, 1734–40; Admiralty 2:469, Secretary's Letter Book, 1736–8, pp. 301, 363, 369, 446–7; Admiralty 2:470, Secretary's Letter Book, 1738–9, pp. 1, 4, 55, 58, 65. See also the London *Daily Gazetteer*, June 28, 1738, p. 1; July 1, 1738, p. 1; July 4, 1738, p. 2.
[5] Oglethorpe to Newcastle, On board the *Blandford* at 'Madera', July 18, 1738, C.O. 5:654, f. 164.
[6] Oglethorpe to Newcastle, On board the *Blandford*, 30 Leagues N.W. from Frederica, Sept. 13, 1738, C.O. 5:654, f. 168.
[7] Oglethorpe to Sir Joseph Jekyll, Jekyll Sound, Sept. 19, 1738, C.O. 5:640, ff. 175–6; Candler, *Col. Rec. Ga.* xxii, part i, p. 251.

same day he arrived at Frederica with his regiment of soldiers and two ships suitable for naval engagements.[1]

The punishment meted out to del Moral Sanchez by the Madrid authorities for his part in the neutrality pact with Oglethorpe of October 1736 made it perfectly plain that, if James Oglethorpe's first sojourn in Georgia had been devoted to the problems of administration and social amelioration, and the second had been marked by evidences of religion, this third period was to be essentially military in character, and the scene of his activities would be not Savannah but Frederica and the Debatable Land.

Before considering the defence of Georgia against Spain, it will be well to follow the other activities in the colony to their not far distant conclusions. Oglethorpe's administration of domestic affairs in Georgia was to profit by the repeated criticisms of the Trustees and the complaints of the colonists. Before leaving England he had persuaded the Trustees to enact legislation providing for the acceptance in colonial courts of Indian evidence,[2] and upon his arrival in September he inaugurated a strict enforcement of the colonial laws, paying particular attention to safeguarding Georgia's credit, and making a prompt survey and report on affairs at Frederica, two moves which greatly pleased the Trustees.[3] For three weeks after his arrival Oglethorpe tarried at Frederica. On October 10 he began a two-week survey in Savannah, after which, except for three days there in November, he remained in the south until March 1739. If his southern residence was military in character, his Savannah visits were administrative and even judicial. Although the colonists had longed for his return,[4] it was not from motives of loyalty and esteem

[1] Oglethorpe to the Trustees, Frederica, Sept. 19, 1738, C.O. 5:640, f. 177; Candler, *Col. Rec. Ga.* xxii, part i, pp. 253–4; *Journal of William Stephens*, Candler, *Col. Rec. Ga.* iv. 206; *Egmont Diary*, ii. 510, 516.

[2] *Egmont Diary*, ii. 368.

[3] Ibid. 516–17; Oglethorpe to the Trustees, Frederica, Oct. 7, 1738, C.O. 5:640, ff. 193–5; Candler, *Col. Rec. Ga.* xxii, part i, pp. 274–81.

[4] *Stephens' Journal*, Candler, *Col. Rec. Ga.* iv. 192; Colonists' Letters, Nov. 15, 1737–Aug. 26, 1738, C.O. 5:640, *passim*; Candler, *Col. Rec. Ga.* xxii, part i, pp. 133–234, *passim*; *Gentleman's Magazine*, ix. 22–3.

alone, for a large number of complaints, varying both in importance and accuracy, greeted him on his arrival at Frederica and during the fortnight spent in Savannah.[1] Next to the critical general situation of the colony, which Oglethorpe freely admitted,[2] the most vital three issues were Thomas Causton's conduct of the colony's stores at Savannah; the land and inheritance question; and the problem of prohibition of both rum and negro slavery.

The responsibility for the serious state of the colony's stores lay entirely in the hands of Thomas Causton, the storekeeper, who, in at least one historian's opinion, was, next to Oglethorpe, the most important functionary at Savannah.[3] Causton was found to be running the trust heavily into debt by unauthorized expenditures, and in addition had not only become insolent and overbearing, but had usurped too great a power, having created, with the aid of Noble Jones, a miniature Tammany dictatorship and oligarchy.[4] Long before Oglethorpe left England, the complaints had come pouring in to the Trustees and their colonial representative had brought with him definite instructions to depose and arrest Causton.[5] Although his accounts were found to be in utter confusion, no proof of fraud could be discovered so that the sole salutary result of his ultimate dismissal[6] was to exhibit anew the slipshod

---

[1] Stephens' Journal, Candler, *Col. Rec. Ga.* iv. 212–18; William Stephens to Verelst, Savannah, Jan. 3, 1739, C.O. 5:640, ff. 244–5; Candler, *Col. Rec. Ga.* xxii, part ii, pp. 1–9.

[2] Oglethorpe to the Trustees, Savannah, March 9, 1738, C.O. 5:640, ff. 287–8; Candler, *Col. Rec. Ga.* xxii, part ii, p. 109.

[3] Osgood, *The American Colonies in the Eighteenth Century*, iii. 52.

[4] *Egmont Diary*, iii. 1–2; Stephens' Journal, Candler, *Col. Rec. Ga.* iv. 52–3, 87–96; Robert Bathurst to Lord Bathurst, Charles Town, Nov. 12, 1737, C.O. 5:640, ff. 3–4; Candler, *Col. Rec. Ga.* xxii, part i, p. 6; Isaac Young to the Trustees, Georgia, March 29, 1738, C.O. 5:640, f. 66; Candler, *Col. Rec. Ga.* xxii, part i, p. 113.

[5] C.O. 5:687, p. 76; Candler, *Col. Rec. Ga.* i. 321–5; C.O. 5:690, p. 166; Candler, *Col. Rec. Ga.* ii. 247.

[6] Oglethorpe to the Trustees, Savannah, Oct. 19, 1738, C.O. 5:640, ff. 198–200; Candler, *Col. Rec. Ga.* xxi, part i, pp. 281–8; Stephens' Journal, Candler, *Col. Rec. Ga.* iv. 213–14, 226–7, 260, 272–4, 295.

methods of internal financial administration[1] and, by comparison, to mitigate, in some degree at least, Oglethorpe's own similar sins of omission. Despite the fact that his arrest of Causton had been ordered by the Trustees, the entire episode in no wise improved Oglethorpe's stature in their eyes, some of them, like Egmont, suspecting their colleague of seeking to curry favour with the populace at their expense.[2]

The second problem was that of land tenure and inheritance. Discouraged to begin with by the oft-times barren soil of Georgia, as in the case of the Salzburgers at Old Ebenezer, the colonists found a further obstacle to success in the laws of inheritance which accorded with the strictest rules of primogeniture and tail male. It was this which in earlier years had brought strong protests from the Salzburgers; it was this which had proven the insurmountable barrier for the Vaudois; it was this which led the Scots at Darien to threaten their departure in a body;[3] it was this which now caused anxiety and trouble for Oglethorpe, who was himself staunchly opposed to female entail;[4] so that in 1739 the Trustees finally determined to make the first changes although absolute inheritance was not permitted until 1750.[5]

The third issue was the prohibition of rum and negro slavery, two restrictions which throughout the decade had led to private grumbling by the colonists despite Oglethorpe's unequivocal assertion in 1739 that, if a petition asking for negro slavery 'is countenanced, the Province

---

[1] Verelst to Causton, London, May 19, 1738, C.O. 5:667, pp. 117–24; Osgood, *The American Colonies in the Eighteenth Century*, iii. 53.

[2] *Egmont Diary*, iii. 4.

[3] Osgood, *The American Colonies in the Eighteenth Century*, iii. 58.

[4] *Egmont Diary*, ii. 478–9; W. Stephens to the Trustees, Savannah, Jan. 19, 1738, C.O. 5:640, ff. 41–4; Candler, *Col. Rec. Ga.* xxii, part i, p. 75.

[5] Oglethorpe to the Trustees, Frederica, July 4, 1739, C.O. 5:640, ff. 324–33; C.O. 5:691, pp. 60, 239–40; Candler, *Col. Rec. Ga.* ii. 392 ff., 500. See also Banks, E. M., *The Economics of Land Tenure in Georgia* (Columbia University Studies in History, Economics and Public Law, xxiii, New York, 1905), pp. 11–13.

is ruined'.[1] But whereas the other two questions of Causton and the inheritance issue had been quietly settled by strategic decisions of the Trustees, the enforcement of these two sumptuary laws led to more serious trouble. Aroused by the enticing gestures of South Carolina, where lands were more fertile, where the labour was performed by negro slaves, and where rum flowed freely,[2] the Georgia colonists awoke and the long-rumbling volcano of public opinion erupted. So strong had become the protests that on April 18, 1737, while Oglethorpe was in England, the Trustees had appointed William Stephens Secretary for the Trust in Georgia, in order to appease the colonists and secure reliable information.[3] In the face of Oglethorpe's continued support of the sumptuary laws, the protests, which to date had come in good faith from substantial citizens of repute, now appeared from the pens of a group of malcontents who pressed their claims in London as well as in Georgia. Nor were the critics only colonists, for in September 1738 a Trustee, Thomas Coram, in a letter to a friend, had inveighed strongly against Oglethorpe,[4] and early in 1739 Egmont, in his diary, noted a malicious letter asserting that 'Oglethorpe had again been shot at, and was so odious to the soldiers that he was forced to confine himself within doors', a tale which the diarist promptly branded as 'another lie invented by our good friends of South Carolina'.[5] Throughout 1739, in fact, Egmont's diary is replete with the content of communica-

[1] Oglethorpe to the Trustees, Savannah, March 12, 1739, C.O. 5:640, ff. 289–90; Candler, *Col. Rec. Ga.* xxii, part ii, p. 111.

[2] W. Stephens to the Trustees, Savannah, May 27, 1738, C.O. 5:640, ff. 106–8; Candler, *Col. Rec. Ga.* xxii, part i, p. 164; Osgood, *The American Colonies in the Eighteenth Century*, iii. 54, 63.

[3] C.O. 5:690, pp. 67–70; Candler, *Col. Rec. Ga.* ii. 190–2; *Stephens' Journal*, Candler, *Col. Rec. Ga.* iv. 3, 7; *Egmont Diary*, ii. 368. See also W. Stephens to the Trustees, Charles Town, Oct. 26, 1737, C.O. 5:639, ff. 410–11; Candler, *Col. Rec. Ga.* xxi. 512; and Elizabeth Jenys to the Trustees, Charles Town, Nov. 5, 1737, C.O. 5:640, f. 1; Candler, *Col. Rec. Ga.* xxii, part i, p. 3.

[4] Thomas Coram to Benjamin Colman, London, Sept. 22, 1738, Ford, 'Letters of Thomas Coram', *Proceedings of the Massachusetts Historical Society*, lvi. 47. [5] *Egmont Diary*, iii. 43.

tions of criticism and complaint to the Trustees from all manner of colonists in Georgia.[1]

Unfortunately for all concerned the first crystallization of personal hostility to Oglethorpe appeared towards the close of 1739 and during the first months of 1740 in a series of vitriolic attacks by Thomas Stephens, son of Secretary William Stephens, who had an imaginary grievance against his father's superior. Leaving Georgia for London in August 1739,[2] young Stephens in March 1740 shocked the Trustees with a verbal attack on Oglethorpe which he expanded into a near crisis by his radical remarks and pro-slavery petitions until in January 1741 Egmont flatly refused ever to see him again because of his 'insolent attack upon the Trustees'.[3] Thomas Stephens's reckless attacks culminated in a petition to Parliament in 1742, charging misapplication of the public funds of Georgia and gross abuse of power—charges heard in committee of the whole and branded as 'false, scandalous and malicious'[4]—and *A Brief Account of the Causes that have retarded the Progress of the Colony of Georgia in America*, published in 1743;[5] but in the meantime other and stronger opposition to Oglethorpe had arisen.

Coming as a counterblast to Benjamin Martyn's *An Impartial Inquiry into the State and Utility of the Province of Georgia*, published in 1741,[6] Thomas Stephens's early

---

[1] *Egmont Diary*, iii. 37–41, 50–5, 60–2, 109–14, 143–4, 196–7, 201–2.

[2] *Stephens' Journal*, Candler, *Col. Rec. Ga.* iv. 382–3.

[3] *Egmont Diary*, iii. 84–8, 109–12, 121, 174–6, 178, 183; Verelst to Oglethorpe, London, March 29, 1740, C.O. 5:667, pp. 310–16; C.O. 5:687, pp. 137, 151, 202–4; Osgood, *The American Colonies in the Eighteenth Century*, iii. 63–6.

[4] *Commons Journals*, xxiv. 192, 194, 216, 218, 221, 229, 247, 268, 276, 280, 284–5, 287–8.

[5] Stephens, Thomas, *A Brief Account of the Causes that have retarded the Progress of the Colony of Georgia in America* (London, 1743); reprinted in *Collections of the Georgia Historical Society*, ii. 87–161. William Stephens, Thomas's father, was so ashamed of his son's actions that in Oct. 1743 he asked the Trustees to accept a reversion of his grants and lands in Georgia, thus disinheriting his son. C.O. 5:687, pp. 267–8; Candler, *Col. Rec. Ga.* i. 431–2.

[6] Martyn, Benjamin, *An Impartial Inquiry into the State and Utility of the Province of Georgia* (London, 1741); reprinted in *Collections of the Georgia Historical Society*, i. 153–201.

attacks on Oglethorpe had been in the nature of a trial balloon sent up to guide three malcontents who, led by Patrick Tailfer, M.D., in that same year issued a pronouncement against the founder of the colony, entitled *A True and Historical Narrative of the Colony of Georgia in America*.[1] Despite the fact that Tailfer had borne none too good a reputation as early as 1735 when he and three others had complained about the quality of their lands,[2] this volume hurt the victim intensely and met with a sufficiently favourable reception in London to demand a reply the next year by Martyn in *An Account Showing the Progress of the Colony of Georgia in America from its First Establishment*.[3] If the malcontents erred too much in their prejudice, Martyn, who knew nothing personally of conditions in Georgia, was too sanguine, and the British public remained without a really moderate and accurate narrative until 1742 when William Stephens, smarting under the attacks of both his prodigal son and the other malcontents,[4] published *A State of the Province of Georgia*, designed to vindicate the Trustees and win further parliamentary appropriations for the colony.[5]

Much of the propaganda cited above was unreliable and, in some cases, merely abusive, but the Trustees were

[1] Tailfer, Pat., M.D., Anderson, Hugh, M.A., Douglas, D., et al., *A True and Historical Narrative of the Colony of Georgia in America* (Charles Town, 1741); reprinted in *Collections of the Georgia Historical Society*, ii. 163–263; *Egmont Diary*, iii. 225–6, 229–30; *Stephens' Journal*, Candler, *Col. Rec. Ga.* iv (Supplement), 80–1.

[2] Charles Town *South Carolina Gazette*, Dec. 27, 1735, pp. 2–3; *Stephens' Journal*, Candler, *Col. Rec. Ga.* iv. 258, 579–80, 604.

[3] Martyn, Benjamin, *An Account Showing the Progress of the Colony of Georgia in America from its Establishment* (London, 1742); reprinted in *Collections of the Georgia Historical Society*, ii. 265–325; and Candler, *Col. Rec. Ga.* iii. 367–432. For the order of the Trustees to Martyn see C.O. 5:687, pp. 169–73; Candler, *Col. Rec. Ga.* i. 377–80.

[4] *Stephens' Journal*, Candler, *Col. Rec. Ga.* iv. 578; iv (Supplement), 239–40, 251–3, 255–6, 259–61, 263, 266–7, 274–5.

[5] Stephens, William, *A State of the Province of Georgia, attested upon Oath in the Court of Savannah, November 10, 1740* (London, 1742); reprinted in *Collections of the Georgia Historical Society*, ii. 67–85; and Candler, *Col. Rec. Ga.* iv. 663–80. See also *Journal of the Commissioners for Trade and Plantations*, vi, 1735–41, pp. 376–80.

often called upon to answer sharp, leading questions in Parliament,[1] and the fact remained that in Oglethorpe the soldier had completely submerged the statesman. Even William Stephens, in a letter to Verelst, complained that 'by degrees he seemed to grow more enamour'd with ye Southern Settlements' and neglected to send up instructions to Savannah as promptly as in the past;[2] while Thomas Jones attributed much of the strife in Savannah to the absence of Oglethorpe's strong personality.[3] But while he still persisted in interfering at most awkward moments, Oglethorpe's administrative activities now became irregular, with marked effect on affairs in general, and his powers were gradually bestowed upon, or assimilated by, other officials.[4] On December 17, 1740, Verelst informed Stephens that 'the Trustees cannot desire General Oglethorpe's interposing in their civil concerns while he is employed in his military ones which are distinct services'.[5] At this time the Trustees, in their attempts to gain further appropriations, had been exposed to all kinds of tales concerning the state of Georgia, so that many had resigned or ceased to attend meetings.[6] As a result of all these factors, the remaining Trustees, at James Vernon's suggestion, determined to divide Georgia into two counties, choosing William Stephens as President of the northern half and temporarily leaving that office in the southern

---

[1] *Egmont Diary*, iii. 106–10.

[2] W. Stephens to Verelst, Savannah, Feb. 7, 1739, C.O. 5:640, f. 264; Candler, *Col. Rec. Ga.* xxii, part ii, p. 46.

[3] Thomas Jones to Verelst, Savannah, Feb. 8, 1739, C.O. 5:640, ff. 265–6; Candler, *Col. Rec. Ga.* xxii, part ii, p. 48. See also W. Stephens to Verelst, Savannah, Oct. 6, 1740, C.O. 5:640, f. 519; Candler, *Col. Rec. Ga.* xxii, part ii, p. 424; W. Stephens to the Trustees, Savannah, Dec. 31, 1741, C.O. 5:641, Document 37 (there is no foliation or pagination in this volume); Candler, *Col. Rec. Ga.* xxiii. 160–94; T. Jones to Verelst, Frederica, April 26, 1742, C.O. 5:641, Document 53; Candler, *Col. Rec. Ga.* xxiii. 296–7; W. Stephens to Verelst, Savannah, June 9, 1742, C.O. 5:641, Document 60 *a*; Candler, *Col. Rec. Ga.* xxiii. 346–9.

[4] See Osgood, *The American Colonies in the Eighteenth Century*, iii. 52.

[5] Verelst to W. Stephens, London, Dec. 17, 1740, C.O. 5:668, pp. 2–3.

[6] *Egmont Diary*, iii. 100, 179–81, 184–6.

half vacant.¹ After October 1740 Oglethorpe was largely ignored by the Trustees, and in the only letter he received from Verelst between October 1740 and September 1741 was not even informed of Stephens's appointment.² Only after an interval was the Presidency of the southern half tendered to Oglethorpe, more as a sop to his vanity than for any profound political reason;³ and by May 1743 that was subordinated to the Savannah hierarchy.⁴ There was indeed much profound truth in Oglethorpe's complaint of February 12, 1743, the tenth anniversary of the creation of Savannah, when he informed the Trustees that the great mistake of administration, both in London and in the colony, 'is speaking of Savannah as if it was the whole Province of Georgia whereas the District of Savannah is but a small portion of it—The Province extends beyond the Mississippi Westward & beyond Frederica Southward, and the Trustees' Orders are obeyed in every part of it except at Savannah'.⁵ By the end of his tenure in Georgia, then, Oglethorpe had thus lost virtually all the great administrative powers which had been his during the past decade.

Although he lost his grip on administrative affairs, nothing was to destroy Oglethorpe's harmonious relations with two great elements in the life of the colony, the Indians and the various religious sects. In the reconstruction of administration in Georgia, he had retained his post of Commissioner for Indian Affairs, although even here in the first letter in five months, Verelst, on September 18, 1741, blandly informed Oglethorpe that, 'as the King's service requires your residence in the Southern part of Georgia, the Trustees have thought it necessary to add

---

¹ Ibid. 169, 171; C.O. 5:691, pp. 17–18; Candler, *Col. Rec. Ga.* ii. 367–8; Osgood, *The American Colonies in the Eighteenth Century*, iii. 42, 67–8.
² Verelst to Oglethorpe, London, April 27, 1741, C.O. 5:668, pp. 18–20.
³ *Egmont Diary*, iii. 169, 171.
⁴ Martyn to W. Stephens, London, May 10, 1743, C.O. 5:668, pp. 121–30; Martyn to Oglethorpe, London, May 21, 1743, C.O. 5:668, pp. 130–1.
⁵ Oglethorpe to the Trustees, Frederica, Feb. 12, 1743, C.O. 5:641, Document 87; Candler, *Col. Rec. Ga.* xxiii. 486.

Mr. Stephens to be another Commissioner besides you for licensing the Traders with the Indians and regulating that trade'.[1] The record of Oglethorpe's relations with the Indians during his previous visits to Georgia affords conclusive proof that Professor McCain did not exaggerate when he asserted that 'Colonel Oglethorpe was a master hand in winning the confidence and support of the red man'.[2] In his first visit he had pacified them and won the friendship of Tomochichi, through whose continued efforts they had since remained faithful. But whereas previous relations had been dictated by local safety, the furtherance of trade, and the protection of Georgia by an Indian barrier from the French in the West, the general situation in the late spring of 1739 compelled Oglethorpe to pay more attention to the Creeks as a military factor against Spain.[3] Having held a highly successful parley with the Indians at Savannah in 1736, Oglethorpe proposed to bind them closer through personal contact in their own environs by making the three-hundred-mile journey, himself, inland to Coweta in August 1739 for a crucial ten-day conference which, despite an interruption due to Oglethorpe's bad attack of fever, assured the loyalty of the Creeks.[4] The death of Tomochichi in October,[5] the renewed activities of the Spaniards, and the underhanded machinations of a few South Carolinians,[6] made it impera-

[1] Verelst to Oglethorpe, London, Sept. 18, 1741, C.O. 5:668, pp. 56–8; C.O. 5:687, p. 188; Candler, *Col. Rec. Ga.* i. 388; C.O. 5:691, p. 25; Candler, *Col. Rec. Ga.* ii. 371.

[2] McCaine, *Georgia as a Proprietary Province*, p. 80.

[3] Oglethorpe to the Trustees, Frederica, July 4, 1739, C.O. 5:640, ff. 324–32; Candler, *Col. Rec. Ga.* xxii, part ii, pp. 166–7.

[4] Oglethorpe to Verelst, Fort Augusta, Georgia, Sept. 5, 1739, C.O. 5:640, f. 362; Candler, *Col. Rec. Ga.* xxii, part ii, p. 208; An anonymous letter, Charles Town, Sept. 11, 1739, C.O. 5:640, f. 366; Candler, *Col. Rec. Ga.* xxii, part ii, pp. 214–15; Stowe MSS. (British Museum), 792, 'A Ranger's Report of Travels with General Oglethorpe, 1739–1742', printed in Mereness, N. D., *Travels in the American Colonies* (New York, 1916), pp. 218–36. See also the New York *Weekly Journal*, June 9, 1740, p. 2; and Martyn, *An Account Showing the Progress of Georgia*, Candler, *Col. Rec. Ga.* iii. 398.

[5] *Stephens' Journal*, Candler, *Col. Rec. Ga.* iv. 428.   [6] *Egmont Diary*, iii. 7.

tive for Oglethorpe to pay particular attention to this problem and, during the next three years, he periodically rode with his rangers to maintain the peace established years before with Tomochichi.[1] In this Oglethorpe in the south ranks with Gooch of Virginia and Clarke of New York in holding the two great Indian confederacies loyal to Britain, an achievement the greatest value of which was not evident until the Seven Years War, two decades later.[2] As the attitude of the Indians during the war indicated, the result was well worth the effort, but Oglethorpe placed his Indian associations on a far higher plane than mere utility. His grief for Tomochichi in 1739 had been unfeigned and deep and, long after the Spanish danger had passed, Oglethorpe continued his correspondence with Mrs. Musgrove and her Indian colleagues.[3] Whatever fault they might find with him in other respects, the Trustees in 1742 wisely appreciated the value of his labours in this field and applauded his work as 'very beneficial' and his plan of Indian union as 'not only very benevolent and judicious, but of the greatest Importance at this critical juncture, when so much danger is to be apprehended from the French'.[4] It was the first bit of praise

[1] Stowe MSS. (British Museum), 792, 'A Ranger's Report of Travels with General Oglethorpe, 1739–1742'; Mereness, *Travels in the American Colonies*, pp. 218–36.

[2] For Clarke in New York see O'Callaghan, *Documents relative to the Colonial History of the State of New York*, vi. 198–9, 211–12, 214, 219, 242–3, 245. For Gooch in Virginia see C.O. 5:1337, Correspondence with Virginia of the Secretary of State, 1714–45, ff. 265–78; C.O. 5:1344, Same, 1727–83, ff. 35–46; C.O. 5:1366, Virginia: Entry Book, 1728–52, pp. 322–6; C.O. 5:1420, Virginia: Sessional Papers: Minutes of Council, 1729–36, and of Council in Assembly, 1736, *passim*; C.O. 5:1423, Virginia: Journal of Council, 1737–52, pp. 27–43; C.O. 5:1425, Virginia: Journal of Council in Assembly, 1738–52, p. 4.

[3] Oglethorpe to the Trustees, Frederica, March 3, 1742, C.O. 5:641, Document 42; Candler, *Col. Rec. Ga.* xxiii. 223–6. In 1751 Vice-President Henry Parker of Georgia confessed to Governor Glen of South Carolina that neither the Choctaws nor the Cherokees 'have visited us in a Body since General Oglethorpe left this country'. Henry Parker to James Glen, Georgia, April 16, 1751, C.O. 5:643, Document No. 62; Candler, *Col. Rec. Ga.* xxvi. 193.

[4] Verelst to Oglethorpe, London, Aug. 9, 1742, C.O. 5:668, pp. 98–9; Martyn to Oglethorpe, London, Aug. 10, 1742, C.O. 5:668, pp. 100–2.

poor Oglethorpe had received in many a moon, and he deserved it!

Perhaps the happiest of all of Oglethorpe's associations in Georgia proved to be with the pious colonists of various denominations, whose decisions and activities were not among the least important factors in this last period of his colonial career. In the spiritual realm these five years were notable for the passing of the Moravians and the departure of many of the Jews, the continued growth of the Anglicans and Lutherans, the arrival of the Calvinists, and the zealous missionary labours of George Whitefield. The pacific Moravians, as Zinzendorf himself told Oglethorpe, had come to Georgia 'not because they were poor, but that they might advance the Gospel'.[1] Opposed to military drill from the very beginning,[2] they had obtained Oglethorpe's promise of exemption therefrom during his second visit to the colony,[3] only to find during his subsequent absence in England that the Trustees were unwilling to grant total exemption, asking for the services of one man from each of Spangenberg's and Nitschmann's cohort.[4] The sole alternative to this was departure from the colony.[5] The outbreak of Spanish hostilities, following hard after Nitschmann's return to Germany and Spangenberg's foray into Pennsylvania,[6] proved an insurmountable barrier to their missionary efforts among negroes, whites, and Indians,[7] and with the courage that is so infinitely greater than the physical, these heroic Christians informed the Trustees that 'they could not in conscience fight and, if expected so to do, they must leave the country'.[8] The situation had become an *impasse* and

---

[1] *Egmont Diary*, ii. 333.
[2] Thomas Causton to the Trustees, Savannah, March 24, 1737, C.O. 5:639, f. 229; Candler, *Col. Rec. Ga.* xxi. 385.
[3] Fries, *The Moravians in Georgia*, pp. 87, 93–4, 161–8, 181–215.
[4] Martyn to Causton, London, Aug. 3, 1737, C.O. 5:667, pp. 50–1.
[5] Martyn to Zinzendorf, London, Sept. 23, 1737, C.O. 5:667, pp. 73–4.
[6] Fries, *The Moravians in Georgia*, p. 141.
[7] *Egmont Diary*, ii. 345.
[8] Ibid. 413.

the Moravians soon sought the quiet, pleasant valleys of Pennsylvania.[1]

If the Moravians migrated for the sake of conscience, many of the Jews in 1740 moved northward for other reasons, but the Sheftall family remained to lay the foundations of a strong and abiding leadership.[2]

Among the denominations that remained in the colony the Anglican Church, except for the activities of George Whitefield, failed to take full advantage of its favoured position. The Salzburger Lutherans had continued to prosper at New Ebenezer, but they invariably relied for secular guidance on Oglethorpe, from whom they extracted innumerable favours until they asked for negro slaves![3] In contradistinction to the Moravians, these Lutherans proved valiant defenders of the colony at all times and fully merited the assiduous attention which Oglethorpe bestowed upon them.[4] While prospering in a material sense, the Salzburgers, feeling the need of further spiritual guidance, had taken the advice of Oglethorpe that they apply to the illustrious Dr. Francke of

---

[1] Ibid. 422; Fries, *The Moravians in Georgia*, pp. 182–5, 215–22; Jordan, J. W., 'The Moravian Immigration to Pennsylvania, 1734–1765', *Pennsylvania Magazine of History*, xxxiii. 229.

[2] *Egmont Diary*, iii. 188, 218; Abrahams, *Some Notes on the Early History of the Sheftalls of Georgia, passim*.

[3] Rev. J. M. Bolzius to Verelst, Ebenezer, Nov. 6, 1738, C.O. 5:640, ff. 206–7; Candler, *Col. Rec. Ga.* xxii, part i, pp. 296–8; Urlsperger, S., editor, *Dritte Continuation der ausführlichen Nachricht von den Saltzburgischen Emigranten* (Halle, Germany, 1740), pp. 2062–5; Urlsperger, S., editor, *Vierte Continuation der ausführlichen Nachricht von den Saltzburgischen Emigranten* (Halle, 1740), pp. 2073–153, *passim*.

[4] Rev. J. M. Bolzius to the Trustees, Ebenezer, July 25, 1741, C.O. 5:641, Document 20; Candler, *Col. Rec. Ga.* xxiii. 75–6; Urlsperger, S., editor, *Fünfte Continuation der ausführlichen Nachricht von den Saltzburgischen Emigranten* (Halle, 1740), *passim*; Urlsperger, S., editor, *Sechste Continuation der ausführlichen Nachricht* (Halle, 1741), *passim*; Urlsperger, S., editor, *Siebente Continuation der ausführlichen Nachricht* (Halle, 1741), p. 591; Urlsperger, S., editor, *Achte Continuation* (Halle, 1742), *passim*; Urlsperger, S., editor, *Neunte Continuation* (Halle, 1743), *passim*; Urlsperger, S., editor, *Zehnte Continuation* (Halle, 1744), *passim*; Urlsperger, S., editor, *Elfte Continuation* (Halle, 1745), *passim*; Urlsperger, S., editor, *Zwölfte Continuation* (Halle, 1746), *passim*.

Halle[1] who, in 1742, sent over to them Heinrich Melchior Mühlenberg, the future Patriarch of the Lutheran Church in America. Because he was in the field when Mühlenberg arrived at Savannah on October 2, 1742, Oglethorpe never met the man whose advent he had advised and who began his historic career among the latter's Salzburger protégés.[2] Seldom has the tolerance of the frontier been better exhibited than in 1741 when the Trustees sent over a band of Strasburger Calvinists. When asked by Egmont whether they could agree with the Salzburger Lutherans, these ancestors of the modern Reformed Church in the United States fittingly replied that 'the Lutherans communicate with a wafer, but they with bread, however, if the Minister be a good man, they believed they should agree well'.[3]

The most outstanding religious character of this period, however, was George Whitefield, like Ingham and the Wesleys, an Oxonian and, not unlike Samuel Johnson, an academic outcast at Pembroke College.[4] As early as March 1737 Egmont had proposed that 'Mr. Whitfield should be appointed for Frederica, Mr. Charles Wesley to be the itinerant minister, Mr. John Wesley, the minister of Savannah, and Mr. Ingham, the Indian minister';[5] and the defection of the others in no wise discouraged Whitefield.[6] On May 10, 1738, the Trustees ratified his election to succeed John Wesley[7] but he had not tarried, either for that formal sanction or to accompany Oglethorpe on his

[1] Oglethorpe to Rev. J. M. Bolzius, Savannah, Nov. 3, 1739, C.O. 5:640, f. 459; Candler, *Col. Rec. Ga.* xxii, part ii, p. 338.
[2] Diary of Heinrich Melchior Mühlenberg, Library of Mount Airy Lutheran Theological Seminary, Germantown, Philadelphia, Pa., U.S.A.; Mann, W. J., *Life and Times of Henry Melchior Mühlenberg* (Philadelphia, 1887), pp. 39–46, 65, 69, 74, 79, 82, 86–7. See also Verelst to W. Stephens, London, June 11, 1742, C.O. 5:668, pp. 89–92.
[3] *Egmont Diary*, iii. 186.
[4] Hill, *Boswell's Life of Johnson* (Powell revision), i. 75; Godley, *Oxford in the Eighteenth Century*, p. 267; Mallet, *History of the University of Oxford*, iii. 119.
[5] *Egmont Diary*, ii. 365.
[6] George Whitefield to Verelst, Stonehouse, Gloucestershire, May 17, 1737, C.O. 5:639, f. 248; Candler, *Col. Rec. Ga.* xxi. 394.
[7] C.O. 5:687, p. 71; Candler, *Col. Rec. Ga.* i. 318; *Egmont Diary*, ii. 484.

return to the colony.[1] Passing the homeward-bound Wesley on the high seas, Whitefield by May 7 had already arrived at Savannah[2] where, during the next six weeks as missionary,[3] he eschewed alike the formalism in the church and the extraneous entangling alliances which had proven so fatal to the Wesleys. As the latters' great labour had been conversion, so Whitefield's *magnum opus* was the Bethesda Orphanage which he modelled upon Francke's orphan house at Halle[4] and which, according to one authority, became the most extensive philanthropic institution of the colonial Protestant Episcopal Church.[5] Beginning, in Dr. Tiffany's words, 'with all Wesley's vigor, but with less rigor of discipline',[6] Whitefield achieved a greater success with the people[7] despite a year's visit to England in 1739,[8] during which he was ordained and made heroic and successful efforts to gain further aid from the Trustees.[9] Upon his return to Frederica in the winter of 1740, after a period at Savannah and an itinerant visit to New England and Pennsylvania,[10] the orphan house, in

---

[1] *Egmont Diary*, ii. 457; London *Evening Post*, Dec. 29, 1737, p. 1; *Universal Spectator*, Dec. 31, 1737, p. 2.

[2] Thomas Causton to the Trustees, Savannah, May 25, 1738, C.O. 5:640, ff. 102–4; Candler, *Col. Rec. Ga.* xxii, part i, pp. 160–1; *Stephens' Journal*, Candler, *Col. Rec. Ga.* iv. 142; Tyerman, *Life and Times of the Rev. John Wesley*, i. 165; Tiffany, *A History of the Protestant Episcopal Church in the United States of America*, pp. 255–6; Tyerman, L., *Life of the Rev. George Whitefield* (2 vols., London, 1876), i. 122.

[3] C.O. 5:690, p. 187; Candler, *Col. Rec. Ga.* ii. 259.

[4] Rev. J. M. Bolzius to Henry Newman, Secretary of the S.P.G., Savannah, Jan. 15, 1740, C.O. 5:640, f. 430; Candler, *Col. Rec. Ga.* xxii, part ii, pp. 297–8; Osgood, *The American Colonies in the Eighteenth Century*, iii. 112–13.

[5] Tiffany, *A History of the Protestant Episcopal Church in the United States of America*, p. 249. [6] Ibid., p. 256.

[7] Tyerman, *Life of the Rev. George Whitefield*, i. 130–46.

[8] Ibid. 146–443.

[9] *Egmont Diary*, iii. 3, 5–6. See also Hartford, Frances, Countess of, *Correspondence with Henrietta Louisa, Countess of Pomfret, 1738–1741* (3 vols., London, 1805), i. 112–34.

[10] For an interesting letter by Whitefield 'on board the *Savannah*, bound from Philadelphia to Georgia, November 30th, 1740', see the MSS. of the Archbishop of Canterbury in the Library at Lambeth Palace, vol. 1123, part i, American Colonies, 1725–54, Document 27.

his biographer's opinion, 'really became Whitefield's parish'.[1] How strong his will power and leadership could be was evinced in 1740 when, on a visit to Philadelphia, he resolutely declined Banjamin Franklin's suggestion to change the location of the orphanage, whereupon the latter, who had a poor opinion of the personnel of the Georgia colony, 'therefore refused to contribute' to the support of the institution.[2] Although immersed in military problems at this time, Oglethorpe had done what he could to keep Whitefield, manifesting a particular interest in the orphanage project,[3] but the cleric's complaints, that Trustees' orders were not carried out and that Oglethorpe's proceedings as to the orphans were arbitrary, engendered much ill will.[4] This, together with the open hostility to Oglethorpe of the malcontents and the serious military situation, made Whitefield's labours so onerous that on January 1, 1741, he left for England where he continued to gather funds for his orphanage.[5] Despite his imperfect personal relations with their leaders, Oglethorpe, in his decade of colonial experience, had witnessed and aided the growth of five Protestant sects, of which at least three were to radiate from their Georgian nuclei into nation-wide denominations of the modern United States.

Important, however, as were its spiritual progress, its administrative problems, and its Indian relations in this period, the vital factor in the life of Georgia was the war with Spain, the certainty of which had been apparent to Oglethorpe when he was still awaiting favourable winds

[1] Tyerman, *Life of the Rev. George Whitefield*, i. 445.
[2] Franklin, B., *Memoirs* (3 vols., London, 1818), i. 85.
[3] *Stephens' Journal*, Candler, *Col. Rec. Ga.* iv. 540.
[4] *Egmont Diary*, iii. 126–7, 204.
[5] *Stephens' Journal*, Candler, *Col. Rec. Ga.* iv (Supplement), 64; Tyerman, *Life of the Rev. George Whitefield*, i. 447–50, 542–6. In August 1739 the Trustees had asked the S.P.G. for two missionaries, one for Savannah, the other for Frederica, to which the latter body agreed. The Rev. William Norris succeeded Whitefield in Frederica while the Rev. William Metcalfe went to Savannah, S.P.G. Journal, viii, 1739–42, pp. 73–4; S.P.G. Archives, Letters Received, Series B, vol. vii, 1738–41, pp. 261, 263.

off England's shores in May and June of 1738.[1] The isolated question of Spanish claims to Georgia had reached a crisis in his brilliant ambiguity as to Fort Saint George and Fort King George in February 1738 only to be completely enveloped and overwhelmed in the maelstrom of the War of Jenkins's Ear. By the Asiento or Contract made with Spain in the Peace of Utrecht in 1713, Britain had gained a monopoly in the slave trade to Spanish colonies, together with the right to send an annual cargo of 500 tons to Spanish ports. Dissatisfaction at the paucity of the trade led to increased smuggling by English traders, many of whom were naturally seized and, not unnaturally, roughly handled, by Spanish coast-guards. The facts of such treatment, magnified and distorted into anti-Spanish propaganda, filled the powder keg to which the match was applied in 1738 when an English merchant mariner named Thomas Jenkins showed Parliament his gory ear, severed by a Spaniard whose sole regret was his inability to perform the same operation on the King of England. But while this particular act proved the Serajevo incident for England and Spain, the resulting war in reality was not a new conflict but rather a continuation of a traditional struggle for supremacy between two great empires—a conflagration which had smouldered and burst into fitful flame down through the centuries. If the exploring and colonizing competition between Spain and England in the era of Cabot and Columbus was peaceful, the religious element in both Spanish Inquisition and English Reformation had led to bloodshed and strife which was far from allayed by the successful raids of Drake upon the last remnants of a once mighty transatlantic empire. In psychology and religion, in temperament and trade, in arts and atmosphere, the Latin and the Anglo-Saxon were alien to each other, and only the ultimate passing of that once proud glory of Charles V and of Ferdinand and

[1] Oglethorpe to Andrew Stone, Southampton, May 21, 1738, C.O. 5:654, f. 139; Oglethorpe to Newcastle, Gosport, June 5, 1738, concluded on board the *Blandford*, Spithead, June 6, 1738, C.O. 5:654, ff. 144-5.

Isabella closed the struggle for supremacy. Thus it was that the personal assault on Captain Thomas Jenkins in 1738 had its reverberations, not only in European chancellories, but in the overhung, mossy marshes of Glyn and along the golden isles of Georgia.[1]

When in September 1737 Walpole had finally sanctioned Oglethorpe's regiment, he had ensured immunity for himself from further colonial complaints of non-co-operation, but he had opened wide the door for Geraldino who never failed to make full use of his opportunities. The Spanish Minister therefore proceeded to make a formal claim on all of Georgia, an act which immediately compelled Oglethorpe and the distracted Trustees to pay an anxious call on Newcastle as Secretary of State for the Colonies.[2] That poor man was of little comfort for he was overwhelmed by Walpole's policy of indecision and a dangerous lack of co-operation from Keene in Madrid. For the first five years of Georgia's existence Benjamin Keene's reports from the Spanish capital were given to Spanish depredation on British commerce and Continental matters of State.[3] Even after 1737 the question of Georgia was handled by Geraldino in London rather than Keene in Madrid, and what little reference he made to Georgia in his reports of Spanish preparations in Cuba during 1738 was soon submerged in the plans for the proposed Anglo-Spanish conference on the boundary question.[4]

---

[1] Temperley, H. W. V., 'The Causes of the War of Jenkins' Ear (1739)', *Transactions of the Royal Historical Society*, 3rd series, iii. 197–236; Richmond, H. W., *The Navy in the War of 1739–1748* (3 vols., Cambridge, England, 1920), i. ix, 1; Rose, J. H., Newton, A. P., and Benians, E. A., editors, *The Cambridge History of the British Empire* (in progress, Cambridge, 1929——), i, chap. xi, Penson, L. M., 'The West Indies and the Spanish-American Trade, 1713–1748', pp. 330–45.

[2] *Egmont Diary*, ii. 382; Bolton and Ross, *The Debatable Land*, pp. 75–6.

[3] S.P. 94 (State Papers, Foreign: Spain, P.R.O.):103–26, Instructions to, and Despatches from, Benjamin Keene in Madrid, 1730–1737; Add. MSS. (British Museum), 43412–43443, Papers of Benjamin Keene.

[4] S.P. 94:127–31, Instructions to, and Despatches from, B. Keene, 1737–1738; S.P. 100 (State Papers, Foreign: Foreign Ministers in England): 59,

GENERAL OGLETHORPE.

from the mezzotint by T. BURFORD, *circa* 1743

In the dawn of the eighteenth century an experienced colonial administrator, William Penn, in a letter to Robert Harley, had lamented the fact that 'we see so little of an American understanding among those whose business it is to superintend ... this American empire'.[1] The situation had in no wise changed for Walpole, trapped between the Scylla of empire and the Charybdis of peace with Spain, now temporized and, to the agonizing fear of the Trustees, used Georgia as a pawn in the manœuvres of 1738 to obtain the Convention of El Pardo with Spain in January 1739.[2] It was fully evident from his tactics that, while Keene might be certain that Spain was bluffing[3] and Horace Walpole might be afraid of the French,[4] Robert Walpole was intent on placating Spain, even to sending Oglethorpe orders to respect whatever boundaries would be fixed by the commissioners.[5] From the evidence at hand it seems not too much to affirm that only the strong and continued protests of the most loyal Trustees 'to keep Georgia out of the Spaniards' hands' and to preserve England's 'possessions' as well as 'rights' in the colony prevented an immediate transfer, and Egmont's *Diary* for the first three months of 1739 is replete with references to

Geraldino's correspondence with Newcastle, April 7 and 11, and June 9, 1738; and report of a conference at the house of Sir Robert Walpole, June 1, 1738, between Geraldino and the Lord Chancellor, Lord Harrington, Secretary at War, Walpole, Sir Charles Wager of the Admiralty, and Newcastle. See also Add. MSS. (British Museum), 32797, Newcastle Papers, ff. 282–8.

[1] William Penn to Robert Harley [*circa* 1701], *Portland MSS.* (H.M.C. Reports), iv, *Harley Papers*, ii. 30.

[2] See also Add. MSS. (British Museum), 9131, Coxe Papers, ff. 199–273, Papers relating to Spanish Depredations, 1738; Bolton and Ross, *The Debatable Land*, pp. 79–80; Brisco, *The Economic Policy of Robert Walpole*, p. 25; Vaucher, P., *Robert Walpole et la Politique de Fleury, 1731–1742* (Paris, 1924), chap. iv.

[3] Keene to Newcastle, Casa del Monte, near Aranjuez, Spain, May 7, 1738, S.P. 94:130; Add. MSS. (British Museum), 32797, ff. 330–3.

[4] Horace Walpole to Sir Robert Walpole, The Hague, April 29, 1735, Coxe, *Memoirs of the Life and Administration of Sir Robert Walpole, Earl of Orford*, iii. 243.

[5] Instructions to Oglethorpe, Whitehall, March 18, 1739, C.O. 5:654, f. 203.

sudden resignations of Trustees and Robert Walpole's indifference, evasions, and unsatisfactory pledges as to increased appropriations for the defence of the colony.[1] What, indeed, could Oglethorpe hope to accomplish in Georgia when four such prominent Trustees and Members of Parliament as Alderman George Heathcote, John White, Robert Moore, and Robert Hucks, within a month turned from supporting the colony to asserting that, 'if we may have a peace with Spain by giving up Georgia, it were a good thing'![2] If Georgia was to be saved to the Empire by Oglethorpe's strong right arm at Frederica and Bloody Marsh and before Saint Augustine in the New World, it was first saved in the House of Commons at Westminster by the persistent, courageous voices of Colonel Bladen, Henry Towers, Henry Archer, and, particularly, the Earl of Egmont.

In January 1739 Benjamin Keene and Abraham Castres represented Britain in the conferences which produced the Convention of El Pardo,[3] but, fortunately, as it proved, for the colony, both the Convention and Oglethorpe's agreement of 1736 with del Moral Sanchez proved void, and Walpole's policy of peace at any price was brought to a sudden end by the popular demand for a maritime war with Spain, which in London was officially declared on October 23, 1739,[4] although Savannah had known of it by September 8 and Oglethorpe had proclaimed it officially on October 3.[5] Even as historians of late years have been compelled to emphasize the fact that, to Britain, the revolt of the thirteen American colonies was but one phase of their imperial problem which included

[1] *Egmont Diary*, iii. 2, 9–45. [2] Ibid. 36.
[3] For the negotiations and convention see Add. MSS. (British Museum), 32798, Newcastle Papers, ff. 165–71, 182–3; Add. MSS., 32799, ff. 89–96, 234–9; Add. MSS., 35406, Hardwicke Papers, ff. 57–88, 108–11, 126–9, 156–63, 170–2; Add. MSS. 35884, Hardwicke Papers, ff. 170–80; Add. MSS. 21438, Collection de différents Mémoires appartenants à la Guerre qui s'est dernièrement allumée en l'Année 1739, entre l'Angleterre et l'Espagne; S.P. 94:133–4.
[4] *Egmont Diary*, iii. 86.
[5] *Stephens' Journal*, Candler, *Col. Rec. Ga.* iv. 406–7, 426–8.

French hostility in India, the West Indies, and on the Continent, so is it here imperative to note that Oglethorpe's was not a casual attack on Florida in a localized struggle for a few isolated acres of marshland in a distant sector of the globe, but was part of the great imperial struggle against Spain known as King George's War, 1739–48.[1]

Nowhere is the scope of this conflict more clearly visible than in the British efforts at colonial interdependence, for it must be remembered that the colonists of South Carolina and Georgia feared not only the Spaniard to the South but also the Frenchman to the West and in Canada where, in August 1739, according to rumours heard by William Stephens, a French and Indian army from Quebec was planning to move against the native allies of Britain.[2] As a result a messenger was sent from Georgia to Connecticut, Rhode Island, and New York, bearing with him the declaration of war and an appeal for aid.[3] During the next four years Oglethorpe made many an appeal to Shirley of Massachusetts,[4] Clarke of New York,[5] Gooch of Virginia,[6] Johnston of North Carolina,[7] and the provincial authori-

[1] Lanning, J. T., 'The American Colonies in the Preliminaries of the War of Jenkins' Ear', *Georgia Historical Quarterly*, xi. 129–55; Lanning, J. T., 'American Participation in the War of Jenkins' Ear', *Georgia Historical Quarterly*, xi. 191–215. For an example of the petitions by English merchants against Spanish depredations in 1738 and 1739, a major incentive for a declaration of war, see Add. MSS. (British Museum), 35909, Hardwicke Papers, ff. 82–5.

[2] *Stephens' Journal*, Candler, *Col. Rec. Ga.* iv. 398–9.

[3] W. Stephens to Verelst, Savannah, Sept. 10, 1739, C.O. 5:640, f. 364; Candler, *Col. Rec. Ga.* xxii, part ii, p. 210.

[4] Wood, G. A., *William Shirley, Governor of Massachusetts, 1741–1756* (Columbia University Studies in History, Economics, and Public Law, xc, New York, 1920), p. 126.

[5] C.O. 5:1059–60; O'Callaghan, *Documents relative to the Colonial History of the State of New York*, vi. 70–1, 147–8, 198–9, 211–12, 214, 219, 242–3, 245; *New York Gazette*, March 1, 1737, pp. 1–2; Hanna, C. A., *The Wilderness Trail* (2 vols., New York, 1911), i. 133.

[6] Oglethorpe to the Trustees, Frederica, May 28, 1742, C.O. 5:641, Document 59; Candler, *Col. Rec. Ga.* xxiii. 333; Charles Town *South Carolina Gazette*, April 30, 1741, p. 2; C.O. 5:1324–5, 1337, 1423, 1426.

[7] Saunders, W. L., editor, *The Colonial Records of North Carolina* (10 vols., Raleigh, North Carolina, 1886–90), iv. 271–2; C.O. 5:323, 344, 346.

ties of Pennsylvania.[1] And his fellow Englishmen in America did not fail him! But it went beyond the mainland, and the colonial records of Antigua, the Bahamas, Barbadoes, Bermuda, Jamaica, and the Leeward Islands bear ample testimony to that co-operative feeling born of the awful fear inspired by Spanish preparations at Havana, at Saint Augustine, and under the aegis of the Archbishop-Viceroy at Mexico City![2]

Nor were those threats and preparations merely the tales of rumour-mongers. The Spanish archives contain numerous documents which indicate irrefutably the staunch determination of all the authorities, from Madrid to Mexico, that 'Don Diego Oglethorpe' should not be permitted to remain in *Florida irredenta* unpunished; and from 1737 to the outbreak of the war itself, there was a constant concentration of the sinews of war. As early as January 1737 Governor Guemes y Horcasitas had submitted to Madrid the project of John Saby, *alias* Don Miguel de Wall, for an overland trek from Saint Augustine to attack Savannah, 'through woods and forests and deserts for a distance of many leagues and with many rivers, all deep and rapid, to cross'. Condemning this as impracticable, Horcasitas added a substitute plan of a threefold attack: by land, with the aid of friendly Indians and Negroes; by water, an attack of 500 regulars on the English forts; and finally a joint attack by both forces along the coast.[3] The receipt of Geraldino's reports and the arrival of Spanish war vessels in August 1737 gave Horca-

---

[1] See the Proclamation by James Logan, President of the Council of Pennsylvania, forbidding aid to the Spaniards, *Pennsylvania Archives*, 4th series: *Papers of the Governors*, i (Harrisburg, Pennsylvania, 1900), 616; *Colonial Records of Pennsylvania: Minutes of the Provincial Council of Pennsylvania*, iv (Harrisburg, 1851), 619.

[2] C.O. 9 (Antigua): 12; C.O. 23 (Bahamas): 4, 14–15; C.O. 26 (Bahamas): 3; C.O. 28 (Barbadoes): 25; C.O. 31 (Barbadoes): 22; C.O. 37 (Bermuda): 13–14, 29; C.O. 40 (Bermuda): 5; C.O. 137 (Jamaica): 20, 56–7; C.O. 140 (Jamaica): 30; C.O. 152 (Leeward Islands): 44; C.O. 177 (Montserrat): 3.

[3] A.I. 87–1–2, No. 4, Governor Guemes y Horcasitas to Patiño, Havana, Jan. 22, 1737.

GEORGIA: THE THIRD PHASE: IMPERIAL DEFENCE

sitas his golden opportunity to plan an offensive, in which the Reverend Archbishop-Viceroy of Mexico seems to have joined with unclerical glee, and 'the task of dislodging the English of Carolina' assumed the aspect of a holy war.[1] By 1738 Horcasitas was issuing sundry instructions for both army and naval units[2] as well as to Montiano in Saint Augustine,[3] while making one final attempt to move Oglethorpe by force of logic and reason rather than arms.[4] From March 18, 1738, it was all serious preparation for 'the impending conflict' and Horcasitas left nothing to chance, even planning for the settlement of Spanish families in the Debatable Land.[5]

If the English colonial administrators on the mainland put to shame the denizens of Whitehall in their support of Georgia, the British West Indies could not complain that

[1] A.I. 87-1-2, No. 77, Horcasitas to Torrenueva, Havana, Aug. 25, 1737; No. 78, Juan Antonio, Archbishop Viceroy of Mexico, to Torrenueva, Mexico, Aug. 28, 1737.

[2] A.I. 87-1-3, No. 26, Horcasitas' printed instructions to various commanding officers; No. 29, Horcasitas' instructions to naval commanders.

[3] A.I. 87-1-3, No. 30A, Horcasitas to Montiano, Havana, March 18, 1738; No. 30C, Horcasitas to Montiano, Havana, March 18, 1738.

[4] A.I. 87-1-3, No. 34, Horcasitas to Oglethorpe, Havana, March 18, 1738.

[5] A.I. 87-1-3, No. 32, Horcasitas to Montiano, Havana, March 20, 1738; No. 33, Unsigned letter, probably Horcasitas, to Montiano, Havana, March 25, 1738; No. 36, Horcasitas to Torrenueva, Havana, April 8, 1738; No. 37, Horcasitas to Torrenueva, Havana, April 8, 1738; No. 38, Horcasitas to Torrenueva, Havana, April 8, 1738; A.I. 87-1-2, No. 111, Horcasitas to Torrenueva, Havana, April 14, 1738; No. 112, Royal officials of Havana to Torrenueva, Havana, April 18, 1738; A.I. 87-1-3, No. 41, Horcasitas to Torrenueva, Havana, April 18, 1738; No. 42, Horcasitas to Torrenueva, Havana, April 18, 1738; No. 43, Horcasitas to Torrenueva, Havana, April 19, 1738; No. 44, Horcasitas to Torrenueva, Havana, April 18, 1738; No. 45, Montiano to Horcasitas, Florida, April 25, 1738; No. 49, Arredondo to Montiano, Saint Augustine, March 28, 1738: Concerning the apportionment of the 200 families; No. 51, Montiano to Torrenueva, Florida, June 12, 1738; No. 54, Horcasitas to Torrenueva, Havana, Dec. 10, 1738; No. 55, Horcasitas to Torrenueva, Havana, Dec. 12, 1738: Concerning the family settlements; No. 57, Horcasitas to Don Joseph de Quintana, Havana, June 20, 1739; No. 59, Horcasitas to Quintana, Havana, July 18-24, 1739 (printed in *Collections of the Georgia Historical Society*, vii, part iii, pp. 7-15); No. 60, Montiano to the King of Spain, Saint Augustine, Aug. 20, 1739.

the Admiralty was asleep. As early as 1737 the Admiralty had transmitted to Newcastle the reports of the Jamaican Naval Commander concerning imminent Spanish hostilities, reports made throughout 1737 with commendable promptness both to London and Georgia.[1] Sir Charles Wager of the Royal Navy had already seen the need for a stronger defence[2] and, on Oglethorpe's return to the colony in 1738, had ordered the three convoy ships to remain, the *Hector* off Virginia, the *Phoenix* at South Carolina, and the *Blandford* at Georgia, while the British Atlantic fleet kept a close watch on Havana after March 1738.[3] And, although war was not officially declared until October 1739, the Commander of the West Indian Squadron was ordered, in August 1738, to 'use all possible means in an hostile manner to act offensively against Spain, and take, sink, burn, or otherways destroy, all ships, sloops or other Vessels belonging to the King of Spain, or his subjects'.[4] Twelve months later every naval unit had orders to 'act hostilities against the Spaniards'.[5]

But despite the wider panorama of this larger imperial struggle, Georgia, by virtue of both its proximity to Florida and its status in Spanish eyes as *terra irredenta*, remained the logical point of first attack; and here the military drama opened in November 1738 with a mutiny among the Gibraltar troops so recently brought over by Oglethorpe. One hundred men marched to the latter's tent to demand full subsistence and back pay. He patiently explained the situation to them and then ordered them to their quarters, whereupon, in Egmont's dramatic description, 'two of them levelled their pieces at him and fired, the shot of one

---

[1] S.P. 42 (State Papers, Domestic: Naval, P.R.O.): 22, part i, 1734–7, f. 229, &c.; part ii, 1737–9, ff. 405–11, &c.

[2] Sir Charles Wager to Admiral Edward Vernon, London, April 25, 1737; June 9, 1737, Vernon-Wager MSS. (Library of Congress, Washington, D.C.), vol. vii.

[3] Richmond, *The Navy in the War of 1739–1748*, pp. 6–7, 10.

[4] S.P. 42:69, Naval Commanders, 1715–58.

[5] Ad. 2 (Admiralty: Secretary's Out-Letters, P.R.O.):55, 1736–9, p. 527: Instructions to Sir Chaloner Ogle, Rear-Admiral of the Blue Squadron, July 17, 1739; S.P. 42:59, f. 67; S.P. 42:85, f. 2.

entirely missed him, but the other passed between his wig and cheek, and providentially missed him'.[1] One rebel was killed on the spot; another was arrested; the mutiny was quelled;[2] and Oglethorpe began his preparations for defence.

The mutiny, however, had certain good effects. The Trustees, who had let him severely alone of late, now sent him their hearty congratulations on his escape and, through Verelst, renewed their expressions of appreciation for his sacrificial labours in the colony.[3] The recent and continued struggles of the Trustees with Walpole for further parliamentary appropriations, struggles which had sapped the strength and loyalty and interest of these supporters, had discouraged Oglethorpe to the point where he saw 'nothing but Destruction to the Colony unless some assistance be immediately sent us'.[4] The mutiny now aroused his fighting instinct and, in a letter to his fellow Trustee, Alderman George Heathcote, he described the difficulties which, in the autumn of 1738, 'rather animate than daunt me':

I am here in one of the most delightful Situations as any man could wish to be. A great number of Debts, empty Magazines, no money to supply them, Numbers of People to be fed, mutinous Soldiers to Command, a Spanish Claim & a large body of their Troops not far from us.[5]

Oglethorpe's visit to the Creeks at Coweta in the summer of 1739 had kept the Indians in line to hold the west, but the calm had been shattered by a negro slave

---
[1] *Egmont Diary*, iii. 6; Oglethorpe to Newcastle, Frederica, Nov. 20, 1738, C.O. 5:654, ff. 174–5; S.P. 42:22, part ii, ff. 405–11.
[2] Thomas Jones to Verelst, Savannah, Nov. 12, 1738, C.O. 5:640, ff. 212–13; Candler, *Col. Rec. Ga.* xxii, part i, pp. 303–4; *Gentleman's Magazine*, ix. 48, 215.
[3] Verelst to Oglethorpe, London, Feb. 5, 1739, C.O. 5:667, pp. 209–10.
[4] Oglethorpe to the Trustees, Frederica, October 19, 1738, C.O. 5:640, ff. 198–200; Candler, *Col. Rec. Ga.* xxii, part i, p. 283; Oglethorpe to the Duke of Montagu, Georgia, *c.* 1742, *MSS. of the Duke of Buccleuch and Queensberry* (H.M.C. Reports), i. 408; *Egmont Diary*, iii. 7–10, 12–15.
[5] Oglethorpe to Alderman George Heathcote, Frederica, Nov. 20, 1738, C.O. 5:640, ff. 218–20; Candler, *Col. Rec. Ga.* xxii, part i, p. 314.

insurrection in South Carolina,[1] attributed to Spanish influences, and a Spanish outrage on Amelia Island which was justified in their eyes by Oglethorpe's establishment of English fortifications in the Debatable Land.[2] Oglethorpe's programme was determined. On October 5 he wrote to the Trustees that 'I have received the King's Commands to anoy the Spaniards and am going to Execute them';[3] and a week later added:

As we every hour expect Action with the Spaniards, I have hardly time to write out the different necessary orders for the Indian Nation, the Rangers, the Garrisons, the Boats, and Letters to Carolina, Virginia, the Northern Colonies and Men of War. As the Safety and Lives of the People, and honour of the English Arms in these parts depend upon using the present Conjuncture, I hope you will excuse my not writing a long letter.[4]

Correctly gauging the struggle on the imperial scale, Oglethorpe decided to 'use the present Conjuncture' for an attack on the very heart of Spanish America, Saint Augustine, the conquest of which had been deemed a necessity by the Board of Trade as early as 1720,[5] and later by Governor Belcher of Massachusetts.[6] The war in Georgia thus developed into an English campaign against Saint Augustine in 1740 and a Spanish *riposte* in 1742, while Vice-Admiral Vernon acquired whatever fame was to be gained in the naval war.

[1] For an account of the insurrection see Oglethorpe to Verelst, Savannah, Oct. 9, 1739, C.O. 5:640, ff. 383–7; Candler, *Col. Rec. Ga.* xxii, part ii, pp. 232–6.

[2] Oglethorpe to Newcastle, Frederica, Nov. 15, 1739, C.O. 5:654, f. 236; Oglethorpe to the Trustees, Frederica, Nov. 16, 1739, C.O. 5:640, ff. 406–7; Candler, *Col. Rec. Ga.* xxii, part ii, p. 266; New York *Weekly Journal*, Jan. 28, 1740, pp. 2–3; McGrady, *History of South Carolina under the Royal Government*, pp. 184–7; Osgood, *The American Colonies in the Eighteenth Century*, iii. 502–4.

[3] Oglethorpe to the Trustees, Savannah, Oct. 5, 1739, C.O. 5:640, f. 372; Candler, *Col. Rec. Ga.* xxii, part ii, p. 217.

[4] Oglethorpe to the Trustees, Savannah, Oct. 11, 1739, C.O. 5:640, ff. 394–5; Candler, *Col. Rec. Ga.* xxii, part ii, p. 242.

[5] Crane, *The Southern Frontier*, pp. 226–7.

[6] Smith, 'The Belcher Papers', *Collections of the Massachusetts Historical Society*, ii. 244–5, 390–1.

The dual attack upon Spain in the New World began late in 1739 with a concentration of British naval forces, neither at Havana nor Cartagena but at Jamaica, where Newcastle evaded his responsibility by empowering a local council of officers to make vital decisions.[1] The result was an over-emphasis on attacking Spain in the Porto Bello expedition of 1739 and a subsequent Cartagena effort instead of securing the defence of Georgia.[2] The Admiralty had ordered all ships on the American station to take part in the offensive[3] but, while Admiral Vernon was refitting at Jamaica, Oglethorpe set out for Saint Augustine. By February 1740 he had gained control of the San Juan or Saint John's River,[4] and had penetrated to within twenty-five miles of his objective. But this had not been achieved by Georgians alone.

When James Oglethorpe had secured his regiment in London he had been given military command over South Carolina troops as well and the executive commissions of both Samuel Horsey and James Glen as Governors of South Carolina recognized that authority.[5] It was in his capacity as General and Commander-in-Chief of South Carolina that Oglethorpe had visited Charles Town in March 1739 to obtain aid for the prospective combat;[6] and he was now loyally supported by the South Carolinians, to whom their former object of hate had become a potential saviour[7] for, as one citizen of Charles Town wrote to his father in England: 'We have nothing here but the Face of

---

[1] Richmond, *The Navy in the War of 1739–1748*, i. 31, 35.

[2] Admiralty 1:232, Jamaica (P.R.O.); 1:233; S.P. 42:90, 92, *passim*.

[3] Admiralty 2:55.

[4] Oglethorpe to W. Stephens, Frederica, Feb. 1, 1740, C.O. 5:640, ff. 440–3; Candler, *Col. Rec. Ga.* xxii, part ii, pp. 312–13.

[5] C.O. 5:197, p. 296; C.O. 5:198, pp. 157–8; Grant and Munro, *Acts of the Privy Council: Colonial Series*, iii. 606, 621–2.

[6] *Stephens' Journal*, Candler, *Col. Rec. Ga.* iv. 298; London *Daily Gazetteer*, June 25, 1739, p. 2.

[7] Oglethorpe to Colonel William Bull, Frederica, Dec. 29, 1739, C.O. 5:439; Colonel William Bull to Newcastle, Charles Town, Feb. 11, 1740, C.O. 5:388, f. 203; S.C. Rec. xx, ff. 251–3; Richmond, *The Navy in the War of 1739–1748*, i. 50.

War between us and Spain.'[1] When, then, in March 1740 Oglethorpe made a hasty visit of a fortnight's duration to Charles Town, the South Carolina legislature, in a magnificent gesture of loyalty and faith, voted to supply him with £120,000 in cash, a regiment of foot, a troop of horse, and men of war, all to aid the attack on Saint Augustine.[2]

It was with such support that James Oglethorpe now led the renewed drive against the Spanish stronghold while a squadron under Captain Vincent Pearce blockaded the harbour. Owing to a failure of co-operation with the fleet, Oglethorpe's programme collapsed when the Spaniards managed to bring succour to the besieged garrison. Despite an artillery attack which won the reluctant praise of the Spaniards and aroused their fears as to the certainty of defeat in a future effort,[3] Oglethorpe failed to dislodge the enemy. Montiano's pessimistic prophecy to Horcasitas that, 'even if necessary to remain one year before this place, General Oglethorpe will do it, until he subdues it',[4] was not realized, and, contrary to his report to Colonel Bull that 'God has been pleased to Bless us with great success',[5] Oglethorpe's thirty-day siege failed. In Admiral Richmond's compact phrases, 'Both Oglethorpe and Pearce proved themselves indifferent leaders; the former, though he developed the idea, was incapable of putting it into execution; the latter saw difficulties everywhere but made little effort to overcome them'.[6] By the end of July

---

[1] London *Daily Gazetteer*, April 7, 1740, p. 1.

[2] Oglethorpe to the Trustees, Charles Town, April 2, 1740, C.O. 5:640, ff. 461; Candler, *Col. Rec. Ga.* xxii, part ii, p. 339; *Stephens' Journal*, Candler, *Col. Rec. Ga.* iv. 535–6.

[3] A.I. 87–1–2, No. 114, Don Pedro Ruiz de Olano to the King of Spain, Saint Augustine, Aug. 8, 1740.

[4] Montiano to Horcasitas, No. 203, Saint Augustine, July 6, 1740, *Collections of the Georgia Historical Society*, vii, part ii, p. 58.

[5] *Report of the South Carolina Committee of Assembly on the Saint Augustine Expedition* (printed in part in *Collections of the South Carolina Historical Society*, iv, Charleston, 1887, balance of appendix in South Carolina Assembly Journal, S.C. Rec. x. 288–340), p. 65.

[6] Richmond, *The Navy in the War of 1739–1748*, i. 50–1; Clowes, W. L., *The Royal Navy* (5 vols., Boston, 1898), iii. 268–70. For a colourful Spanish

GEORGIA: THE THIRD PHASE: IMPERIAL DEFENCE 235

the English failure was patent and only the weakness of the Spanish forces prevented the return attack which stratagem demanded.[1] While Montiano indulged in a voluminous descriptive epistle to Horcasitas, full of joy at the rather unexpected raising of the siege,[2] a South Carolinian, in utter despair, had expressed the opinion that 'the consequence of abandoning the Siege of Saint Augustine will most certainly be the entire loss of the whole Province of Georgia',[3] and Oglethorpe's party had begun their return journey to the north only to find that, owing to this failure, the amity between South Carolina and Georgia had vanished in a cloud of charges and countercharges.

James Oglethorpe was an ambitious soul who seldom accepted criticism and never succumbed to a defeat. Smarting under this blow to his national pride, his optimism and his vanity, and justifiably embittered by an irritating paucity of aid from the homeland, the Georgia leader now proceeded without justification to vent his spleen upon his late allies from South Carolina. He not only accused them of failure to co-operate in crises but, in a letter to the Duke of Montagu, affirmed that 'Carolina has above 40,000 negroes and not 4,000 white men that can bear arms, and those mere militia. If they remove us, all that country is at their pleasure; yet there is a kind of stupid security that makes them not believe they are in danger, and not thank those who would prepare against it.'[4] The South Carolinians quite naturally resented these insinuations and authorized their Assembly to make a full

account of the attack see Francisco de san Buenaventura, Señor Don Fray, *Ave Maria: A Relacion* (Saint Augustine, 1740).
[1] Montiano to Horcasitas, No. 205, Saint Augustine, July 28, 1740, *Collections of the Georgia Historical Society*, vii, part ii, pp. 62–3.
[2] A.I. 86–6–5, No. 55, Montiano to Horcasitas, Saint Augustine, July 28, 1740.
[3] An anonymous South Carolinian's letter to Peregrine Fury, Colonial Agent at London, South Carolina, Aug. 1, 1740, C.O. 5:654, ff. 299–300.
[4] Oglethorpe to the Duke of Montagu, Georgia, *c.* 1742, *MSS. of the Duke of Buccleuch and Queensberry* (H.M.C. Reports), i. 408.

investigation.[1] After a full year of preparation, the legislators presented a notably impartial report which not only cleared their own troops and refuted Oglethorpe's contentions, but proceeded, unfortunately, to hurl a heated charge of incompetency at the Georgian. Although the signatories 'purposely avoid taking any particular notice of many Imprudent Steps of the General in the Expedition',[2] the report, after properly praising Colonel Alexander Vanderdussen and his Carolinians, affirmed that 'neither this government nor the forces in the pay thereof have been in the last degree the cause of the ill Success of the Expedition'.[3] The dispute waxed so warm that an anonymous critic of Oglethorpe, who signed his communication, 'A.B.', revealed to Newcastle a plot by James Oglethorpe to massacre all British subjects in the West Indies and South Carolina in order to aid the French and Spanish Indians and 'mulattos' with whom he was said to be in constant correspondence! To support this charge, 'A.B.' directed attention to the fact that one of his sisters was Maid of Honour to the Queen of Spain, one was in France (Eleanor), one in Savoy (Frances), and Anne in England constantly plotted with the others by correspondence.[4] The only possible connexion of actuality with this fable was the fact that it was Anne Oglethorpe's keen mind which prevented the publication in England of a Carolinian version of the siege, whereby the Assembly, in Egmont's words, 'proposed to blast' her brother's reputation.[5] But in all this welter of words the indisputable fact remained that Colonel Vanderdussen had been a hearty friend and loyal colleague of Oglethorpe;[6] that

---

[1] C.O. 5:439, S.C. Assembly Journal; S.C. Rec. xiii. 31, 40, 56; xiii, part ii, pp. 57–94; xiv. 1–115, 253, 338–9; xv. 37, 56, 59, 83–5, 88–90.

[2] 'Report of the South Carolina Committee of Assembly', *Collections of the South Carolina Historical Society*, iv. 130.

[3] Ibid. iv. 1–177.

[4] 'A.B.' to Newcastle, undated, Add. MSS. (British Museum), 32992, Newcastle Papers, f. 114.

[5] *Egmont Diary*, iii. 238.

[6] *Stephens' Journal*, Candler, *Col. Rec. Ga.* iv. 635.

the work of South Carolina in appeasing the Creeks had helped materially in making possible Oglethorpe's later achievements;[1] that the South Carolina troops were with Oglethorpe at the time of attack and there is not one iota of evidence of non-co-operation; and that Carolina had always been watchful in warning[2] and generous with aid, both in men and money.[3]

The failure of the expedition and his unquestioned loss of prestige now affected Oglethorpe's health as well as his temper. As William Stephens noted in his journal, the commander was 'reduced to an extraordinary Weakness by a continual Fever' and 'the Disappointment of Success (it is believed) now galled him, and too great Anxiety of Mind preyed upon him'.[4] The fever raged for two months but the spirit was still alive, and it hastened his recovery.[5]

Well again, his administrative troubles returned, for it was obvious that a commander on Saint Simon's Island could not simultaneously be the efficient executive at Savannah.[6] But the war must go on: always the preparation for the attack which he knew must come; always the appeal for more support. On November 20, 1738, Oglethorpe had addressed an appeal to the Right Honourable Thomas Winnington, Paymaster of the Forces, in a letter which indicates clearly the former's problem with Parliament:

Give me leave to acquaint You with the Situation of the Colony of Georgia, and at the same time desire your Assistance.

The Parliament, to defray the Charges of the Improvements of the Colony of Georgia, and the Military Defence thereof, used to grant £20,000 for a year. The King ordered a Reg^t for the defence of the Colony, and thereupon the Trustees were

[1] Crane, *The Southern Frontier*, pp. 272–5.
[2] e.g. *An Account Showing the Progress of the Colony of Georgia*, Candler, *Col. Rec. Ga.* iii. 389–91.
[3] C.O. 5:439, S.C. Assembly Journal; S.C. Rec. xii. 295–323.
[4] *Stephens' Journal*, Candler, *Col. Rec. Ga.* iv. 635.
[5] Ibid. 653.
[6] *Egmont Diary*, iii. 119–40.

contented to abate £12,000 in their demands, and £8,000 only was granted to them. But as the Regiment did not arrive till near a year afterwards, the Trustees were obliged to support the Military Charge of the Colony during that whole time, which was very dangerous by reason of the threatened Invasion from the Spaniards; of which You received so many accounts. No Officer of the Trustees dared abandon a Garrison, reduce any men, or dismiss the Militia, whilst the Spaniards threatned the Province, and the King's Troops were not arrived to relieve them. A Debt of near £12,000 is contracted because by unforseen accidents the Regiment was delayed, and the Military Expence was continued till their Arrival though the Parliamentary Grant ceased.

I must entreat therefore your Assistance to the Trustees on their Application to Parliament for a Sum sufficient to discharge this Debt; for if the people who furnished with necessaries a Colony then threatned with Invasions, and the people who then bore Arms for the Defence of it, and thereby secured that Important Frontier till the Arrival of the King's Troops, should be ruined by not being paid their just Demands, It would prevent hereafter any Frontier Colony from receiving Assistance.[1]

If that were the case in 1738, the situation had become but intensified in eighteen months and, despite his faithfulness in keeping them fully informed of conditions and his campaigns, the Trustees, disturbed at his extravagance in military expenditures, failed Oglethorpe; the British Government, in the person of Walpole, again willing in May 1740 to yield Georgia for peace at any price,[2] failed him. In vain had he sent Lieutenant Horton to England to plead for succour.[3] In desperation Oglethorpe had instructed Harman Verelst to 'raise money on all his estate, real and personal, without limitation of the sum, as also to employ all his salary from the Government for answering the bills he should draw on him for the service of the public'. Egmont well lauded this as 'a real instance of zeal for his country'; but, with both

---

[1] James Oglethorpe to Thomas Winnington, Frederica, Nov. 20, 1738, *Notes and Queries*, 3rd series, x. 64.
[2] *Egmont Diary*, iii. 142–3.   [3] Ibid. 135–40, 145, 154–5, 159.

Whitehall and the Trustees failing him, Oglethorpe's providence was sorely needed, for South Carolina had been unable, on her own credit, to raise the funds pledged towards the pay of the troops, and it was her hated enemy, Oglethorpe, who now personally supplied the money![1]

If in May 1740 Walpole had been willing to lose Georgia for the sake of peace, the failure before Saint Augustine and the prospect of an imminent Spanish reply had stirred the Admiralty to action. Up to now its instructions had been 'to harass the Spaniards' in offensive tactics; on October 7, 1740, orders were issued to all officers in the American service to 'have a particular attention to the Security of South Carolina and Georgia' and 'at all times to give all the assistance in your Power to the People of that Province and Colony, against their enemies, and particularly against the Spaniards at Saint Augustine'.[2] But at the same time the second period of propaganda to raise further funds in Parliament was well under way,[3] and Thomas Stephens, Patrick Tailfer, and their fellow malcontents were assailing Oglethorpe in London. By April 1741 the latter was suffering a second illness at Frederica 'through fatigue and vexation',[4] a break-down which continued into July,[5] while his recovery was retarded by the pronounced hostility of a subordinate officer in the Saint Augustine campaign, Lieutenant-Colonel Cooke,[6] whom Oglethorpe himself had promoted from the rank of Major a bare year before.[7]

While Oglethorpe was thus regaining his strength, the international picture had greatly changed. The mercantilist system of colonial polity which, in Admiral Richmond's opinion, was the primary cause of the war with

---

[1] Ibid. 146.
[2] Admiralty 2:56, pp. 443–4. See also Ad. 1:4109.
[3] Crane, *The Promotion Literature of Georgia*, pp. 16–20.
[4] *Egmont Diary*, iii. 214–15.
[5] Urlsperger, *Neunte Continuation der ausführlichen Nachricht von den Saltzburgischen Emigranten*, pp. 1050–1.   [6] *Egmont Diary*, iii. 213, 216.
[7] W.O. 4 (War Office, Secretary-at-War: Out-Letters, P.R.O.): 36, 1740–1, p. 291, Secretary Yonge to Oglethorpe, War Office, Nov. 8, 1740: Approving promotions.

Spain, had made England's chief rival not really Spain but France, which nation late in 1740 threw in her naval strength on the side of her Latin sister.[1] What was of far greater effect on Oglethorpe, however, was the eruption in 1741 of warfare on the European continent, the necessities of which were henceforth to deprive him of valued aid. All the evidence in the Newcastle and Hardwicke correspondence, together with the stony silence of Whitehall, leads one to the conclusion that the British Government from 1738 to 1742 was infinitely more interested in the preservation, first of the 'freedom of the seas' for British trade, then of peace with Spain, and finally, if necessary as the only alternative to peace, of the reduction of Spanish power in the West Indies—than it was concerned with the preservation and perpetuation of Georgia. Admirals Vernon and Wager and the West Indian fleet were to receive official support as a matter of imperial concern; Oglethorpe must needs shift for himself. By 1741, moreover, the problems of France, the King of Prussia, the Queen of Hungary, the Greffier of Holland, the House of Austria, and the Holy Roman Empire, found Britain too involved on the continent to pay much attention to the lone defender of the Southern Frontier deep in the Debatable Land.[2] By the close of 1741, then, Oglethorpe was virtually compelled to rely on himself[3] for, that autumn, a committee of officers and government authorities, composed of Sir Charles Wager, the Duke of Montagu, General Wade, and Martin Bladen, considering Verelst's presentation of Oglethorpe's request for further resources, rejected it for being 'couched in such general and uncertain terms'![4]

[1] Richmond, *The Navy in the War of 1739–1748*, i. ix, 1, 101–37.
[2] Add. MSS. (British Museum), 35406–7, Hardwicke Papers, *passim*, especially ff. 125–34, 'Consideration upon the Present State of Affairs', Nov. 1, 1741.
[3] Oglethorpe to Newcastle, Frederica, July 19, 1741, C.O. 5:654, f. 351; Richmond, *The Navy in the War of 1739–1748*, i, chap. vii.
[4] C.O. 5:5, ff. 170–4; Lansdowne MSS. (British Museum), 820, ff. 61–88; Vernon-Wager MSS. (Library of Congress), xv, *passim*.

As a result of the failure of the British West Indian naval expeditions,[1] Oglethorpe had fitted out two privateers and a schooner,[2] but his chief reliance was on the British ships at Jamaica and on his own defences at Frederica, the citizenry of which were now to realize the truth of Harman Verelst's censure of them to Causton in 1737 for having cut down the wood outside the town: 'That wood was a better defence than any fort. ... The real defence of the town is the Woods and the Swamps.'[3] His defensive measures were needed, for Montiano had wasted no time in seeking and obtaining reinforcements and the necessary orders from Madrid to proceed against the English,[4] relying chiefly on naval privateers.[5] Despite the havoc wrought on English commerce by Spanish privateers over the entire extent of the Atlantic coast,[6] James Oglethorpe did not fear the enemy. His previous encounters had confirmed his views as to their ultimate impotency, and in April 1741 he had confidently written to the Trustees: 'As God has been pleased hitherto to overcome all these oppositions, I think from thence we are much more likely to succeed than we were before we knew what opposition we were to receive.'[7] The calm

[1] Richmond, *The Navy in the War of 1739–1748*, i, chap. vi.
[2] Chapin, H. M., *Privateering in King George's War, 1739–1748* (Providence, Rhode Island, 1928), pp. 208–12.
[3] Verelst to Causton, London, Aug. 11, 1737, C.O. 5:667, pp. 51–62.
[4] A.I. 86–7–21, No. 27, Montiano to Don José de la Quintana, Saint Augustine, Sept. 10, 1740; A.I. 86–6–5, No. 60, Royal order to Montiano, Madrid, Oct. 4, 1740; No. 61, Royal order to Montiano, Madrid, Nov. 7, 1740.
[5] A.I. 86–7–21, No. 29, Montiano to de la Quintana, Saint Augustine, Jan. 2, 1741; No. 31, Montiano to de la Quintana, Saint Augustine, Oct. 1, 1741.
[6] For interesting foreign comment on British misfortunes in the war with Spain, 1739–41, see the dispatches of Giovanni Giacomo Zamboni, Resident in England for the Duke of Modena, the Landgrave of Hesse-Darmstadt, and the King of Poland, to Ludwig V, Landgrave of Hesse-Darmstadt, and his Ministers, Rawlinson MSS. (Bodleian Library), H (Letters), 119, ff. 336–9, 365–6, 414–17.
[7] Oglethorpe to the Trustees, Frederica, April 28, 1741, C.O. 5:641, Document No. 4; Candler, *Col. Rec. Ga.* xxiii. 23–5; *Collections of the Georgia Historical Society*, iii. 113.

of the succeeding months merely increased the tension, for across the Caribbean Horcasitas was quietly, though thoroughly, completing the arrangements for attack which had been suspended in 1737.[1] In obeying the royal orders of October 31, 1741,[2] Horcasitas proposed to make the advance between April and June of 1742, and the Spanish correspondence of this period bears eloquent testimony to the high efficiency and industry of the Governor of Cuba and Montiano in Saint Augustine.[3]

While the Spaniards foregathered in Florida, Oglethorpe had been seeking all possible assistance, and only too often in vain. The strategic situation was now the reverse of that in 1740 and he made the most of it. Early in June 1742, while the Spaniards were advancing northward by sea and land, Oglethorpe warned South Carolina of the great reinforcements from Cuba[4] and, in a letter to Colonel Bull, once again vigorously besought their aid.[5] The Carolinians had acquired a fear of France in the West and were unimpressed,[6] so that on June 7, in a pathetic letter, Oglethorpe reminded Newcastle of the aid which had been sought but never sent:

I hope Your Grace will remember that I long ago acquainted you that I expected an Invasion as soon as the affair of Cuba was ended, and pray'd for succours which are not yet arrived.

---

[1] A.I. 87–1–3, No. 62, Horcasitas to Don Joseph del Campillo, Havana, Feb. 24, 1742.

[2] A.I. 87–1–3, No. 61, Royal orders to Horcasitas and Montiano, Madrid, Oct. 31, 1741.

[3] A.I. 87–1–3, No. 63, Montiano to Campillo, Saint Augustine, March 12, 1742; No. 66, Horcasitas to Campillo, Havana, April 4, 1742; No. 67, Horcasitas to Campillo, Havana, April 6, 1742; No. 64, Montiano to Horcasitas, Saint Augustine, April 13, 1742; No. 69, Report of a Council of War, Havana, May 10, 1742; No. 70, Horcasitas to Montiano, Havana, May 14, 1742; No. 71, Horcasitas to Montiano, Havana, June 2, 1742; No. 73, Horcasitas to Campillo, Havana, June 8, 1742.

[4] Oglethorpe to the Council of South Carolina, Frederica, June 4, 1742, C.O. 5:441, p. 94; S.C. Rec. viii, ff. 81–2.

[5] Oglethorpe to Colonel Bull, Frederica, June 5, 1742, C.O. 5:441, pp. 95–6; S.C. Rec. viii, ff. 84–5.

[6] S.C. Petition, June 3, 1742, C.O. 5:384, Document No. 1; S.C. Rec. xx, ff. 574–80.

... It is too late now to desire Your Grace to represent this to His Majesty and ask succours; before they can arrive the matter will be over. I hope I shall behave as well as one with so few men and so little Artilery can.[1]

The silence of South Carolina now brought back a touch of his pessimism and asperity, and on June 26 he frankly informed the Carolinians that, 'if we should be defeated and they take Fort William and Frederica, I know nothing can stop them on this side Virginia'.[2] This dire prophecy proved effective and Colonel Bull, although still haunted by the French nightmare, successfully sought aid from Governor Gooch of Virginia and provided Carolinian assistance which enabled Oglethorpe to lay his plans of defence.[3]

On June 22, Montiano, aided by a pilot who had deserted from South Carolina, made his advance. Oglethorpe retreated from Saint Simon's Island, which was promptly occupied by the Spaniards. The former retired to Frederica where, as Colonel Bull so unsympathetically wrote Newcastle, "'tis not expected he can long hold against so great a Force'.[4] Flushed with their easy advances and the prospect of an ultimate, sweeping, victory, the Spaniards began to cut their way through the marsh woods towards Frederica. Oglethorpe was relying on the Jamaica troops and fleet, last reported at Charles Town, to encircle the Spaniards off Saint Simon's Island, much as Rochambeau and Washington were to cut off Cornwallis at Yorktown four decades later.[5] But despite the reputation of the Jamaican coast-guard which had so impressed the Spaniards in 1737,[6]

[1] Oglethorpe to Newcastle, Frederica, June 7, 1742, C.O. 5:655, f. 29.
[2] Oglethorpe to the Council of South Carolina, Frederica, June 26, 1742, C.O. 5:441, pp. 103–4; S.C. Rec. viii, f. 91.
[3] C.O. 5:441, p. 107; S.C. Rec. viii, ff. 190–7.
[4] Bull to Newcastle, Charles Town, July 7, 1742, C.O. 5:388, f. 153; S.C. Rec. xx, ff. 585–7.
[5] For this *einkreisung* policy see W. Stephens to the Trustees, Savannah, July 13, 1742, C.O. 5:641, Document No. 63; Candler, *Col. Rec. Ga.* xxiii. 377–8.
[6] A.I. 87–1–2, No. 77, Horcasitas to Torrenueva, Havana, Aug. 25, 1737.

the Jamaica contingent retired to their island from Charles Town without firing a shot,[1] while the Carolina fleet arrived after the battle.[2] The Spaniards, numbering nigh three thousand, pressed on; by July 7 they were within a mile of Frederica near Bloody Marsh where, in what has not unjustly been called 'the highwater mark of his career',[3] James Oglethorpe ambushed a large part of the invaders to such good effect that, with the aid of diplomatic strategy, the superior Spanish force was led to withdraw;[4] and in characteristic manner the victorious commander celebrated the preservation of Georgia by ordaining that July 25, 1742, be set apart 'as a day of public thanksgiving to Almighty God for His great deliverance in having put an end to the Spanish invasion'.[5]

In the words of Professor Coulter, 'the withdrawal of the Spaniards in July 1742 was the last act of Spanish Florida in the drama of the War of Jenkins' Ear'.[6] The

---

[1] New York *Weekly Journal*, Dec. 13, 1742, pp. 2–3; Boston *Weekly News Letter*, Dec. 30, 1742, p. 1. For evidence of Jamaican fears of Spanish depredations see Add. MSS. (British Museum), 12431, A volume of Jamaica documents; and Add. MSS., 34207, Letters of Colonel W. Burrard, 1740–66.

[2] W. Stephens to Verelst, Savannah, Aug. 13, 1742, C.O. 5:641, Document No. 66; Candler, *Col. Rec. Ga.* xxiii. 383–4.

[3] McCain, *Georgia as a Proprietary Province*, p. 86.

[4] For the various accounts of the Spanish attack and retreat see Oglethorpe to Newcastle, Frederica, July 30, 1742, C.O. 5:655, ff. 127–9; Francis Moore to the Trustees, Charles Town, July 13–14, 1742, C.O. 5:655, ff. 53–4; Oglethorpe to Captain William Thomson, Frederica, July 9, 1742, C.O. 5:655, f. 55; 'An Account of the late Invasion of Georgia drawn out by Lieutenant Patrick Sutherland', C.O. 5:655, f. 85–9; W. Stephens to Verelst, Savannah, July 18, 1742, C.O. 5:641, Document No. 63A; Candler, *Col. Rec. Ga.* xxiii. 378–82; Add. MSS. (British Museum), 32699, Newcastle Papers, ff. 543–4: Deposition of Samuel Cloake, Frederica, Aug. 3, 1742; Urlsperger, *Neunte Continuation der ausführlichen Nachricht*, pp. 1252–8; Charles Town *South Carolina Gazette*, July 5, 1742, p. 2; July 12, 1742, p. 1; July 19, 1742, pp. 1–3; July 26, 1742, pp. 1–3; August 2, 1742, pp. 1–2; August 16, 1742, p. 2; Willcox, C. de W., editor, 'Spanish Official Account of the Attack on the Colony of Georgia in America and of its Defeat on St. Simons Island by General James Oglethorpe', *Collections of the Georgia Historical Society*, vii, part iii, pp. 52–96.

[5] Oglethorpe to the Trustees, Frederica, July 30, 1742, C.O. 5:655, ff. 127–9; *Collections of the Georgia Historical Society*, iii. 139.

[6] Coulter, *A Short History of Georgia*, p. 48.

importance of the battle of Bloody Marsh has been variously estimated. The Boston *Post* in derision printed these lines:

They both did meet, they both did fight, they both did run away;
 They both did strive to meet again, the quite Contrary Way.[1]

It may perchance be asserted that, had the battle of Bloody Marsh not been fought—and won, no matter how fortuitously[2]—by Oglethorpe, the Carolinas or even Virginia would later have been the scene of the decisive Anglo-Spanish struggle for American continental supremacy. But that is fatuous. This was the decisive battle, as decisive for Spain as two decades later the Plains of Abraham proved for France, or Yorktown two decades later yet for Britain.

'Deeply mortified' at the turn of events, Horcasitas, in his report to the Madrid authorities, admitted that he had expected a victory which was to include the complete destruction of all English communities 'as far as Port Royal' or Charles Town.[3] And Antonio de Arredondo, who had had contact with Oglethorpe and his forces five years before, had been so certain of a Spanish conquest that he had prepared and published *An Historical Proof of Spain's Title to Georgia*, which was a very full and remarkably sound refutation of the English claim to the Debatable Land.[4]

Thus it was that, despite their defeat at Bloody Marsh,

---

[1] Boston *Post*, Oct. 4, 1742, p. 2.

[2] Samuel Ogle in May 1743 expressed to Newcastle the very sound judgement that, 'notwithstanding General Oglethorpe's good conduct and personal bravery, the preservation of that province was rather owing to the ill management and disagreement of the Spanish commanders, than to any human means employed on our part for our defence'. Samuel Ogle to Newcastle [no place], May 17, 1743, C.O. 5:655, ff. 201–6.

[3] Willcox, 'The Spanish Official Account of the Attack on the Colony of Georgia', *Collections of the Georgia Historical Society*, vii, part iii, pp. 48–51. See also A.I. 87–1–3, No. 78, Montiano to Triviño, Saint Augustine, Aug. 3, 1742; No. 81, Horcasitas to Campillo, Havana, Aug. 19, 1742; No. 83, Montiano to Horcasitas, Saint Augustine, Sept. 6, 1742.

[4] For the English version see Bolton, *Arredondo's Historical Proof of Spain's Title to Georgia*.

the Spaniards remained an ever-present danger in Florida, where they reunited their forces for a future attack on Saint Simon's, Frederica, and, if they were fortunate, perchance on Savannah itself. Fully aware of the future dangers and his present responsibilities, Oglethorpe turned his attention to local defensive measures, and renewed appeals for definitive aid. Within the colony itself he appealed to the President and Assistants of the Northern Province at Savannah for assistance[1] and then turned to his fellow Britons in Jamaica. Unfortunately for Oglethorpe, Governor Edward Trelawny was deep in a dispute on etiquette and the need of an apology from Admiral Sir Chaloner Ogle,[2] and the Jamaican force which, at the instigation of Colonel Bull, had come to Charles Town in the summer of 1742,[3] returned to its base without even visiting Georgia. There is some evidence that, although he desired that visit, Oglethorpe acquiesced in their return home,[4] but in a letter to Newcastle's secretary, Andrew Stone, the Georgia commander lashed out at the Carolinians, whom he blamed for being 'so stupid (not to say worse) that they prevented the Men of War from coming hither tho' I gave them very near a Month's Notice'.[5]

But the ultimate source of aid must be Whitehall and, dismayed by the utterly apathetic attitude of the government, Oglethorpe now appealed directly to the Duke of Newcastle who, with his brother, Henry Pelham, in 1742 displaced Walpole in control of the Whig oligarchy. In a series of remarkable letters he explained the vital importance of Georgia as a buffer state and vividly portrayed the dire consequences of its conquest by Spain,

---

[1] C.O. 5:692 (no pagination); Candler, *Col. Rec. Ga.* vi. 40.
[2] C.O. 137 (Jamaica): 37, *passim.*
[3] C.O. 5:42, Nos. 161–77.
[4] Oglethorpe to Colonel A. Duroure, commanding the Jamaican contingent at Charles Town, Frederica, Oct. 21, 1742, C.O. 5:388, f. 172; S.C. Rec. xx, ff. 641–3.
[5] Oglethorpe to Andrew Stone, Frederica, Nov. 24, 1742, C.O. 5:655, ff. 94–5; *Collections of the Georgia Historical Society,* iii. 126.

the knowledge and fear of which, he wrote, 'has made me expend my fortune and expose my person much more than by the strictest rules of duty I should have been obliged to'. Praying that the frontier be properly protected, he declined to 'be blamed if I dye in an unsuccessful defence of it for the being killed in one's duty is all that the bravest man or best officer that wants the necessary means of war, can do'.[1] At the same time he bluntly informed Andrew Stone that 'my remaining in uncertainty may not only prove fatal to myself but very probably the consequence of it may be the loss of two or three Provinces'.[2] Two months passed without a reply. If the comment of Philip Yorke, later second Lord Hardwicke, that 'the money we have spent in that chimerical project is all thrown away'[3] is a criterion, then the silence—and ignorance—of London is explicable. But Oglethorpe persisted and in January 1743 again appealed directly to Newcastle, reminding him that 'it was by the great Blessing of God that we defeated the Enemy' for 'they had all Preparations, numbers, and time sufficient to have destroyed us and had I been as incredulous and as unprepared, they had in all human probability not only conquered Georgia, but both Carolinas, for the Negroes could have certainly revolted, and if the Spaniards had defeated us, they had nothing but what would have run from them'. In measured phrases he boldly declared:

I would not trouble Your Grace with these Reflexions were it not necessary to prevent future ill Consequences by dear bought experience. I hope this good use may be made of a bad accident that it may give weight to the representations of those who are near danger and who can certainly perceive the

[1] Oglethorpe to the Duke of Newcastle, Frederica, Nov. 24, 1742, C.O. 5:655, f. 92; *Collections of the Georgia Historical Society*, iii. 124.
[2] Oglethorpe to Andrew Stone, Frederica, Nov. 24, 1742, C.O. 5:655, ff. 94–5; *Collections of the Georgia Historical Society*, iii. 126.
[3] Philip Yorke to Dr. Thomas Birch, Wimpole, Sept. 19, 1742, Add. MSS. (British Museum), 35396, Correspondence of Philip Yorke, later second Lord Hardwicke, and Dr. Thomas Birch, 1740–1745, f. 62.

danger and take the measures necessary for defence sooner than those at a distance can.[1]

Again the rather plain hint was lost on Whitehall, and in February Oglethorpe warned the Duke that, inasmuch as 'every day confirms the imminent danger', further aid was badly needed, for he had 'reason to apprehend the worst of consequences from the great numbers of the enemy if I have not timely support'.[2] But all his efforts were in vain: Whitehall preserved its silence and the Trustees continued to ignore him.[3]

Despite this, or rather because of his isolation, Oglethorpe now concluded that the best defence was a strong attack and decided to make another raid upon Saint Augustine early in March 1743.[4] From his campaign on the Saint John's River in Florida, he informed Newcastle that 'I should think myself inexcusable if I did not inform Your Grace of the dangerous situation of His Majesty's Colonies'.[5] Oglethorpe's efforts were as ardent as ever but the Spaniards, convinced that 'it is very necessary to expel General Oglethorpe from the islands he is occupying so near this city',[6] proved to have as stout a defence as ever; they refused to surrender; the expedition failed; and Oglethorpe returned to Georgia on April 1 to ponder the situation[7] and complain of South Carolina to Newcastle.[8]

It was true that his defence of the colony had made

---

[1] Oglethorpe to Newcastle, Frederica, Jan. 22, 1743, C.O. 5:655, f. 118; *Collections of the Georgia Historical Society*, iii. 128–9.

[2] Oglethorpe to Newcastle, Frederica, Feb. 16, 1743, C.O. 5:655, f. 163.

[3] No letter went out to Oglethorpe from Verelst or Martyn between Aug. 10, 1742, and May 20, 1743, C.O. 5:668.

[4] Charles Town *South Carolina Gazette*, March 21, 1743, p. 2.

[5] Oglethorpe to Newcastle, Saint Johns River, Florida, March 12, 1743, C.O. 5:655, f. 177; *Collections of the Georgia Historical Society*, iii. 150.

[6] A.I. 87-1-3, No. 84, Montiano to Campillo, Saint Augustine, Feb. 16, 1743. See also A.I. 87-1-2, No. 115, Ruiz Deslano to the King, Saint Augustine, March 20, 1743.

[7] Charles Town *South Carolina Gazette*, April 18, 1743, p. 2.

[8] Oglethorpe to Newcastle, Frederica, April 22, 1743, C.O. 5:655, f. 192.

him Georgia's idol,[1] but in Carolina, despite memorials of thanks and congratulation from the citizens of Beaufort, Port Royal Island,[2] and Charles Town,[3] his name was anathema.[4] Andrew Rutledge of Charles Town wrote Verelst that 'the majority of this Town are delighted with nothing more than to lay hold on all occasions to vilify the Man, to whom they owe their preservation';[5] while Berenger de Beaufain in March 1743 wrote to Egmont that 'there is no prospect of a better understanding between General Oglethorpe and the people of this Province'.[6] At home, the Government, to be sure, had at last promoted him to the rank of Brigadier-General,[7] but his mainstay on the Board of Trustees, the Earl of Egmont, had resigned from the Council 'partly by reason of my ill health', as he noted in his diary, 'and partly from observing the ill behaviour of the Ministry and Parliament with respect to the colony'.[8] By June of 1743 Newcastle was far more engrossed in the latest casualty reports of the battle of Dettingen and its possible effect on British hegemony in the continental balance of power[9] than in the importunities of James Oglethorpe, but on

---

[1] Thomas Causton to Verelst, Oxted, Georgia, November 16, 1742, C.O. 5:641, Document No. 75; Candler, *Col. Rec. Ga.* xxiii. 428; John Dobell to the Earl of Egmont, Savannah, Jan. 5, 1743, C.O. 5:641, Document No. 82; Candler, *Col. Rec. Ga.* xxiii. 460; Causton to Verelst, Oxted, May 10, 1743, C.O. 5:641, Document No. 106; Candler, *Col. Rec. Ga.* xxiv. 27; Rev. J. M. Bolzius to B. Martyn, Ebenezer, Sept. 15, 1743, C.O. 5:641, Document No. 124; Candler, *Col. Rec. Ga.* xxiv. 106.

[2] C.O. 5:655, ff. 47–8; S.C. Rec. xxi, ff. 166–9.

[3] New York *Weekly Journal*, Nov. 1, 1742, pp. 1–2; Boston *Evening Post*, Dec. 6, 1742, pp. 1–2. For a poem lauding Oglethorpe and deriding Carolina see the New York *Weekly Journal*, Dec. 20, 1742, pp. 1–2.

[4] Charles Town *South Carolina Gazette*, July 25, 1743, p. 2; *Egmont Diary*, iii. 218.

[5] Andrew Rutledge to H. Verelst, Charles Town, April 27, 1743, C.O. 5:655, f. 219.

[6] H. Berenger de Beaufain to the Earl of Egmont, Charles Town, March 6, 1743, C.O. 5:641, Document No. 96; Candler, *Col. Rec. Ga.* xxiii. 532.

[7] S.P. 44:183, p. 219; W.O. 25:20, p. 231; Dalton, *English Army Lists*, vi. 53.

[8] *Egmont Diary*, iii. 265.

[9] See Add. MSS. (British Museum), 35407, ff. 218–22.

June 23 the recruiting of further volunteer troops for Oglethorpe's regiment was ordered—too late.[1] The Trustees also showed more interest, Martyn reporting in May that, on receipt of Oglethorpe's latest letters, they 'met in a fuller Common Council than there has been for a long time',[2] while Verelst, in next to the last letter sent to him in Georgia, on May 20 wrote the General that 'they have been very much concerned to find you left destitute of support so long, and that the affairs of North America have been so neglected'.[3] But their pious phraseology proved a hollow mockery for, like the War Office, they were—too late.

Soon after Egmont's resignation Oglethorpe found to his sorrow that his rebellious subordinate, Lieutenant-Colonel William Cooke, having received a twelve-months' leave of absence 'to come to England for the Recovery of his health',[4] seized the opportunity to bring charges against him, as Egmont recorded them, 'of defrauding his regiment by making them pay for the provisions the Government sent them over gratis'.[5] As a result the War Office asked Oglethorpe to answer these charges.[6] In addition a new series of complaints concerning unsatisfied bills of exchange had poured in to the Lords Commissioners of the Treasury.[7] As early as August 1740 Oglethorpe, 'having affairs of very great moment depending in England', had sought a discretionary leave of absence to return to Britain;[8] on April 22 he had written to George Clarke of New York that 'all looks very black

---

[1] W.O. 26:20, p. 30. See also pp. 41–2, 50.
[2] Martyn to Oglethorpe, London, May 21, 1743, C.O. 5:668, pp. 130–1.
[3] Verelst to Oglethorpe, London, May 20, 1743, C.O. 5:668, pp. 132–3.
[4] Will Yonge to Oglethorpe, War Office, Jan. 29, 1742, W.O. 4:37, p. 146.
[5] *Egmont Diary*, iii. 266.
[6] Will Yonge to Oglethorpe [London], Feb. 28, 1743, W.O. 4:38, p. 35.
[7] Add. MSS. (British Museum), 32700, Newcastle Papers, ff. 19–22.
[8] Peregrine Fury to Andrew Stone, London, Aug. 27, 1740, C.O. 5:654, f. 305; *Egmont Diary*, iii. 141–2; Verelst to Stone, London, April 10, 1742, C.O. 5:654, f. 17; Verelst to Stone, London, April 13, 1742, C.O. 5:654, f. 21.

GEORGIA: THE THIRD PHASE: IMPERIAL DEFENCE 251

around us';[1] and in July he made inquiries in Charles Town as to the next boats sailing for home.[2] The weight of all these forces was overwhelming and Oglethorpe's decision was inevitable. On July 23, 1743, James Oglethorpe, despondent at heart, turned his face towards England. His career in Georgia had closed.

When for the last time he bade farewell to his colonial colleagues, Oglethorpe was given ample proof of the esteem in which he was held by the better element in Georgia. Praised as 'an excellent & blessed instrument of God' by Pastor Bolzius of the Salzburgers,[3] to whom alone he confided the real reason for his return to London,[4] Oglethorpe departed after having given to this colony a decade of his best years and a fortune which, owing to parliamentary parsimony, he was wellnigh unable to replenish. Despite the criticism of the malcontents, Oglethorpe had made his impress on the people, and as late as 1748 James Habersham, in a letter to Harman Verelst, referred feelingly to 'the many instances we have had of General Oglethorpe's unwearied applications to serve us'.[5]

Upon his safe arrival on September 28 in London, which, in the words of Pastor Bolzius, 'is to us a great matter of Satisfaction & Thanksgiving to God',[6] Oglethorpe was well received by his old friends,[7] but the old South Carolina feud as to responsibility for the Saint Augustine failure of 1740 again cropped up. His oppo-

---

[1] Oglethorpe to George Clarke, Frederica, April 22, 1743, O'Callaghan, *Documents relative to the Colonial History of the State of New York*, vi. 242–3.

[2] W. Stephens to Verelst, Savannah, July 18, 1743, C.O. 5:641, Document No. 116; Candler, *Col. Rec. Ga.* xxiv. 60.

[3] Pastor J. M. Bolzius to B. Martyn, Ebenezer, Sept. 15, 1743, C.O. 5:641, Document No. 124; Candler, *Col. Rec. Ga.* xxiv. 106.

[4] Urlsperger, *Zwölfte Continuation der ausführlichen Nachricht*, p. 2216.

[5] James Habersham to Verelst, Savannah, Dec. 29, 1748, C.O. 5:642, Document No. 91; Candler, *Col. Rec. Ga.* xxv. 342.

[6] Pastor J. M. Bolzius to Verelst, Ebenezer, Feb. 20, 1744, C.O. 5:641, Document No. 160; Candler, *Col. Rec. Ga.* xxiv. 220.

[7] *Egmont Diary*, iii. 275, 279; London *Daily Post*, Sept. 27, 1743, p. 1; *Evening Post*, Sept. 27, 1743, p. 2.

nents in 1742 had prepared *An Impartial Account of the Late Expedition against St. Augustine*[1] which evoked a reply the next year by Oglethorpe's subordinate, Lieutenant George Cadogan,[2] but the General went a step farther. Cadogan had ascribed the failure to Carolina; according to Dr. Birch, 'General Oglethorpe is return'd with high Resentments against those who have censur'd his conduct in his absence; & has begun with Governor Glen of South Carolina, whom he severely bastinado'd one night this week at the Governor's own house. If he should proceed in that way, he has certainly a very tedious campaign to go thro'; & after all, he had better reserve his courage for the Spaniards.'[3] While awaiting the court martial, Oglethorpe again besought Parliament for the advances he had made in the defence of Georgia. By March 1744 he had spent of his own resources £91,705 13s. 5d., of which £25,595 19s. 7d. had been repaid up to the previous December, leaving Britain indebted to her loyal son for £66,109 13s. 10d.[4] This time Oglethorpe's appeal was successful, for on March 20, 1744, Egmont recorded the fact that 'this day the House of Commons granted the sums expended by General Oglethorpe, in defence of Georgia, amounting to above 60,000*l*. without any division. Sir Jo. Cotton, who was ever an enemy to the colony, desired to know what use the colony was of to England, which gave the General an opportunity to showing that on the preservation of it depends that of all the northern provinces. He was well heard by the House.'[5]

On May 24, 1744, the War Office requested the Judge

[1] *An Impartial Account of the Late Expedition against St. Augustine* (London, 1742).
[2] Cadogan, G., *The Spanish Hireling detected* (London, 1743).
[3] Dr. Thomas Birch to Phillip Yorke, London, Oct. 1, 1743, Add. MSS. (British Museum), 35396, Hardwicke Papers, f. 162.
[4] *Commons Journals*, xxiv. 613–15; S.P. 41 (State Papers, Domestic: Military, P.R.O.):14, No. 9, Petition of Harman Verelst for and on behalf of Brigadier General James Oglethorpe. As late as 1791 a declared account showed that Oglethorpe owed the government £841 17s. 8d. as overdrawn. A.O. 1:162, Roll. 441; Add. MSS. (British Museum), 41064.
[5] *Egmont Diary*, iii. 293.

Advocate General to summon a Board of General Officers[1] to consider the charges of Lieutenant-Colonel Cooke, who claimed that 'he has suffered great Indignities, and unjust Impositions and Deductions of his Pay, together with an ill State of Health, contracted and confirmed in a great Measure by a Series of Injuries'.[2] A distinguished Board, presided over by Lord Mark Kerr and including Generals Dalzell and Churchill, met at the Horse Guards at 11 a.m. on June 7, heard four allegations, adjourned to 10 a.m. the next day, when they considered fifteen more charges, and promptly issued a report, declaring that 'not any one Article thereof is made out, and every one of them is either ffrivolous, Vexatious or Malicious, and without ffoundation', and recommending Cooke's dismissal from the service.[3] The triumph was complete, and in August the victor again addressed Newcastle, complaining that no one paid any attention to his ideas and offering his services if needed for the protection of his beloved colony.[4]

During the ensuing decade Oglethorpe continued his interest in Georgia by an erratic attendance at both Board and Council meetings, where, however, he at all times maintained his right of dissent from the accepted proceedings of the Trustees.[5] The colony managed to struggle along despite the disaffection of the Trustees, who save for Egmont, Vernon, and Oglethorpe gave up almost all interest therein. In July 1742 the Act prohibiting rum had been repealed;[6] on February 6, 1745,

[1] W.O. 71 (War Office: Judge Advocate General: Proceedings of the Board of General Officers, P.R.O.):7, ff. 118 verso–119.
[2] W.O. 71:7, f. 119 verso. See also W.O. 81:3, pp. 66–7.
[3] W.O. 71:7, ff. 120–30. See also W.O. 4:39, p. 241; *Egmont Diary*, iii. 300; and the *Gentleman's Magazine*, xiv. 336.
[4] Oglethorpe to Newcastle, London, Aug. 24, 1744, C.O. 5:655, ff. 270–1; *Collections of the Georgia Historical Society*, iii. 155.
[5] C.O. 5:687, pp. 324, 327; Candler, *Col. Rec. Ga.* i. 463, 465; C.O. 5:691, pp. 144–7; Candler, *Col. Rec. Ga.* ii. 442–5. See also Oglethorpe to Newcastle, Westminster, April 15, 1744, Add. MSS. (British Museum), 32702, Newcastle Papers, f. 347.
[6] C.O. 5:687, pp. 208–27, 270; Candler, *Col. Rec. Ga.* i. 398–400, 410–11, 433; *Journal of the Commissioners for Trade and Plantations*, vii. 34, 37.

Oglethorpe attended the meeting of the Trustees at which they decided to separate the civil and military authority;[1] in 1746 he expressed to the Secretary of State for War his 'great Concern that that Colony is like to suffer severely' from parliamentary delay in appropriations;[2] as late as 1748 he sent orders to the officers of his regiment in Georgia;[3] on January 19, 1749, Oglethorpe attended his last Council meeting[4] and on March 16 his last Board meeting;[5] the next year the anti-slavery law was repealed;[6] and in June 1752 the colony, in accordance with the terms of its charter, reverted to the Crown.[7] The place of Oglethorpe in these later days of the trust has been justly defined by Dr. McCain:

> Had he been as interested after 1743 as he was when the work was first begun, he would have ranked with Vernon and Egmont in his attendance, and his right to the first place among the Trustees could hardly have been questioned. As it is, the position of honor assigned him is based on his activities during the first decade of the Trust.[8]

James Oglethorpe had continued a more than desultory interest in his colony and its welfare after his return to England in 1743, but his life at home now expanded into far different spheres of activity, which were to include not only another phase of the military career but matrimony and two decades in the Johnsonian literary circle as well. He was but 46 years of age when he closed his colonial career, and much in life lay still before him.

---

[1] B. Martyn to W. Stephens, London, Feb. 6, 1745, C.O. 5:668, pp. 174–6.

[2] Oglethorpe to Sir William Yonge, Bt., Secretary of State for War, London, May 20, 1746, S.P. 41:17.

[3] C.O. 5:656, f. 108. On November 24 his Georgia regiment was disbanded and on Dec. 27, 1748, Henry Fox, Secretary at War, informed Oglethorpe that the King had no further need for a General and Commander-in-Chief in South Carolina and Georgia, and therefore gave Oglethorpe his thanks for services rendered and called in his commission, W.O. 4:45, pp. 262, 348.

[4] C.O. 5:691, p. 219; Candler, *Col. Rec. Ga.* ii. 490.

[5] C.O. 5:688, p. 96; Candler, *Col. Rec. Ga.* i. 529.

[6] C.O. 5:688, p. 98; Candler, *Col. Rec. Ga.* i. 530–40.

[7] For the proclamation of June 25 see the London *Gazette*, July 4, 1752, p. 1.

[8] McCain, *Georgia as a Proprietary Province*, p. 51.

CHAPTER VIII

THE 'FORTY-FIVE AND OBLIVION

His return from Georgia marked the apex of James Oglethorpe's career. The remainder was largely an anti-climax. The controversy which had beclouded his later days in the colony had passed, and by July 1744 the Charles Town correspondent of the *Westminster Journal* could express the hope of seeing him again in America.[1] Oglethorpe in fact sent out a ship to the colony at his expense, but he remained in England.[2] As a Brigadier General, Oglethorpe had attended the Board sessions and served in various courts martial, but after his own trial, despite his acquittal, his attendance was spasmodic.[3] In April 1744 Dr. John Burton, his college-mate at Corpus thirty years before, dedicated to him a sermon on *The Folly and Wickedness of misplacing our Trust and Confidence*, preached at St. Mary's, Oxford.[4] In May the General was elected to the Board of Directors of the Children's Hospital,[5] and in June it was rumoured that he was going to campaign in Flanders.[6] But something far more important was afoot.

As early as 1728 Samuel Wesley, junior, in *An Ode to James Oglethorpe, Esq.*, had urged him to marry.[7] But the suggestion had not been enthusiastically received. In August 1744 the usually accurate *Gentleman's Magazine*

[1] London *Westminster Journal*, Sept. 15, 1744, p. 3.
[2] Ibid., Sept. 8, 1744, p. 3; *Daily Gazetteer*, Sept. 15, 1744, p. 1.
[3] W.O. 71:7, ff. 99–142.
[4] Burton, John, *The Folly and Wickedness of misplacing our Trust and Confidence: A Sermon Preached before the University of Oxford, at St. Mary's, on Wednesday, April 9, 1744, Being the Day appointed for a General Fast* (Oxford, 1744).
[5] London *Evening Post*, May 10, 1744, p. 1.
[6] Ibid., June 9, 1744, p. 1.
[7] 'Tis single, 'tis imperfect Light,
   The World from Worth unwedded shares,
He only shines compleatly bright
   Who leaves his Virtues to his Heirs.
              Wesley, Samuel, junior, *Poems*, p. 167.

erroneously reported his marriage to Miss Elizabeth Sambrooke, the sister and heiress of the late Sir Jeremy Sambrooke, Baronet, for many years Oglethorpe's colleague in Parliament.[1] True, the magazine erred, but only in the identity of the bride. On Friday, September 14, 1744, a marriage-licence was issued at the Faculty Office of the Archbishop of Canterbury in London to 'Hon. James Oglethorpe, of St. Margaret's, Westminster, Esq., Bachelor, above 40 and Elizabeth Wright, of Cranham, Essex, spinster, above 25'.[2] The next morning, in the King Henry VII Chapel in Westminster Abbey, James Oglethorpe after almost fifty years of celibacy married the only daughter of the late Sir Nathan Wright, Baronet, and grand-niece of the Sir Nathan who was Lord Keeper of the Seal under Queen Anne. Far from its being a romance, the impoverished imperialist, in a frank *mariage de convenance*, had won the heiress to her unmarried brother, Sir Samuel Wright, a lady worth £1,500 a year in her own right![3] While the press broke forth in epithalamial verse,[4] the bride and groom immediately set out for Westbrook Place, Surrey, where the honeymoon was spent.[5] On November 17 they returned to their house near Whitehall,[6] but, accompanied by the Chickasaw Indian Chief who had crossed with Oglethorpe in 1743, spent Christmas at Westbrook Place.[7] On January 6, 1745, General and Mrs. Oglethorpe returned to London[8] but the happy bridegroom was not permitted to enjoy his new state in uninterrupted

---

[1] *Gentleman's Magazine*, xiv. 451; *Commons Journals*, xxi. 246; xxv. 323.

[2] Armytage, 'Allegations for Marriage Licences issued from the Faculty Office of the Archbishop of Canterbury at London, 1543 to 1869', Harleian Society Publications, xxiv. 254.

[3] London *Evening Post*, Sept. 15, 1744, p. 4; *Daily Gazetteer*, Sept. 17, 1744, p. 2; *Westminster Journal*, Sept. 22, 1744, p. 4; Lipscomb, *History and Antiquities of the County of Buckingham*, iv. 151.

[4] *Gentleman's Magazine*, xiv. 558, October verse: 'On the Marriage of General Oglethorpe'; *London Magazine*, xiii. 460, 512.

[5] London *Daily Gazetteer*, Sept. 15, 1744, p. 1.

[6] Ibid., Nov. 19, 1744, p. 1.

[7] Ibid., Dec. 25, 1744, p. 1.   [8] Ibid., Jan. 7, 1745, p. 1.

peace. Once more the shadow of Jacobitism was to cross James Oglethorpe's path, this time, however, in hostile mien.

When in 1719 James III's pathetic sequel to the 'Fifteen had crashed in Spain, the Jacobite movement entered a period of outward quiescence. Perhaps it is too strong to say that 'the prospect of a Stuart restoration and the problem of the English Jacobites dominated English domestic and foreign policy from 1715 to 1745'.[1] But the failure of the 'Nineteen had by no means meant the end of the movement; and if, as the authority on Jacobitism has shown, Sir Robert Walpole, by playing on the fears of all who had aught to gain thereby, successfully checked any possibilities of James's return to England, the latter was able to continue his activities on the Continent, where the movement smouldered until fanned into flame by the loyal labours of a Paris circle, not least among whom was Eleanor Oglethorpe de Mézières.[2]

The departure of young James Oglethorpe for England and a Hanoverian Parliament had not dimmed the spirit of his sisters, Eleanor and Anne, who after 1720 continued a desultory correspondence with James III at Rome, while Theophilus, junior, preened himself on an influence he no longer possessed. Anne Oglethorpe was a regular correspondent under the cipher name of 'Mr. Newlands' and frequented Rotterdam, Brussels, and Paris in the cause until advised in 1727 to retire to England, whither she proceeded the next year. Although in 1722 James was rather effusive to Eleanor de Mézières, the latter rarely wrote to Italy, preferring to labour with Thomas Carte behind the scenes for the great restoration; so that, after Anne's departure in 1728, the Oglethorpe connexion was lost until 1737, when the de Mézières family joined in formulating the plans which matured in the programme of 1743 whence sprang the invasion

[1] Pimlott, 'The English Jacobites under the Hanoverian Kings', p. 1.
[2] Petrie, *The Jacobite Movement*, pp. 155-76.

of Scotland in 1745 by Charles Stuart, son of the Old Pretender.[1]

By 1744 the situation had become serious. As one student of Jacobitism has so well phrased it, 'if the Jacobites had been negligible, the English Government could have laughed them to scorn'.[2] But negligible they were not. Although Horace Walpole affirmed of the Stuart threat that 'everybody seems as much unconcern'd as if it were only some Indian King brought over by Oglethorpe',[3] the Government became alarmed. Whether because of the absence on the Continent of the flower of the British army or by mere coincidence, the Hanoverian regency, forgetting the Jacobite connexions of his youth, now called upon James Edward Oglethorpe to defend England against one who, according to the Shaftoe narrative, would have been his own nephew, an invader in whose troops was actually serving the son of Eleanor Oglethorpe de Mézières.[4] In March 1744 Oglethorpe

[1] The King's Collection of Stuart Papers at Windsor Castle, 1721-43; Add. MSS. (British Museum), 20310, Gualterio MSS., ff. 275, 296, 299-300, 331; Add. MSS. 31140, Strafford Papers: Political Correspondence, viii, ff. 143-4; Add. MSS. 31260, Papers of Cardinal Gualterio: Letters of David Nairne, Secretary to the Pretender, ii, ff. 159, 180-1, 218, 242, 256, 261; Add. MSS. 31261, ff. 19, 233; Add. MSS. 9144, Coxe Papers, f. 24; Coxe, *Memoirs of the Life and Administration of Robert Walpole, Earl of Orford*, iii. 460; Colin, J., *Louis XV et les Jacobites: Le Projet de Débarquement en Angleterre de 1743-1744* (Paris, 1901), pp. viii, 37-40; Boislisle, *Mémoires de Saint-Simon*, xiv. 321, note 5; xxxviii. 181-2; Dussieux and Soulié, *Mémoires du Duc de Luynes*, v. 343, 370-1; *Commons Journals*, xx. 466; *MSS. of Charles F. W. Underwood* (H.M.C. Reports), pp. 225, 427; Bell, R. F., editor, *Memorials of John Murray of Broughton, Sometime Secretary to Prince Charles Edward, 1740-1747* (The Scottish History Society, Edinburgh, 1898), pp. 130, 392; Lang, A., *Prince Charles Edward, The Young Chevalier* (new ed., London, 1903), pp. 327, 379; Ruvigny and Raineval, Marquis of, *The Jacobite Peerage*, p. 138; Shield, A., *Henry Stuart, Cardinal of York, and his Times* (London, 1908), pp. 36-65; Shield and Lang, 'Queen Oglethorpe', *Blackwood's Edinburgh Magazine*, clxiii. 231-4; Shield and Lang, *The King Over the Water*, pp. 361-6, 373, 387-9, 404; Petrie, *The Jacobite Movement*, pp. 177-217.

[2] Pimlott, 'The English Jacobites under the Hanoverian Kings', p. 3.

[3] Toynbee, Paget, editor, *Supplement to the Letters of Horace Walpole* (3 vols., Oxford, 1918-25), iii. 385.

[4] Dussieux and Soulié, *Mémoires du Duc de Luynes*, vii. 152.

received a commission to raise 'a regiment of hussars to defend the coasts'[1] and was ordered to Gravesend and the southern district.[2] On March 30, 1745, he was created Major-General.[3]

The summer passed in silence, but on September 20 the War Office ordered Oglethorpe to the north;[4] and he left, as one Whitehall official asserted, 'for Burlington Bay this evening to march the Dutch Battalion northward in case the winds have proved unfavourable for its proceeding by sea'.[5] The regiment proceeded by water to Hull,[6] while Oglethorpe himself hastened overland to the Yorkshire of his forefathers.[7] In a letter to the Duke of Newcastle, written at York, September 24, he explained how the northern situation prevented him from joining Sir John Cope, whose orders he was awaiting at York. Here the citizens, after an impassioned plea by Archbishop Thomas Herring, had raised a defence-fund of £30,000 with which to greet the General, who, without much difficulty, was persuaded to remain at York to convert a body of fox-hunters into the Yorkshire Light Horse, a volunteer cavalry unit later known as 'The Royal Regiment of Hunters', which became 'the germ of the yeomanry'.[8] Oglethorpe meanwhile had received

---

[1] Toynbee, Mrs. Paget, editor, *The Letters of Horace Walpole* (16 vols., Oxford, 1903–5), ii. 10; London *Evening Post*, March 6, 1744, p. 2.

[2] Add. MSS. (British Museum), 20005, Earl of Stair's Military Order Book, 1744.

[3] W.O. 25:21, p. 101; W.O. 25:135, p. 35; S.P. 44:186, p. 12; Dalton, *English Army Lists*, vi. 53.

[4] Sir William Yonge to Oglethorpe, War Office, Sept. 20, 1745, W.O. 4:40, p. 493.

[5] Jesse, J. H., *Memoirs of the Pretenders* (3 vols., Boston, 1901), iii. 266; London *Evening Post*, Sept. 21, 1745, p. 1; *Daily Advertiser*, Sept. 23, 1745, p. 1.

[6] W.O. 5:37, Marching Orders, p. 45.

[7] S.P. 36:68, No. 95, Newcastle to William Osbaldeston, Whitehall, Sept. 21, 1745.

[8] Oglethorpe to Newcastle, York, Sept. 24, 1745, S.P. 36:69, No. 4; Yorke, P. C., *Life and correspondence of Philip Yorke, earl of Hardwicke, lord high chancellor of Great Britain* (3 vols., Cambridge, 1913), i. 461, 465; Harris, G., *Life of Lord Chancellor Hardwicke* (3 vols., London, 1847), ii. 167; Montefiore, C. Sebag, *History of Volunteer Forces* (London, 1908), pp. 74–5;

fresh orders to join Marshal Wade and Sir John Cope in the field,[1] but his plea for royal approval of the regiment of hunters proved successful[2] and, at the regiment's request, he was appointed their Colonel.[3] On September 25 the Earl of Malton informed Newcastle that the defensive 'Association' was a great success and that Oglethorpe 'was very much contributing by his Behaviour in encouraging & keeping up that Spirit which he so eminently himself possesses, & have prevailed upon him to be willing (with His Majesty's Approbation) to let the Ship called the *Success*, now bound to Georgia, to be ordered Down to Hull' and its soldiers, stores, and arms transferred for use in the defence of York.[4] The next day this notice appeared throughout the community:

September 26th, 1745
Advertisement
THE Gentlemen Volunteers under General OGLETHORPE, have concluded to meet on *Monday* the 30th *Instant* arm'd; upon Knavesmire, and serve at their own Expence.[5]

The news soon spread that 'the bucks . . . to the number of twenty or thirty, have listed under a mad general—Oglethorpe. . . . They make more noise than they deserve, their numbers being much magnified'.[6] What-

---

Manners, W. E., *John Manners, Marquis of Granby* (London, 1899), p. 16; Toynbee, Mrs. Paget, *The Letters of Horace Walpole*, ii. 140; Page, *Victoria County History of Yorkshire*, iii. 434. In forming the Royal Hunters, Oglethorpe was assisted by John Hall-Stevenson, a young Yorkshireman, whose close friend, Laurence Sterne, wielded a mighty pen rather than a sword for the House of Hanover. Cross, W. L., *Life and Times of Laurence Sterne* (3rd ed. with alterations and additions, New Haven, 1929), p. 126.

[1] Sir William Yonge to Oglethorpe, War Office, Sept. 26, 1745, W.O. 4:40, p. 502; W.O. 26:20, p. 289.

[2] Sir William Yonge to Oglethorpe, War Office, Sept. 28, 1745, W.O. 4:40, p. 504.

[3] W.O. 25:135, p. 65; S.P. 36:69, No. 68, Newcastle to Oglethorpe, Whitehall, Sept. 28, 1745; No. 69, Oglethorpe to Newcastle, York, Sept. 28, 1745.

[4] Earl of Malton to Newcastle, York, Sept. 25, 1745, S.P. 36:68, No. 31.

[5] Add. MSS. (British Museum), 35598, p. 140.

[6] Stephen Thompson to Vice-Admiral Medley, London, Nov. 8, 1745,

ever some of the natives may have thought of his judgement, Oglethorpe, never averse to publicity, had decided that the volunteers 'are to rendezvous at Knavesmire on Monday morning, have a Ball at night and march on Tuesday morning'. Little wonder that Archbishop Herring wrote to Lord Chancellor Hardwicke: 'We must leave it to the General to consider whether a Ball will inspire or enfeeble his myrmidons; but let the spirit of defence go forward.'[1]

In October the Archbishop was still of the opinion that 'Oglethorpe is very alert, wants to collect our Lord Lieutenants & their forces together'.[2] In mid-October Oglethorpe conferred with General Wade, who ordered him to Newcastle,[3] whence he marched his troops in four days,[4] so that on October 29, when the British troops, pursuant to orders of the 1st, gathered at Newcastle under Wade to resist the Stuart invasion set for the 30th, Oglethorpe was there with a body of his Georgia rangers[5] and his Yorkshire hunters, who 'made a grand Shew'[6] and 'a fine appearance and do honour to their

MSS. of the Lady Du Cane (H.M.C. Reports, xvi), p. 77; Edward Montagu to his wife, Elizabeth Montagu, Allerthorpe, Yorkshire, Sept. 27, 1745; Oct. 1, 1745, Climenson, Emily J., editor, *Elizabeth Montagu, the Queen of the Blue-Stockings: Her Correspondence from 1720 to 1761* (2 vols., London, 1906), i. 210, 213.

[1] Garnett, Richard, 'Correspondence of Archbishop Herring and Lord Hardwicke during the Rebellion of 1745', *English Historical Review*, xix. 544.
[2] Ibid. 720.
[3] London *General Evening Post*, Oct. 26, 1745, p. 2; General Wade to Newcastle, Camp near Doncaster, Oct. 19, 1745, S.P. 36:72, No. 20.
[4] Edwin Lasceles to Hardwicke, Newcastle, Oct. 25, 1745, Add. MSS. (British Museum), 35889, Hardwicke Papers, f. 14; Harris, *Life of Lord Chancellor Hardwicke*, ii. 179. Oglethorpe was accompanied by Thomas Bosomworth, the errant husband of Mary Musgrove of Georgia, Bosomworth to Verelst, York, Oct. 12, 1745, C.O. 5:641, Document No. 197; Candler, *Col. Rec. Ga.* xxiv. 428.
[5] Seton, Sir Bruce, Baronet, editor, 'The Orderly Book of Lord Ogilvy's Regiment in the Army of Prince Charles Edward Stuart, 10 October, 1745, to 21 April, 1746', *Journal of the Society of Army Historical Research*, ii. 11 note; *Gentleman's Magazine*, xv. 624; Harris, James, Third Earl of Malmesbury, editor, *Letters of the First Earl of Malmesbury* (2 vols., London, 1870), i. 24.
[6] London *Evening Post*, Oct. 29, 1745, p. 1; *Daily Post*, Oct. 29, 1745, p. 1.

King and country'.[1] In November Wade's army was reviewed at Newcastle with Oglethorpe's contingent in the centre between the British regulars and the Dutch allies,[2] and on the 19th Newcastle, asking him to send regular reports of all military activities, both of his own troops and of the enemy, assured him that 'His Majesty is extremely well satisfied with the Zeal you have shewd for His Service, and is fully persuaded, That Nothing will be omitted on Your Part, that can contribute to it, in the present critical Conjuncture'.[3] Oglethorpe's star, which had been under a cloud on his return from Georgia, was again in the ascendant, and he promptly replied, promising an expeditious news-service and acknowledging his happiness 'in his Majesty's and your Grace's gracious acceptance of my poor Endeavours'.[4] But December was to be the bleakest month for him in many a year.

As November closed Oglethorpe was ordered by Wade to join Ligonier with his cavalry.[5] As the former informed the Duke of Cumberland, he had with him at this time regular cavalry, 'St. George's Draggoons' numbering 270, a detachment of 520 men from Lord Montagu's and Wade's forces, and the two irregular bodies, the Royal Hunters and the Georgia Rangers.[6] Oglethorpe had had a poor opinion of the Dutch troops for some time,[7] and on December 3 expressed himself strongly on the subject to the Archbishop of York, with whom he and his soldiers, 'who were prodigiously welcome to my ale & bread &

---

[1] Letter of an unknown author, Morpeth, Nov. 4, 1745, *MSS. of Sir William Fitzherbert* (H.M.C. Reports, xiii, Appendix, part vi), p. 161.
[2] London *General Advertiser*, Nov. 15, 1745, p. 1; S.P. 36:73, No. 124.
[3] Newcastle to Oglethorpe, Whitehall, Nov. 19, 1745, S.P. 36:74, No. 20.
[4] Oglethorpe to Newcastle, Durham Castle, Nov. 24, 1745, S.P. 36:74, No. 92.
[5] Oglethorpe to Newcastle, Darlington, Nov. 26, 1745, S.P. 36:75, No. 25.
[6] Oglethorpe to the Duke of Cumberland, Barnesby, Nov. 1745, Cumberland Papers, Windsor Castle.
[7] Archbishop Herring to Lord Chancellor Hardwicke, Bishopthorpe, Nov. 9, 1745, Add. MSS. (British Museum), 35889, Hardwicke Papers, ff. 27–8.

cheese', breakfasted.[1] On December 6 the Jacobite retreat began with Wade sending in pursuit Oglethorpe,[2] who had been with the horse and dragoons at Richmond.[3] Winning an engagement at Manchester, the latter now forced his way ahead of the rebels to join Wade at Wakefield.[4] On his arrival there on the 10th Wade found himself unable to trap the enemy under existing conditions and ordered Oglethorpe with the Dragoons, Royal Hunters, and a detachment of two cavalry regiments, nearly 500 men in all, to harass the enemy's flank and small detached parties, and then join the Duke of Cumberland at Preston.[5] On the 13th Oglethorpe reported to the Duke of Newcastle his arrival at Preston,[6] where he was just behind the rebels and 'would follow them as soon as his Detachment was refreshed';[7] the next day he was at Garstang with orders to pursue the rebels if they fled.[8] But unfortunately for him he had been checked in an earlier encounter, whereby Prince Charles

[1] Garnett, 'Correspondence of Archbishop Herring and Lord Hardwicke during the Rebellion of 1745', *English Historical Review*, xix. 733; Harris, *Life of Lord Chancellor Hardwicke*, ii. 198–9.
[2] Wood, A. W., Prothero, G. W., and Leathes, S., editors, *Cambridge Modern History* (14 vols., Cambridge, 1902–12), vi, *The Eighteenth Century*, chap. iii, Terry, C. S., 'Jacobitism and the Union', p. 115; Ray, James, *A Compleat History of the Rebellion* (Bristol, 1752), pp. 194–7; Whyte, F., and Atteridge, A. H., *A History of the Queen's Bays, the Second Dragoon Guards, 1685–1929* (London, 1930), p. 70. See also Eardley-Simpson, L., *Derby and the Forty-Five* (London, 1933), pp. xiii, 1, 79–130, 204–5; and Buchan, J., *Midwinter*, a novel.
[3] MSS. of Charles F. W. Underwood (H.M.C. Reports), p. 287.
[4] MSS. of Sir William Fitzherbert (H.M.C. Reports), pp. 165–6, 169, 173–5; Dalton, *English Army Lists*, vi. 53; Toybnee, Mrs. Paget, *The Letters of Horace Walpole*, ii. 162; Ewald, A. C., *Life and Times of Prince Charles Stuart* (London, 1883), p. 184.
[5] General Wade to the Duke of Cumberland, Wakefield, Dec. 11, 1745, Cumberland Papers, Windsor Castle; Yorke, *Life . . . of Philip Yorke, earl of Hardwicke*, i. 480; MSS. of the Earl of Buckinghamshire (H.M.C. Report, xiv, Appendix, part ix), *The Trevor MSS.*, p. 138.
[6] Oglethorpe to Newcastle, Preston, Dec. 13, 1745, S.P. 36:77, No. 4.
[7] Wade to Newcastle, Ripon, Dec. 15, 1745, S.P. 36:77, No. 43.
[8] Wade to Newcastle, Preston, Dec. 14, 1745, Cumberland Papers, Windsor Castle; Sir Everard Fawkener to Newcastle, Preston, Dec. 14, 1745, S.P. 36:77, No. 45.

was enabled to escape, and each day from December 13 to 17, at Preston, Wigan, and Lancaster, Oglethorpe was just too late.[1] But on the 17th, after Cumberland and Wade had held him back from Lancaster owing to inability to support him,[2] Oglethorpe proceeded to Shap, near Penrith, where he allowed the rebels to get away.[3] In the words of one who was at Shap, 'General Oglethorpe with the Corps from Major Wade's army which was advanced before us, had orders to cut off the retreat of the rear guard . . . but by what—accident—I know not—the affair was neglected and gave us more trouble.'[4] With the escape of Prince Charles, Oglethorpe turned to Carlisle, where he spent Christmas Day.[5] The pursuit of the Jacobite retreat was accomplished without him, and he had no part in the final English victory at Culloden in April 1746. But he was not forgotten. His failure to check the rebel escape at Shap was to cost him dear.

The Christmas holidays were spent in the north. From Carlisle he went to Newcastle in the new year[6] and then to York on January 20,[7] where Archbishop Herring 'saw poor Oglethorpe.... He looks dismally and I judged of the

---

[1] Seton, 'The Orderly Book of Lord Ogilvy's Regiment', *Journal of the Society of Army Historical Research*, ii. 26 note; Charteris, E., editor, *Lord Elcho's Short Account of the Affairs of Scotland in the Years 1744, 1745, 1746* (Edinburgh, 1907), pp. 345–6; Terry, C. S., editor, *The Forty-Five: A Narrative of the Last Jacobite Rising by Several Hands* (Cambridge, 1922), p. 78; Farrer and Brownbill, *Victoria County History of Lancaster*, vii. 78; viii. 19; Roper, W. O., *Materials for the History of Lancaster* (2 vols., Chatham Society Publications, new series, lxi–lxii, Manchester, 1907), i. 93; Yorke, *Life . . . of Philip Yorke, Earl of Hardwicke*, i. 484.

[2] Wade to Newcastle, Preston, Dec. 16, 1745, Cumberland Papers, Windsor Castle; Cumberland to Newcastle, Preston, Dec. 16, 1745, S.P. 36:77, No. 60.

[3] Ferguson, R. S., 'The Retreat of the Highlanders through Westmorland in 1745', *Transactions of the Cumberland and Westmorland Antiquarian and Archaeological Society*, x. 186–228.

[4] Joseph Yorke to Lord Hardwicke, Penrith, Dec. 19, 1745, Add. MSS. (British Museum), 35354, Hardwicke Papers, ff. 161 verso–162.

[5] *MSS. in Various Collections* (H.M.C. Reports), viii, *MSS. of the Honourable F. L. Wood*, pp. 151, 155.

[6] London *Evening Post*, Jan. 9, 1746, p. 1.

[7] Ibid., Jan. 25, 1746, p. 1.

sore place by his falling instantly upon the affair of Shap'.[1] By February 6 he was back in London,[2] where his misfortunes at Shap and the old family taint of Jacobitism subjected him to severe criticism. It is true that his failure at Preston has been laid to a negative order from the Duke of Cumberland;[3] it is true that the Reverend John Bisset, a clergyman at Aberdeen, had lauded his military character on the basis of his 'virtue and probity';[4] it is true that a lady in Preston could write that the rebels, who hated the Duke of Cumberland, 'don't seem to mind anybody else in particular, except General Oglethorpe, whose vivacity they are no strangers to. They seem to hope his forwardness may outrun his judgment, in which I don't doubt, they will be fatally mistaken';[5] it is true that the Duke of Cumberland considered his journey to Preston 'a laborious march of one hundred miles, over ice and snow, through a dangerous and almost impassable road in less than three days';[6] and it is true that Cumberland and Wade both restrained him at Garstang.[7] But there was another side to the shield. Since his Georgia days Oglethorpe had been well known among the Scots who became the Jacobites of the 'Forty-five[8] and had corresponded with Duncan Forbes, Lord Presi-

[1] Archbishop Herring to Lord Chancellor Hardwicke, Bishopthorpe, Jan. 21, 1746, Garnett, 'Correspondence of Archbishop Herring and Lord Hardwicke', *English Historical Review*, xix. 740.

[2] *London Magazine*, xv. 97; *European Magazine*, viii. 90.

[3] Seton, 'The Orderly Book of Lord Ogilvy's Regiment', *Journal of the Society of Army Historical Research*, ii. 26 note.

[4] 'Diary of the Reverend John Bisset, Minister at Aberdeen, 1745-46', *Miscellany of the Spalding Club*, i (Aberdeen, 1841), 345-400, especially p. 351.

[5] London *Westminster Journal*, Dec. 21, 1745, p. 3; Banner, Rev. F. S., 'The "Going-Out" of Prince Charlie in 1745', *Transactions of the Historical Society of Lancashire and Cheshire*, lvii (Liverpool, 1906), 91.

[6] *Historical Memoirs of his late Royal Highness, William Augustus, Duke of Cumberland* (London, 1767), p. 316.

[7] Wade to Newcastle, Preston, Dec. 16, 1745, Cumberland Papers, Windsor Castle; Cumberland to Newcastle, Preston, 4 a.m., Dec. 16, 1745, S.P. 36:77, No. 60.

[8] Warrand, D., editor, *More Culloden Papers* (5 vols., Inverness, 1923-30), iv. 65.

dent of the Court of Session in Scotland.[1] In a letter to Forbes, Henry Fane, a loyal supporter of the Hanoverian government, affirmed that, 'had it not been for the mismanagement of Oglethorpe', the Jacobites could have been conquered by an England unprepared;[2] while Joseph Yorke hinted broadly to Lord Hardwicke that Oglethorpe's failure to cut off the enemy was owing to his latent Jacobitism.[3] Even his old friend, the Earl of Egmont, regretfully noted that 'he is an unfortunate man, his vanity and quarrelsomeness rendering him incapable to preserve the friendship of his acquaintance or make new friends, and every mouth is now open against him with a kind of satisfaction'.[4] In any event, the army administration was adamant in its hostile judgement of his errors, for he was struck off the staff of the Duke of Cumberland and exposed to the possibilities of a court martial. Whereas in 1685 Sir Theophilus Oglethorpe had brought the good news from Sedgemoor to receive a knighthood, his son, James, sixty years later, returned to London from a northern campaign to face a court martial instigated by the most popular officer in the British army, the Duke of Cumberland!

In March Oglethorpe's command was handed over to General Cadogan[5] and the first steps taken to ensure a trial. In April a London journal reported that he was leaving within three weeks for Georgia;[6] but he remained in London, where on August 7, 1746, Oglethorpe accepted

---

[1] e.g. Oglethorpe to the Lord President, Duncan Forbes, Frederica in Georgia, Feb. 21, 1740, Forbes, Duncan, *The Culloden Papers* (London, 1815), p. 155.
[2] Henry Fane to Duncan Forbes, Jan. 9, 1746, Warrand, *More Culloden Papers*, iii. 234.
[3] Colonel the Honourable Joseph Yorke to Lord Chancellor Hardwicke, Penrith, Dec. 19, 1745, Yorke, *Life . . . of Philip Yorke, earl of Hardwicke*, i. 485–6.
[4] *Egmont Diary*, iii. 312–13.
[5] Archbishop Herring to Lord Hardwicke, York, March 11, 1746, Add. MSS. (British Museum), 35598, Hardwicke Papers, f. 198.
[6] London *Evening Post*, April 15, 1746, p. 1. Two days later it retracted this statement, London *Evening Post*, April 17, 1746, p. 1.

THE 'FORTY-FIVE AND OBLIVION 267

service for attendance at a court martial;[1] on the 9th he sent in his list of twenty-four witnesses;[2] and, at 9 a.m. on August 21, the court met only to grant Oglethorpe's request for an extension of time to secure distant witnesses.[3] As Dr. Thomas Birch, a very interested attendant, wrote to Philip Yorke:

> Oglethorpe's Tryal for Disobedience of the Duke's orders was appointed before a Court martial of which Gen. Wentworth was President on Thursday last, but put off till the 29th of next month at his Request, he alledging, that he wanted a Witness. I find by a Friend of his, that his Defence against one of the main Articles will be denying his having received one of the Duke's orders.[4]

While Henry Fox of the War Office was summoning the witnesses on whose word Oglethorpe relied for acquittal,[5] the accused, according to Dr. Birch,

> behaves himself very decently during the Suspence of his Tryal. He does not appear at all in public, & avoids all occasions of talking of his Affair, & only answers, when he is ask'd about it, that he is satisfied, the Duke was obliged by his Informations to bring him to a Tryal; but that the Tryal will be a thorough Vindication of his Character.[6]

At last, on Monday morning, September 29, began the trial of James Oglethorpe, in the words of the royal warrant, 'for having disobey'd or neglected his orders and suffered the Rear of the Rebells near Shap to escape'.[7] This was no ordinary hearing of charges before a Board

[1] W.O. 71:126, No. 2. [2] Ibid.
[3] Ibid.; W.O. 81:3, pp. 132, 144.
[4] Dr. Thomas Birch to Philip Yorke, London, Aug. 26, 1746, Add. MSS. (British Museum), 35397, Hardwicke Papers, ff. 15 verso–16.
[5] Terry, C. S., editor, *The Albemarle Papers, being the Correspondence of William Anne, Second Earl of Albemarle, Commander-in-Chief in Scotland, 1746–1747* (2 vols., New Spalding Club, Aberdeen, 1902), i. 168, 174; *MSS. of Mrs. Frankland-Russell-Astley* (H.M.C. Reports, xv), p. 346.
[6] Dr. Thomas Birch to Philip Yorke, London, Sept. 20, 1746, Add. MSS. (British Museum), 35397, Hardwicke Papers, f. 29 verso.
[7] Royal warrant of Sept. 9, 1746, W.O. 71:19, p. 195. For evidence see pp. 195–284.

of General Officers like the case Lieutenant-Colonel Cooke had brought in 1743. This was a formal court martial composed of Lieutenant-General Thomas Wentworth as President and twelve other officers, a distinguished body including Major-Generals Pulteney, Churchill, Wolfe, and 'Lord De Lawar'. Oglethorpe was brought in under arrest and the prosecution opened its case. The court did not meet on Wednesday, but throughout Monday, Tuesday, and Thursday the prosecution built up its charges. On Friday October 3, Oglethorpe's defence began, and was still presenting witnesses when the court adjourned the next day for the week-end. Although Philip Yorke later chided Dr. Birch that 'for one that was present your Account of Oglethorpe's Tryal is a very superficial one',[1] the latter's report on the first week's sessions contained the essence of the evidence:

> I have been this week a constant attendant at Mr. Oglethorp's Tryal. . . . It appears that his troops, which were about 600, were within half a mile of Shap on the Evening before the Action at Clifton; that they retir'd thence to Orton, five miles on this side of Shap; & the next day did not begin their March till near eleven o'Clock, so that when the Duke had pass'd that Village near two Miles, he perceiv'd General Oglethorpe's Corps a mile & a half to the Rear; upon which he sent for, & reprimanded him in these words, 'If you had done what I order'd you, few of the Rebels had escap'd'; to which the General made no reply, but retir'd with a low bow. His defence, which he enter'd upon yesterday, turns upon the excessive Fatigue of the troops, the Want of Forage on the night they came before Shap, and the Reports of the Rebels being there to the number of about 2000; whereas the Assistant to the Duke's Quarter Master, who pass'd thro' Shap the next day at noon, was assur'd that they were not above 300, as he perceiv'd them to be an hour after. The Court proceeds next week, having sat every day this week except Wednesday.[2]

---

[1] Philip Yorke to Dr. Thomas Birch, Wrest, Oct. 12, 1746, Add. MSS. (British Museum), 35397, Hardwicke Papers, f. 39 verso.

[2] Dr. Thomas Birch to Philip Yorke, London, Oct. 4, 1746, Add. MSS. (British Museum), 35397, Hardwicke Papers, ff. 35 and verso.

THE 'FORTY-FIVE AND OBLIVION 269

Having presented his case in a remarkably sound paper on October 3, Oglethorpe on October 6 and 7 presented witnesses whose evidence seems to Dr. Birch to have been of questionable value. On October 11 Birch reported to Philip Yorke that

> General Oglethorpe's Tryal ended on Tuesday, after the Court had sat seven days upon it. I heard the whole Proceedings, & think it will leave some Imputation upon his Character, tho' he should escape Punishment. His not marching till near noon the day of the Action at Clifton is wholly unaccountable; & he would fix the Blame of it upon Lieutenant Colonel Arabin of St. George's Dragoons, who, I am assur'd, could retort a much severer Charge upon him for his Conduct that very evening near Clifton, which, according to the Account I have had of it, was a complication of Cowardice and a thorough Ignorance of his Profession.[1]

Noting in a letter to Horace Mann that courts martial 'are all in fashion now', Horace Walpole, who had no great love for the General, observed that 'Oglethorpe's sentence is not yet public, but it is believed not to be favourable', gratuitously adding that 'he was always a bully, and is now tried for cowardice'.[2] Contrary to Walpole's cherished hopes, and despite the overwhelming popularity of Cumberland, Oglethorpe was promptly and 'most honourably' acquitted.[3] Dr. Birch, however, was 'still of my former opinion, that his reputation will suffer by what appear'd on his Tryal'.[4]

Dr. Birch's conclusions proved sound, and Oglethorpe, despite his acquittal, became somewhat of a 'forgotten man'. Although in September 1747 he received the sop of promotion to the rank of Lieutenant-General,[5] he no

---

[1] Dr. Thomas Birch to Philip Yorke, London, Oct. 11, 1746, Add. MSS. (British Museum), 35397, Hardwicke Papers, ff. 38 and verso.
[2] Toynbee, Mrs. Paget, *The Letters of Horace Walpole*, ii. 245–6.
[3] W.O. 71:19, pp. 282–3; London *General Advertiser*, Oct. 21, 1746, p. 1; *Westminster Journal*, Oct. 25, 1746, p. 3.
[4] Dr. Thomas Birch to Philip Yorke, London, Oct. 18, 1746, Add. MSS. (British Museum), 35397, Hardwicke Papers, f. 41 verso.
[5] S.P. 44:186, p. 498; W.O. 25:22, p. 129; W.O. 25:136, p. 118; Dalton, *English Army Lists*, vi. 53.

longer was appointed to the Board of General Officers[1] nor did his name appear in a list of general officers who 'are to command in the next Campaign' of 1747 in Flanders.[2] His isolation in England seems to have become social as well as strictly professional, for his house at Whitehall was taken over by Lord and Lady Coke[3] and he no longer served as a director of the Children's Hospital.[4] His interest in America, however, had not waned, and when in this same year Cadwallader Colden, philosopher, scientist, and later Lieutenant-Governor of New York, and correspondent of Linnaeus, Franklin, and Samuel Johnson, was expanding his *History of the Five Indian Nations*, Oglethorpe promised his aid and 'was so kind as to overlook [the] manuscript, and approved it very much'.[5] But at home, even in his solitude, one interest remained. James Oglethorpe still represented Haslemere in the British House of Commons.

In the first session of the House after his return from Georgia in 1743 he had served on various committees as of old and had been the colleague of Fox, Pelham, Winnington, and Sir Charles Hanbury-Williams.[6] The next year he was appropriately made chairman of the committee on recruiting the army, but, with the 'Forty-five, Oglethorpe found himself far from Westminster. His return to committee-work in 1746 proved a boon during and after his court martial, even though he no longer received the choicest assignments. On June 26, 1747, despite the publicity of the trial and the candidacy of a third contestant, he and Burrell were re-elected,[7] but

[1] W.O. 71:9, pp. 2-3, 12-13.
[2] London *Westminster Journal*, Jan. 24, 1747, p. 2.
[3] London *Whitehall Evening Post*, April 7, 1747, p. 3.
[4] Ibid., May 14, 1747, p. 2.
[5] Thomas Osborne to Cadwallader Colden, London, June 12, 1747, *Letters and Papers of Cadwallader Colden*, . . . *1711–1775* (7 vols., Collections of the New York Historical Society, l–lvi, New York, 1918–23), iii (lii), 403. See also iv (liii), 64.
[6] Ilchester, Earl of, and Mrs. Langford Brooke, *Life of Sir Charles Hanbury-Williams* (London, 1928), p. 87.
[7] Oglethorpe, 52; Burrell, 45; Mr. Huggins, 12, London *Evening Post*,

Oglethorpe's name seldom appears in the *Commons Journals* for that year and 1748, his sole important assignment during the latter year being to the chairmanship of the committee to encourage the growth of 'Indico'.[1] By 1749 the clamour against him seems somewhat to have receded, and he returned from the rural solitude of Godalming and Cranham to the life of London, where he lived in Lisle Street, Leicester Fields.[2] His humanitarian instincts were appealed to in at least one case,[3] and he renewed his friendship with that staunch old Jacobite and Oxonian antiquarian, Thomas Carte.[4] But his most notable achievement lay in the realm of arts and science. Although never elected to the Society of the Dilettanti, as were his later friends, Topham Beauclerk, Bennet Langton, David Garrick, and Sir Joshua Reynolds,[5] Oglethorpe did become a Fellow of the Royal Society. Despite the fact that he never attended any of its sessions as a guest previous to his nomination, his application for membership on April 6, 1749, was sponsored by seven

June 30, 1747, p. 1; *Whitehall Evening Post*, June 30, 1747, p. 2; *Penny London Post*, July 1, 1747, p. 3; Smith, *Parliamentary Representation of Surrey*, p. 93; Swanton and Woods, *Bygone Haslemere*, pp. 195–6. It was at this time that T. Edwards, the critic, in a letter concerning plans for a ball, suggested as to dance-tunes that 'America may be called by Oglethorpe'. T. Edwards to Daniel Wray, Turrick, Nov. 12, 1747, Bodleian MSS. 1011, Letters of T. Edwards, v. 20.

[1] For Oglethorpe's parliamentary record, 1743 to 1745, see Add. MSS. (British Museum), 35337, Parliamentary Journal of Philip Yorke, 1743–5, ff. 8, 13 verso, 30 verso, 71; and *Commons Journals*, xxiv. 518, 534, 621, 674, 688–9, 720, 729, 781, 783, 786, 807, 823, 829; xxv. 58, 128, 131, 151, 161, 169, 183, 188–9, 309, 345, 369, 375, 382, 400, 419, 519, 525, 537, 564, 623, 632–5, 640, 643, 647–8, 651–2.

[2] Osborn, J., *A Complete Guide to all Persons who have any Trade or Concern within the City of London and Parts Adjacent, 1749* (London, 1749), p. 148; Certificate Book of the Royal Society, 1731–50, p. 396.

[3] In 1749 Zachary Williams, when expelled from the Charterhouse at the age of 78, turned to Oglethorpe with his complaint in a long, bombastic letter which, from all the evidence at hand, failed to elicit any response. *Gentleman's Magazine*, lvii. 1158–9.

[4] Carte MSS. (Bodleian Library, Oxford), ccxxxvii, f. 35, Thomas Carte's Memorandum of a talk with General Oglethorpe, Feb. 3, 1749.

[5] Cust, L., *History of the Society of the Dilettanti* (revised ed., London, 1914), pp. 262–72.

distinguished Fellows, including his friend Sir Hans Sloane, a former President; Dr. Martin Folkes, the President at the time; William Hanbury, the cleric and musician; Cromwell Mortimer, the secretary of the Society; Peter Collinson, the antiquarian; Mark Catesby, the naturalist; and Lord Cadogan, Sloane's son-in-law.[1] Described as 'a Gentleman well versed in Natural History, mathematicks and all branches of Polite Literature', Oglethorpe attended only the session of June 15 as a candidate,[2] although his name was read at ten successive meetings.[3] On November 9 he was elected a Fellow,[4] and on November 16 gave the usual bond, signed the obligation, and was admitted.[5] Yet, although his certificate of nomination stated that he was 'desirous of becoming a member' and he was recommended 'as one who will be a usefull member & every way qualified to promote the designs of our Institution',[6] there is no evidence in the *Philosophical Transactions* that Oglethorpe ever read a paper; there is no record that he ever brought a guest; and it is extremely doubtful if he himself ever attended any sessions of the Royal Society.[7] In 1749 he was a guest at the Royal Society Club, but he never became a member.[8]

[1] Certificate Book of the Royal Society, 1731–50, p. 396. At the same time there was proposed for membership Philip Carteret Webb, who later became Oglethorpe's successful political rival in Haslemere. Journal Book of the Royal Society, xxi, 1748–51, p. 92.
[2] Even this one attendance was at the express desire of President Folkes. Journal Book of the Royal Society, xxi, 1748–51, p. 139.
[3] April 13 to June 15, weekly except for April 27, and Oct. 26 and Nov. 2. Certificate Book of the Royal Society, 1731–50, p. 396.
[4] Certificate Book of the Royal Society, 1731–50, p. 396; Journal Book of the Royal Society, xxi, 1748–51, p. 162.
[5] Journal Book of the Royal Society, xxi, 1748–51, p. 167.
[6] Certificate Book of the Royal Society, 1731–50, p. 396.
[7] Journal Book of the Royal Society, xxi, 1748–51; xxii, 1751–4; xxiii, 1754–7; Church, A. H., *Some Account of the 'Letters and Papers' of the Period, 1741–1806, in the Archives of the Royal Society* (Oxford, 1908), pp. 9–14.
[8] Oglethorpe was 'one of the most attractive personalities that appeared at the Club' in 1749, Geikie, Sir Archibald, *Annals of the Royal Society Club* (London, 1917), pp. 35–6.

Oglethorpe's interest still lay in his parliamentary duties, and the session of 1749 saw his renaissance, both as a speaker and in committee-work. In 1747 his interest in the welfare of numerically small, but spiritually potent, denominations had led him to advise Count Zinzendorf and the Moravians to appeal to Parliament for greater privileges and recognition of their communion both in England and America by a release of its members from the obligations of bearing arms and taking oaths. Not only did he write to the Board of Trade and submit letters from Conrad Weiser, the great Lutheran missionary to the Indians of Pennsylvania, and Thomas Penn, both of whom could testify to the standing of the sect in their own colony, but he held numerous personal conferences with Zinzendorf, both at the latter's home and his own, and in 1749, as chairman of the parliamentary committee, successfully spoke in the House and personally influenced Lord Halifax to secure passage of the measure.[1]

Oglethorpe's committee-work now centred in the chairmanship of the very important committee on the state of the British Fisheries, including the herring, cod, and whaling industries. On April 10, 1750, he and Admiral Vernon, 'at the Star and Garter Tavern, Pall Mall', received the Freedom of the City of Edinburgh for their efforts on behalf of the White Herring Fishery Bill;[2] and for the next two years he took a marked interest in the Council for the Encouragement of British Fisheries. He

---

[1] *Commons Journals*, xxv. 728, 804, 812, 816, 818, 855, 859; *Journal of the Commissioners for Trade and Plantations*, viii, 1742–9, pp. 152, 213–14; the Moravian *Hütten Diarium* for 1749 (predecessor of the Moravian *Nachrichten*) and the *Acta Fratrum Unitatis in Anglia* (London, 1749), Document No. 4 in the Archives of the Moravian Church, Bethlehem, Pennsylvania; Hutton, J. E., 'The Moravian Contribution to the Evangelical Revival in England, 1742–1755', *Historical Essays commemorating the Jubilee of Owens College, Manchester* (edited by T. F. Tout and James Tait, Manchester, 1907), pp. 423–52; Hutton, J. E., *History of the Moravian Church* (London, 1909), pp. 337–9.

[2] London *Evening Post*, April 12, 1750, p. 4; *Whitehall Evening Post*, April 12, 1750, p. 1.

was asked to make the address to the Prince of Wales on the presentation to the Free British Fishery of the Royal Charter,[1] and he enthusiastically subscribed for a quantity of stock in the enterprise. It has been asserted that, after 1750, Oglethorpe was so reduced in circumstances that he practised the science of physic as a profession for the next decade and a half.[2] Whether that be true or not, on March 16, 1752, stock to the value of £1,450 in his name was sold as defaulted and on August 18 £400 worth more came on the market because he had not paid for it[3] —action which naturally closed his connexion with the fisheries.[4]

More as an ornament of the House during these years than for his utility, Oglethorpe from 1749 to 1752 served on various committees, but he spoke once more on the floor of the House. It was singularly appropriate that the final major parliamentary battle of one who had been born and bred in the military tradition should deal with the subject so dear to his heart: the good of the army. For well-nigh thirty years James Oglethorpe upheld the honour and welfare of the British soldier. The army had been the theme of one of his earliest parliamentary addresses. In 1744 he had returned to the subject,[5] and in the debate on the Mutiny Bill in 1750 he supported the soldiers' cause by speaking for parliamentary revision of mutiny cases. Taking first the part of the officers, he upheld their right of honourably refusing to tell the Lords how each had voted in a court martial, for

---

[1] *London Magazine*, xix. 510–11.

[2] *European Magazine*, viii. 91.

[3] Add. MSS. (British Museum), 15154, Minutes of the Council for the Encouragement of British Fisheries, pp. 219, 276.

[4] For the fisheries question see Add. MSS. (British Museum), 15154, Minutes of the Council for the Encouragement of British Fisheries, pp. 21–6, 38, 40–60, 65; Add. MSS., 15156, Minutes of the Committee on Shipping, pp. 1, 24, 51–8, 71; Add. MSS., 32721, Newcastle Papers, ff. 105–6, 169–70; Add. MSS., 32722, Newcastle Papers, ff. 175–8; London *Whitehall Evening Post*, Sept. 22, 1750, p. 2; Oct. 22, 1751, p. 2; *Public Advertiser*, Dec. 5, 1753, p. 2; *Evening Post*, Dec. 6, 1753, p. 1.

[5] Cobbett, *Parliamentary History of England*, xiii. 463 ff., 1268.

the House of Lords was not a court of justice. Concerning complaints, he opposed the doctrine that

this House is never to take notice of the complaints made by the army or by any man or any sort of men, in the army. I hope both the officers and soldiers of the army are all subjects of Great Britain; and it is our duty to take notice of every complaint made to us by any British subject, unless upon the face of it, it appears to be frivolous or unjust. Nay farther, as we are the great inquest of the nation, it is our duty to inquire diligently if any of the subjects of Great Britain be exposed to, or labouring under any and what oppressions, and to take the most effectual methods for procuring them relief.

This duty, he felt, should be more frequently attended to, 'especially with regard to that part of the British subjects who serve in our armies either by sea or land; for they are by the nature of the service more exposed to oppression than any other part of his majesty's subjects, and it is likewise much more dangerous for them to complain'. Taking now the side of the ordinary soldier, who 'has common understanding as well as other men' and who would not abuse the right of protest or complaint, Oglethorpe attacked the preservation of tyranny in the army which encouraged brutal officers to use the soldiers ill by refusing them parliamentary investigations: 'I shall always be jealous of a power, the exercise whereof is trusted to the absolute and arbitrary will of a single man; nor do I think that any such power can ever be necessary in time of peace; for though in time of war such a power must often be granted, yet even then it ought to be as little made use of as possible.'[1] The erstwhile Jacobite had developed a healthy opposition to entrenched bureaucracy.

At this same time a bill for limiting the time of military service gave him an opportunity to renew the expression of his views of twenty years before, when he advocated the granting of discharges to the soldiers upon demand

---

[1] Cobbett, *Parliamentary History of England*, xiv. 622, 638–41, 666–9.

after one year's service, so that the troops in the colonies would settle as servants or tradesmen in that part of the world, thereby increasing the white population of the sugar colonies and serving as protection against the French navy. Oglethorpe felt that the bill was a step towards an ideal in the welfare and advancement of the common soldier, who now often served a lifetime in the army with virtually no hope of promotion. He also proposed that the term of service in the colonies be shortened, and soon after advocated a bill to increase the efficiency of the British militia at home.[1]

These expressions of concern for the welfare of soldiers and the protection of distant colonies proved to be Oglethorpe's parliamentary valediction. The remainder of his time was spent in committee-work. Strangely enough, although on the committee to consider the exportation of salt to the American colonies, he was omitted from the group to which was referred a petition from Georgia silk-raisers on the growth of silk in America! For the rest his attention was engrossed by the Royal African Company, municipal problems, economic questions, the state of British highways including the paving of Pall Mall (on which committee he was associated with that famous fop, George Bubb Dodington),[2] and his favourite subject, the naturalization of foreigners.[3] In February 1752 Oglethorpe was made chairman of a committee on the King's Bench Prison to consider a petition of its prisoners, and once again the old crusading spirit flamed in the committee recommendations for the alleviation of distressful conditions which were self-evident and demanded cleans-

---

[1] Cobbett, *Parliamentary History of England*, xiv. 758–9, 1204, 1207.
[2] Wyndham, H. P., editor, *The Diary of the late George Bubb Dodington* (4th ed., London, 1809), p. 103.
[3] *Commons Journals*, xxv. 664, 668, 719, 725, 733, 804, 808–9, 813, 829, 838, 854, 860, 864–5, 869, 871–2, 877, 881–8, 890, 892, 911, 917–18, 923, 925, 928, 932–4, 937–8, 940–2, 950, 968, 974, 992, 996–7, 999, 1015, 1018, 1023, 1030, 1032–6, 1040, 1057–8, 1066, 1090, 1092, 1102, 1116; xxvi. 4, 27, 41, 51, 113, 115, 127, 130, 148, 157, 187, 208–9, 215, 227, 242, 244–60, 273–4, 287.

ing as much as had those of a quarter-century before.[1] The subsequent months of 1752 and 1753 were taken up with such topics as 'distemper among the horned cattle in this kingdom', the importation of gum senega, the regulation of 'taylors and stay-makers' and of framework knitters at their trade, the lighting and condition of streets and roads, and the state of workhouses and chapels, of advowsons and estates.[2]

Not the least of James Oglethorpe's multifarious committee appointments during his three decades in the House of Commons proved to be one of his last, for in December 1753 he took a prominent part in the committee which arranged the lottery from the proceeds of which the British Government purchased the Sloanean, Harleian, and Cottonian Collections, which became the nucleus of the British Museum.[3] Oglethorpe's friend of thirty years, Sir Hans Sloane, had died on January 11[4] and had been buried a week later.[5] On January 19 the publication of his will revealed his desire that the famous museum he had built up be offered to the King and Parliament for £20,000.[6] On Saturday morning, January 27, the group of over forty trustees, chosen by Sloane, met at the Manor House of Chelsea at the call of Sloane's son-in-law, Lord Cadogan, and the other executors of the estate, to arrange for the disposal of his museum. After Cadogan had welcomed them and the Earl of Macclesfield had read the will and codicils, James Oglethorpe, a trustee

[1] *Commons Journals,* xxvi. 457, 505-13. The report 'revealed a continuance of the well-known evils'. Webb and Webb, *English Prisons under Local Government,* p. 27.
[2] *Commons Journals,* xxvi. 296-300, 312, 315, 330-2, 335, 345, 356, 376-7, 382, 389-90, 404, 417, 437, 453, 459, 470-1, 518-19, 521, 535, 537, 539, 550, 554, 560, 584, 593, 626, 630-1, 643-6, 650, 655, 659, 666, 670-1, 673, 678-80, 695-7, 704, 711, 713-15, 717, 725, 733, 744, 750, 762, 795, 802, 808, 815, 817, 819, 822, 840-2, 865, 868, 928, 933, 944, 946, 950, 1003, 1008, 1011, 1019.
[3] *Commons Journals,* xxvi. 873.
[4] London *Public Advertiser,* Jan. 12, 1753, p. 1.
[5] Ibid., Jan. 19, 1753, p. 1; *Evening Post,* Jan. 20, 1753, p. 4.
[6] London *Public Advertiser,* Jan. 22, 1753, p. 1.

of the estate and one of the pall-bearers at Sloane's funeral,[1] 'gave an Account of the Intention of Sir Hans, of the Nature and the Value of the Museum, and produced an Abstract of the Articles it contained'.[2] Although on its purchase by Parliament[3] Oglethorpe was not made a Trustee of the Museum,[4] his part both in the settlement of the estate and the committee-work for the State lottery entitles him to recognition as one of those who assisted in the founding of the British Museum.

Fortune now turned against James Oglethorpe. Whether it was because he now spent most of his time in London in winter and in Essex during the summer, or because of agitation against the naturalization of Jews,[5] Oglethorpe seems to have sensed the imminence of defeat in Haslemere in the spring of 1754. He therefore attempted to safeguard his seat in Parliament by standing both in Haslemere and in Westminster, London. The results were equally unfortunate: at Westminster the returns on the first day were: Colonel Cornwallis, 333; Sir John Crosse, 305; Lord Middlesex, 24; General Oglethorpe, 10![6] And the next five days made the defeat only so much heavier: Colonel Cornwallis, 3,385; Sir John Crosse, 3,184; General Oglethorpe, 261; Lord Middlesex, 209.[7] In Haslemere the contest was closer but the defeat hurt far more. The General's long period in opposition to the bureaucrats of Whitehall had led them to enter two of their strongest supporters at Haslemere, Philip Carteret Webb,[8] Secretary to the Commissioners

---

[1] London *Evening Post*, Jan. 20, 1753, p. 4.
[2] London *Daily Advertiser*, Jan. 30, 1753, p. 2; *Evening Post*, Jan. 30, 1753, p. 1.
[3] London *Public Advertiser*, Feb. 1, 1753, p. 2; *Evening Post*, Feb. 1, 1753, p. 1; *Public Advertiser*, March 8, 1753, p. 1; March 21, 1753, p. 1.
[4] London *Evening Post*, Dec. 13, 1753, p. 1; *Public Advertiser*, Dec. 13, 1753, p. 1.
[5] London *Evening Post*, Dec. 8, 1753, p. 4; *Public Advertiser*, Dec. 8, 1753, p. 2; Swanton and Woods, *Bygone Haslemere*, pp. 196, 199.
[6] London *Public Advertiser*, April 17, 1754, p. 1.
[7] Ibid., April 22, 1754, p. 1.
[8] A decade later, when Webb had become solicitor of the Treasury, John

for Bankrupts, and James More Molyneaux, of an old Surrey family. At the declaration of the poll Webb and Molyneaux were each accredited with 73 votes as against 45 each for Oglethorpe and Burrell. The General seems at first to have been content with the result, but Burrell on November 18, 1754, petitioned the Commons to have the election voided. This evidently aroused Oglethorpe, for ten days later he too submitted a petition of contest, charging that the Bailiff of Haslemere, Edward Upfold, 'in taking the poll, behaved in a very partial and illegal manner, particularly in admitting persons to vote in favour of the said James More Molyneaux and Philip Carteret Webb, who had no right so to do, and refusing to accept the votes of others who had a right, and tendered their votes for the petitioner', Oglethorpe.[1] The petition, which included charges against both Molyneaux and Webb of 'several undue practices', was referred, together with Burrell's, to the committee on privileges and elections. Unfortunately for their case, Burrell and Oglethorpe had not agreed on a common procedure, and this had its effect on the hearing and the decision. The main issues were the right of freeholders to vote and the natural corollary thereof, the proper definition of 'freeholders' as by Burgage Tenure. The committee soon handed down a decision affirming the suffrage rights of freeholders. This ruling led Burrell to withdraw his petition at once, but Oglethorpe stubbornly determined to fight the issue to a conclusion. The committee therefore granted him time until January 21, 1755, to add further evidence, but he failed to appear for any further hearing, and on April 24, 1755, the day before Parliament was prorogued, the committee on elections reported its agreement to seat Molyneaux and Webb on the basis of

Wilkes called him 'the most infamous of all the tools of that administration'. Almon, John, editor, *Correspondence of John Wilkes* (5 vols., London, 1805), iii. 208.

[1] *Commons Journals*, xxvii. 35. See also the London *Evening Post*, April 16, 1754, p. 4; *Whitehall Evening Post*, April 16, 1754, p. 3; *London Gazette*, April 20, 1754, p. 1.

the official poll, which gave each of the successful candidates 70 votes as against 46 for Burrell and 45 for Oglethorpe.[1] This was the third time in thirty years that Oglethorpe was a participant in a contested election, but it was the first time that he was the petitioning loser; and it marked the end of his parliamentary career.

Bereft of all those interests which had meant life and vigour to him, Oglethorpe once again bethought himself of the army. Since the court martial he had had no regimental connexion. In December 1754 the press reported a rumour that he was at last to have a regiment 'upon the British Establishment',[2] but the power of the Duke of Cumberland was still effective and a rumour it remained. In September 1755, when the Seven Years War loomed imminent upon the American horizon, Oglethorpe begged Newcastle to revive and restore his Georgia regiment for service in America,[3] but when the appointments were announced the next month the name of Oglethorpe did not stand with those of Cumberland, Sir John Ligonier, and the Earl of Loudoun.[4] It is an interesting question whether, had he not evoked the wrath of Cumberland and been court-martialled in 1746, James Oglethorpe, and not James Wolfe, might have led Britain to victory on the Heights at Quebec in 1759.

While his professional, parliamentary, and social house of cards was falling about him, Oglethorpe had turned back to his own family. His sister, Anne, had remained at Westbrook after his marriage and the 'Forty-five, while Eleanor Oglethorpe de Mézières, undaunted by the failure of Prince Charles in 1746, had continued steadfast in the

---

[1] *Commons Journals*, xxvii. 13, 20, 91, 112, 169, 291–3; Smith, *Parliamentary Representation of Surrey*, p. 28; Swanton and Woods, *Bygone Haslemere*, p. 198.
[2] London *Whitehall Evening Post*, Dec. 17, 1754, p. 3; *Public Advertiser*, Dec. 17, 1754, p. 1.
[3] James Oglethorpe to Newcastle, London, Sept. 22, 1755, Add. MSS. (British Museum), 32859, Newcastle Papers, ff. 185–6.
[4] London *Gazette*, Oct. 21, 1754, pp. 2–4; Oct. 28, 1754, pp. 2–3; *Whitehall Evening Post*, Nov. 8, 1754, p. 1.

THE 'FORTY-FIVE AND OBLIVION 281

cause,[1] although one Jacobite historian has asserted that, by 1746, Eleanor 'was regarded, both by James and the Prince, as a reckless and feather-brained conspirator'.[2] In 1749 Lord Nairne and the Oliphants of Gask visited her in Paris,[3] where as late as 1752 she was considered a leader in French society and accepted as such by English visitors.[4] Having failed to secure a passport from Newcastle for a visit to England in 1740,[5] Madame de Mézières came over without one in September 1752, ostensibly to visit her sick sister, Anne, at Westbrook, Godalming,[6] where tradition had it that Prince Charles was paying a secret visit at the same time. Promptly upon her arrival in Surrey, Eleanor wrote an appealing letter in appalling French to Newcastle,[7] who, from all the evidence, paid no attention to it. She then sought his sanction to go to Bath for a cure of her rheumatism,[8] and only succeeded in drawing upon herself deep suspicion of implication in the Elibank Plot[9] which caused so much commotion from 1752 to 1754 and, in the words of the historian of the Jacobite movement, 'was the last definite scheme to restore the Stuarts to the throne of Great Britain by means of a movement within the country itself'.[10] Al-

[1] Shield, 'The Loyal Oglethorpes', *The Royalist*, p. 44; Shield, *Henry Stuart, Cardinal of York*, pp. 114, 121; Bell, *Memorials of John Murray of Broughton*, p. 353; Rathery, E. J. B., *Journal et Mémoires du Marquis d'Argenson* (9 vols., Paris, 1859–67), v. 318, 367; Johnstone, Chevalier de, *Memoirs of the Rebellion in 1745 and 1746* (2nd ed., London, 1820), p. 311.
[2] Lang, *Prince Charles Edward Stuart, The Young Chevalier*, p. 327.
[3] Oliphant, T. L. K., *The Jacobite Lairds of Gask* (London, 1870), p. 246.
[4] Countess of Westmorland to the Countess of Denbigh, Mereworth, June 12, 1752, *MSS. of the Earl of Denbigh* (H.M.C. Reports), p. 278.
[5] Shield, *Henry Stuart, Cardinal of York*, p. 40.
[6] Ibid., pp. 152–3; Shield and Lang, 'Queen Oglethorpe', *Blackwood's Edinburgh Magazine*, clxiii. 203–6.
[7] La Marquise de Mézières to Newcastle, 'de Wess Broke, le 5 d'octobre, 1752', Add. MSS. (British Museum), 32840, Newcastle Papers, f. 268.
[8] Madame de Mézières to Newcastle, London, Jan. 28, 1753, Add. MSS. (British Museum), 32731, Newcastle Papers, f. 112.
[9] H. V. Jones to Newcastle, Whitehall, Dec. 1, 1753, Add. MSS. (British Museum), 32733, Newcastle Papers, ff. 353–6.
[10] Petrie, *The Jacobite Movement*, pp. 229–48; Petrie, Sir Charles, Bt., 'The Elibank Plot', *Transactions of the Royal Historical Society*, 4th series, xiv. 175–96.

though George Selwyn's account of this remarkable woman deeply impressed Horace Walpole,[1] she accomplished nothing beyond a last visit to her sister, Anne, who did not survive long after. In 1759 Eleanor was supposed to have plotted a restoration during the Seven Years War,[2] but the movement was ended.

To what degree James Oglethorpe took part in the Jacobite conversations of this period we know not, but the ties of family loyalty were so strong that it is reasonable to suppose that his sister's illness drew him into the family reunion. With no other interests at hand, Oglethorpe now turned to an old friend. In 1755, while a young Virginian named George Washington was extricating the sad remnants of Braddock's brigades from the Indian ambush in western Pennsylvania, the former commander in Georgia and friend of Indians was writing again to his comrade of Paris student days, now the illustrious Field-Marshal Keith.[3] That winter must have witnessed an improvement in his financial condition, for in spring the *Wanderlust* seized him and in May 1756 he was in Rotterdam, Holland. We know not why he went or whether he visited his sister, Eleanor, in France; whether he made the Grand Tour, or whether he called on Frederick the Great for whom he expressed such profound admiration. There is no record of his Dutch visit[4] other than his superb letter of May 3 to Keith, who had acknowledged Oglethorpe's of December 1755. James Oglethorpe was a true Briton, phlegmatic and self-con-

---

[1] Horace Walpole to Hon. Henry Seymour Conway, Strawberry Hill, May 5, 1753, Toynbee, Mrs. Paget, *Letters of Horace Walpole*, iii. 155.
[2] Shield and Lang, *The King Over the Water*, p. 463.
[3] James Oglethorpe to Field-Marshal Keith, [no place], Dec. 9, 1755, *MSS. of Lord Elphinstone* (H.M.C. Reports, ix, Appendix, part ii), p. 229.
[4] Although she was in Holland at this time, Mrs. Calderwood of Polton, the friend of Marshal Keith, makes no reference to Oglethorpe. Fergusson, Alexander, editor, *Letters and Journals of Mrs. Calderwood of Polton* (Edinburgh, 1884), pp. 362-3. Nor is there any reference to Oglethorpe in the correspondence of the Earl of Hardwicke, British Minister to The Hague, and his son, Joseph Yorke, Add. MSS. (British Museum), 35357, 35364, 35388, Hardwicke Papers.

tained, and this letter is a unique example of a slightly garrulous, widely read, and deep-thinking elderly gentleman unburdening his philosophic mind to a friend. Expressing his ardent desire to visit Berlin, Oglethorpe justified his 'violent inclination to see your King' by his youthful memories of other rulers. Of Frederick the Great he wrote that

> Your King by his actions and writings apears a character superior to any this age has produced. He seems most like the Roman Varro, or the English Sir Walter Rauleigh, soldier, poet, philosopher, mathematitian and musitian in his private character, and besides these, in his publick a politick King and wise lawgiver. I should not thinck my colection of characters compleat without his drawn from the life.

Lewis the 14th was made considerable by having great generals, great subjects and great dominions, all laying round and contiguous and improved to the utmost. Your King has made dispersed and unimproved dominions considerable. He formed his troops and Generals and affter conquered with those instruments of his own making. In short a powerful Kingdom made Lewis the 14th a great King. Your King's genious has created and made his Kingdom great and powerful.

The wourld also say he has judgment and a brilliant wit, agreeable in private conversation, to which he gives what the Antients call Atick Salt. Had he not been a King he would have made shining character in comon life as an agreeable companion, and, as Shakespear says of Henry the 5th, would have been the king of good fellows. This part Lewis the 14th entirely wanted. His perfection was fast. He was a pompous figure on the throne, but nothing but dull form in private life....

You commend my having encouraged trade and speak of it as equal to arms in which permit me to differ. I thinck it a thing low in its nature but very necessary now that wars are carried on by mony as well as by men. I made myself therefore acquainted with the nature of trade, publick credit, funds, fisheries and plantations, being facilitated by the three voiages I made to America, one to the Levant, and travels by land through most part of Europe. Also by sitting thirty years in Parliament which made me acquainted with the method by which 15 millions, which is all England has of mony in specie, is made to performe the service and answer 80 millions of mony.

You mention that we got the fishery encouraged. We did so and carried several other laws through the House which have succeeded, and encreased the trade, fisheries and plantations, the great suports of naval power.

Yet even encouragements given to trade may be pushed too far. Trade must be subservient to the end for which it is suported, that is the good of the State. Such as occation luxury and effemenancy are to be avoided, and even plantations may be too dear bought by expensive wars.

Had Sir Robert Wallpole kept his power he had carried into execution a plan he made me form, which would have established a plantation more advantageous than any England yet has, and which neither France nor any other European power had the least clame to pretence to apose. That country is still vacant from Europeans, and England has as yet no pretention but must acquire them by first possession.

On his retreat the young men run into the war and other measures the world knows, and since strove to make a settlement in Nova Scotia and other disputed countries. They have lay'd out there 20 times as much as I proposed, and have got nothing but a ruinous war. I must desire you would excuse my tedious letter and believe me to be, Dear Sir, your most humble and most obedient servant,

JO[1]

Although the length of his continental visit is unknown, it is quite probable that he was already abroad when his parliamentary colleague of thirty years, Peter Burrell, died in April 1756,[2] and his sister, Anne, 'a lady well known for her extensive humanity and benevolence', passed away on September 5, at her home in Strand-on-the-Green near Brentford.[3] Since 1750 Oglethorpe had lost his seat in Parliament, his holdings in, and place on, the British Fisheries Commission, and now a favourite

[1] James Oglethorpe to Field-Marshal Keith, 'Roterdam, May 3, 1756', *MSS. of Lord Elphinstone* (H.M.C. Reports, ix, Appendix, part ii), p. 229. Where was Oglethorpe's idyllic colony? Was it the 'Lost Atlantis' or the Samoa of Robert Louis Stevenson, Tahiti or Bali?
[2] London *Evening Post*, April 17, 1756, p. 1.
[3] *London Magazine*, xxv. 452.

THE 'FORTY-FIVE AND OBLIVION

sister and long-time colleague. But his cup was not yet full. In 1757 the Royal Society 'took into consideration the cases of those who are in arrears in dues', and on June 9 'ejected' Oglethorpe, who owed £18 10s., virtually his entire obligation since election.[1] By the end of 1757 Oglethorpe became indeed the 'forgotten man', and the records, archives, and newspapers are devoid of any reference to him during the next two years. On the accession of King George III in 1760 his commission as Lieutenant-General was, indeed, renewed,[2] but promotion was denied to one who was anathema to the Duke of Cumberland and who had decried the achievements of Wolfe and Amherst as 'nothing but a ruinous war'.[3] In 1760 General and Mrs. Oglethorpe came to Soho Square, where they lived for some years.[4] The next year his influence and support were sought by another candidate for Haslemere;[5] but Oglethorpe was forgotten. How deeply he felt it all, and how disgusted he was with the national trend of affairs, are evident from two letters he addressed to William Pitt in 1761.

Henry Pelham, who had succeeded Walpole in 1743, had died in 1754, to be followed by his brother, the Duke of Newcastle, who for three years held sway as Prime Minister. With the progress of the Seven Years War, William Pitt the elder had become Secretary of State in 1756 and the next year brought about a coalition

[1] At a shilling per week, Oglethorpe probably paid the first month or so, and the balance due made up the total in the seven-year interval. Oglethorpe's case was mild: The Earl of Sandwich owed £31 8s.; the Earl of Buchan £59 13s.; Lord Delawar £67 16s.; John Warburton £90 7s.; and Sir Alexander Cuming, who preceded Oglethorpe in dealing with the Indians on the Carolina border in 1730, £92 4s. This meant a debt of about forty years! All were ejected with Oglethorpe, Journal Book of the Royal Society, xxiii. 585.
[2] S.P. 44:192, p. 7; W.O. 25:139, p. 1; London *Gazette*, Nov. 29, 1760, p. 11; *Evening Post*, Dec. 2, 1760, p. 1.
[3] Oglethorpe to Field-Marshal Keith, Rotterdam, May 3, 1756, *MSS. of Lord Elphinstone* (H.M.C. Reports), p. 229.
[4] Chancellor, E. Beresford, *The Romance of Soho* (London, 1931), p. 59.
[5] *Transactions of the Essex Archaeological Society*, new series, xv (Colchester, 1921), 99–100.

ministry with Newcastle as First Lord of the Treasury. This was the state of affairs when on October 6, 1761, Oglethorpe addressed to Pitt the following letter:

The present threats like the Tumultus Galicus obliges every man even the Old to offer their Service.

Gratitude requires my utmost regard to you as well as an hereditary affection to your Family. But there is a stronger motive. You are the suport of the libertys of England & of all Europe. This makes me offer my Service to his Majesty Through You Sir.

The treatment I met with made me retier from a wourld that did not want men who prefferd the publick to their privat intrest.

My Spirit rose in me when I heard in the place of my retierment that you were attaked & pushed at for the highest effort of virtue For Saving your Country from a distructive submission to certain ruin.

Commanding long on the Frontiers of ye Spanish America rendered me perfectly acquainted with their weakness in Mexico. And had Admiral Vernon & I been Suported by such a Minister as you the Last Spanish war had been ended as soon as began.

Their fear for that Tender part may in your hands S^r be so managed as to prevent any Spanish minister thô never so corrupt, or never so daring from persisting in Measures that risk the loss of what interests every Family in Spain as well as the King's Revenue.

I could give many useful hints on this head, but shall not trespass on your time. If you should thinck them Usfull you will honour me with your commands & believe me to be

S^r
Your most obedent
Humble Servant

if you honor me with y^r orders
Direct Inclosed under cover
to Mr Oglethorpe at Lady
 Sambrooks Hanover Square.[1]

Unfortunately for Oglethorpe, Pitt had resigned the day before, news of which reached the General before he had sealed the letter; and he now took the opportunity to

[1] James Oglethorpe to William Pitt, London, Oct. 6, 1761, Chatham Papers (P.R.O.), G.D. 8:51.

'lament England & Europe who have lost your assistance at this Critical time'. Affirming that Pitt had 'raised your country to an high pitch of Glory & by a timely retreat given a shining testemony against yielding to impudent fears', Oglethorpe withdrew his offer of services, since 'Honour requires not to serve, but under Vertuous Ministers, & Addison justified that there is a time when
—The Poast of honour is a private Station.
I shall continue in my retreat being justified in renouncing a Wourld where one of the ablest & best of men sees there is no good to be done.'[1]

Oglethorpe now relapsed into silence. Now and then a ripple broke on the placid waters, as when in December 1762 a letter, signed 'Britannicus et Americus' from Soho, appeared in the press on the value of South Carolina and Georgia,[2] or again in 1764 when the wine books of Edward Turnour, Baron Winterton of Gort, county Galway, indicate the sporadic emergence into London social life of the General and Mrs. Oglethorpe.[3] In the same year it was rumoured that a general officer had been offered a regiment but would not accept until it had been cleared up why he lost his last one.[4] There was no proof that either referred to Oglethorpe, but it looked like a possibility. At last in 1765, as the Duke of Cumberland was dying, Oglethorpe was promoted to the rank of General.[5]

[1] Oglethorpe to William Pitt, London, Oct. 6, 1761, Chatham Papers (P.R.O.), G.D. 8:51.
[2] In July Oglethorpe wrote an account of the Cherokees, London *Lloyd's Evening Post and British Chronicle*, July 30, 1762, p. 99; for the 'Britannicus' article, see issue of Dec. 8, 1762, p. 544.
[3] There are references to General Oglethorpe, April 6 and May 4, and to Mrs. Oglethorpe, April 13, 1764; one to the General, March 29, 1765; one to the General, April 30, 1766; another to him, April 12, and one to Mrs. Oglethorpe, May 22, 1769. In the Town Wine Books, giving names of visitors, of Edward Turnour, Baron Winterton of Gort, County Galway, 1761, Viscount Turnour and Earl Winterton, 1766. I am indebted for these references to the kindness of the Right Honourable the Earl Winterton and to Richard Holworthy, Esq.
[4] London *Evening Post*, Sept. 18, 1764, p. 2.
[5] S.P. 44:196, p. 128; W.O. 25:30, p. 139; W.O. 25:141, p. 268; Dalton, *English Army Lists*, vi. 53.

The Grenville ministry which had been formed after the successful Peace of Paris in 1763 had fallen in July 1765, and on January 18, 1766, Oglethorpe wrote at great length to Robert Clive, then Governor of Bengal in India, detailing not only the changes in personnel but all the gossip and rumours concerning the personal and political predilections and manipulations of the Cabinet. In a welter of words perhaps the most important message for Clive lay in this line: 'Little of India is now talked of. America is now the Object of all attention.' Ascribing the American colonial disturbances to the 'usual Dexterity & undermining intrest & Influence' of the French, Oglethorpe noted the creation of the American Stamp Act Congress of October 7, 1765, 'where under pretence of opposing the Act of Parliament Passed Last year for Laying a stamp duty on America, They have indeed disowned the Power of the English Parliament over them in matters of taxes & have stoped trade with England till that act be repealed'. There was cause for Oglethorpe to add: 'This occations all thought to be turned that way. The East Indias with all its wealth is not now the occupation of Government'; but he consolingly concluded: 'It matters not if you have but Strength to do your business.'[1]

Having written to Clive, Oglethorpe seems to have withdrawn into his Essex shell again, and for over a year there is no word from Cranham Hall. In August 1766 Pitt, now Earl of Chatham, formed a new ministry, succeeding the Marquis of Rockingham, and on February 6, 1767, Oglethorpe in London wrote to ask his advice as to what candidates he should support in the approaching parliamentary elections of 1768:

Were I not teased with applications not only for the Burough of Haslemire, but for some other Buroughs, and for the Counties of Surry, Sussex and Essex, where I have some little Interest, Your Lordship should not have been troubled with this, but that I would not engage the little Interest I have, till I know

[1] Oglethorpe to Lord Clive, Cranham Hall, Essex, Jan. 18, 1766, India Office, Miscellaneous, 808, Clive Papers: Home Series, ff. 267–9.

whom of the Candidates would be the most usefull to the Publick Good in the House of Commons, of which I know Your Lordship to be the best Judge; and in this I joine with the Opinion of the People and the Common Voice.

For notwithstanding the floods of impertinence and Nonsense vomited out by hireling Scriblers, some set on by the Envious, some by the Enemies of the Kingdom, the Opinion, and Affections of the best and most active part of the people, are greater to Your Lordship, than I ever knew it to any Man, it is founded on Reason, Gratitude, and Self Interest.

Common Sense is the Characteristick of the real Gentlemen and the middle people of England, all who have honesty & common Sense, are attached to you, because you saved them, and their Posterity. They feel the ill consequence of the prevalence of those who would not follow your Advice, and men of the best understanding know that the Safety of the Nation rests on you, as much as that of Thebes did on Epimenondas, whose Character of all the Antients seems most yours.[1]

Whether or not Chatham fell a victim to Oglethorpe's flattery and asked Oglethorpe to stand we know not, but the gentleman who was 'teased with applications' from Surrey, Sussex, Essex, and a few boroughs, began to cast longing eyes upon his old seat at Haslemere. Returning to his London house in Lower Grosvenor Street for the Christmas holidays of 1767,[2] Oglethorpe perfected his political plans. The veteran was intent on one more effort in the political arena. On February 27, 1768, Oglethorpe set out for Haslemere 'where he has been invited as a Candidate'. Accompanied by many friends, he 'was received with the utmost Joy'. His victorious opponent in 1754, Philip Carteret Webb, declined to stand again, and supported Oglethorpe and Johnson against Colonel Molyneaux and Peter Burrell, junior, son of James Oglethorpe's former colleague. Surely, as Americans have it, 'politics makes strange bed-fellows'! In the words of a press report, 'since the General's

[1] Oglethorpe to the Earl of Chatham, Lower Grosvenor Street, London, Feb. 6, 1767, Chatham Papers (P.R.O.), G.D. 8:51.
[2] London *Evening Post*, Dec. 19, 1767, p. 4.

Arrival the four Candidates met each other with great Civility; the Canvassing is carrying on with Decency, and they have jointly agreed, that the Company should retire from the Public Houses by Ten o'Clock at Night to prevent Disorders'. This plan succeeded, for another report noted that 'the uproars are over, and all goes on very quietly'. What a change from 1722! Polling began on March 16 and closed on the nineteenth. Peter Burrell having declined to stand, William Burrell was substituted. On the count Molyneaux and Burrell won by 22 votes, 71 to 49. As the former lived at the house of the Bailiff who announced the vote, that worthy official was promptly accused of 'partiality and taking bad votes'. Once again Oglethorpe threatened to contest the result before the House of Commons, but the verdict was impregnable, and Oglethorpe's parliamentary campaigning was for ever ended.[1]

With this defeat Oglethorpe returned to his rural solitude again. The public forgot him in their interest in John Wilkes and No. 45 of his *North Briton*. But if Oglethorpe was pessimistic about the political future of England, his own future at the age of 72 was just dawning in the first rays of Johnsonian splendour, which now rose over literary England to warm and irradiate James Oglethorpe's last two decades.

[1] London *Public Advertiser*, March 1, 1768, p. 2; March 5, 1768, p. 3; March 12, 1768, p. 3; March 23, 1768, p. 3; April 14, 1768, p. 4; *Gazetteer and New Daily Advertiser*, March 5, 1768, p. 2; *St. James's Chronicle*, March 24, 1768, p. 4; Swanton and Woods, *Bygone Haslemere*, pp. 200–1.

CHAPTER IX

OTIUM CUM DIGNITATE IN JOHNSON'S LONDON

WITH his final defeat at Haslemere in March 1768, Oglethorpe passed from that strenuous life which had engrossed his every attention for forty years. The strife of conquest was ended; the burden of imperialism had been lifted; even the bitterness of personalities and recrimination, of neglect and ridicule, of resentment and stubborn pride, had been assuaged by the healing hand of time; the mellow days of old friendships and old books had come.

For fifteen years after he retired from the political arena James Oglethorpe found contentment and pleasure in the society of the literary and artistic giants of that period in English life which has so properly been called the Age of Johnson—the good Doctor himself; James Boswell, his *fidus Achates*; Edmund Burke, M.P.; Dr. Oliver Goldsmith, exponent of both medical and dramatic science; David Garrick, who gave dignity and honour to the stage; and Sir Joshua Reynolds, the creator of beauty on canvas.

At first blush it may seem strange that a veteran warrior, a creator of empire, a lonely wanderer in distant climes, inured to hardships and accustomed to arms, should be at ease in the realm of arts and letters; but not without cause could James Boswell assert of him that 'this extraordinary person was as remarkable for his learning and taste, as for his other eminent qualities; and no man was more prompt, active, and generous, in encouraging merit'.[1] We must remember, moreover, that among his forebears was Owen Oglethorpe, President of Magdalen College, Oxford, and Vice-Chancellor of the University; that two distant cousins were Cambridge Fellows; that his grandfather and two elder brothers were Oxonians;

[1] Hill, *Boswell's Life of Johnson* (Powell revision), i. 128.

and that James Oglethorpe himself could proudly boast of that allegiance than which there is none higher in the halls of Academe, Eton and Oxford. He need not retire even before the great Cham himself, nor did he.

In 1733 Nathanael Johnson, charging his brother Samuel with an unfraternal attitude in some private matter, had said: 'I believe I shall go to Georgia in about a fortnight.'[1] Whether or not he did so is of no consequence here. Whether he met Oglethorpe at that time is an absorbing but, at least for the present, an unanswerable question. But whether James Oglethorpe met or heard of Samuel Johnson through his brother before 1738, the son of Corpus was one of the first in that year properly to appraise and welcome the son of Pembroke on the appearance of his poem, *London*.[2] As already a famous Briton, Oglethorpe proved a benefactor to the twenty-nine-year-old *inconnu*, who ever after acknowledged his obligation to his fellow Oxonian. Thus it was that two years before the birth of his future biographer, Boswell, the sage of Lichfield had been recognized by Oglethorpe, who, thirty years later, now drew himself into the circle of the *litterati*. If, as Boswell put it,

it is painful to think that he [Oglethorpe] had but too much reason to become cold and callous, and discontented with the world, from the neglect which he experienced of his publick and private worth, by those in whose power it was to gratify so gallant a veteran with marks of distinction—

then was it particularly appropriate that Oglethorpe should find an intellectual haven among such good companions.[3]

Three decades after, the episode with Johnson was repeated on the publication by a Scottish youth, named

---

[1] *Notes and Queries*, 1st series, xii. 266; Hill, *Boswell's Life of Johnson* (Powell revision), i. 90 note 3.

[2] Hill, *Boswell's Life of Johnson* (Powell revision), i. 127–8; Collins, A. S., *Authorship in the Days of Johnson* (London, 1927), p. 188. In 1738 Oglethorpe also subscribed ten guineas to the *History of England* by that eminent historian and Jacobite family friend, Thomas Carte. Nichols, John, *Illustrations of the Literary History of the Eighteenth Century* (8 vols., London, 1817–58), v. 166.   [3] Hill, *Boswell's Life of Johnson* (Powell revision), i. 128.

SAMUEL JOHNSON
from the painting by SIR JOSHUA REYNOLDS, 1778, in the Tate Gallery

James Boswell, of *An Account of Corsica*, a volume inspired by the Corsican patriot, General Pasquale de Paoli, to whom Boswell had been introduced by Jean-Jacques Rousseau, and who in 1769 made his permanent home in England, entering like Oglethorpe the Johnson circle. The work appeared in February 1768, two months before Oglethorpe lost the Haslemere election, and it was a propitious moment for both men when the elder introduced himself to the rising young Scot, who soon was sufficiently familiar to have both the General and Dr. Johnson to dinner.[1]

By April Oglethorpe was tendering advice, but the circumstances make the situation most interesting. In 1763 James Boswell had met a young Dutch maiden of great beauty, charm, and intellect, named Isabella van Serooskerken van Tuyll, but better known to literature and fame as Zélide. Enraptured by this brilliant and unconventional spirit, he promptly planned marriage, only to find his capricious idol in 1765 writing that she expected to marry François-Eugène Robert, Comte de Bellegarde, son of James Oglethorpe's sister Fanny, a young man who fondly expected to be the legatee of his Uncle James![2] We know not whether Oglethorpe's solicitude was for his nephew's success in romance or his new friend's literary career and future fame, but in April 1768 Boswell recorded, in a letter to his friend, the Rev. William J. Temple, that

Old General Oglethorpe, who has come to see me and is with

[1] Scott, G., and Pottle, F. A., editors, *The Private Papers of James Boswell... from Malahide Castle* (hereinafter cited as *Boswell Papers*, 18 vols., New York, 1928–34), i. 149; vi. 87; vii. 150, 187; Rogers, the Rev. Charles, editor, *Boswelliana: The Commonplace Book of James Boswell* (London, 1874), p. 62; Hill, *Boswell's Life of Johnson* (Powell revision), ii. 350, note 2.

[2] Scott and Pottle, *Boswell Papers*, ii. 106; Scott, Geoffrey, *The Portrait of Zélide* (London, 1925), pp. 17, 21–40, 48–52; Godet, Philippe, *Madame de Charrière et ses amis* (2 vols., Geneva, 1906), i. 54, 67–127, particularly p. 97; Godet, Philippe, editor, *Lettres de Belle de Zuylen (Madame de Charrière) à Constant d'Hermenches, 1760–1775* (Paris, 1909), pp. ix, note 1, 50, 57, 61–4, 69–70, 74, 80–1, 88, 112, 117, 153–4, 295, 326–30, 334, 336, 340, 342, 346, 348, 359.

me often, just on account of my book, bids me not marry till I have first put the Corsicans in a proper situation. You may make a fortune in the doing of it, said he; or, if you do not, you will have acquired such a character as will entitle you to any fortune.[1]

Whether or not owing to Oglethorpe's advice, by June discord had ended Boswell's friendship with the Belle de Zuylen who subsequently married Monsieur de Charrière and reigned for many years in the social and literary world of Madame de Staël, Benjamin Constant, Necker, and Sainte-Beuve.[2]

One of the surest antidotes to regret and unrequited love is professional success, and Boswell found it easy to forget Zélide in his growing reputation. By May 1768 he could write to Temple that 'I am really the *great man* now', for, through the patronage of Johnson and Oglethorpe, the literary world was knocking at his door.[3] Throughout 1768 Boswell's journal and notes in London reveal his close contact with the General, whose mind, according to one critic, was 'rich, but like an upholsterer's shop: carpets high up, glasses below, etc.'[4] To Boswell the old soldier had turned pragmatist and philosopher. In May he commented on conditions in London: 'The mob was now the best blood, being composed of old families sunk. Mortimers are sweeping the streets.' The next day Boswell found him 'tedious but instructive', so that, when he came a third time three days later, the Scot 'was too eager with the worthy General and raged on subjecting inferiours' in such a manner that he 'was

---

[1] Boswell to the Rev. W. J. Temple, London, April 26, 1768, Seccombe, Thomas, editor, *Letters of James Boswell to the Rev. W. J. Temple* (London, 1908), p. 119; Tinker, Chauncey B., editor, *Letters of James Boswell* (2 vols., Oxford, 1924), i. 154.

[2] Scott, *Portrait of Zélide*, p. 57; Godet, *Madame de Charrière et ses amis*, p. 170.

[3] Boswell to the Rev. W. J. Temple, London, May 14, 1768, Seccombe, *Letters of James Boswell to the Rev. W. J. Temple*, p. 121; Tinker, *Letters of James Boswell*, i. 160.

[4] Scott and Pottle, *Boswell Papers*, vii. 188.

sorry at opposing too much the worthy man, so full of age and spirit'.[1]

How full of spirit James Oglethorpe at 73 could be was amply and convincingly demonstrated in 1770. When in 1769 Sir Francis Bernard returned to England after his recall as Governor of Massachusetts, that most unpopular of colonial governors loudly continued to assert his autocratic and aristocratic snobbishness towards the colonists, only to find that there were certain Englishmen who refused to permit such expressions. A London letter of June 5, 1770, published in both the Boston *Gazette* and *Evening Post* of September 3, reported that

> Bernard was drove out of the Smyrna Coffee-House not many Days since, by General Oglethorpe, who told him he was a dirty, factious Scoundrel, who smelt cursed strong of the Hangman; that he had better leave the Room, as unworthy to mix with Gentlemen of Character, but that he would give him the Satisfaction of following him to the Door, had he any Thing to reply.—The Governor left the House like a guilty Coward.[2]

The years passed and Oglethorpe's friendships strengthened and widened. If the period to 1769 was one of introductions, the seventeen-seventies proved to be a period of fulfilment, the glorious decade of comradeship for one who was to survive most of his close associates. Possibly the year of his greatest influence was 1772. Although he retained the Cranham estate in Essex as a summer home, Oglethorpe was occupying a house in Lower Grosvenor Street, London, where he now was able to entertain, and be of service to, his friends Dr. Johnson, General Paoli, and Boswell,[3] the latter of whom noted that at Oglethorpe's 'we had many a valuable

---

[1] Ibid. 190-2.
[2] Boston *Evening Post*, Sept. 3, 1770, p. 3; *Gazette*, Sept. 3, 1770, p. 2. This story has been stoutly denied by the Bernard family historian (Higgins, Mrs. Napier, *The Bernards of Abington and Nether Winchendon: A Family History* (2 vols., London, 1903), ii. 216-17), but the consensus of historical opinion concerning Bernard's colonial career makes it not improbable.
[3] Scott and Pottle, *Boswell Papers*, ix. 51.

day'.[1] Boswell's papers reveal in amazing amplitude the sordid details of his own social lapses throughout the years, and it was largely due to the steadfast loyalty and encouragement of Oglethorpe, who often would call of a morning at eight, that the errant Scot managed to remain within the bounds of rectitude. Not the least effective means of aiding Boswell was to give him frequent invitations for dinner, where the daughters of Eve could not lead him astray, and where his bibulous nature might be curbed or at least concealed. Not the least important gathering at Oglethorpe's home, on Friday, April 10, 1772, inspired this note in Boswell's journal:

I dined at General Oglethorpe's, at his house in Lower Grosvenor Street. His Lady, whose fortune is his support while our court shamefully neglects him, was a good civil old Lady, with some affectation of wit, with which however she troubled us but little. Mr. Johnson and Dr. Goldsmith and nobody else were the company. I felt a completion of happiness. I just sat and hugged myself in my own mind. Here I am in London, at the house of General Oglethorpe who introduced himself to me just because I had distinguished myself, and here is Mr. Johnson whose character is so vast; here is Dr. Goldsmith so distinguished in literature. Words cannot describe our feelings. The finer parts are lost, as the down upon a plumb; the radiance of light cannot be painted.

It was at this meeting that Dr. Johnson's observation, that armorial bearings were as ancient as the Siege of Thebes, led Goldsmith to the question, 'if duelling was lawfull'.[2] This created the opening, first for Johnson and then for Oglethorpe. Boswell noted that 'the brave old General at once fired at this, and said that undoubtedly a man had a right to defend his honour', whereupon, after a further brief, timorous question by Goldsmith, the Thunderer held sway and philosophized. Johnson, however, soon threw the conversation back on Oglethorpe by

[1] Chapman, R. W., editor, *Boswell's Journal of the Tour to the Hebrides* (Oxford, 1924), p. 247 note.
[2] Boswell, in his *Life*, uses the phrase, 'consistent with moral duty'. Hill, *Boswell's Life of Johnson* (Powell revision), ii. 179.

persuading him to narrate his reminiscences of service under Prince Eugene of Savoy, in which he drew a plan of the siege of Belgrade on the tablecloth in wine. After he had concluded with the assertion that 'he neither believed nor disbelieved apparitions', the company forsook philosophy for Bacchus: 'We sat till past eight, only sipping a little wine; that is to say, the General and Goldsmith and I; for Mr. Johnson never tastes wine now, but drinks only lemonade. I had a full relish of life today. It was like being in London in the last age. I felt myself of some real personal consequence while I made one of such a company.'[1]

While Oglethorpe thus began what were to become annual reunions with Boswell, Johnson, and Goldsmith, he did not limit his friendship to conversational and gastronomic delicacies, nor did he restrict the circle of friends. When in 1737 Samuel Johnson, the schoolmaster of Edial, had come to London he had brought with him one of his pupils, named David Garrick, whose subsequent career in the art of the drama in every way proved as brilliant as his mentor's in letters.[2] Although neither his correspondence nor his biography indicates any friendship whatsoever with Oglethorpe,[3] the two were together at least once in their capacity of common friend to James Boswell. A week after the illustrious dinner-party described above, Boswell the barrister had a vital case in court and noted in his journal that 'General Oglethorpe, with the activity of a young Soldier, and the zeal of a warm friend, was with me this morning by eight o'clock', and subsequently attended the trial with Garrick, solely to encourage the Scot in his professional practice.[4]

The next year saw Oglethorpe's life and fondness for

[1] Scott and Pottle, *Boswell Papers*, ix. ii–iii, 68–73, 259; Hill, *Boswell's Life of Johnson* (Powell revision), ii. 179–83.
[2] Hill, *Boswell's Life of Johnson* (Powell revision), i. 97–103.
[3] Little, D. M., editor, *Pineapples of Finest Flavour; or, a Selection of unpublished Letters of D. Garrick* (Cambridge, Mass., 1930); Fitzgerald, Percy, *The Life of David Garrick* (2 vols., London, 1868).
[4] Scott and Pottle, *Boswell Papers*, ix. 78, 80.

298   JAMES EDWARD OGLETHORPE

Boswell continued on the same high plane. On April 4 the Scot, returning from a winter's legal practice in the north,

found him in his usual spirits. He had a Bible lying upon the table before him. Whenever I appeared, 'My dear Boswell', cried the fine old Gentleman, and prest me in his arms. I value his acquaintance very highly and it is the more pleasing to me that I owe it entirely to my own merit; for he came and introduced himself to me at my lodgings in half-moon street, piccadilly, the spring when my *Account of Corsica* came first out.[1]

Nine days later, on April 13, 1773, the group forgathered at the General's for a dinner which had become an annual event. Boswell, remembering that 'last year we had a noble day there, . . . was anxious a little lest this should fall far short; but it did not'.[2] While his beloved Georgia was passing through the first paroxysms of the American Revolution, Oglethorpe was thus entertaining Johnson and Boswell at dinner and listening to one, Dr. Oliver Goldsmith, a mutual friend, singing Tony Lumkin's song, 'The Three Jolly Pigeons', and the Irish air, 'Ah! Me! When shall I marry me?' written for Mrs. Bulkeley, in the role of Kate Hardcastle, in his new play, *She Stoops to Conquer*,[3] which had opened brilliantly on the same night in March on which had arrived a daughter in Boswell's family.[4] Two days after that dinner, this group met again, this time at General Paoli's house.[5]

As in 1738 Oglethorpe had sponsored Johnson, so after 1765 he had encouraged Goldsmith, calling on him in

---

[1] Ibid. vi. 87; Rogers, *Boswelliana*, p. 85.
[2] Scott and Pottle, *Boswell Papers*, vi. 113.
[3] The latter song was dropped when it was found that Mrs. Bulkeley could not sing. Scott and Pottle, *Boswell Papers*, vi. 118; ix. 109–10; Hill, *Boswell's Johnson* (Powell revision), ii. 217–19; Prior, James, *Life of Oliver Goldsmith, M.B.* (2 vols., London, 1837), ii. 380.
[4] Boswell to Oliver Goldsmith, Edinburgh, March 29, 1773, Adam, R. B., *Catalogue of the Adam Collection of Johnsoniana* (4 vols., London, 1930), i, *Letters of James Boswell*, p. 14.
[5] Forster, John, *Life and Times of Oliver Goldsmith* (2nd ed., 2 vols., London, 1854), ii. 391–2.

his chambers with Topham Beauclerk,[1] and, through Goldsmith, indulging his expression of the true meaning of the Greek word χάρις. Oglethorpe had been a director of the Westminster Hospital and the Children's Hospital; in 1750 he had been a guest at a dinner to the Board of Governors of Saint Bartholomew's Hospital,[2] and his humanitarian interests were well known. As one interested in medicine Goldsmith had offered to distribute such sums as might be sent him, and Oglethorpe contributed five pounds and a letter of strong commendation for such agencies of human welfare.[3] As an author Goldsmith was attacked in the London press, and here Oglethorpe suggested that, 'if a farm and a mere country scene will be a little refreshment from the smoke of London, we shall be glad of the happiness of seeing you at Cranham Hall'.[4] Thus it was that, both in Essex and in London, Goldsmith often had the pleasure of meeting his literary colleagues at Oglethorpe's bounteous table.[5]

Ten days after Goldsmith's introduction of his new play, Boswell took his friend Topham Beauclerk, a great-grandson of Charles II and Nell Gwynne, to see Oglethorpe, who treated his guests to 'fine sack', noted a marked physical resemblance of his guest to Charles II, and 'harangued on the mischief of enclosing, by depopulating'. Beauclerk, according to Boswell, 'was delighted. Said at my lodgings he had heard him called General Oglethorpe, but had no more idea 'twas that General, than that 'twas Julius Caesar'.[6] Although he might at times find Oglethorpe 'tedious', Boswell never declined an opportunity to see him, and on April 29 again set out

[1] Ibid. 163–5.
[2] London *General Advertiser*, July 6, 1750, p. 2; *Evening Post*, July 7, 1750, p. 1; *Whitehall Evening Post*, July 7, 1750, p. 2.
[3] Oglethorpe to Goldsmith, Cranham Hall, no date, Goldsmith, Oliver, *Miscellaneous Works* (4 vols., London, 1801), i. 95–6. See also the London *European Magazine*, xxiv. 260.
[4] Goldsmith, *Miscellaneous Works*, i. 95–6; Forster, *Life and Times of Oliver Goldsmith*, ii. 165; Prior, *Life of Oliver Goldsmith*, M.B., ii. 422–3.
[5] Prior, *Life of Oliver Goldsmith*, M.B., ii. 421–3, 452.
[6] Scott and Pottle, *Boswell Papers*, vi. 123.

on foot with Johnson bound for the General's home. In Berkeley Square they met Goldsmith and Sir Joshua Reynolds, who, in Boswell's words, 'told us they were at a loss where to go. "So", said I, "you took us as guides" ', to which the irrepressible Johnson added, 'I wondered, indeed, at their great civility.' These four celebrities, together with a Miss Lockwood, Bennet Langton, and Henry Thrale, husband of his more illustrious wife, Hester Lynch Salusbury Thrale, made up the company. Thrale was too quiet for the Doctor, who, five months later, during his tour to the Hebrides, told Boswell that 'he was angry at Thrale for sitting at General Oglethorpe's without speaking',[1] but the general conversation proved intellectual, covering such diverse topics as the edible quality of dogs as found in a custom of Otaheite or New Zealand,[2] the brilliant qualities of Goldsmith's new comedy, *She Stoops to Conquer*, and a critical, though heartily favourable, review of the dramatic art of David Garrick.[3]

Oglethorpe's hospitality proved to be popular, and, if the 'fine sack' which had been served to Boswell and Beauclerk had made an impression, his stock of 'rich Canary wine' was equally appreciated by the Scot, who indulged in a generous potation when he called on May 10 to bid the General farewell before returning to his native northern heath.[4] Despite Boswell's departure for Scotland Oglethorpe found much to do, for in June 1773, when Sir Joshua Reynolds set out to review the fleet with the King at Portsmouth, the artist dined *en route* at

[1] Chapman, *Boswell's Journal of the Tour to the Hebrides*, p. 345; Hill, *Boswell's Life of Johnson* (Powell revision), v. 277.

[2] This interest in Otaheite was occasioned to a great extent by the arrival in England during 1774 of Omai, a native brought over by Captain Furneaux, who had visited the South Sea Islands in 1772. Omai was returned to the South Seas by Captain Cook on his third voyage in 1777. Peake, R. B., *Memoirs of the Colman Family* (2 vols., London, 1841), i. 354–78.

[3] Scott and Pottle, *Boswell Papers*, vi. 126; Hill, *Boswell's Life of Johnson* (Powell revision), ii. 232–5.

[4] Scott and Pottle, *Boswell Papers*, vi. 140; Hill, *Boswell's Life of Johnson* (Powell revision), ii. 260.

Godalming, and mentions Oglethorpe in the same entry of his journal as 'at the George', Portsmouth.[1] The next eighteen months saw the death of Goldsmith, and Boswell absorbed in his own family and his law practice, conducting Johnson's journey to the Hebrides and the Western Isles of Scotland, where he gave Cocker's *Arithmetick* to the young lady of Anoch.[2] As a result, references to Oglethorpe's activities are correspondingly meagre. Despite his humanitarian interests, and although Goldsmith and Dr. J. C. Lettsom, later his physician, were charter founders, Oglethorpe is not listed as a founder of the Royal Humane Society in 1774.[3] In February Johnson wrote to his Edinburgh associate that Oglethorpe had called and 'was not unwelcome',[4] but Boswell was unaffected by this allusion until on June 20 he himself 'received a long letter from General Oglethorpe. It stirred my mind, revived my idea of my own consequence in London, and made me impatient to be there, and not lost in this provincial corner where I find nothing to engage me warmly'.[5] Despite a letter from Johnson which gave him 'the same sensation tonight as on hearing from General Oglethorpe: that it was hard that I should not be in London',[6] and much as he relished the General's communication, there is no record of a reply, and the months passed in silence with Boswell in Scotland and Johnson with the Thrales in Wales, meeting Paoli at Caernarvon.

On Tuesday, March 21, 1775, Boswell returned to

[1] Notebook of Sir Joshua Reynolds for 1773, Royal Academy of Arts; Leslie, C. R., and Taylor, T., *Life and Times of Sir Joshua Reynolds* (2 vols., London, 1865), ii. 27 note.
[2] See Johnson to Mrs. Thrale, Skie, Sept. 6, 1773, Hill, G. B., editor, *Letters of Samuel Johnson, LL.D.* (2 vols., Oxford, 1892), i. 243; and Hill, *Boswell's Life of Johnson* (Powell revision), v. 138 and note 2.
[3] Pettigrew, T. J., *Memoirs of J. C. Lettsom* (3 vols., London, 1817), i. 186–7.
[4] Johnson to Boswell, London, Feb. 7, 1774, Hill, *Boswell's Life of Johnson* (Powell revision), ii. 272.
[5] Scott and Pottle, *Boswell Papers*, ix. 124.
[6] Ibid. 128.

London, and the next Sunday, 'in the forenoon... found General Oglethorpe. He had Thuanus' history and Nelson's *Feasts and Fasts* lying on the table before him. He was reading Thuanus.[1] He received me with his usual cordiality, and we drank Chocolade. He told me that Basil Kennet was his Tutor and told him that a man who follows a learned profession, as a Lawyer, should have a common-place book; but a man who is only intended for a general scholar should not, as it hurts the memory'; with which sage observation Boswell agreed.[2]

Omitted in 1774, owing largely to Boswell's sojourn in Edinburgh, the annual April conclave was renewed on the tenth of that month. Nine days before Lexington and Concord, and only four months before his Georgia joined the other colonies in open rebellion against the Crown, James Oglethorpe was entertaining Boswell, Johnson, Bennet Langton, the Rev. Dr. Thomas Campbell, a touring cleric and *littérateur* from Ireland,[3] and a young relative of Mrs. Oglethorpe. Goldsmith had died the previous year, and although he noted that 'we had a good dinner and Sicilian wine as usual', Boswell sadly added, 'but I missed poor Goldsmith'. Dr. Johnson, as usual, had the floor, although before dinner Mrs. Oglethorpe, with amazing temerity, had 'plagued Mr. Johnson about his giving such a book as *Cocker's Arithmetick* to the young woman at Anoch. He said it was the only book he had. But I said, "How came you to buy it, to take it in a Post-chaise?" He said, "Sir, it is inexhaustible." ' If an arithmetic was inexhaustible, Johnson, despite Boswell's opinion that 'he was not much in the humour of talking', on this occasion, at least, likewise had that doubtful virtue, and he merrily held forth on suicide, on his failure at dancing, on the

---

[1] The edition was probably that of his friend, Thomas Carte, who had been editing the work during the period 1724–8, Carte MSS. (Bodleian Library, Oxford), ccxxv, ff. 131, 144–8. A new edition appeared in 1733, Carte MSS., ccxxvi, ff. 110–11.

[2] Scott and Pottle, *Boswell Papers*, x. 148–9.

[3] Hill, G. B., editor, *Johnsonian Miscellanies* (2 vols., Oxford, 1897), ii. 51–2.

Abyssinians, and then on the prospective reception of his works in America, expecting to be hanged in effigy. Finally he considered the happiness of man, particularly probing Pope's pessimistic proposition that 'man never *is*, but always *to be* blest'. Boswell having asked, 'Is a man never happy for the present?', the oracle replied, 'Never but when he is drunk'—and immediately turned to Oglethorpe, urging him to give the world his biography: 'I know no man whose Life would be more interesting. If I were furnished with materials, I should be very glad to write it.'[1] But the General, according to Dr. Campbell, 'excused himself, saying the life of a private man was not worthy public notice', and merely asked Boswell 'to bring him some good Almanack, that he might recollect dates, and seemed to excuse himself also on the article of incapacity'. The Scot now pleaded with him to 'furnish the skeleton' for 'Dr. Johnson would supply bones and sinew'; at which Oglethorpe was of the opinion that 'He would be a good Doctor who would do that'; whereupon Campbell said *he* was a good Doctor, at which Johnson 'laughed very heartily'.[2] Despite these pleasantries, Oglethorpe was adamant, and although Boswell himself in later years twice took copious notes from the General's own lips[3]—notes which have completely disappeared[4]—the world is the loser for his modesty and reserve.

On May 22, 1775, while the Continental Congress met in Philadelphia, Boswell again set out for Scotland,[5] and the summer, which saw the battle of Bunker Hill and the rise to supremacy in the American army of George Washington, passed in Britain with Johnson's strong protest against the colonists, entitled *Taxation no Tyranny*, and from Boswell an expression of sympathy, together

[1] Scott and Pottle, *Boswell Papers*, x. 202–3; Hill, *Boswell's Life of Johnson* (Powell revision), ii. 350–2.
[2] Hill, *Johnsonian Miscellanies*, ii. 51.
[3] Scott and Pottle, *Boswell Papers*, xiii. 233; xiv. 218.
[4] Ibid. xiii. 233 note 1; xiv. 218 note 1.
[5] Hill, *Boswell's Life of Johnson* (Powell revision), ii. 377.

with Oglethorpe's, for the colonial cause.[1] While the months passed in silence and the old friendship with Boswell and Johnson rested on faith, Oglethorpe continued his keen interest in the colonial situation in South Carolina and Georgia,[2] and his support was suspected in the publication, in the *London Magazine* for January 1776, of an impassioned appeal for the colonies, signed by the Reverend Dr. Zubly, pastor of the Independent Church, Savannah, Georgia, and a member of the Second Continental Congress.[3] The statement has been made that about this time Oglethorpe was offered command of the British expeditionary force, a post which he declined on being refused the power to treat with the colonists. Despite its use by three writers,[4] this story is unsupported by any evidence in the War Office records,[5] and Oglethorpe's well-known views on the colonial rights of Englishmen would hardly have recommended him to the authorities. This is clearly indicated by the fact that when, in April 1776, the composition of a proposed Commission for the Conciliation of America was announced, the name of James Oglethorpe, than whom no one was better qualified for the post, was missing.[6]

While Oglethorpe was thus interested in the American Revolution, Boswell was in Scotland welcoming a son and heir, Alexander, and Johnson was touring France with the Thrales. The autumn of 1775 was particularly lonely for the General. There was no correspondence

[1] Scott and Pottle, *Boswell Papers*, x. 229.
[2] *Calendar of Home Office Papers*, George III, iv. 448; C.O. 5:134 (P.R.O.), No. 15dd, Extracts of Letters from the American Rebellion, Mr. De Brahm to General Oglethorpe, Charles Town, South Carolina, Oct. 17, 1775.
[3] *London Magazine*, xlv. 35-9.
[4] McCall, H., *History of Georgia* (2 vols., Boston, 1818), i. 325; Holmes, Abiel, *The Annals of America* (2 vols., Cambridge, Massachusetts, 1829), ii. 235; Bancroft, George, *History of the United States* (1st ed., 5 vols., London, 1848), iii. 166.
[5] All the pertinent War Office records, army lists, letter-books, and orders to American expeditionary forces have been consulted, and Oglethorpe's name never appears. See especially W.O. 65, now Index 5604, List of General and Staff Officers in North America.
[6] London *Public Advertiser*, April 17, 1776, p. 2.

with either Boswell or Johnson;[1] Goldsmith was no more; and Eleanor Oglethorpe de Mézières, last of his family, had died at the age of 91.[2] Finding few of his associates in London, he retired for a while to Cranham Hall, where the state of affairs in Britain led him, in a letter to a friend, to attack 'the Landed and Church Interest throughout the Kingdom' for 'designing to plunder the rich and imprison and starve the poor'.[3]

On February 19, 1776, Boswell recorded in his Edinburgh journal his vexation that, owing to his all-absorbing law practice, he had not once written to the old soldier since he left London in the previous May.[4] Four days later he was suddenly moved to write to Oglethorpe, General Paoli, and other London associates, men whose quality led him to note with pride that 'my mind was enlivened by such variety of connections'.[5] London again called him, and, after a brief visit with Johnson at Ashbourne,[6] he returned to the metropolis on March 29,[7] but only twice did he see Oglethorpe. Not until April 21 did he call and breakfast with him on 'Chocolade, etc. Was in high spirits'.[8] A fortnight later, on May 8, Boswell, Johnson, and Dr. Markham of Whitechapel, who had achieved some current fame in his work for London

---

[1] See Tyson, M., and Guppy, H., editors, *The French Journals of Mrs. Thrale and Doctor Johnson* (Manchester, 1932); and Hill, *Boswell's Life of Johnson* (Powell revision), ii. 389–401.

[2] Toynbee, Mrs. Paget, *Lettres de la Marquise du Deffand à Horace Walpole* (*1776–1780*), iii. 119. One of her daughters became the Princess de Ligne; another Abbess of Panthemont; and a son became Bishop of Urés. See Toynbee, Mrs. Paget, *Lettres de la Marquise du Deffand à Horace Walpole* (*1776–1780*), i. 304–5; ii. 399–404; vii. 312; Coke, Lady Mary, *Letters and Journals* (4 vols., Edinburgh, 1889–96), iii. 401; Add. MSS. (British Museum), 34636, Stuart Papers, ff. 47–8, Henri de Béthisy de Mézières, Bishop of Urés, to Henry, Cardinal Duke of York, Brussels, April 4, 1794.

[3] Oglethorpe to George Scott, Cranham Hall, Essex, Sept. 12, 1775; Nichols, *Illustrations of the Literary History of the Eighteenth Century*, iv. 522–3.

[4] Scott and Pottle, *Boswell Papers*, xi. 101.

[5] Ibid. 103.

[6] Hill, *Boswell's Life of Johnson* (Powell revision), ii. 473–5; iii. 1.

[7] Ibid. iii. 5–7; Scott and Pottle, *Boswell Papers*, xi. 209.

[8] Scott and Pottle, *Boswell Papers*, xi. 262.

hospitals, dined at Oglethorpe's house.[1] Pressed concerning the qualities of his late wife, Johnson deemed her as good as General Oglethorpe's, whereupon the latter, 'now thirty years married, professed subjection, and was glorying in it'.[2] As Boswell later put it, 'the uncommon vivacity of General Oglethorpe's mind and variety of knowledge, having sometimes made his conversation seem too desultory', Johnson, walking with the Scot to Charing Cross, observed, 'General Oglethorpe never compleats what he has to say',[3] a failing of which the learned and weighty Doctor seems never to have been guilty! But if such was his estimate of the General, Mrs. Oglethorpe proved more caustic concerning Johnson himself, when she said of his rolling before speaking, 'He's charging himself.'[4]

As was well known, London was always delightful to 'Bozzy', but stern Scottish legal duty called, and he shortly returned to Edinburgh, where his Journal during 1776 and much of 1777 yields nothing about Oglethorpe.[5] The absence of Boswell, and Johnson's attentions to the creation of his masterpiece, *The Lives of the Poets*, seem to have turned the founder of Georgia and author of *The Sailor's Advocate* more fully towards Edmund Burke and the American Revolution, and Granville Sharp and the impressment evil. When in 1775 Johnson had upheld the right of Parliament to tax the colonies, an impetuous Irishman named Edmund Burke had pleaded the cause

[1] This was Johnson's second of three consecutive dinner engagements. See Johnson to Mrs. Thrale, London, May 6, 1776, Hill, *Letters of Samuel Johnson, LL.D.*, i. 393; Piozzi, H. L., editor, *Letters to and from the late Samuel Johnson, LL.D.* (2 vols. in 1, Dublin, 1788), i. 225. Mrs. Thrale noted the event in a reply written on that very day, Mrs. Thrale to Johnson, Bath, May 8, 1776, Letters from H. L. Thrale to S. Johnson (Thraliana in the John Rylands Library, Manchester), i, No. liv.
[2] Scott and Pottle, *Boswell Papers*, xi. 272–3; Hill, *Boswell's Life of Johnson* (Powell revision), iii. 52.
[3] Hill, *Boswell's Life of Johnson* (Powell revision), iii. 56–7; Scott and Pottle, *Boswell Papers*, xi. 273.
[4] Scott and Pottle, *Boswell Papers*, xi. 273.
[5] Ibid. xii, *passim*, especially p. 238.

of conciliation.[1] Some time in May 1777 Oglethorpe expressed his hearty approval of Burke's courageous stand, for on June 2, 'from the Planting of Georgia, 45', as he put it, the latter replied in gratitude for what he called 'the most flattering mark of honour which I have ever received'. Expressing a sincere wish for the welfare of Georgia as 'once more a free & flourishing member of a free & flourishing empire', Burke feared that 'too much to hope from a country which seems to have forgot the true source of its dignity & greatness'; but he concluded with the hope that 'better things I trust await your honourable age & their generous youth. I am happy in having known & admired the last of the English legislators in America.'[2]

The American Revolution, together with the age-old problem of slavery, was now the means of an introduction to one of the most interesting men of the late eighteenth and early nineteenth centuries, Granville Sharp, whose grandfather, like Oglethorpe's, was a Yorkshireman. The climax of Oglethorpe's efforts on behalf of the Americans came between June 1777 and April 1778. While the scene was being set for Ticonderoga, James Oglethorpe joined Sharp in a futile attempt to win Chatham and the Duke of Richmond to a plan for peace without victory, wherein the colonists, instead of being completely alienated, would receive their full and ancient rights as Englishmen. The fact that the effort failed in no wise dims the glory of Oglethorpe's efforts,[3] nor did it affect his sentiments, for a year later he expressed before a group of learned and distinguished Englishmen his disgust at the official British attitude toward the colonists.[4]

[1] London *Saint James's Chronicle*, Oct. 10, 1775, p. 4.
[2] Edmund Burke to Oglethorpe, Westminster, June 2, 1777, Fitzwilliam, Charles William, Earl, and Bourke, Sir R., editors, *Correspondence of the Right Honourable Edmund Burke* (4 vols., London, 1844), ii. 157–8.
[3] Hoare, Prince, *Memoirs of Granville Sharp, Esq.* (London, 1820), p. 179; Lascelles, E. C. P., *Granville Sharp and the Freedom of Slaves in England* (London, 1928), p. 45. There is nothing relating to Oglethorpe in the Sharp papers, owned by Miss Olive Lloyd-Baker at Hardwicke Court, Gloucester, other than what is printed in these two volumes.
[4] Scott and Pottle, *Boswell Papers*, xiii. 222.

The American Revolution had not, however, been the sole meeting-ground for Oglethorpe and Sharp. Granville Sharp in 1772, by the use of the Habeas Corpus plea, had compelled Lord Mansfield in the Somerset case to acknowledge as a legal precept that a man of colour was a free man on English soil. Subsequently he had worked with Dr. Fothergill, Oglethorpe's own physician, in the anti-slavery and anti-slave-trade crusades.[1] In 1775 he resigned his post in the Ordnance Office, and when impoverished thereby was supported by his two brothers, in his biographer's words, 'until an accidental acquaintance with General Oglethorpe . . . restored him to independence'.[2] By the autumn of 1776 his *Law of Retribution* had been brought to the attention of Oglethorpe, who, in much the same manner as with Boswell, introduced himself to the author, this time in a learned letter on retribution in ancient and modern times.[3] Delighted with this attention, Sharp sought his judgement as to his new tracts on human rights, drawing Oglethorpe over to the ethical consideration of slavery.[4] This gave the founder of Georgia the opportunity he so long had craved to make it clear that slavery in Georgia had been due to the machinations of the British Government, not the Trustees. In an illustrious letter Oglethorpe, after inviting Sharp to visit him in Grosvenor Street, launched into an historical survey of slavery in Rome, Greece, Persia, Africa, under Goths and Moors, in Spain and Portugal, and even under Louis XIV in France; and quoted Tacitus and 'Sir Walter Rawleigh'. All the spirit of the prison-investigation half a century before lay in his last lines:

[1] Dr. J. Johnston Abraham to the author, London, Sept. 12, 1933; Sept. 27, 1933. For Fothergill's labours with Benjamin Franklin for mediation and peace between England and America see Donne, W. B., editor, *Correspondence of King George the Third with Lord North from 1768 to 1783* (2 vols., London, 1867), i. 203–4.

[2] Hoare, *Memoirs of Granville Sharp, Esq.*, pp. 91, 105–7, 126–8.

[3] Oglethorpe to Sharp, Cranham Hall, Essex, Sept. 1776, Hoare, *Memoirs of Granville Sharp, Esq.*, pp. 155–6.

[4] Sharp to Oglethorpe, Wicken Park, Sept. 27, 1776, Hoare, *Memoirs of Granville Sharp, Esq.*, pp. 156–7.

'I am exceedingly glad that you have entered the lists in opposition to these horrors. It is a proper time to bring these abominable abuses under consideration.'[1]

Sharp, with the aid of William Wilberforce and Thomas Buxton, guided the anti-slavery movement to a logical and successful conclusion some years after Oglethorpe's death, but this initial meeting on the subject of slavery led the two men to a natural consideration of impressment and a reconsideration of Oglethorpe's publication of 1728, *The Sailor's Advocate*. It has been asserted that brutality was the chief evil in the British Navy; that Oglethorpe's labours for prison reform 'will show how callous our ancestors could be in the early eighteenth century'; and finally that 'the Navy produced no General Oglethorpe'.[2] The last statement may be literally correct, but Oglethorpe had done a great deal for the British sailor in his *Sailor's Advocate* of 1728. In 1759 Francis Barber, Dr. Johnson's negro servant, had been impressed as a sailor, and Tobias Smollett had sought the influence and aid of John Wilkes to secure his freedom.[3] Whether or not this influenced them almost two decades later, Sharp and Oglethorpe in 1776 planned a deliberate attack on press-gangs and the impressment evil, which, owing to the incipient war with France, was again beginning to flourish. Throughout December of that year Sharp organized his ideas while Oglethorpe delved into Bracton's *De Legibus*.[4] The immediate result was a bulky document entitled 'General Oglethorpe's Memorandums on the Illegality of pressing Seamen, with Remarks by G. S.';[5] their position was publicly announced in 1777 in a new and enlarged edition of *The Sailor's Advocate*, of

---

[1] Oglethorpe to Sharp, Cranham Hall, Oct. 13, 1776, Hoare, *Memoirs of Granville Sharp, Esq.*, pp. 157–9.
[2] Hannay, D., *A Short History of the Royal Navy, 1217–1815* (2 vols., London, 1898–1909), i. 82.
[3] Tobias Smollett to John Wilkes, Chelsea, March 16, 1759, *MSS. of the late Colonel Macaulay* (H.M.C. Reports, iii), p. 400.
[4] Hoare, *Memoirs of Granville Sharp, Esq.*, pp. 159–64.
[5] Ibid., p. 164.

which Oglethorpe's share was the complaint, on professional grounds, that commissioned officers, often of the best old English families, were compelled to serve as policemen, warders, and jailers.[1] If the adoption of Oglethorpe's colonial policy might have prevented the American Revolution, can it not with equal justice be claimed that, had Britain accepted his views on impressment, the War of 1812 might in large part have been avoided? Johnson had given Sharp and Oglethorpe his whole-hearted support in their campaign against slavery, but he could not reach an accord with them in their hostility to the press-gang,[2] and their appeal failed to rouse public interest. Even less successful was Sharp's attack on duelling, for, despite his citation of Blackstone, Chief Justice Holt, and the Levitical Law,[3] he received no aid from General Oglethorpe, who stoutly supported this 'ancient and honourable' mode of settling disputes.[4]

The summer of 1777 thus passed, and in September Johnson persuaded Boswell to join him for a few weeks at Ashbourne, where the latter confided to his master his project for a *History of the Civil War in Great-Britain in 1745 and 1746*, a volume which, although it never appeared, held peculiar possibilities. Johnson was ever a Jacobite at heart, and shortly after this expressed his belief that, 'if England were fairly polled, the present king would be sent away tonight, and his adherents hanged tomorrow'.[5] But what would Boswell the Scot have said of Oglethorpe's part in the 'Forty-five? He had in the old veteran an unrivalled source, but their very intimacy might have been an embarrassment. Perhaps it was as well that the project never materialized.

---

[1] Lascelles, *Granville Sharp and the Freedom of Slaves in England*, pp. 88–94.
[2] Ibid., p. 92.
[3] Sharp, G., *A Tract on Duelling* (1st ed., London, 1773; 2nd ed. with additions, London, 1790).
[4] Lascelles, *Granville Sharp and the Freedom of Slaves in England*, p. 95.
[5] Scott and Pottle, *Boswell Papers*, xii. 33–4; Hill, *Boswell's Life of Johnson* (Powell revision), iii. 135, 155–7, 162, 493–4, 499–500.

Boswell returned to Scotland at the end of September,[1] and again the friendship with Oglethorpe survived without aid of written lines.[2] Spring brought the usual yearnings for London and his friends, and on March 18, 1778, the barrister from Edinburgh arrived to enjoy the company of his comrades, the Thrales, Johnson, General Paoli, Reynolds, Garrick, Hannah More, and, of course, Oglethorpe,[3] whom he saw at least twice. On April 14 the annual reunion at the latter's home was attended by Johnson, Boswell, Langton, and General Paoli. Oglethorpe and the learned Doctor were in fine fettle, the former declaiming against luxury,[4] whereupon Johnson, with the wisdom gained by experience, affirmed that 'every state of society is as luxurious as it can be. Men always take the best they can get.' Oglethorpe, however, proved idealistic, claiming that 'the best depends much upon ourselves; and if we can be as well satisfied with plain things, we are in the wrong to accustom our palates to what is high-seasoned and expensive'; and lauded the luxury of the Numidian as portrayed by Addison in his *Cato*. The conversation now turned to governments and their powers, Johnson abhorring government by despots and therefore approving that of Britain,'which is founded on the parliament, then is in the privy council, then in the King'. Boswell having claimed that it was far easier, however, to destroy the power of a single despot than to curb the people, Oglethorpe sprang to the attack against the bureaucratic usurpation of powers, adding, 'don't you think that we see too much of that in our own Parliament?'[5] Ten days later Boswell, dining at General Paoli's, saw Oglethorpe once again.[6] The next month

[1] Hill, *Boswell's Life of Johnson* (Powell revision), iii. 208.
[2] Boswell's Journal in Edinburgh, Sept. 1777 to March 1778, Scott and Pottle, *Boswell Papers*, xiii. 67–99.
[3] Hill, *Boswell's Life of Johnson* (Powell revision), iii. 222–82, *passim*.
[4] Cf. Stephen, Leslie, *English Literature and Society in the Eighteenth Century* (Ford Lectures for 1903, London, 1904), pp. 200–1.
[5] Hill, *Boswell's Life of Johnson* (Powell revision), iii. 282–3.
[6] Boswell to the Rev. Dr. Percy, London, April 25, 1778, Hill, *Boswell's Life of Johnson* (Powell revision), iii. 278.

he returned to Edinburgh,[1] but before his departure was responsible for the introduction of Oglethorpe to the publishing side of the literary life.

Boswell's *Account of Corsica* had been published by Edward and Charles Dilly, whose partner in the ownership of the *London Magazine* Boswell had become in 1769. Now, a decade later, the Scot introduced to them James Oglethorpe, who also became a partner in that literary enterprise. The General as early as 1768 had given support and encouragement to a political writer named Sayre[2] and was interested in other scribes as well.[3] Thus he turned to literature when on January 20, 1779, the death of Garrick removed the one slender thread which linked him to English dramatic art.[4] When, then, in December 1778 Charles Dilly wrote to Boswell that they all hoped to see him again the next spring, 'when the Venerable Genl. Oglethorpe will no doubt again honour us with his company',[5] the invitation could not be resisted, and March 15, 1779, found the erstwhile Edinburgh lawyer again in the midst of his friends.[6] For two months he revelled in their company, and Oglethorpe, now 82, was as lively as ever, missing few if any of the gatherings. The annual dinner at his home on April 12 with the usual quartet—Johnson, Boswell, Langton, and Paoli—where, among other subjects, they analysed the House of Commons and the population problem in Britain,[7] was overshadowed the next evening by a remark-

[1] Hill, *Boswell's Life of Johnson* (Powell revision), iii. 359–72; Scott and Pottle, *Boswell Papers*, xiii. 123–203.

[2] Esther de Berdt to Joseph Reed, London, May 20, 1768, Matthews, Albert, editor, 'The Letters of Dennys de Berdt, 1757–1770', *Transactions of the Colonial Society of Massachusetts*, xiii (Boston, 1912), 293–461, especially p. 438 and note.

[3] See Taylor, John, *Records of My Life* (2 vols., London, 1832), ii. 326–7.

[4] London *Evening Post*, Jan. 21, 1779, p. 3. There is nothing in the various biographies of the Colmans, Jordan, Kemble, Siddons, or Inchbald to indicate Oglethorpe's interest in the theatre.

[5] Charles Dilly to Boswell, London, Dec. 15, 1778, Scott and Pottle, *Boswell Papers*, xiii. 308–9.

[6] Hill, *Boswell's Life of Johnson* (Powell revision), iii. 373.

[7] Scott and Pottle, *Boswell Papers*, xiii. 219.

JAMES BOSWELL
from the portrait by SIR JOSHUA REYNOLDS, 1786, in the
National Portrait Gallery

able gathering of the British aristocracy of the mind at the home of Sir Joshua Reynolds. Here at one time were Reynolds, Boswell, Burke, Langton, Lord Portmore, the Marquis of Lothian, and Oglethorpe. The conversation seems to have turned markedly towards the American Revolution, for 'Oglethorpe harangued on the constitutional mode of redress; angry at our warmth against the colonies when we were affraid of Spain and France; like a Man affraid to fight who comes home and kicks his servant'. It is no wonder that Boswell added, 'Talked till I was exhausted.'[1] But the exhaustion wore off, and a week later he 'supt with Oglethorpe'.[2] Although there is no immediate evidence to sustain such a theory, it seems that Boswell must have made overtures concerning a biography of the General, for on April 24 he recorded in his Journal that he called 'and took down notes of his life. . . . Home and wrote Oglethorpe's notes of his life hitherto ommitted.' The tragedy of these lines lies in Professor Pottle's terse sentence: 'These notes have disappeared.'[3] That evening 'Oglethorpe called in coach and carried me to Beauclerk's. Lady Di[ana] not with us. Johnson, Sir Joshua, Langton, Jones, Stevens, Paradise and Dr. Higgins were the company', which discussed the attack on the late David Garrick by that brilliant if notorious journalist John Wilkes.[4]

Boswell spent the summer as usual in Scotland, and there is no evidence that he saw Oglethorpe while in London that October.[5] During the period from November 1779 to March 1781, Oglethorpe was singularly alone, a solitude emphasized by certain cardinal facts. In 1764 Sir Joshua Reynolds and Johnson had founded a social and intellectual organization which at Garrick's funeral in January 1779 had become known for the first time

[1] Ibid. 222.
[2] Ibid. 231. [3] Ibid. 233 note 1.
[4] Ibid. 233. Boswell does not mention Oglethorpe's presence, in his lengthy account of the affair in the *Life*. Hill, *Boswell's Life of Johnson* (Powell revision), iii. 386–90.
[5] For this period see Scott and Pottle, *Boswell Papers*, xiv. 1–165.

as the Literary Club. Six of Oglethorpe's friends were charter members: Reynolds, Johnson, Burke, Beauclerk, Langton, and Goldsmith. Before Oglethorpe's death Bishop Percy, George Colman the actor, Garrick, Boswell, Charles James Fox, Edward Gibbon, Adam Smith, Sheridan, Malone, and Dr. Burney were admitted; but Oglethorpe is never mentioned. On Garrick's death they decided to wait a year before electing his successor, but applications were made.[1] Did Oglethorpe, who is not mentioned as attending his funeral,[2] apply and receive the snub of rejection? No evidence is known, but it is singular that Oglethorpe never entered Brooks's, the membership of which included Garrick, Walpole, Gibbon, Sheridan, Burke, and Reynolds.[3] And although he was acquainted with the Thrales, his name does not appear in the table of characters and virtues of the various members of the Streatham circle.

But one or two events stand out. Beauclerk died in 1780; Boswell was in Edinburgh; and Johnson was absorbed in completing his volume on the poets; but in February and March 1780 Oglethorpe sat five times to Reynolds for his portrait. On seeing it in April, Oglethorpe must have found something to criticize, for on May 25 he had one further appointment.[4] If friends were distant and few, Oglethorpe found a full measure of

[1] Malone MSS. (Bodleian Library, Oxford), 36. Fragments relating to the Literary Club, 1764–1811; *Annals of the Club, 1764–1914* (London, 1914), pp. 1, 6, 11, 15, 43; Peake, *Memoirs of the Colman Family*, i. 333.
[2] London *Evening Post*, Feb. 2, 1779, p. 3; *Morning Chronicle*, Feb. 3, 1779, p. 4. Johnson, Burke, Gibbon, Reynolds, Langton, and George Colman rode in the funeral procession.
[3] Williamson, V. A., editor, *Memorial of Brooks's* (London, 1907), pp. 19–33.
[4] Note Book of Sir Joshua Reynolds for 1780, Royal Academy of Arts. The dates are Feb. 29, March 2, 7, 10, 17, and May 25. The first four were at 12 o'clock noon, that of March 17 no hour stated, the last at ten o'clock in the morning. Reynolds painted this for the Duke of Rutland's collection at Belvoir Castle, where it was subsequently destroyed in a fire. The Duke paid £52 10s. for the portrait. *MSS. of the Duke of Rutland* (H.M.C. Reports, xii), iv. 245, 350. See also Cotton, William, *Sir Joshua Reynolds and his Works* (London, 1856), p. 149.

interest in the London life about him. When, in June, London was shaken by those riots which bear the name of Lord George Gordon, the rabid Protestant opponent of the then pending bill for removing Catholic disabilities, Dr. Johnson's vivid description of the scenes thus enacted led Mrs. Thrale to tender an urgent invitation for him to fly for safety to Bath.[1] But Oglethorpe had to see it all. As the learned Mrs. Montagu, 'Queen of the Blues', wrote to William Weller Pepys: 'General Oglethorpe in the restlessness of youth determined to go down to Westminster Hall this morning and engaged Montagu [her nephew and adopted son] to go with him in apprehension of mob and violence, I am uneasy at this expedition and wish *both* these *young* gentlemen safe at home.'[2] Oglethorpe survived the mob, and in January 1781 renewed his acquaintance with the Wesleys by going to hear Charles Wesley's two sons give a violin recital at their father's home, where the founder of Georgia again met the illustrious John Wesley 'and kissed his hand in token of respect'.[3]

At last on March 19, 1781, after an absence from London of almost a year and a half, Boswell arrived for a visit of over two months. Five days later he dined at General Paoli's, visited Thrale who was in his final illness, and then called on Oglethorpe, who to him 'seemed much older and visibly failing or decayed. But perhaps I was mistaken', he added.[4] Whether because of this or owing to two years' neglect, the errant Scot this time saw much of the aged veteran, who, as was to be expected, now acquired some popularity in London.[5] Despite the

---

[1] Johnson to Mrs. Thrale, London, June 9, 1780; Mrs. Thrale to Johnson, Bath, 3 a.m., June 10, 1780, Piozzi, *Letters to and from the late Samuel Johnson, LL.D.*, ii. 100-6.
[2] Blunt, Reginald, editor, *Mrs. Montagu, 'Queen of the Blues': Her Letters and Friendships from 1762 to 1800* (2 vols., London, 1923), ii. 89-90. See also de Castro, J. P., *The Gordon Riots* (London, 1926).
[3] Curnock, *John Wesley's Journal*, vi. 303 and note.
[4] Scott and Pottle, *Boswell Papers*, xiv. 173.
[5] Ibid. 188, 208, 210, 212, 218, 233.

death of Thrale on April 4,[1] Oglethorpe continued his social rounds and introduced Boswell to new friends.[2] On May 2 he attended a dinner as the latter's guest, together with Reynolds, the Right Reverend Thomas Barnard, Bishop of Killaloe, David Boswell, the host's brother, and others; and two days later Oglethorpe and James Boswell visited the House of Lords, where they met Lord Mansfield and Edmund Burke.[3] On May 9 Boswell again 'sat a while with General Oglethorpe and took notes of his life', which, like an earlier set, have disappeared;[4] and on May 29 he paid his farewell visit before leaving again for the north. What was said we know not, but Boswell must have been fatigued, for, as he noted in his Journal, he 'drank canary, which acted as a restorative'.[5] On June 2 he went to Scotland, where, owing largely to the death of his father the next summer, he remained until March 1783.[6]

The silence of these twenty-one months was broken rarely. There is no allusion to Oglethorpe in Johnson's diary for 1782,[7] and the only item of Boswell's journal likely to interest Oglethorpe was this note of December 1, 1781: 'I restrained my joy on Lord Cornwallis's surrender, not to give offence. But it inspirited me, in so much that though for some time I have been quite lazy in the morning, relaxed and unable to rise, I this day sprung up.'[8] If Boswell restrained his joy 'not to give offence', Oglethorpe, during these later years of the Revolution the senior General in the British Army, had been even more careful, maintaining a discreet silence in public. Only when Lord North's ministry was threatened and

[1] Scott and Pottle, *Boswell Papers*, xiv. 190.
[2] Hill, *Boswell's Life of Johnson* (Powell revision), iv. 112.
[3] Scott and Pottle, *Boswell Papers*, xiv. 212.
[4] Ibid. xiv. 218 and note 1; xv. v.
[5] Ibid. xiv. 233.
[6] Hill, *Boswell's Life of Johnson* (Powell revision), iv. 118, 153-4, 163-4, 500; Scott and Pottle, *Boswell Papers*, xv. 3-165, especially pp. 120-1.
[7] Johnson Diary of 1782, owned by Miss E. G. Dowdell of Edinburgh. This statement is made on the authority of L. F. Powell, Esq.
[8] Scott and Pottle, *Boswell Papers*, xv. 45.

finally fell in March 1782, did Oglethorpe break into print with one letter supporting North's ministry as the best available, and two others, publicly addressed to that Lord, the one in his favour, the other lauding him for his policy of taxation for revenue only, and proposing a licence-tax on public houses and taverns, but not on theatres.[1]

Early in 1783 one important friendship was established. Although he mentioned Oglethorpe not once in his journals from 1771 to 1782,[2] Horace Walpole, who in 1746 had called him a bully and rejoiced in his court martial, was now evidently his good friend. Walpole's notebook records that on February 16, 1783, Oglethorpe told him that

In Ch[arles the] 2ds time they called Philosophers Foolosophers. That one day before the King of Prussia, Voltaire having attacked Marshal Keith pretty freely, the King s[ai]d. 'Marshal, do you say nothing in return?' 'Oh', s[ai]d the Marshal, 'I have nothing to say to him but that he is a Poet in history and an historian in Poetry.'[3]

Whether it was the whimsical appeal of Oglethorpe's conversation or for some other cause, Walpole waxed quite enthusiastic about his friend. Two days after the conversation reported above he wrote to the Countess of Upper Ossory that

I am a Methusalem from the scenes I have seen; yet, t'other day, I made an acquaintance with one a little my senior; yet we are to be very intimate for a long time for my new friend is but ninety-four. It is General Oglethorpe; I had not seen him these twenty years, yet knew him instantly. As he did not recollect me, I told him it was a proof how little he was altered and I how much. I said I would visit him; he replied, 'No, no;

---

[1] London *Public Advertiser*, March 14, 1782, p. 2; March 19, 1782, p. 1; March 22, 1782, pp. 1-2.

[2] Steuart, A. F., editor, *The Last Journals of Horace Walpole during the Reign of George III from 1771-1783* (2 vols., London, 1910). See especially vol. ii. 476-533.

[3] Lewis, W. S., editor, *A Note Book of Horace Walpole* (New York, 1927), p. 48.

I can walk better than you; I will come to you'. He is alert, upright, has his eyes, ears, and memory fresh. If you want any particulars of the last century, I can procure them.[1]

Boswell's visit to London in the spring of 1783 coincided with Johnson's grave illness,[2] and the latter's irritability was evident when the Scot, having visited Oglethorpe on the second day after his arrival in order to invite him to Johnson's, informed the Doctor of his act. The sick man's 'anger suddenly kindled, and he said with vehemence, "Did you not tell him not to come? Am I to be *hunted* in this manner?"' To which poor Boswell could merely reply that he, of all persons, could not forbid the General's advent. That evening Oglethorpe came and the change in Johnson's demeanour was marked. He 'attended him in the parlour, and was as courteous as ever'. After discussing the literature which at the time absorbed him, Oglethorpe adverted to the present state of the House of Commons which, he said, 'has usurped the power of the nation's money, and used it tyrannically. Government is now carried on by corrupt influence, instead of the inherent right in the King'. Johnson now did a *volte-face*. The day before he had rejoiced that 'this Hanoverian Family is Isolée here'.[3] Now, seeing his friend returning in old age to the Jacobite doctrine of divine right, Johnson himself temporarily forsook his strong Jacobite prejudices which in 1764 had so shocked Rousseau,[4] and, ascribing the current disturbance to 'the want of inherent right in the King', solemnly affirmed that 'what we did at the Revolution was necessary'; to which the staunch old scion of the Oglethorpes of Yorkshire, with great and

---

[1] Horace Walpole to the Countess of Upper Ossory, Berkeley Square, London, Feb. 18, 1783, Toynbee, Mrs. Paget, *Letters of Horace Walpole*, xii. 406.

[2] For Johnson's views on his serious illness see an unpublished letter to his friend, Robert Chambers, in India, from Bolt Court, Fleet Street, London, April 19, 1783. Johnsonian collection of R. B. Adam, Photo-print copy in the Bodleian Library, Oxford.

[3] Scott and Pottle, *Boswell Papers*, xv. 172–3.

[4] Ibid. iv. 109.

simple dignity, replied: 'My Father did not think it necessary.'[1]

Despite his age, Oglethorpe continued to move among his friends and their friends, both at his and their homes and at the Club, where, the day after this discussion, his presence caused Boswell to feel that 'Time was borne up on a thousand wings'.[2] At this time also Granville Sharp called to report his latest efforts in the movement against African slavery,[3] and cemented those relations which in later years were to reap him no mean reward.[4] Soon after this, Oglethorpe put in a good word for the Edinburgh barrister to his friend the Lord Chief Justice, Lord Mansfield,[5] and later the Scot called on the General with his friend William Johnston Temple, grandfather of a recent Archbishop of Canterbury and great-grandfather of the present Archbishop of York. On May 8 Temple noted 'a visit to General Oglethorpe, a surprising character at his age. What he said of the present state of our country, not to the purpose; though near 90 quoted several of the Latin poets.'[6] Exactly three weeks later Boswell took leave of Johnson, and the next day, despite his 'anxious apprehensions' at parting with the Doctor for so long a time, set out for Scotland.[7]

The years were passing, but Boswell's apprehensions were not being justified when Johnson wrote to him in March 1784 to report progress in recovery and joy at

[1] Ibid. xv. 177-8; Hill, *Boswell's Life of Johnson* (Powell revision), iv. 163-4, 170-1.
[2] Scott and Pottle, *Boswell Papers*, xv. 179.
[3] Hoare, *Memoirs of Granville Sharp, Esq.*, p. 236.
[4] Mrs. James Oglethorpe, on her death in 1787, bequeathed the manor of Fairstead in Essex to Sharp with a recommendation to settle it in his lifetime to charitable uses after his death, leaving the appropriation to his own direction and choice. But it reverted to the Oglethorpe family heirs. Hoare, *Memoirs of Granville Sharp, Esq.*, pp. 384-5, 392 note.
[5] Scott and Pottle, *Boswell Papers*, xv. 183, 194.
[6] Bettany, Lewis, editor, *Diaries of William Johnston Temple, 1780-1796* (Oxford, 1929), pp. 29, 38; Scott and Pottle, *Boswell Papers*, xv. 213.
[7] Hill, *Boswell's Life of Johnson* (Powell revision), iv. 224-6; Scott and Pottle, *Boswell Papers*, xv. 235, 239-40.

the former's imminent return to London.¹ On May 5 the devoted Scot arrived and, after a brief visit during which he and Oglethorpe met at the Dilly bookshop, carried the greatly improved Johnson off to Oxford.² Oglethorpe, meanwhile, had found new interests, and his last two years proved as vigorous as any since the 'Forty-five. In February 1784 he again attended a concert at the home of Charles Wesley, renewing his friendship with the brothers,[3] and about this time entered the feminine literary circles known as the Georgian Ladies' Clubs.[4] In a playful letter of 1782, Oglethorpe at 86 had essayed the role of dress-reformer to Mrs. Montagu,[5] at whose home two years later Dr. Charles Burney, the father of Fanny, Madame D'Arblay, met 'the antique General Oglethorpe' who 'was pointed out to him by Mr. Walpole for a man nearly in his hundredth year; an assertion that, though exaggerated, easily gained credit, from his gaunt figure and appearance'. Walpole, intent on having Fanny Burney observe this rare specimen of humanity, deliberately put Oglethorpe on exhibition for her at Mrs. Montagu's home. Fanny left no record of the occasion in her own diary,[6] but in the memoir of her father called the General

pleasing, well bred, and gentle. . . . At the side of General Oglethorpe, Mr. Walpole, though much past seventy, had almost the look, and had quite the air of enjoyment of a man who was yet almost young: and so skeleton-like was the

---

[1] Hill, *Boswell's Life of Johnson* (Powell revision), iv. 264–5, 527–8.
[2] Ibid. 271–311, 494.
[3] Curnock, *John Wesley's Journal*, vi. 474.
[4] This statement is based on the authority of Dr. Hubert Hall. There is no allusion to Oglethorpe before his death in the correspondence of Mrs. Elizabeth Carter with Miss Catherine Talbot, 1741–70, Mrs. Vesey, 1763–87, and Mrs. Montagu, 1755–1800: Pennington, Montagu, editor, *Memoirs of the Life of Mrs. Elizabeth Carter* (2 vols., London, 1808), i. 467–9; Pennington, Montagu, editor, *Letters of Mrs. Elizabeth Carter to Mrs. Montagu, between the Years 1755 and 1800* (3 vols., London, 1817), *passim*.
[5] Oglethorpe to Mrs. Montagu, 'Written in a very clear firm hand', Blunt, *Mrs. Montagu, 'Queen of the Blues'*, ii. 194.
[6] *Diary and Letters of Madame D'Arblay* (7 vols., London, 1842), i–ii.

General's meagre form, that, by the same species of comparison, Mr. Walpole almost appeared, and again, almost seemed to think himself, if not absolutely fat, at least not despoiled of his *embonpoint*.[1]

But the most important of Oglethorpe's later associates was the poetess Hannah More, who in 1784, at the age of 39, was quite enamoured of her 88-year-old 'new admirer', with whom she flirted 'prodigiously', and who, as she wrote to her sister, was

the finest figure you ever saw. He perfectly realizes all my ideas of Nestor. His literature is great, his knowledge of the world extensive, and his faculties as bright as ever; he is one of the three persons still living who were mentioned by Pope. . . . He was the intimate friend of Southern, the tragic poet, and of all the wits of that time. He is perhaps the oldest man of a *gentleman* living. . . . He is quite a preux chevalier, heroic, romantic, and full of the old gallantry.[2]

Having been introduced by Miss Reynolds, Sir Joshua's niece, Hannah More had known the other members of the Johnson circle since 1773 but did not meet Oglethorpe until the spring of 1784.[3] Her cultural contacts were such that it is not strange that in her presence Oglethorpe discussed politics with Edmund Burke, who thought him the most extraordinary man of whom he had ever read, 'for that he had founded the province of Georgia; had absolutely called it into existence, and had lived to see it severed from the empire which created it, and become an independent state'.[4] As she informed a friend, Hannah More's refusal to read the old romances evoked regret from Oglethorpe, who assured her that 'it was the only way to acquire *noble sentiments*'. She maintained that she must have '*men and women*' with whom she could feel affections and interests in common, and whose stories, however romantic, 'contained *probable* adventure and

[1] D'Arblay, Mme, *Memoirs of Dr. Burney* (3 vols., London, 1832), ii. 273–4.
[2] Roberts, William, *Memoirs of the Life of Mrs. Hannah More* (2 vols., London, 1836), i. 256.
[3] Ibid. i. 33–249, *passim*.
[4] Ibid. 287.

possible perfection'.[1] Despite their intellectual disagreement, or perhaps because of its stimulus, they remained warm friends, and as late as 1785 Hannah More wrote to her sister that 'I am just going to flirt a couple of hours with my beau, General Oglethorpe'.[2] But Hannah More was not the sole attraction. Mary Hamilton recorded her presence on May 18, 1784, at the home of Mrs. Agmondesham Vezey, the 'Blue-stocking of Mayfair', where she met 'a select party' including Horace Walpole, Mrs. Garrick, Burke, Miss Hannah More, and 'Genl *Oglethorpe* who in his 97th Year retains his *faculties*, is very active & walks some miles every day, goes with his Waistcoat almost entirely unbuttoned in ye midst of Winter'.[3]

Oglethorpe's winter activities indicated the sportsman, and such he was. In his youth he had shot snipe in Conduit Mead, now Conduit Street and Bond Street,[4] and had practised archery 'in the neighbourhood of London';[5] and in 1782, when the Finsbury Archers had the use of the Artillery grounds, he was elected an honorary member of the Royal Toxophilite Society of London.[6] When, on May 26, 1784, this body besought the Honourable Artillery Company to grant them permission to shoot on the Artillery grounds, the petition bore, among the names of its signers, that of James Edward Oglethorpe.[7]

While Oglethorpe was thus intent on sport and society, Johnson had been enjoying what was to prove his last visit to Oxford. For a full fortnight he revelled in those

[1] Gaussen, A. C. C., *A Later Pepys: Correspondence of Sir William Weller Pepys* (2 vols., London, 1904), ii. 244, 246 note; Roberts, *Memoirs of the Life of Mrs. Hannah More*, i. 272.

[2] Roberts, *Memoirs of the Life of Mrs. Hannah More*, i. 320.

[3] His age, of course, was only 87, but the record was notable even at that figure. Anson, E. and F., *Mary Hamilton* (London, 1925), p. 185.

[4] London *Morning Post*, July 5, 1785, p. 2; *Public Advertiser*, July 5, 1785, p. 3; *Whitehall Evening Post*, July 5, 1785, p. 2.

[5] Add. MSS. (British Museum), 29791, W. Latham's Anecdotes of Archery, f. 28.

[6] *A History of the Royal Toxophilite Society* (1st ed., Taunton, 1867), p. 14; 2nd ed. (Taunton, 1870), p. 202.

[7] Raikes, G. A., *History of the Honourable Artillery Company* (2 vols., London, 1878–9), ii. 104.

honours which meant so much to this son of Pembroke, but if the heart and mind and spirit were the gainers, his body paid the penalty. The recovery of May had been deceptive and incomplete; the peace and rest and quiet which London might have given him was broken in July by Mrs. Thrale's confession of her matrimonial intentions with regard to Signor Piozzi; and it was completely shattered at the end of the month by her marriage. By November Johnson, bereft of the devotion of Mrs. Thrale, had very faint hopes of recovery; and on December 13, 1784, died one who not unjustly has been called 'the most abnormally English creature God ever made',[1] one of the last of James Oglethorpe's friends of many years.[2] And yet, despite their friendship, it is an amazing fact that Oglethorpe not only was not an executor,[3] not only received nothing in Johnson's will,[4] but in no record of the event is mentioned as having been a pall-bearer, having participated in the funeral procession, or having attended the ceremonies on December 20, in Westminster Abbey.[5]

James Oglethorpe's last months were unmarked by any indication of an imminent decline in health. From February 16 to 19, 1785, he attended the four days' sale of Johnson's library at Christie's; and, if the portrait of him conning the catalogue may be construed as presaging that famous poem, *The Last Leaf on the Tree*, written over half a century later by an American poet, Dr. Oliver

[1] Dr. G. M. Trevelyan in Turberville, A. S., editor, *Johnson's England* (2 vols., Oxford, 1933), i. 6.
[2] Hill, *Boswell's Life of Johnson* (Powell revision), iv. 283-311, 417.
[3] 'Sir Joshua Reynolds, Sir John Hawkins and Dr. Scott of the Commons', London *Public Advertiser*, Dec. 14, 1784, p. 2.
[4] London *General Advertiser*, Dec. 24, 1784, p. 2; *Public Advertiser*, Dec. 25, 1784, p. 3; Hill, *Boswell's Life of Johnson* (Powell revision), iv. 402-4, 440-5.
[5] London *Public Advertiser*, Dec. 21, 1784, p. 4; Dec. 23, 1784, p. 3; Dec. 30, 1784, p. 3; *Annals of the Club*, p. 28; Baring, Mrs. Henry, editor, *Diary of the Right Honourable William Windham* (London, 1866), p. 35; Broaden, James, *Memoirs of the Life of John Philip Kemble, Esq.* (2 vols., London, 1825), i. 228-9; Colman, George, junior, *Random Records* (2 vols., London, 1830), ii. 272-3.

Wendell Holmes,[1] his mind showed no diminution in the expression of his literary tastes: he purchased some early editions of the classics, *The Acts and Deeds of Sir William Wallace*, 'the learned Mrs. Carter's *Epictetus*, and three portraits, one of them of Mrs. Montagu'.[2] At this sale he proved an object of veneration to the youthful Samuel Rogers, who ever after recalled that, 'at the sale of Dr. Johnson's books, I met General Oglethorpe, then very, very old, the flesh of his face looking like parchment. He amused us youngsters by talking of the alterations that had been made in London and of the great additions it had received within his recollection.'[3]

In April Horace Walpole enthusiastically wrote to his friend, Sir Horace Mann, that Oglethorpe 'has the activity of youth when compared to me. His eyes, ears,

[1]
My grandmamma has said—
Poor old lady, she is dead
    Long ago—
That he had a Roman nose,
And his cheek was like a rose
    In the snow.

But now his nose is thin
And it rests upon his chin
    Like a staff,
And a crook is in his back
And a melancholy crack
    In his laugh.

I know it is a sin
For me to sit and grin
    At him here;
But the old three-corned hat,
And the breeches, and all that,
    Are so queer.

Carman, Bliss, *The Oxford Book of American Verse* (New York, 1927), pp. 149–51.

[2] Roberts, S. C., *An Eighteenth Century Gentleman and Other Essays* (Cambridge, 1930), pp. 47, 59. Oglethorpe spent £2 17s. 6d., buying five lots on February 16, two lots on February 18, and one lot on February 19. His own copy of the sale catalogue is now in Yale University Library, see Newton, A. Edward, editor, *Sale Catalogue of Dr. Johnson's Library* (Philadelphia, 1925), and Hill, *Boswell's Life of Johnson* (Powell revision), iv, pp. 444–5.

[3] Dyce, the Rev. A., editor, *Recollections of the Table-Talk of Samuel Rogers* (New Southgate, 1887), p. 10; Roberts, R. E., *Samuel Rogers and his Circle* (London, 1910), p. 3.

JAMES EDWARD OGLETHORPE
aged 88, at the sale of the Library of Dr. Johnson, from
the pen-and-ink sketch by S. IRELAND, 1785

articulation, limbs, and memory would suit a boy, if a boy could recollect a century backwards. His teeth are gone; he is a shadow, and a wrinkled one; but his spirits and his spirit are in full bloom; two years and a half ago he challenged a neighbouring gentleman for trespassing on his manor.'[1]

In a contemporary collection of anecdotes concerning illustrious Britons, it was recorded of Oglethorpe that, 'as soon as he gets out of bed he throws himself upon the Floor, & exercises his Limbs for some time'.[2] Such activity at 88 is not incredible in the light of this letter of May 14 from Jonathan Williams, junior, to his Philadelphia friend, Benjamin Franklin, once the colonial agent for Georgia:

I dined yesterday at Mr. Paradise's and was very much surprised at the activity & lively conversation of an old military man. He danced about the Room with gaiety, kissed & said pretty things to all the Ladies, & seemed to feel all he said as much as any young man could do. He put me in mind of your *cribbidge* old Lady when he talked of being an ensign in the Guards in Queen Anns reign. This youthful old gentleman was General Oglethorpe whom I believe you know. He spoke of you with the strongest marks of esteem.[3]

For two years he had heard nothing of Boswell, who on May 22 suddenly 'sent word to General Oglethorpe I'd dine with him if at home, and was made welcome'. The Scot took along his younger brother, David, who 'was very well received'. Although there were some others present, including 'Col. Johnson (irish) from America' and 'Mr. Baillie (scotch) from India', Boswell's 'spirits sank as Oglethorpe talked it almost all himself'.[4]

[1] Horace Walpole to Sir Horace Mann, Berkeley Square, London, April 8, 1785, Toynbee, Mrs. Paget, *Letters of Horace Walpole*, xiii. 259.
[2] Add. MSS. (British Museum), 18559, Note Book of the Rev. Sir Richard Kaye, Bart., Rector of Kirkby, Notts., and Dean of Lincoln (in 22 vols.), x, Anecdotes of the Nobility and Distinguished Persons of England, f. 55 verso.
[3] Jonathan Williams, junior, to Benjamin Franklin, London, May 14, 1785, Franklin Papers (American Philosophical Society, Philadelphia), xxxviii, f. 154. [4] Scott and Pottle, *Boswell Papers*, xvi. 94.

But if the critical Scotsman was disappointed in his old friend, Oglethorpe's greatest triumph of spirit, mind, and body was yet to come. On June 1, 1785, to the horror of much of the British press, John Adams had been received by King George III as the first Minister to the Court of Saint James's from the new United States of America.[1] Within three days after that auspicious event, James Edward Oglethorpe, who, as the *Gentleman's Magazine* affirmed, had

> ... founded Georgia, gave it laws and trade,
> He saw it flourish, and he saw it fade,[2]

called, at the age of 88, on the new Minister, who later described him as 'very polite and complimentary'. Oglethorpe 'had come to pay his respects to the first American Ambassador and his family, whom he was very glad to see in England; expressed a great esteem and regard for America, much regret at the misunderstanding between the two countries, and was very happy to have lived to see the termination of it'. Adams, fully cognizant of the unique significance of this occasion, returned the visit and enjoyed a conversation of over two hours' duration with the old hero.[3]

Within the next three weeks Oglethorpe fell ill, but the air was full of Warren Hastings and India, of ignominy in America and revolutionary rumblings in France, and not a word of his illness appeared in the press.[4] On June 30 he was dead and of no further interest to one like Walpole, who could write thus of Samuel Johnson: 'How little will Dr. Johnson be remembered when confounded with the masses of authors of his own calibre!'[5] The

---

[1] London *Public Advertiser*, June 2, 1785, p. 3; June 7, 1785, p. 3; June 11, 1785, p. 2. [2] *Gentleman's Magazine*, lv. 573.

[3] John Adams to Abiel Holmes, Quincy, Massachusetts, Nov. 14, 1807, Holmes, *The Annals of America*, ii. 530, note xii.

[4] The following London journals have been thoroughly examined for June 1785: London *Public Advertiser*; *General Evening Post*; *Whitehall Evening Post*; *Morning Post*; *Morning Herald*; *Morning Chronicle*; *General Advertiser*; *St. James's Chronicle*; *London Chronicle*; and *The Gazetteer*.

[5] Horace Walpole to the Countess of Upper Ossory, Strawberry Hill, July 9, 1785, Toynbee, Mrs. Paget, *The Letters of Horace Walpole*, xiii. 290.

silence was profound. The British press emphasized the novelty of his great age, which was usually exaggerated,[1] and noted that by his death 'the Administration have a regiment to give away'.[2] Only the *Public Advertiser* paid tribute to him as 'not only an instance of longevity, but of every civil and military virtue'.[3] The American press was not much better.[4] His 'friends' were worst of all.

In 1774, on the death of Goldsmith, Boswell had made the statement that 'the death of one friend endears to us still more those who survive';[5] and nine years later, in 1783, the Scotsman, in *A Letter to the People of Scotland, on the Present State of the Nation*, had proudly acclaimed 'my intimacy with the excellent and much honoured General Oglethorpe, who himself settled one of the American Colonies, and still lives with all his faculties and all his benevolence in full vigour'.[6] But his journal for June 30, 1785, reads merely: 'Long with Malone. Not well at all.'[7] Not until eight years later, when in London on August 10, 1793, did Boswell 'reflect how sadly London was changed to me of late: no General Paoli—no Sir Joshua Reynolds—no Sir John Pringle—no Squire Godfrey Bosville—no General Oglethorpe'.[8]

Forgotten by all the others, Oglethorpe was sincerely mourned by two of the feminine intellectuals of the day. On September 9, 1785, in the midst of much news and

[1] e.g. London *General Evening Post*, July 2, 1785, p. 4; *Morning Chronicle*, July 2, 1785, p. 3; *Morning Herald*, July 2, 1785, p. 3; *Morning Post*, July 2, 1785, p. 2; *Public Advertiser*, July 2, 1785, pp. 3–4; *St. James's Chronicle*, July 2, 1785, p. 4; *Whitehall Evening Post*, July 2, 1785, p. 3.
[2] London *Public Advertiser*, July 6, 1785, p. 4.
[3] Ibid., July 19, 1785, p. 4.
[4] e.g. Philadelphia *Pennsylvania Journal*, Sept. 7, 1785, p. 3; *Packet and Daily Advertiser*, Sept. 7, 1785, p. 2; Sept. 8, 1785, p. 2; Trenton *New Jersey Gazette*, Sept. 19, 1785, p. 2.
[5] Boswell to [Bennet Langton?], Edinburgh, April 10, 1774, Add. MSS. (British Museum), 38510, f. 54; Tinker, *Letters of James Boswell*, i. 197–200.
[6] Boswell, James, *A Letter to the People of Scotland, on the Present State of the Nation* (1st ed., Edinburgh, 1783), pp. 5–6; 2nd ed. (London, 1784), p. 5.
[7] Scott and Pottle, *Boswell Papers*, xvi. 103. See also Wraxall, Sir N. W., Bart., *Posthumous Memoirs of his own Time* (3 vols., London, 1836), i. 323–57.
[8] Scott and Pottle, *Boswell Papers*, xviii. 198.

gossip, Mrs. Montagu wrote to Mrs. Carter: 'I was very sorry to part with my old Love the General, and heartily pity Mrs. Oglethorpe'.[1] Two weeks later 'the learned Mrs. Carter' fully concurred in her friend's sentiments:

It is no wonder your spirits should be so much depressed by the loss of an old and valuable friend. You have my most sincere congratulations, that you are in possession of the best of consolations under such a misfortune, in the conviction that he not only lived, but left this world with such dispositions as were the best qualifications for the happiness of a better. I quite grieve for poor Mrs. Oglethorpe. The good old General and she seemed to be so happy, and to have such a cordial affection for each other, that the separation must be very grievous.[2]

The rest is silence;[3] and yet the death of James Oglethorpe on June 30, 1785, removed a man who had touched life at many points, and was just coming into his own, a fine character who, like Abou ben Adhem, 'loved his fellow-men', a rare soul of whom Austin Dobson justly avowed: 'He prosecuted Philanthropy in

---

[1] Mrs. Montagu to Mrs. Carter, Sandelford [near Newbury, Berkshire], Sept. 9, 1785, Blunt, *Mrs. Montagu, 'Queen of the Blues'*, ii. 193.

[2] Mrs. Carter to Mrs. Montagu, Deal, Sept. 22, 1785, Pennington, *Letters of Mrs. Elizabeth Carter to Mrs. Montagu*, iii. 252. Mrs. James Oglethorpe died at Cranham Hall, Essex, on Oct. 26, 1787, at the age of 74. London *Public Advertiser*, Nov. 5, 1787, p. 4; *Whitehall Evening Post*, Nov. 6, 1787, p. 3.

[3] Within six months of Oglethorpe's death, his two French nephews made overtures to claim any lands he might still have owned in Georgia. The Chevalier de Mézières, Eleanor's son, as heir, persuaded Thomas Jefferson, as American Minister to France, to consult Vergennes at Versailles, Adams in London, and the Governor and Congressional Delegates of Georgia, as to the availability of Oglethorpe's Georgia property, while Fanny's son, the Marquis de Bellegarde, approached Adams in London through Granville Sharp, and finally addressed President Washington, who, on Jan. 15, 1790, expressed his regret that he 'never was so happy as to have any personal acquaintance with' Oglethorpe, but was certain Georgia in the Revolution would have protected, not confiscated any property its founder might still have held there. See Washington, H. A., editor, *Writings of Thomas Jefferson* (9 vols., New York, 1854), i. 499–502; ix. 235–8; Adams, C. F., editor, *Works of John Adams* (10 vols., Boston, 1856), viii. 365; and Sparks, Jared, editor, *Writings of George Washington* (12 vols., Boston, 1837–46), x. 76–7.

the spirit of a Paladin, rejoicing in the obstacles, the encounters, the nights *sub Jove frigido*.'[1]

Thus closed a career which had been full of promise and replete with achievement; a career ushered in as a phoenix upon the smouldering embers of the Jacobite ruins of 1688, nurtured on Jacobite precepts and aspirations, exposed to treasonable temptations, evolved in Georgian parliaments, developed in humanitarian movements, and brought to maturity in the expansion of the British Empire beyond the seas: the career of an imperial philanthropist. Nor was that all. For forty years after he left his beloved Georgia, James Oglethorpe was at home among an illustrious company, a fellowship dispersed only by death, a group one of the last survivors of which was Oglethorpe himself. He dared to argue with Johnson; he pitied Boswell in his moral lapses; he debated the politics of the American Revolution with Burke; he sustained Goldsmith in adversity and acclaimed him in achievement; and he joyously and wholeheartedly applauded Garrick and Reynolds in their respective arts.

In his delightful autobiography, Edward Bok tells the story of his grandfather, who created a garden isle out of a barren rock in the North Sea, five miles from the coast of Holland. Here, while the father laboured, a courageous Dutch mother reared thirteen children. One day, when they had grown to man's and woman's estate, the mother called them together and told them the story of their father's successful struggle on 'The Island of Nightingales'. 'And now', she said, 'as you go out into the world I want each of you to take with you the spirit of your father's work, and each in your own way and place, to do as he has done: make you the world a bit more beautiful and better because you have been in it. That is your mother's message to you.'

If on these pages is found a true record of his active life; if, though imperious, hasty, irascible, and tactless, as at

[1] Dobson, *A Paladin of Philanthropy*, pp. 12, 31.

times he admittedly was, the soul of that man be understood; if, finally and above all, he did aught to procure and protect a nobler England and a greater Empire—then has James Edward Oglethorpe, imperial idealist, merited the fame he has attained, for his labours have made the world 'a bit more beautiful and better'.

INDEX

The abbreviation O. is used for Oglethorpe.

'A. B.', 236.
A Brief Account of the Causes that have retarded the Progress of the Colony of Georgia in America, 212.
A Discourse concerning the designed establishment of a New Colony to the South of Carolina, the most delightful country in the Universe, 114.
A Letter to the People of Scotland on the Present State of the Nation, 327.
A New and Accurate Account of the Provinces of South Carolina and Georgia, 121, 121[8], 122.
A State of the Province of Georgia, 213.
A True and Historical Narrative of the Colony of Georgia in America, 213.
Aberdeen, 265.
Abou ben Adhem, 328.
Abraham, Heights of, 280; Plain of, 245.
Abyssinians, 303.
Acolf, 2.
Acton, William, 93–5.
Aculf, 2.
Acwulf, 2.
Adams, E. D., 110.
Adams, John, 102, 326, 328[3].
Addison, Joseph, 110, 311.
Admiralty, British, 129, 230, 233, 239.
Africa, 308.
'Ah! Me! When shall I marry me?', 298.
Ailesbury, Thomas Bruce, 2nd Earl of, 22, 37, 40–1; quoted, 77.
Alberoni, Giulio, Cardinal, 77.
Albuquerque, 119.
Aldborough, the ship, 144.
Alexander, Prince of Württemberg, 67[5].
d'Allone, Abel Tassin, secretary to Queen Mary, 36, 36[3], 112, 112[1]; his bequest, 112, 115, 122, 124.
Altamaha river, 114–15, 157, 169, 173, 190, 204–5.
Amatis brothers, the, 136.
Amelia Island, 232.
American Revolution, the, 298, 302–4, 306–8, 310, 313, 316.
Amesbury, 31.
Amherst, Jeffrey, Baron, 113, 285.
An Account of Corsica, 292–4, 298, 312.
An Account Showing the Progress of the Colony of Georgia in America from its First Establishment, 213.
An Essay on Plantations, 121.
An Historical Proof of Spain's Title to Georgia, 245.
An Impartial Account of the Late Expedition against St. Augustine, 252.
An Impartial Inquiry into the State and Utility of the Province of Georgia, 212.
An Ode to James Oglethorpe, Esq., 225, 225[7].
Anabaptists from Saxony, 168.
Anglicans in Georgia, 129, 139, 159–61, 218.
Anglo-Spanish Boundary Commission, 201–3, 224–6.
Ann, the frigate, 130.
Anne, Princess, afterw. Queen of England, 29, 30; as Queen, 50, 53–4, 56, 58–9, 69–70, 256, 325; death, 64, 70.
Anoch, the young lady of, 301–2.
Anti-slave-trade crusade, 308.
Anti-slavery crusade, 308.
Antigua, 228.
Arabin, Lt.-Col., 269.
d'Arblay, Fanny Burney, Madame, 320–1.
Archer, Henry, M.P., 226.
Argyll, Fort, 136.
Argyll, House of, 17.
Arithmetick, Cocker's, 301–2.
Armada, Spanish, 9–10, 10[1].
Army, British, James Oglethorpe and, 58, 67, 259–69, 280.
Arran, Earl of, 126.
Arredondo, Antonio de, 175–6, 204, 245.
Arthur, Sir George C. A., 24[1].
Ashbourne, 305.
Ashton, John, 37.
Asiento, the, 223.
'Association', Yorkshire, 260.
Athenian democracy, 104.
Athens, 66.
Atkinson, C. T., 24[1].
Atlantis, Lost, 284[1].
Atterbury, Francis, 65, 85–6.
Ausführliche Nachricht, 140.
Austen, Jane, 63.
Austria, House of, 240.
Austrians, 68.
d'Autremont, Marquis, 76.
Avignon, 76.
Azilia, Margravate of, 114, 119, 122, 132.

Bacchus, 297.
Bahamas, 228.
Baillie, Mr., 325.
Balfour, Arthur James, 1st Earl of, 100–1.
Bali, 284[1].
Bambridge, Warden Thomas, 91–4.
Bank of England, 125.
Bar-le-Duc, 76–7.

INDEX

Barbadoes, 228.
Barber, Francis, 309.
Barclay, Sir George, 43.
Barnard, Thomas, Bishop of Killaloe, 316.
Barnwell, Col. John, 114, 157.
Bartholomew Fair, Indians at, 145.
Bastille, the, 44.
Bateman, William, 143[1].
Bath, 30, 30[1], 281, 315.
Beauclerk, Lady Diana, 313.
Beauclerk, Topham, 271, 299–300, 313–14.
Beaufain, Berenger de, 249.
Beaufort, South Carolina, 132, 249.
Beer, George Louis, 136.
Belcher, Jonathan, Gov. of Massachusetts, 127–8, 135, 232.
Belgrade, battle of, 68, 297.
Belle de Zuylen, the, 294.
Bellegarde, François-Eugène Robert, Comte de, 293, 328[3].
— Jean François de, Marquis des Marches, 76.
Bellingham, Thomas, 35.
Belvoir Castle, 314[4].
Bengal, 288.
Benson, Arthur, 59.
Berkeley, George, Irish cleric, 70, 123–5.
Berlin, 283.
Bermuda, 123, 228.
Bernard, Sir Francis, 295.
Bersompierre, Marquis de, 77.
Berwick, James Fitz-James, Duke of, 43.
Bethesda Orphanage, 221–2.
Beverston Castle, 11.
Bienville, Jean Baptiste Le Moyne, Sieur de, 113, 183.
Bills of credit, 177–8.
Birch, Dr. Thomas, 252, 267–9.
Bisset, Rev. John, 265.
Blackstone, Sir William, 310.
Bladen, Col. Martin, M.P., 226, 240.
Blandford, the ship, 207, 230.
Blathwayte, William, 27.
Blenheim, 51.
Bloody Marsh, battle of, 226, 244–5.
Blundell, Lord, 81.
Board of Trade, 116, 157, 183, 232, 273.
Bohemia, 170.
Bois de Boulogne, 71.
Bok, Edward, 329.
Bolingbroke, Henry St. John, 1st Viscount, 71.
Bolton, H. L., 114, 119, 173, 175.
Bolzius, Pastor J. M., 134, 139–40, 158, 168, 251.
Bosomworth, Thomas, 261[4].
Boston *Evening Post*, 295.
— *Gazette*, 295.
— *Post*, 245.

Bosville, Squire Godfrey, 327.
Boswell, Alexander, 304.
— David, 316.
— James, relates story of O. and Prince of Württemberg, 67–8; writes *An Account of Corsica*, 292–4; and Zélide, 293–4; and O., 293–327; and life of O., 303, 313, 316; and American Revolution, 303–4; father of Alexander Boswell, 304; proposes *History of the Civil War in Great-Britain in 1745 and 1746*, 310; and O. in later years, 312–19; neglects O. after Johnson's death, 325, 327; mentioned, 58, 291, 295, 314, 329; quoted, 291–5, 296, 296[2], 297–303, 305, 311, 313, 315–16, 318, 325, 327.
Bothwell Brigg, battle of, 16, 20, 72.
Boyer, Abel, 146.
Boyne, battle of the, 39.
Bracton, Henry de, 309.
Braddock, Gen. Edward, 282.
Bramham, Yorkshire, 2–3, 10, 14, 158.
Bramston, Sir John, 26.
Brawls and duels, 20–1, 81–3.
Bray, Rev. Thomas, 111–12.
Brentford, 284.
Bridge, George Rodney, 48.
Bristol Channel, 186–7.
'Britannicus et Americanus', 287.
British Fishery, the, 273–4, 284.
Brooks's Club, 314.
Broughton, Thomas, Lt.-Gov. of S. Carolina, 155, 179, 181, 183, 195.
Bruce, Henry, 93.
Bruges, 70.
Brussels, 257.
Bryant, Arthur, 15.
Buchan, Earl of, 285[1].
Bulkeley, Mrs., 298, 298[3].
Bull, Col. William, of S. Carolina, 131, 234, 242–3, 246.
Bunker Hill, 303.
Burgage Tenure, 279.
Burghley, William Cecil, 1st Baron, 8.
Burke, Edmund, 101, 291, 306–7, 313–14, 316, 321–2, 329.
Burlington Bay, 259.
Burney, Dr. Charles, 314, 320.
— Fanny, 320–1.
Burrell, Peter, 81–2, 107, 270, 279–80, 284, 289.
— Peter, jun., 289–90.
— William, 290.
Burton, John, 63, 161, 255.
Buxton, Thomas, 309.

'Cabbot, Sebastian', 174–5.
Cadillac, Antoine de la Mothe, 113.
Cadogan, Gen. 266.
— Charles, Baron, 272, 277.
— Lieut. George, 252.

INDEX

Caernarvon, 301.
Caesar, Julius, O. compared with, 299.
Calderwood, Mrs. Margaret, of Polton, 282[4].
Calvinists, 218, 220.
Cambridge University, Oglethorpes at, 10, 61, 291.
— Sidney Sussex College, 10, 61; Trinity College, 61, 66.
Campbell, Rev. Dr. Thomas, 302–3.
Canada, 179, 227.
Cape La Hogue, 40.
Carlisle, 6, 11, 14, 264.
Carlyle, Thomas, 100.
Carolina, 113–15; divided, 115, 117–20.
Carolina border, 285[1].
Carolinas, the, 193.
Caroline, Princess of Wales, 70; as Queen of England, 146, 149, 149[3], 152, 188.
Carpenter, George, Lord, 126.
Cartagena, 233.
Carte, Thomas, 23[1], 26[2], 187, 257, 271, 292[2], 302[1].
Carter, Mrs. Elizabeth, 324, 328.
Carteret, John, Lord, 117, 120.
Castell, Robert, 90, 93, 131[5].
Castres, Abraham, 226.
Catesby, Mark, 272.
Catholic question, the, Charles II and, 20; James II and, 29.
Catholics, Oglethorpes as, 8–9.
Cato, 311.
Causton, Thomas, 151, 155–6, 166, 186–7, 209–11, 241.
— Mrs. Thomas, 165–6.
Channing, Edward, 141.
Charitable Corporation, the, 91[1], 105.
Charles I, 11.
Charles II and the Oglethorpes, 13–23; death of, 23, 23[1]; mentioned, 37, 47, 65, 175, 175[1], 189, 299.
Charles V of Spain, 223.
Charles Edward, the Young Pretender, *see* Stuart.
Charles Town, S. Carolina: threatened by Spaniards (17th c.), 113; O. at (1733), 130–1, 135, 138–9; O. reported coming to (1736), 181; O. criticizes, 183–4, 248; O. visits (1739–40), 233–4; reviles O. (1743), 249; mentioned, 136, 164, 166, 173–4, 195, 243–6, 251, 255.
Charles Town *South Carolina Gazette*, 130, 141, 156–7.
Charrière, Monsieur de, 294.
Charter, Georgia, 116–19.
Charterhouse, the, 271[3].
Chatham, William Pitt, Earl of, 101, 110, 285–9, 307.
Chelsea, Manor House of, 277.
Cherokee Indians, 115, 217[3].

Chester, 35, 35[5].
Cheyney, E. P., 178.
Chickesaw Indians, 114, 181–2.
Chiffinch, Dorothy, 18.
— William, 18.
Children's Hospital, the, 255, 270, 299.
China, 52.
Chocktaw Indians, 217[3].
Christ Church, Savannah, 164.
Christie's, 323–4.
Church, L. F., quoted, 88.
Churchill, Gen., 253, 268.
— Arabella, 43.
— Charles, 32.
— Capt. George, 27.
— John, Duke of Marlborough, 19, 25–6, 32, 51–4, 58–9, 67–9.
— Sarah Jennings, Duchess of Marlborough, 19, 56.
— William, 32[4].
— Winston, 44[3].
— Sir Winston, 27.
Citters, Arnout van, Dutch Minister to England, 35[5].
Clarendon, Edward Hyde, Earl of, 25–6, 41.
Clarke, George, Lt.-Gov. of New York, 176, 217, 227, 250.
Clifton, 268–9.
Clive, Robert, Baron, Governor of Bengal, 110, 288.
Cobbett's *Collection of State Trials*, 94.
Cobbett's *Parliamentary History*, 86, 93, 101–4.
Coke, Lord and Lady, 270.
Colden, Cadwallader, 270.
Collinson, Peter, 272.
Colman, George, 314.
Cologne, 167.
Columbus, Christopher, 3.
Common Council for Georgia, 118, 120, 206, 250.
Commons, *see* House of Commons.
Commons Journals, 271.
Commonwealth, the, Oglethorpes under, 11–13.
Compagnie des Indes, 56[3].
Conciliation of America, Commission for, 304.
Concord, 302.
Connecticut, 227.
Constant, Benjamin, 294.
Continental Congress, 303; 2nd, 304.
Conway, Lady, 35.
Cook, James, 300[2].
Cooke, Lt.-Col. William, 239, 250, 253, 268.
Cope, Sir John, 259–60.
Coram, Thomas, 112, 120, 123, 211.
Cornish, Francis Warre, 59.
Cornwallis, Charles, 1st Marquis, 243, 278, 316.

INDEX

Cotton, Sir John, 252.
Cottonian Collection, the, 277.
Coulter, E. M., 244.
Counter-Reformation, the, 6.
Coupland, R., 101.
Covenanters, Scottish, 15–16, 20, 23.
Cowes, O. at, 152–4, 167, 171.
Coweta, Indian conference at, 1739, 215–18, 231.
Crane, Verner W., 121, 121[8], 122[4], 157.
Cranham Hall, 271, 288, 295, 299, 305, 328[2].
Cranmer, Thomas, 5.
Creek Indians, 114, 134, 216, 231, 237.
Cromwell, Oliver, 11, 13.
— Thomas, 5.
Crookham, 15–16.
Crosse, Sir John, 278.
Crown, the, O. on, 98–9.
Cuba, 173, 194–5, 197, 224, 242.
Culloden, battle of, 264.
Cumberland, William Augustus, Duke of, 262–9, 280, 285, 287.
Cuming, Sir Alexander, 115, 115[1], 285[1].
Cunningham, Alexander, 73.

Dale, Robert, 71.
Dalzell, Gen. Robert, 253.
Dante, 93.
Darby, John, 94.
Darien, 169.
Debatable Land, the, 174, 208, 229, 232, 240, 245.
Declaration of Indulgence, 29.
De La Warr, John West, 1st Earl, 268, 285[1].
Dempsey, Capt. Charles, 174–5.
Derby, Earl of, 35[3], 150.
Dettingen, battle of, 1743, 249.
Devon, 187.
Dickens, Charles, 89.
Dickerson, O. M., 134.
Digby, Hon. Edward, 120.
Dilly, Charles, 312.
— Edward, 312.
Disarmament, O. on, 99.
Dober, John Andrew, 153.
Dobson, Austin, 1, 97, 120, 147[2], 168, 328–9.
Doddington, George Bubb, 276.
Domesday Book, 2.
Donauwörth, battle of, 51.
Dorset, Charles Sackville, 6th Earl of, 46.
Dover, Treaty of, 16.
Doyle, J. A., 78, 110.
Drake, Sir Francis, 174–5, 175[1], 176, 205.
— S. G., 113[1].
Duelling, 296.
Dunbar, Capt. George, 168.
Duras, Marshal de, 26.

Dutch allies, O.'s, 262.
Dutch Battalion, the, 259.
Dutch in New York, 113.

East India Company, the, 52, 125.
Ebenezer, Old, 139, 168, 210; New, 168–9, 219.
Edial, 297.
Edinburgh, 86, 106, 301–2, 305–6, 311–12, 314, 319.
Edisto river, 176, 190.
Edward the Confessor, 1, 79[4].
Edward II, 3.
Edwards, H. J., 25–6.
— T., 270[7].
Egmont, Earl of, *see* Percival, Sir John.
Egmont Diary, 97, 105, 110, 115–19, 123, 125, 130, 132, 140, 146, 152, 159–60, 166, 171, 180, 183, 185, 187–9, 193–4, 199, 205–6, 210–12, 218, 220, 225–6, 230–1, 236, 238–9, 249, 252, 266.
El Pardo, Convention of, 1739, 225–6.
Elections, *see* Parliamentary elections.
Elibank Plot, the, 281.
Elizabeth, Queen, 7, 174, 176.
Ellis, John, Under-Secretary of State, 51.
English Reformation, 223.
Epictetus, 324.
'Epimenondas' (Epaminondas), 289.
Essex, 278, 288–9, 295, 299, 319[4], 328[2].
Essex, Arthur, 1st Earl of, 35[3].
Eton College, 59–61, 145, 292.
Eugene, Prince of Savoy, James O.'s memory of, 57; service under, 67–8; mentioned, 73, 170, 297.
Eveleigh, Sam, 156, 177.
Eyre, Sir Robert, 92.

Fairfax family and O. Manor, 12.
— Anne, 12, 12[1].
— Ferdinando, 2nd Lord, 12.
— Henry, of Bolton Priory, 12.
— Thomas, 3rd Lord, 12.
— Thomas, 27.
Fairstead, Manor of, 319[4].
Fane, Francis, consultant Privy Councillor for S. Carolina, 180.
Fane, Henry, 266.
Farmer, Anthony, 29.
Feasts and Fasts, Nelson's, 302.
Feiling, Keith, 84.
Fénelon, François de Salignac de la Mothe, 69.
Fenwick, Sir John, 32, 34, 38, 43[3], 46.
Ferdinand V of Spain, 223.
Ferguson, Robert, 22, 41.
Ferguson Plot in Edinburgh, 37.
Feversham, Louis Duras, 2nd Earl of, 15–16, 25, 32, 35[3].
'Fifteen, the, 65, 71, 75, 257.
Finsbury Archers, the, 322.

INDEX

Fishery, British, the, 273-4, 284.
Fitz-Harris case, the, 20.
Flanders, 58, 69-70, 255, 270.
Fleet Prison, 90-4.
Flodden Field, 15-16.
Florida, 113, 136, 173-7, 190-1, 195-6, 200-5, 227, 230, 232-5, 242, 244, 246, 248.
Folkes, Dr. Martin, 272, 272[2].
Foot Guards, 58, 67, 69[4].
Forbes, Duncan, Lord President of Council of Scotland, 265-6.
Foreign affairs, O. on, 99.
Fort Argyle, 136.
— King George, 114-15, 204-5, 223.
— Saint George, 173, 177, 200, 204-5, 223.
— Saint George, Madras, 52.
— William, 243.
Fortescue, Sir John, 44[3], 199-200, 200[1].
'Forty-five, the, 77, 257-70, 280, 310, 320.
Fothergill, Dr. John, 308.
Founders and Coppersmiths Company, 22.
Fowler, Thomas, 66, 79.
Fox, Charles James, 270, 314.
— Henry, 109, 254[3], 267.
France, 15-16, 32, 39, 41, 43-4, 67, 69, 72, 75, 77, 99, 106, 113, 135, 149, 185, 193, 236, 240, 242, 245, 282, 284, 304, 308, 313, 326.
Francis I of France, 67.
Francke, August Hermann, of Halle, 139, 219-21.
Franklin, Benjamin, 101, 222, 270, 325.
Fratres Bohemiae, the, 170.
Frederica in Georgia, 156-7, 163-6, 173, 175, 186, 205, 208, 215, 220-2, 222[5], 226, 239, 243-4, 246.
Frederick, Prince, of England, 157.
Frederick, Prince of Württemberg, 67[5].
Frederick II of Prussia ('Frederick the Great'), 240, 282-4, 317.
Frederick William I of Prussia, 138.
Free British Fishery, the, 273-4, 284.
French, the, 40, 42, 46, 71, 76, 100, 113, 115, 134, 136-7, 149, 151, 172, 178, 180, 182, 184, 193, 216-17, 227, 281, 288.
Frontier, southern, 113-15, 156-7, 173-4, 240, 286.
Fuller, William, 39.
Fullerton, Rev. Mr., 149.
Furneaux, Capt., 300[2].

Galway, 287, 287[3].
Gambia, Africa, 148.
Garrick, David, 271, 291, 297, 300, 311-14, 329.
Garrick, Mrs. David, 322.
Garstang, 263, 265.

'General Oglethorpe's Memorandums on the Illegality of pressing Seamen, with Remarks by G. S.', 309.
Gentleman's Magazine, 130, 147, 155-6, 255, 326.
George I of England, 65, 67, 69, 79.
George II of England, 145, 149, 198-9, 201, 206.
George III of England, 89, 102, 274, 285, 300, 326.
George, Prince of Denmark, 29-30, 30[1].
Georgia, origins of, 110-28; founding of, 129-31; 1st period in, 131-42; internal administration of, 132-42; 2nd period in, 155-85; religion in, 158-72; and S. Carolina, 151, 178-90; no Quakers in, 169; division of, 214-15; and the Spaniards, 222-7; defence of, 227-46; becomes a royal province, 254; referred to, 1, 109, 262, 265-6, 270, 276, 282, 287, 292, 298, 302, 304, 306-7, 315, 321, 326, 328[3], 329; *see also* Immigration.
Georgia Rangers, the, in the 'Forty-five, 261-2.
Georgia regiment, the, 280.
Georgian Ladies' Clubs, 320.
Geraldino, Don Tomás, Spanish Minister to England, 174-5, 184, 190-1, 193, 195-8, 200-2, 224, 228.
Germans, the, 74.
Germany, 170.
Ghent, 70.
Gibbon, Edward, 314.
Gibraltar troops, 230.
Gibson, Edmund, Bishop of London, 171.
Glen, James, Gov. of S. Carolina, 217[3], 233, 252.
'Glorious Revolution', the, 31-3.
Glyn, Marshes of, 113, 224.
Godalming, Surrey, 33-4, 36, 40, 44, 51, 67, 77, 79, 79[4], 144, 271, 281, 301.
'Godbold, Mr.', 79[4].
Goddard, John, 173.
Godolphin, Charles, 27.
— Henry, Provost of Eton, 59.
— Sidney, Earl of, 27, 54, 59.
Godolphin House, 28, 38.
Goethe, Johann Wolfgang von, 100.
'Golden Isles' of Georgia, the, 113, 224.
Goldsmith, Dr. Oliver, author of *The Deserted Village*, 157; at reunions, 296-8; produces *She Stoops to Conquer*, 298, 300; O. befriends, 298-9; death of, 301, 327; mentioned, 291, 299-302, 305, 314, 329.
Gooch, William, Gov. of Virginia, 217, 227, 243.
Goodrick, Sir Henry, 38.
Gordon, Lord George, 315.
Gordon, Peter, 142.

INDEX

Gordon of Earlstoun, 27.
Gort, 287, 287[3].
Goths, 308.
Gramont, Philibert, Comte de, cited, 19.
Gravesend, 130, 146, 162.
Greece, 308.
Green, J. R., 62, 65.
Greffier of Holland, the, 240.
Grenville ministry, the, 288.
Griffin, John, Lord, 34.
Gronau, Rev. Israel Christian, 138–9.
Guale, 113, 115, 174.
Gualterio, Card., 72, 77.
Guemes y Horcasitas, Juan Francisco de, Gov. of Havana, 196, 202, 204, 228–9, 234–5, 242, 245.
Guy's Charities, 87.
Guy's Hospital, 87.
Gwynne, Nell, 299.

Habersham, James, 251.
Hague, The, 42, 51, 201.
Hales, Dr. Stephen, 112, 120, 161.
Halifax, George Savile, Marquis of, 31–2.
— George Montague Dunk, 2nd Earl of, 273.
Hall, Dr. Hubert, 320[4].
Hall-Stevenson, John, 259[8].
Halle, 138, 220–1.
Hamilton, Mary, 322.
Hanbury, William, 272.
Hanbury-Williams, Sir Charles, 109, 270.
Hannay, D., quoted, 309.
Hardcastle, Kate, 298.
Hardin, William, 131[5].
Hardwicke, Philip Yorke, 1st Earl of, Lord Chancellor, 261, 266, 284[4].
Hardwicke correspondence, 240.
Harleian Collection, the, 277.
Harley, Edward, 39.
— Robert, Theophilus O., jun., and, 53; and Anne O., 55; mentioned, 64, 225.
Harrington, William Stanhope, 1st Earl of, 138[2].
Haslemere, Surrey, Theophilus O., sen., M.P. for, 48–50; Lewis O. M.P. for, 50–1; Theophilus O., jun., M.P. for, 53–4, 54[1], 70; James O. M.P. for, 81–109, 270–80; mentioned, 272[1], 278–80, 285, 288–9, 291.
Hastings, Lady Margaret, 163.
— Warren, 326.
Hat Bill, 105.
Havana, 173–5, 203, 228, 230, 233.
Hearne, Thomas, 63, 71.
Heart of Midlothian, 106.
Heath, Nicholas, Abp. of York, 7.
Heathcote, George, Georgia Trustee, 226, 231.

Hebrides, Tour to the, 300–1.
Hector, the ship, 207, 230.
Heinsius, Grand Pensionary of Holland, 112[1].
Henrietta, Duchess of Orléans, 16–17.
Henry V of England, 283.
Henry VII of England, 3, 174.
Henry VIII of England, 5, 174.
Henry Esmond, 76.
Herbert, Edward, Baron, of Cherbury, 129.
— Rev. Henry, 129, 159–60.
Hermann und Dorothea, 100.
Herring, Thomas, Abp. of York, 259, 261–2, 264.
Herrnhut in Saxony, Moravians at, 170.
Hessians, the, 97–8.
Hickes, Bishop George, 60.
Higgins, Dr., 313.
— Mrs. Napier, 295[2].
Highlanders, Scottish, 169.
Hispaniola, 28.
History of the Civil War in Great-Britain in 1745 and 1746, 310.
History of the Five Indian Nations, 270.
Hocclestorp, Hugh de, 2.
Hocclestorp, William de, 2.
Hoffmann, Johann Philipp von, 30, 34.
Holdsworth, Sir W. S., 89.
Holland, 54, 100, 138, 240, 282, 282[4], 329.
Holland, Greffier of, 240.
Holland Regiment, 27–33.
Holmes, Oliver Wendell, 323–4.
Holt, Lord Chief Justice, 40, 310.
Holworthy, Richard, 287[3].
Holy Club of Oxford, the, 161.
Holy Roman Empire, the, 240.
Honourable Artillery Company, the, 322.
Hopkey, Sophia, 165–6.
Horcasitas, *see* Guemes y Horcasitas.
Horsey, Samuel, Gov. of S. Carolina, 233.
Horton, Lieut., sent to England, 238.
Hounslow Heath, 30.
House of Commons, 23, 26–7, 30–1, 48–51, 53–4, 54[1], 84–109, 226, 289–90, 312, 318; Theophilus O., sen., in, 23, 26–7, 30–1, 48–50; Lewis O. in, 50–1; Theophilus O., jun., in, 53–4; James O. in, 84–109, 270–80.
House of Lords, 316.
Howard, John, 95.
Howard of Escrick, William, 3rd Baron, 13, 22.
Hucks, Robert, Georgia Trustee, 226.
Huddleston, Father John, 23[1].
Huggins, John, 94.
Hull, 8, 259–60.
Hungary, 73.
Huss, John, 170.

INDEX

d'Iberville, Pierre Le Moyne, Sieur, 113.
Ilfracombe, 187.
Immigration to Georgia, English, 118, 122, 125, 129–31, 136–7; continental, 125, 136–40, 168–72, 218, 220; Amatis brothers from Savoy, 136–7; Jews, 137, 139; Salzburger Lutherans, 125, 137–40, 168–9; Scottish Presbyterians, 169; Moravians, 170–2; Calvinists (Reformed), 218, 220.
Imperial Conference of 1926, 100–1.
Impressment evil, the, 306, 309–10.
Indentured servants, 122, 150[6].
India, 52–3, 227, 228, 326.
Indian trade, 150–1, 189–90.
Indians, in and around Georgia, 113–15, 131–3; conciliation of, 1733, 134, 141–2; in England, 1734, 144–6; regulation of trade with, 150–1; O.'s conference with Chickasaw, 1736, 181–2; conference with Creek, at Coweta, 1739, 215–16; O. retains loyalty of, 1738–43, 215–18; in service of Georgia, 177, 217–18; mentioned, 177, 183–4, 189, 236, 273, 282, 285[1].
Industrial Revolution, the, 102.
Ingham, Rev. Benjamin, 153–4, 157, 161–3, 171, 220.
Inverness, 147.
Ireland, 35–6, 39, 70, 302.
Isabella of Spain, 227.
Island of Nightingales, the, 329.
Isle of Wight, 144.
Italy, 257.

Jablonsky, Bishop, 171[3].
Jacobite movement, the, 1688–96, 33–44, 46; 1698–1714, 54–61; 1715–20, 64–79; 1720–40, 85; 1740–50, 257–69, 280–2.
Jacobitism, the Oglethorpes in, 33–44, 46, 54–79, 257–65, 280–2; at Oxford, 60–6; after 1719, 85, 257–65, 280–2, 310, 318; mentioned, 170, 329.
Jail Inquiry, 89–95, 110.
Jamaica, 228, 230, 233, 241–4, 246.
James, Duke of York, opinion of, concerning Ellen Wall, 18[1]; mentioned, 20; as James II of England, 24–32; flight to France, 1688, 32, 34; quoted, 33; and Jacobitism, 35, 41–5, 54; death, 50; referred to, 38, 42–3, 54.
James I of England, 8.
Jefferson, Thomas, 101, 328[3].
Jekyll, Sir Joseph, 207.
Jekyll Island, 207.
Jenkins, Thomas, 223–4.
Jenkins's Ear, war of, 222–46.
Jews, German, in Georgia, 137;

Sephardic, in Georgia, 137, 137[2], 139, 159, 164, 218–19; naturalization of, in England, 278.
Joar Factory in Gambia, 148.
Job ben Solomon, 148.
Job Jalla, 148.
John, King of Portugal, 57.
Johnson, Col., 325.
— Mr., Haslemere candidate, 1768, 289.
— Nathanael, 292.
— Robert, Gov. of S. Carolina, 125, 127, 129–31, 143, 150, 156, 177–9.
— Samuel, at Pembroke College, Oxford, 63, 220, 292; fascinated by O.'s account of the battle of Belgrade, 68; aided by O., 200, 292; and O., 292–323; and Mrs. O., 302, 306; and a life of O., 303; on the American Revolution, 303, 306; a Jacobite, 310, 318–19; in later years, 318–19; death, 323; library sold, 323–4; mentioned, 270, 291, 294–8, 300–6, 309–16, 318–20, 322–4, 326, 329.
Johnston, Gabriel, Gov. of N. Carolina, 227.
Jones, Noble, 151, 209.
Jones, Thomas, 214.
Jones, Sir William, 313.
Joseph in Egypt, 104.

Keene, Benjamin, 173, 192, 197, 201, 203, 224–6.
Keith, George, Earl Marischal, 76.
— James, Field-Marshal, 67, 76, 282, 282[4], 317.
Kennett, Basil, Pres. of Corpus Christi College, Oxford, 63, 302.
Kensington, Indians at, 145.
Kent, Men of, 49.
Kenyon, Roger, 35[3].
Kerr, Lord Mark, 253.
Keynsham, 24–5.
King, the haberdasher, 111–12, 115, 122.
King George's War, 1739–48, 227.
King in Council, the, 182.
King's Bench Prison, Southwark, 92–3, 276–7.
Kingsale, Lord, 126.
Kirke, Percy, 25.
Knavesmire, 260–1.
Königsmark, Philip, Count, 22, 22[1].
Kouli Kan, Thomas, 115[1].

Lamb, Sir Thomas, 102–3, 103[1], 149.
Lancaster, 264.
Lang, A., 45, 86[1], 281.
Langton, Bennet, 271, 300, 302, 311–14.
Lanier, Sir John, 32.
Lanning, J. T., 173[1], 173[5].

INDEX

La Salle, René Robert, Cavalier de, 113.
Latimer, Hugh, 5.
Law, John, 76.
Law, Levitical, 310.
Law of Retribution, 308.
Lecky, W. E. H., 89–90.
Lee, Col. George, 12.
— Robert E., 12[1].
Leeward Islands, 228.
Leigh, Theophilus, 63.
Leopold I, Emperor, 34, 46.
Leopold Anton, Abp. of Salzburg, 100, 138.
Lettsom, Dr. John C., 301.
Levant, the, 283.
Levitical Law, 310.
Lexington, Robert Sutton, 2nd Baron, 38.
Lexington, battle of, 302.
Leyden, University of, 62.
Lichfield, 292.
Lichfield, Earl of, 37.
Ligne, Claude-Lamoral, Prince de, 77.
Ligonier, Gen. John, 262, 280.
Ligulfe, Theane of Oglethorpe, 1, 79[4].
Limerick, Viscount, 150.
Lincoln, Abraham, 150.
Linn, C. A., 139[3].
Linnaeus, Carolus, 270.
Lisle Street, 271.
Literary Club, the, 314.
Locke, John, 62–3, 65.
Lockhart, Sir William, 36.
Lockwood, Miss, 300.
Logan, James, Pres. of Council of Pennsylvania, 228[1].
London, 167, 173, 187, 191, 194–5, 201, 206, 212, 215, 224, 226, 230, 233, 239, 251, 256, 265–6, 271, 278, 287–9, 295, 299, 301–2, 305–6, 311, 313, 315, 318, 320, 322, 327–8, 328[3].
— Berkeley Square, 300; Bond Street, 322; British Museum, 277–8; Charing Cross, 306; Conduit Mead, 322; Conduit Street, 322; Gray's Inn, 9, 13; Hanover Square, 286; Hyde Park, 37, 39; Leicester Fields, 271; Lincoln's Inn, 10; Lower Grosvenor Street, 289, 295, 308; Old Palace Yard, 188; Pall Mall, 276; St. Bartholomew's Hospital, 299; St. James's Church, Piccadilly, 35–6, 50[1]; St. James's Palace, 22–3, 23[1]; St. James's Park, 27; St. Martin-in-the-Fields, 20–1, 47, 86[1]; St. Paul's, 28; Soho Square, 285, 287.
— Westminster, 107, 112, 173, 184, 186, 226, 270; election of 1754, 278; Abbey, 323; Hall, 315; Hospital, 299; Infirmary, 200; Prison, 91.
— Whitehall, 8, 38, 42, 129, 173, 229, 239–40, 246, 248, 259, 278.

London, a poem by Samuel Johnson, 200, 292.
London Magazine, 304, 312.
London *Daily Courant*, 146.
— *Daily Gazetteer*, 233–4.
— *Daily Journal*, 81–3.
— *Evening Post*, 206.
— *Gazetteer*, 188.
— *Grub-Street Journal*, 126–7.
— *Hooker's Weekly Miscellany*, 141–2, 187, 206.
— *London Journal*, 182.
— *Public Advertiser*, 327.
— *Weekly Miscellany*, 159.
— *Westminster Journal*, 255.
Lords Commissioners for Trade and Plantations, the, 190.
Lort, Dr. Michael, 79[4].
'Lost Atlantis', the, 284[1].
Lothian, William Henry Kerr, 4th Marquis of, 313.
Lotteries: for Georgia, 117, 123; for the British Museum, 277–8.
Loudoun, John Campbell, Earl of, 280.
Louis XIV of France, 15–17, 44, 57, 69, 283, 308.
Louisiana, 119.
Lowndes, Thomas, 149.
Lubbock, Percy, 59.
Lumkin, Tony, 298.
Luther, Martin, 170.
Lutherans, 99–100, 125, 138–40, 168–70, 218–20.
Luttrell, Narcissus, 38–9, 41.

Macaulay, Thomas Babington, Lord, 26.
McCain, J. R., 119, 140–1, 147, 216, 254.
Macclesfield, Charles Gerard, 1st Earl of, 36.
Macclesfield, George Parker, 2nd Earl of, 277.
McConnell, S. D., 124.
MacKay, Gen., 25.
— Patrick, 180, 189.
McKinley, A. E., 132, 140.
Macky, John, 45.
'Madame Carwell', 17.
Madeira, 207.
Madras, 52.
Madrid, 173–4, 193, 195–7, 201, 203, 224, 228, 241, 245.
— *Gaceta de Madrid*, 192.
'Magick Lanthorn', the, Tomochichi and, 146.
Malcontents, 184–5, 211–13, 239, 250–1.
Malone, Edmund, 314, 327.
Malta, 58[4], 75.
Malton, Earl of, 260.
Manchester, 263.
Mann, Horace, 269, 324.

INDEX 339

Manor House of Chelsea, the, 277.
Mansfield, William Murray, 1st Earl of, 308, 316, 319.
Mar, John Erskine, Jacobite Earl and Duke of, 71–5.
Marches, Jean François de Bellegarde, Marquis des, 76.
Margravate of Azilia, 114, 119, 122, 132.
Maria Theresa of Hungary, 240.
Markham, Dr. Peter, 305.
Marlborough, Duke of, see Churchill, John.
— Duchess of, see Churchill, Sarah.
Marshalsea Prison, 91–4.
Marshes of Glyn, 113, 224.
Martyn, Benjamin, Secretary of the Georgia Trustees, 120–1, 121[8], 131–2, 142–4, 144[3], 168, 177, 190, 212–13, 250.
Mary, Catholic Queen of England, 6–7.
Mary, Princess, wife of William of Orange, 29–31; Queen of England, 36–40, 112, 112[1]; death of, 42.
Mary of Modena, Queen of England, 32, 44; at Saint-Germain, 76, 78.
Maryland, 111, 148.
Massachusetts, 113, 127–8; invites O., 135–6; mentioned, 232, 295.
Mather, John, Pres. of Corpus Christi College, Oxford, 63.
Mathew, Abp. of York, 13.
— John, 13.
Meath Home for Incurables, 79[4].
Melfort, John Drummond, 1st Earl of, 44.
Men of Kent, the, 49.
Messina, 70.
Metcalfe, Rev. William, 222[5].
Mexico, 286.
Mexico City, 228.
Mézières, Athanase de, 56[3].
— Chevalier de, 328[3].
— Eleanor O. de, see Oglethorpe, Eleanor.
— Eugène-Marie de Bethisy, Marquis de, 56, 56[3], 76.
— Henrietta Eugénie de, 77.
Mickva Israel Temple, 137.
Middlesex, Charles Sackville, 1st Earl of, 278.
Middleton, Charles, 2nd Earl of, 27, 31[3], 41–2, 44.
Missions, Spanish, 113–14.
Mississippi, French in, 113–14, 134–6, 172, 178, 180, 180–2, 225, 227, 242.
Mississippi scheme of John Law, 76.
Mississippi Valley, 113.
Mobile, French at, 149, 151, 183.
Molyneaux, James More, 279–80, 289–90.

Molyneaux, More, 81.
Monmouth, James Scott, Duke of, 16, 18–20, 23–5, 29.
Monmouth's Rebellion, 23–6.
Montagu, George Brudenell, Duke of, 235, 240, 262.
— Mrs. Elizabeth, 'Queen of the Blues', 315, 320, 324, 328.
Montaubon, Charles de Rohan, Prince, 77.
Montcalm, Louis Joseph, Marquis de, 113.
Montgomery, Sir James, 40.
— Sir Robert, 114, 122.
Montiano, Don Manuel de, Gov. of Florida, 202[5], 203, 229, 234–5, 241–3.
Montijo, Conde del, 202.
Moore, Francis, 148, 153, 158.
— Robert, Georgia Trustee, 226.
Moors, the, 308.
Moravians, the, in Georgia, 170–2, 218–19; in England, 273.
More, Hannah, 311, 321–2.
Morley, John, 84.
Morpeth, Northumberland, 15, 23, 26–7, 30–1.
Mortimer, Cromwell, 272.
'Moville', French at, 149, 151, 183.
Mühlenberg, Heinrich Melchior, 220.
Musgrave, Sir Philip, 11.
Musgrove, Mary, 134, 217, 261[4].
Muskerry, Lord, 126.
Mutiny, in Savannah, 139; in the army, 230–1.
Mutiny Bill, the, 274–5.

Nairne, David, Secretary to James III, 72, 74, 77.
— John, Lord, 281.
Naples, 74.
National defence, 99, 106.
Naturalization of foreigners, 98, 276.
Naval expeditions, 241.
Navy, the British, Pepys and, 27; Theophilus O., sen., and, 27; Theophilus O., jun., and, 74; James O. and, 88, 106, 309.
Necker, Jacques, 294.
Negro insurrection in S. Carolina, 231–2.
Nevill, R., 79[4].
New England, 221.
New Inverness, 169.
New Mexico, 119.
New York, 113, 227.
New Zealand, 300.
Newcastle, Thomas Pelham-Holles, Duke of, Secretary of State for the Colonies, 117, 120, 129–30, 174–6, 179, 183–4, 191–2, 194–5, 197–8, 200–4, 207, 224, 230, 233–4, 240, 242, 245[2], 246–9, 253, 259–60, 262, 280–1;

as Prime Minister, 285; as 1st Lord of the Treasury, 286.
Newcastle, town of, 261-2, 264.
Newgate Jail, 92.
'Newlands, Mr.', Jacobite *alias* of Anne O., 257.
Newton, A. Edward, 324.[2]
Newton Kyme, 5, 9.
Nichols, John, 108.
Nicholson, Col., 157.
'Nineteen, the, 76, 257.
Nitschmann, David, Moravian Bishop, 153, 171-2, 218.
Noble, Rev. Mark, 2[2].
Norris, Rev. William, 222[5].
North, Sir Dudley, 27.
— Frederick, Lord, 102, 316-17.
— Sir Henry, 27.
North Briton, No. 45, 290.
North Sea, 329.
Nottingham, Daniel Finch, 2nd Earl of, 40.
Nova Scotia, 284.
'Nymphs', the, 71.

Oates, Titus, 20.
Occlesthorp, Hugh de, 2.
Ocele, 2.
Ocelestorp, 2.
Ockelesthorp, Petrus de, 2.
Oclestorp, Elyas, 2.
Oclestorpe, Nicholas de, 2.
— Nicholaa de, 2.
Ogilsthorp, Willelmo de, 3.
Ogle, 2.
Ogle, Sir Chaloner, British Adm., 246.
— Samuel, 245[2].
Oglesthorp, John, 3.
Oglestorp, 2.
Oglethorpe, Andrew, 4.
— Anne Henrietta, James Edward's oldest sister, birth, 19; on father's knighthood, 262[2]; Jacobite career, 50, 54-6; relations with Robert Harley, 55; with Lord Treasurer Godolphin, 55, 59; and Frances Shaftoe case, 55, 55[3], 56; later Jacobite career, 57, 69-78, 86, 257; seeks baronetcy, 71-2; created Countess of O., 77; awaits her brother, 1736, 187; protects her brother's repute, 236; at Westbrook, 280-2; death, 284-5.
— Eleanor, James Edward's second sister, birth, 19; at Jacobite court, 54; and Shaftoe case, 55; marriage, 56, 68; Jacobite activities, 68-78, 257; in the 'Forty-five, 257-8; in England, 281; and the Elibank Plot, 281; a Jacobite in 1759, 282; death, 305; mentioned, 98, 236, 280, 282, 328[3].
— Eleanor Wall, mother of James Edward, birth and ancestry, 17; as Ellen Wall, maid to Duchess of Portsmouth, 17-18; head laundress and 'sempstriss', 18; marriage, 18-19; children, 19, 35, 40, 43, 46-7; created Lady O., 27; and death of Charles II, 23[1]; in Revolution of 1688, 31-2; friendship with Dean Swift, 34, 42, 57; Jacobite activities of, 35-6, 50-60, 68-77; labours for her children, 50-8; for James Edward, 58-61; seeks a baronetcy, 71-2; death, 126; tributes to, 126-7; mentioned, 65.
— Elizabeth, James Edward's aunt, 14.
— Elizabeth Wright, marries James Edward O., 256; heredity, 256; financial position, 256, 296; and Dr. Johnson, 302, 306; bequeaths Fairstead to Granville Sharp, 319[4]; death, 328[2]; mentioned, 285, 287, 296, 328.
— Frances Charlotte (Fanny), James Edward's fourth sister, birth, 43; Jacobite career, 57, 69-76; and John Law, 76; maligned by Thackeray, 76; marries Jean François de Bellegarde, 76; mentioned, 236, 293, 328[3].
— George, of Newton Kyme, father of Bishop Owen O., 4-5.
— Henry, of Bishopsfield, 1572, a Catholic, 8.
— James, James Edward's third brother, 35-6, 55.
— James Edward, ancestry 1-46; birth, 46-7; youth, 47-57; youthful impressions, 57; military career, 58, 67; at Eton, 59-60; at Oxford, 61-7, 79; M.A. (Oxon.), 66; at the Paris Academy, 67; under Prince Eugene in the Balkans, 67-8; in France, 67-73, 75-9; heir to baronetcy, 72; a Stuart messenger in Italy, 73-5; a Jacobite, 78-9; Squire of Westbrook, 79, 79[4], 80; candidate for Parliament, 1722, 81; elected, 81; in trouble, 81-4; letter to London *Daily Journal*, 82-3; committee work, 84-7, 96, 96[1]; on Atterbury, 85-6; re-elected, 1727, 86; and *The Sailor's Advocate*, 88; in jail inquiry, 89-95; on temperance and politics, 97-8; on the army, 97; on international affairs, 98-100; on colonial polity, 100-2; and industry, 102-3; on the Charitable Corporation, 103-4; on finance, 97, 103-4; on constitutional questions, 98, 104; re-elected, 1734, 105; on navy estimates, 106; on Edinburgh riots, 106; re-elected, 1741, 107-8; as an estate trustee, 1727-31, 111-12, 115, 122; in organization of the Georgia movement, 111-28; author of *An Essay on*

INDEX 341

Plantations, 121; reputed author of *A New and Accurate Account*, 121; resolves to go to Georgia, 127-8; at Charles Town, 130; founds Savannah, 131-3; pacifies the Indians, 134; and European immigration, 136-9; and various sects, 136-40; and the colonists, 139-43; leaves for England, March 1734, 144; and the Trustees, 143-4; and Indians in England, 144-6; in England, 1734-5, 144-52; and the Royal African Company, 147-8; and Job Jalla, 148, 150; and the Trustees, 1735, 149-52; advocates temperance, 150; opposes negro slavery, 150; regulates trade with Indians, 151; second voyage to Georgia, 153-5; and southern expansion of Georgia, 156-7; founds Frederica, 157; and religion, 158-72; and the Wesleys, 158-68; and Lutherans at New Ebenezer, 168-9; and Presbyterian Scottish Highlanders, 169-70; and Zinzendorf, 170-2; and the Moravians, 170-2; and the Spaniards, 172-7; and Arredondo, 175-7; treats with del Moral Sanchez, 177; and financial problems, 177-8; and South Carolina-Georgia Indian trade dispute, 178-84, 188-90; confers with Chickasaw Indians, 1736, 181-2; recalled by Trustees, 1736, 185-6; and Trustees, 1737, 188-206; compromises with South Carolina, 188-90; replies to Spanish charges, 190-2; prepares for defence of Georgia, 192-200; appointed Colonel and General, 194-5; overcomes Walpole, 199; a Governor of Westminster Infirmary, 200; aids Samuel Johnson, 200; deludes Britain on Fort Saint George, 200-5; third voyage to Georgia, 205-8; and domestic affairs in Georgia, 208-22; and Causton, 209-10; and sumptuary laws, 210-11; and William Stephens, 211-15; and Thomas Stephens, 212; and other malcontents, 213-14; just criticism of, 214-15; President of the Southern half of Georgia, 215; and Indians, 215-18; and the religious groups, 217-22; and Whitefield, 220-2; defends Georgia against Spain, 222-46; deserted by Trustees and Walpole, 225-6, 238-9; and war of Jenkins's Ear, 226-44; and mutiny of soldiers, 230-1; attacks Saint Augustine, 234-5; reviles the Carolinians, 235; criticized by S. Carolina, 235-7; appeals for aid, 237-8, 246-50; defends Georgia, 238-46; at Bloody Marsh, 244-6; presses Newcastle for aid, 246-9; isolated, 248; raid on Saint Augustine, 1743, 248; recalled for court martial, 250-1; sails for home, 251; repaid by Parliament, 252; acquitted, 253; end of Georgia Trusteeship, 253-4; in London, 255-6; marriage, 255-6; and the 'Forty-five, 257-66; Major-General, 259; in Yorkshire, 259-62; pursues the rebels, 263-4; a failure in the 'Forty-five, 264-5; second court martial of, 266-9; Lieut.-General, 269; in House of Commons, 1743-54, 270-80; Fellow of the Royal Society, 271-3, 285; aids the Moravians, 273; and the British Fishery, 273-4, 284; financial straits of, 273-4; helps to found the British Museum, 277-8; defeated for re-election, 1754, 278-80; family relations, 1750-6, 280-2; in Holland, 1756, 282-4; on Frederick the Great, 283-4; ejected from the Royal Society, 1757, 285; the 'forgotten man', 285; and William Pitt the elder, 285-7; General, 1765, 287; and Clive, 1766, 287-8; on the Stamp Act, 288; defeated at Haslemere, 1768, 288-90; literary interests of, 291-2; in the Johnsonian circle, 292-326; and Boswell, 292-327; and Boswell's romance, 293-4; and Sir Francis Bernard, 1770, 295; annual dinner reunions at home of, 295-313; on duelling, 296-7; and Garrick, 297, 313-14; and the American Revolution, 298, 303-4, 306-8, 313, 316; befriends Goldsmith, 298-9; and charity, 298-9; and Topham Beauclerk, 299-300; and Reynolds, 300-1, 314, 314[4]; Boswell and Johnson contemplate life of, 303, 313, 316; and Granville Sharp, 306-10, 319; and impressment, 306-10; and Edmund Burke, 306-7; on slavery, 309-10; and Hannah More, 311, 321-2; and the Dilly brothers, 312; and political writing, 312; and the theatre, 313; and clubs, 313-14; and the Gordon Riots, 1780, 315; and the Wesleys, 1781-4, 315, 320; on Lord North and the American Revolution, 316-17; and Horace Walpole, 317-18, 324-5; and the Georgian Ladies' Clubs, 320-2; and archery, 322; and the death of Johnson, 322-3; at the sale of Johnson's library, 323-4; at 88, 325; welcomes John Adams, 326; death, 326-8; mourned by ladies, 327-8; estimate, 328-30.

— John, 146[4], 4, 9.
— John, 10[2], 61.

INDEX

Oglethorpe, John, son of Sutton O., jun., 14.
— Lewis, James Edward's oldest brother, birth, 19; in Parliament, 50–1; Deputy Lieut. for Surrey, 51; under Marlborough, 51; death, 51; mentioned, 53, 58, 70, 83; and Eton, 59; and Oxford, 60.
— Ligulfe, Theane of, 1, 79[4].
— Louisa Mary (Molly), James Edward's third sister, birth, 40; Jacobite career, 57, 69–77; proposed for Hanoverian court honour, 70–1; later Jacobite career, 77; marries the Marquis de Bersompierre, 77; last years, 77, 236.
— Martin, adventurer, 9.
— Owen, of Newington, 8.
— Bishop Owen, 5–8, 53, 291.
— Richard, *obit.* 1546, 9.
— Robert, of Rawdon, 4.
— Sir Robert, Baron of the Exchequer, 9.
— Robert, 10[1].
— Sutton, the first, James Edward's grandfather, 10–13, 15.
— Sutton, jun., James Edward's uncle, 13–14.
— Sutton, the third, James Edward's cousin, 14.
— Sutton, James Edward's fourth brother, 40.
— Theophilus, James Edward's father, birth, 14; early career, 15–20; marriage, 19–21; children, 19, 35, 40, 43, 46–7; career under Charles II, 20–4; M.P. for Morpeth, 23, 26–7, 30; knighted, 26; career under James II, 24–32; the Jacobite, 32–44; Deputy Lieut. for Surrey, 47; M.P. for Haslemere, 48–50; death, 50, 50[1]; and Count Zinzendorf, 170; mentioned, 65, 72, 83, 100, 126, 266.
— Theophilus, jun., James Edward's second brother, birth, 19; in India, 52, 55; in Parliament, 53–4, 54[1], 57; and Robert Harley, 53; at Eton, 59; Jacobite career, 69–77, 257; in Flanders, 69–70; on the continent, 69–77; created Baron (Jacobite), 71–2; death, 77; Squire of Westbrook, 79; referred to, 78, 123; views concerning Owen O., 5, 8.
— Ursula, James Edward's aunt, 14.
— William, 15th century, 4.
— William, son of Richard, 16th century, 9, 9[3].
— William, of O. Grange, son of William, 1584, 9, 10.
— William, son of William of O. Grange, 10, 10[3].
Oglethorpe, Yorkshire, 1–14.

Oglethorpe, the ship, 147.
Oglethorpe Grange, 9.
— Hall, Bramham, Yorkshire, 61[4].
— Manor, 2, 12.
Oglethorpes of Rawdon, 4; of Yorkshire, 318.
Ohio river valley, 113.
Okelesthorp, John de, 3.
Okelesthorpe, Hugh, 2[4].
Oliphants of Gask, the, 281.
Omai, 300[2].
Omry, Mrs. Hester van, 123.
Onslow, Arthur, Lewis O.'s duel with, 51; and Theophilus O. jun., 54; and James O., 81–3, 91; on O.'s election in 1734, 105.
Order of the Garter, the, 6.
Ormonde, James Butler, 2nd Duke of, 69, 69[4], 77–8.
Orton, 268.
Osgood, H. L., 114, 121, 140, 147, 151.
Otaheite, 300, 300[2].
Oxford, battle near, 12; James O. comes to, 61–2; Jacobite riots in, 60–6; mentioned, 75, 320, 322–3.
— Bear Lane, 62; Constitution Club, 65; High Street, 61; Cherwell, 63; Magdalen Bridge, 61; Mitre Hotel, 62; Plain, 61.
Oxford University, Owen O. at, 5–6; Sutton O., jun., at, 13; Lewis O. at, 60; James O. at, 61–7; state of education at, 62; customs and social life at, 62–3; Jacobitism in, 60–6; and Job Jalla's Arabic letter, 148; derides the Wesleys, 162; mentioned, 4–6, 75, 291–2, 322–3.
— All Souls College, 64; Bodleian Library, 62; Brasenose College, 61[4], 162; Christ Church, 60, 65, 85, 161; Clarendon Building, 64; Codrington Library, 64; Corpus Christi College, 60, 61–7, 79, 161, 255, 292; Exeter College, 60; Gloucester Hall, 64; Lincoln College, 161, 167[5]; Magdalen College, 5–6, 61, 291; Merton College, 60; Merton Walk, 63; Pembroke College, 63, 220, 292, 323; Queen's College, 64, 161; St. Mary's Church, 255; Sheldonian Theatre, 28, 64; University College, 60, 64; University Press, 64; Wadham College, 60; Worcester College, 64.
Oxfordshire, Oglethorpes in, 8–9.

Page, M., 24[2].
Palatines, German, 137.
Palermo, 70.
Paoli, Gen. Pasquale de, 293, 295, 298, 301, 305, 311–12, 315, 327.
Paradise, John, 313, 325.
Paris, 67–77, 257, 281–2.

INDEX

Parker, Henry, Vice-Pres. of Georgia, 217[3].
Parliament, early Oglethorpes in, 4, 8; Theophilus O. in, 23, 26–7, 30–1, 48–50; Lewis O. in, 50–1; Theophilus O., jun., in, 53–4, 54[1]; James O. in, 81–109, 270–80.
Parliamentary elections: 1722, 81; 1727, 86; 1734, 105; 1741, 107; 1747, 270, 270[7]; 1754, 278–80; 1768, 288–90, 293.
Patiño, Don José, Spanish Minister for Colonies, 191, 196.
Peace of Paris, 1763, 288.
Pearce, Capt. Vincent, 234.
Pelham, Henry, 108, 246, 270, 285.
Penn, Thomas, Proprietor of Pennsylvania, 127, 143, 273.
— William, 36–7, 41–2, 44, 225.
Pennsylvania, 37, 87, 218–19, 221, 227–8, 273, 282.
Penrith, 264.
Pension Bill, the, O. on, 98.
Pepys, Samuel, 27, 48, 58, 88.
— William Weller, 315.
Percival, Sir John, later Earl of Egmont, on Prison Committee, 91, 112; Associate of Dr. Bray, 112; and Georgia movement, 115–20, 122–3, 143–4, 150, 159, 178, 180, 185, 188–9, 210, 226, 252–4; and Berkeley, 123; quoted, 97, 105, 159–60, 166, 171, 180, 185, 187, 189, 193–4, 211–20, 230–1, 236, 238, 249, 266; mentioned, 107, 249; and Thomas Stephens, 212.
— Lord, son of prec., 107–8.
Percy, Earls, 2.
— Bishop Thomas, 314.
Persia, 308.
Peterborough, Charles Mordaunt, 3rd Earl of, 70, 123.
Petre, Father Edward, 44.
— Lord, 120.
Petrie, Sir Charles, Bt., 257, 281.
Philadelphia, 37, 143[1], 222.
Philip II of Spain, 6.
Philip V of Spain, 196, 198, 202.
Philosophical Transactions, 272.
Phoenix, the ship, 230.
Pickering, Frances Mathew, wife of Sutton O., the first, 13.
Pimlott, J. A. R., 257–8.
Piozzi, Signor Gabriel, 323.
Pitt, Thomas, Gov. of Fort Saint George, Madras, 52.
'pitt, mr.', 73.
Pitt, William, Earl of Chatham, 101, 110, 285–9, 307.
Plymouth Sound, 207.
Pococke, Dr. Richard, 79[4].
Poland, 76, 170.

Pope, Alexander, 147, 147[2], 159, 303, 321.
Popish Plot, the, 20.
Port Royal, 115, 176, 245, 249.
Porteous affair, 106.
Portmore, Charles, 2nd Earl of, 313.
Porto Bello expedition, the, 1739, 233.
Portsmouth, Louise de Quérouaille, Duchess of, 17, 19–21, 31.
Portsmouth, 206–7, 300–1.
Portugal, 308.
Pottle, F. A., 313.
Pragmatic Sanction, the, 99.
Presbyterians, Scottish, 169.
Preston, Richard Graham, Viscount, 31[3], 34, 37.
Preston, 263–5.
Pretender, Old, *see* Stuart, James.
Pretender, Young, *see* Stuart, Charles.
Prince of Wales, the ship, 146, 169.
Pringle, Sir John, 327.
Prior, Matthew, 42.
Privy Council, 115–17, 190.
Prohibition of rum and negro slavery, 179, 210–11.
Proprietors of Carolina, 205.
Public Record Office, 115.
Pulteney, Maj.-Gen. William, 268.
Pury, Jean Pierre, 115.
Purysburg, 115, 166.

Quakers, none in Georgia, 169.
Qualification Bill, the, 104.
Quebec, 227, 280.
Quérouaille, Louis Renée de Penencovet de, 16–17, 19–21, 31.
Quincy, Edmund, 160.
— Rev. Samuel, 160, 184.

Radcliffe, Dr. John, 64.
Raleigh, Sir Walter, 141, 283, 308.
Rand, B., 124.
Randolph, Thomas, Pres. of Corpus Christi College, Oxford, 63.
Rawdon, Oglethorpes of, 4.
Rawlinson, John, 63.
— Thomas, 59[1].
Read Bluff, 168.
Reasons for Establishing the Colony of Georgia, 122[2].
Reck, Baron Georg Philip Friederich von, 138–9, 139[1], 168.
Recusants, Catholic Oglethorpes as, 8–9.
Reformed Church of the United States, 220.
Regensburg, 138.
Restoration, the, 13–17.
Revolution of 1688, 31–3.
Reynolds, Miss Frances, 321.
— Sir Joshua, 271, 291, 300, 311, 313–14, 327, 329.
Rhode Island, 124, 135–6, 227.

INDEX

Richardson, John, 20–1.
Richmond, Charles Lennox, 2nd Duke of, 120.
— Charles Lennox, 3rd Duke of, 307.
Richmond, H. W., 234, 239–40.
Richmond, town of, 263.
Ridley, Nicholas, 5.
Riots, Jacobite, at Oxford, 65; Gordon, 315.
Rising of 1715, the, 65, 71, 169.
'Rising of the North', the, 8.
Roberts, R. E., 146[5].
Robinson, Elizabeth, wife of Sutton O., jun., 13.
Rochambeau, Jean Baptiste Donatien de Vineur, Comte de, 243.
Roche, Maurice, 17.
Rockingham, Charles Watson-Wentworth, 2nd Marquis of, 288.
Rogers, Samuel, 324.
Roman Catholics barred in Georgia, 119, 159.
Rome, 72, 74–6, 122, 257, 308.
Ross, Mary, 114, 119.
— William, Lord, 36.
Rotherhithe, 147.
Rotterdam, 257, 282.
Round, Dr. J. H., 1.
Rousseau, Jean Jacques, 293, 318.
Royal African Company of England, the, 96[1], 147–8, 150, 276.
Royal Humane Society, 301.
'Royal Regiment of Hunters', the, 259, 259[8], 261–3.
Royal Society, 271–2, 285, 285[1].
Royal Society Club, 272, 272[8].
Royal Toxophilite Society, 322.
Rutland, Charles Manners, 4th Duke of, 57, 314[4].
Rutledge, Andrew, 249.
Rye House Plot, the, 22.

Sacheverell, Henry, 54.
Sackville, Gen. Charles, 25.
Saint Augustine, 173–6, 191, 193, 197, 203, 226, 228–9, 232–3, 235, 239, 242, 248, 251.
Saint Catherine's, 173.
'St. George's Draggoons', 262–3, 269.
Saint-Germain, Jacobite court at, 32, 39–45, 69–76; Oglethorpes at, 39, 41, 43–5, 54, 69–76.
Saint Helena Sound, 176.
Saint John's river, 173, 175, 177, 195, 200, 203–5, 233, 248.
Saint Mary's river, 173.
Saint Simon's Island, 136, 157, 169, 237, 243, 246.
Sainte-Beuve, Charles A., 294.
Salmon, Rev. Matthew, 162.
Salzburg, Austria, 99–100.
Salzburgers, in Austria, 99–100, 170; apply to Trustees, 125; in Europe, 138; in Georgia, 138–40, 168–9, 210, 219–20; mentioned, 182.
Sambrook, Lady, 286.
Sambrooke, Elizabeth, 256.
— Sir Jeremy, Bt., 256.
Samoa, 284[1].
San Ildefonso, 190.
Sanchez, Franciso del Moral, Gov. of Florida, 177, 188, 190–1, 193, 196–7, 201–2[5], 204, 208, 226.
Sancroft, William, Abp. of Canterbury, 32, 39.
Sandwich, Earl of, 285[1].
Sardinia, Victor Amadeus, King of, 77.
Savannah, O. founds, 131–2; O. at, 134–44; in 1734, 142–3; in 1736, 155–6, 159; O. seldom at, after 1737, 208; O.'s criticism of, 215; mentioned, 163, 165, 167, 172, 180, 214, 216, 220–2[5], 226, 228, 237, 246, 304.
Savannah river, 113.
Savoy, 136, 297.
Savoy, Victor Amadeus, Duke of, 57, 70.
Savy, John, *alias* Miguel Wall, 176, 197, 228.
Sayre, Mr., 312.
Schellenberg, battle of, 51.
Schwenkfelders, the, 170.
Scotch-Irish in Georgia, no, 169.
Scotland, 36, 65, 69, 71, 75, 258, 300–1, 303, 311, 313, 316, 319.
Scott, Captain John, 32.
Scott, Sir Walter, 106.
Sedgemoor, battle of, 24, 24[1-2], 25, 266.
Seifert, Anton, Moravian pastor, 172.
Selwyn, George, 282.
Serajevo, 223.
Servants, white indentured, 122, 150[6].
Seven Years' War, 217, 280, 282, 285.
Shaftesbury, Anthony Ashley Cooper, 4th Earl of, 150.
Shaftoe, Frances, 55, 55[3], 56.
Shaftoe narrative, 258.
Shakespeare, 283.
Shap, 264–5, 268.
Sharp, Granville, 306–10, 319, 319[4], 328[3].
Sharpe, Mr., 81–2.
She Stoops to Conquer, 298, 300.
Shearness, 30.
Sheftall family, 137, 219.
Sheridan, Richard Brinsley, 314.
Shield, A., quoted, 45, 86[1].
Shirley, William, Gov. of Massachusetts, 227.
Shotover Hill, near Oxford, 61.
Sicily, 123.
Sicily, Victor Amadeus, King of, 70, 74, 76.
Sidney, Henry, 18, 23.

INDEX

Simmonds, the ship, 152–3, 162, 171.
Slave trade, British monopoly in, 223.
Slavery, prohibition of negro, 139, 150, 179, 219, 307–9, 319.
Sloane, Sir Hans, 120, 145–6, 148, 152, 272, 277–8.
Sloanean Collection, the, 277.
Smith, Adam, 101, 314.
Smollett, Tobias, 309.
Smyrna Coffee-House, 295.
Sobieski, Clementina, wife of James III, 76.
Society for the Promotion of Christian Knowledge, 111, 161.
Society for the Propagation of the Gospel in Foreign Parts, 111, 160, 222[5].
Society of the Dilettanti, 271.
Socorro, 119.
Some Account of the Designs of the Trustees for Establishing the Colony of Georgia in America, 121.
Somerset case, the, 308.
Sotheby, Anne, wife of William O., of O. Grange, 10.
South Carolina, legislature of, 130–1, 155, 181, 189, 235–7; welcomes O., 130–1; amicable relations with, 131–2, 135; aids O., 131–2, 135; dispute with Georgia over Indian trade, 151, 178–90; lauds O., 181; appeals to Westminster, 184–6, 188–96; O. and Governorship of, 194; O. General for, 195, 199; negro insurrection in, 231–2; aids Georgians against St. Augustine, 234–5; reviled by O., 235; investigates O., 235–6; replies, 236–7; aids defence of Georgia, 242–4; mentioned, 119–20, 177, 211, 216, 251–2, 287, 304.
South Sea Bubble, 76, 84, 87.
South Sea Company, 105.
South Sea Islands, 300[2].
Southampton, 206.
Southern Frontier, 113–15, 156–7, 173–4, 240.
Southerne, Thomas, poet, 321.
Spain, James III in, 76; Molly O. at court of, 77; in Florida, 113, 132, 134–6, 151, 157, 172–7; British negotiations with, 173–7; protests to London, 184–5, 190–2, 195–205; charges against O. by, 185, 190–2, 195–205; in war of Jenkins's Ear, 222–46; outrage on Amelia Island by, 232; attacks Georgia, 241–4; mentioned, 76–7, 157, 188, 257, 286, 308, 313.
Spangenberg, August Gottlieb, Moravian, 171–2, 218.
Spaniards, the, 73, 113, 115, 134, 149, 151, 159, 172–7, 183, 190–3, 195–205, 222–5, 227–30, 232–46.

Spanish America, 286.
— Armada, 9–10, 10[1].
— claims, 173, 185, 188, 190–3.
— Council of State, 195–6.
— depredations, 1732, 99; 1736, 172; 1738, 223–4; 1739, 232.
— Inquisition, 223.
Spence, Nicholas, 161.
Staël, Anne Louis Necker, Madame de, 294.
Stamp Act Congress, American, 288.
Stanhope, Gen. James, 54.
Star Chamber, 91.
Starenbergh, Count, 73.
Staughton Magna, Huntingdonshire, 28.
Steevens, George, 313.
Stephen, Sir Leslie, 109.
Stephens, Thomas, 212, 212[5], 213, 239.
— William, 211–14, 216, 227, 237.
Sterne, Laurence, 259[8].
Stert, Arthur, 173.
Stevens, W. B., 114.
Stevenson, Robert Louis, 284[1].
Stone, Andrew, secretary to Newcastle, 246.
Strafford, Thomas Wentworth, Earl of, 77.
Strand-on-the-Green, 284.
Strasburg, 220.
Streatham, 314.
Street, Mr. Justice, 83.
Stuart, Charles, the Young Pretender, 85, 258, 263–4, 280–1.
Stuart, James, the Old Pretender, or James III, birth, 29, 55; flight to France, 32; and substitution story, 55; and the Oglethorpes on the continent, 69–78; and the 'Fifteen, 71; creates Theophilus O., jun., a baronet, 72; in exile, 74–8; and James O., 74–6; and the 'Nineteen, 76, 257; mentioned, 65, 77, 281.
Success, the ship, 260.
Sugar Colonies, the, 100–2.
Sunderland, Charles Spencer, Earl of, 30.
Surrey, 281, 288–9.
Sussex, 288–9.
Sutton, Sir Robert, 103, 105, 126.
— Susan, wife of William O. the third, 10.
— Sir William, Bt., 10.
Sweden, 138.
Swedes on the Delaware, 113.
Swift, Dean Jonathan, 34, 42, 57[2], 70[4].
Swiss emigrationists, 125.
Sydney, Henry, Viscount, 38.

Tacitus, 308.
Tadcaster, 5.
Tahiti, 284[1].

INDEX

Tail male in Georgia, 132, 137, 139, 210.
Tailfer, Patrick, 213, 239.
Tammany, 209.
Tangier, 16, 16[1].
Tanner, J. R., 48.
Tanner, Mr., jun., 187.
Taxation no Tyranny, 303.
Taylor, Frank, 24[2].
Temperance, 150.
Temple, Rev. Frederick, 319.
— Rev. William, 319.
— Rev. Wiliam J., 293-4, 319.
Tenison, Thomas, Abp. of Canterbury, 47.
Texas, 119.
Thackeray, W. M., 76.
Thanet, the Earl of, 125.
The Acts and Deeds of Sir William Wallace, 324.
The Deserted Village, 157.
The Folly and Wickedness of misplacing our Trust and Confidence, 255.
The Last Leaf on the Tree, 323-4[1].
The Lives of the Poets, 306.
The Sailor's Advocate, 1728, 88, 100, 106; revived with Sharp, 1777, 306, 309-10.
'The Three Jolly Pigeons', 298.
The Wealth of Nations, 101.
Thebes, 289, 296.
Theodore, King of Corsica, 115[1].
Thicknesse, Philip, 146[5], 184.
Thomson, James, poet, 95, 147.
Thoresby, Ralph, Yorkshire antiquarian, 71.
Thrale, Henry, 300-1, 304, 311, 314-16.
— Hester Lynch Salusbury, 300-1, 304, 306[1], 311, 314-15, 323.
Thuanus, 302, 302[1].
Thwaites, Adam, 2[4].
Ticonderoga, 307.
Tiffany, C. C., 160, 166-7, 221.
Tipperary, 17, 20.
Tomochichi, and O. in Georgia, 134; in England, 144-6; departure, 146; affection for O., 146, 216; and the Blarney Stone, 146[5]; death, 216-17; mentioned, 182, 217.
Torbay, 31.
Tories, the, 69, 84.
Torrenueva, Marquis de, Minister of State for Colonial Affairs, successor to Patiño, 196, 210-12, 204.
Towers, Henry, M.P., 226.
Townshend, Charles, 2nd Visc., 81.
Trade, Indian, 150-1; legislation for, 150-1; conflict with South Carolina over, 178-90.
Treaties: Anglo-Spanish, 1670, 200; of Dover, 16; of Utrecht, 69, 75, 175, 223; of Vienna, 99; with Indians, 134; with Governor del Moral Sanchez, 177, 190, 196-7, 201, 208, 226.
Trelawny, Edward, Gov. of Jamaica, 246.
Trevelyan, G. M., 1, 45, 66, 323.
— Sir George Otto, 66.
Trustees, the Georgia, 117-22, 124-6, 128-32, 136, 138-9, 143-4, 146-7, 149-50, 155-6, 159-61, 161[7], 162, 166-8, 170, 177-9, 183, 185-6, 188-9, 192, 194-5, 199, 204-6, 208-15, 218, 220-2, 222[5], 224, 226, 231-2, 237-9, 241, 248-50, 253-4, 308.
Tucker, Reginald, 27.
Tunstall, W. C. B., 58[4].
Turenne, Henri, Vicomte de. Marshal of France, 15.
Turin, 73-4, 77.
Turks, the, 67-8, 73.
Turner, Bishop Francis, 60.
— Thomas, Pres. of Corpus Christi College, Oxford, 60, 60[2], 63.
Turnour, Edward, Baron Winterton of Gort, 287, 287[3].
Tuyll, Isabella van Serooskerken van, 293-4; and Boswell, 293-4; and Bellegarde, 293; marries M. de Charrière, 294.
Twist, Oliver, 132.
Two Brothers, the ship, 186.
Tybee, 133.
Tyerman, L., 221-2.
Tyrconnel, Earl of, 150.
Tyrol, the, 138, 170.

Ugelbert, 2.
Union with Scotland, the, 69.
Unitas Fratrum, the, 170.
Unity of Brethren, the, 170.
Upfold, Edward, 279.
Upper Ossory, Countess of, 317.
Urban, Sylvanus, 147.
Urbino, 74-6.
Urlsperger, Samuel, 138, 140.
Utrecht, Treaty of, 69, 75, 175, 223.

Val Dery, Richard, Seigneur de, 17.
Vanderdussen, Col. Alexander, 236.
Varro, Terentius, Roman scholar, 283.
Vaudois, French Protestant, 137, 168, 210.
Verelst, Harman, 153, 156, 160-1, 185-6, 214-15, 231, 238, 240-1, 249-51.
Vergennes, Charles Gravier, Comte de, 328[3].
Vernon, Edward, Vice-Adm., 232, 240, 273, 286.
— James, 42, 48, 91, 120, 144, 178, 185, 206, 214, 253-4.

INDEX

Versailles, 328[3].
Verses on the Prospect of planting Arts and Learning in America, 123.
Vesey, Mrs. Agmondesham, the 'Blue-Stocking of Mayfair', 322.
Victor Amadeus II, Duke of Savoy, 57, 70; King of Sicily, 70, 74, 76; King of Sardinia, 77.
Vienna, Treaty of, 99.
Virginia, Council of, 176, 193, 230, 232, 243, 245.
Voltaire, François Marie Arouet de, 317.
Vuarron y Eguiarreta, Don Juan de, Abp. Viceroy of New Spain in Mexico, 196, 228-9.

Waddington, Samuel, 61[4].
Wade, Gen. George, 91, 240, 260-5.
Wager, Sir Charles, Adm., 195, 230, 240.
Wakefield, 263.
Wales, 187, 301.
Wall, Catharine Roche, grandmother of James O., 17.
— Eleanor, see Oglethorpe, Eleanor Wall.
— Matthew, brother of Eleanor Wall O., 42.
— Miguel, alias John Savy, 176, 197, 228.
— Richard, of Rathkenny, grandfather of James O., 17.
Wallingford, Berkshire, 8.
Walpole, Horace, on O. in 1742, 108-9; and the Georgia project, 118; in Hanover, 192; and Geraldino, 198; at The Hague, 201; fears the French, 225; on the 'Forty-five, 258; on O.'s court martial, 269; friendship with O. in later years, 317-18, 320-2, 324-5; on O.'s death, 326; mentioned, 79[4], 110, 282, 314.
— Robert, and Atterbury, 84-5; and prison investigation, 92[2], 92[3]; policy, 1732, 99-100, 104; fall, 1742, 108, 246, 285; and creation of Georgia, 116-17; and support of Georgia, 143, 188, 191, 193-5, 198-202, 204-5, 224-6, 231, 238-9; criticizes O., 191-2; criticized by O., 193-4, 284; reverses himself, 199; capitulates, 199; willing to use Georgia as a pawn, 204, 225-6, 238-9; and Jacobitism, 257; mentioned, 54, 184, 246.
Walsbergen, 53.
Walters, Lucy, 24.
Wandsworth Parish Cemetery, Surrey, 14.
War of 1812, 310.
War of Jenkins's Ear, 222-46.

War Office, the, 250, 252-3.
Warburton, John, 285[1].
Warminster, 31.
Warre, Edmond, 59.
Washington, George, 12, 243, 282, 303, 328[3].
— Col. Henry, royalist, 12[1].
— Lawrence, 12.
Webb, Beatrice, 89, 92, 277[1].
— Philip Carteret, 272[1], 278, 278[8], 279-80, 289.
— Sidney, 89, 92, 277[1].
Weiser, Conrad, 273.
Welch, Mrs., 154.
Wentworth, Lt.-Gen. Thomas, 267-8.
Wesley, Charles, in Georgia, 161-4; on the Moravians, 171; and O. in later years, 167, 200, 315, 320; and report on Georgia, 186, 188; mentioned, 167, 171, 183, 186, 220.
— John, on Eleanor Wall O. and death of Charles II, 23[1]; on Jacobite Oxford, 64; on voyage to Georgia, 153-5, 162; on O., 155, 158, 166; in Georgia, 161-8; and the Moravians, 171-2; and O. in later years, 315; mentioned, 171, 183, 220-1.
— Rev. Samuel, sen., 161.
— Mrs. Samuel, sen., 161.
— Samuel, jun., on Eleanor Wall O. at death of Charles II, 23[1]; on O. in prison inquiry, 95; on Lady O.'s death, 127; O.'s friend, 161; urges O. to marry, 255, 255[7].
— Samuel, 3rd, son of Charles Wesley, 167, 167[5].
West, Dr., 161.
West Indies, the, 110, 123-4, 227, 229, 236, 240.
Westbrook, Manor of, Godalming, Surrey, 33, 45, 66, 79, 79[4], 80, 257, 280-1.
Westbrook Place, Surrey, 256.
Western Isles, the, 301.
Westminster, see London.
Whig oligarchy, the, 116, 246.
White, Gilbert, 79[4].
— John, Georgia Trustee, 226.
White indentured servants, 122, 150[6].
Whitechapel, 305.
Whitefield, George, 218; an Oxonian, 220; at Frederica, 221-2, 222[5]; founds Bethesda Orphanage, 221-2; and Benjamin Franklin, 222.
Whitelamb, Rev. John, 161.
Wigan, 264.
Wilberforce, William, 309.
Wilkes, John, 278[8], 290, 309, 313.
William of Orange, and the Duke of Monmouth, 24; and the Revolution of 1688, 31-3; and Theophilus O., sen., 35, 38-9, 44[3], 45-9; and Lady

INDEX

O., 35–6, 39; death, 50; and Abel Tassin d'Allone, 112[1].
William the Conqueror, 2.
Williams, Jonathan, 325.
— Zachary, 271[3].
Williamson, Capt., 41.
— William, 165–6.
Windham, William, 78, 84, 91.
Windsor, 6, 53, 57–8.
Windsor Castle, 57.
Winn, Watkyn Williams, 91.
Winnington, Thomas, Paymaster of the Forces, 109, 237–8, 270.
Winterton, Edward Turnour, Baron, 287, 287[3].
— Edward Turnour, 6th Earl, 287[3].
Wolfe, Gen. James, 110, 113, 268, 280, 285.
Woodcock, Thomas, 69[4].
Worcester Fly, the, 61.
Wren, Sir Christopher, 27–8.
Wright, Elizabeth, *see* Oglethorpe, Elizabeth Wright.
— Sir Nathan, Lord Keeper of the Seal, grand-uncle of Elizabeth Wright O., 256.
— Sir Nathan, Bt., father of Elizabeth Wright O., 256.

Wright, Robert, quoted, 94, 102–3.
— Sir Samuel, brother of Elizabeth Wright O., 256.
Württemberg, Prince of, 67.
Wycombe, Buckinghamshire, 8.

Yale, Elihu, 52, 52[2].
Yale University, 52[2].
Yamacraw Indians, 134.
Yamassee Indian War, 114.
York castle, 3.
York city, 3, 259–62, 264.
Yorke, Joseph, 266, 282[4].
— Philip, later 2nd Earl of Hardwicke, 247, 267–9.
Yorkshire, 318; Oglethorpes in, 1–14, 79[4], 158, 259–64.
Yorkshire Association, the, 260.
Yorkshire Light Horse, the, 259, 261.
Yorktown, 243, 245.

Zélide, 293–4.
Zinzendorf, Nicholaus Ludwig, Count, 170–2, 218, 273.
Zubly, Rev. Dr., 304.
Zuylen, the Belle de, 294.